Managing Equality and Diversity

Managing Equality and Diversity

Theory and Practice

Savita Kumra and

Simonetta Manfredi

OXFORD

UNIVERSITY PRESS

OXFORD
UNIVERSITY PRESS

Great Clarendon Street, Oxford OX2 6DP

Oxford University Press is a department of the University of Oxford.
It furthers the University's objective of excellence in research, scholarship,
and education by publishing worldwide in

Oxford New York

Auckland   Cape Town   Dar es Salaam   Hong Kong   Karachi
Kuala Lumpur   Madrid   Melbourne   Mexico City   Nairobi
New Delhi   Shanghai   Taipei   Toronto

With offices in

Argentina   Austria   Brazil   Chile   Czech Republic   France   Greece
Guatemala   Hungary   Italy   Japan   Poland   Portugal   Singapore
South Korea   Switzerland   Thailand   Turkey   Ukraine   Vietnam

Oxford is a registered trade mark of Oxford University Press in the
UK and in certain other countries

Published in the United States
by Oxford University Press Inc., New York

© Oxford University Press, 2012

British Library Cataloguing in Publication Data

Data available

Library of Congress Cataloging in Publication Data

Data available

Typeset by TNQ Books and Journals Pvt. Ltd.
Printed in
Great Britain on acid-free paper by
CPI Group (UK) Ltd, Croydon, CR0 4YY

ISBN 978-0-19-9591404

10 9 8 7 6 5 4 3 2 1

Contents

Dedication and acknowledgements

From Simonetta Manfredi:

I would like to dedicate this book to my son Enrico who is becoming a wonderful young man with a great sense of humor.

Acknowledgements

I would like to thank the following colleagues:

- Michelle Montgomery for sharing her expertise and knowledge of implementing equality and diversity in the workplace;
- Bob Price for supporting and encouraging my work in the area of equality and diversity, and for contributing to my professional development;
- Rohini Sampath for her support at work;
- Emma Rundall for dealing with the time-consuming task of seeking permissions to reproduce copyright materials;
- Lucy Vickers for taking the time to read some of my writing and providing me with most valuable feedback;
- Teresa Woodbridge for kindly proofreading some of my chapters.

I would also like to thank Oxford Brookes University for allowing me to reproduce some of its equality documentation which has enabled me to provide some real-life examples of policies and practices in the workplace. I also wish to acknowledge Professor Janet Beer, Vice-Chancellor at Oxford Brookes University, whose strong commitment to gender equality has been a source of inspiration for me.

I would like to thank John Lulham and EntrepriseMouchel for taking the time to talk to me and enable me to include in this book an interesting case study on the use of procurement to advance equality in the private sector.

A special thanks to my son Enrico for helping me with IT and design, and especially for his infinite patience in supporting me with these tasks.

From Savita Kumra:

I would like to dedicate this book to my husband Julian and our sons Kieran and Aron for their love, support, and the daily joy they bring to my life.

Acknowledgements

- I would like to thank Professor Susan Vinnicombe, OBE for being a wonderful role model and sparking my interest and passion in equality and diversity work.

- I would like to thank Charlotte Sweeney and Geraldine Hailey for sharing their insights into equality and diversity issues from a practitioner perspective. This was invaluable and enabled me to ground key concepts in a more holistic way.

- I would like to thank colleagues in the British Academy of Management Gender in Management Special interest group, particularly Adelina Broadbridge, Sandra Fielden, Sharon Mavin, and Carol Woodhams who have all listened with great patience and offered invaluable help and advice at each key challenge I have faced in the writing of this book.

- Thanks to Emma Rundall for dealing with the time-consuming task of seeking permissions to reproduce copyright materials.

- A special thanks to my family who have accepted my working many weekends and countless holidays with grace and seemingly infinite patience.

I would like to thank Brunel Business School for their support in the writing of this book in terms of time and expert support from countless colleagues.

From Simonetta and Savita:

Last but not least we would like to thank the OUP team who have worked on the preparation of this book for their support and helpfulness. A special thanks to Angela Adams who encouraged us to take on this project and Francesca Griffith for her most valuable support and guidance throughout this project. We are grateful to our anonymous reviewers for providing helpful and constructive feedback on our chapters, and to all the colleagues and organizations that have given permission to reproduce copyright materials.

Preface

In today's globalized business environment, the effective management of organizational diversity has never been more critical. With the publication of the 'Workforce 2000' report by the Hudson Institute; which showed that by the year 2000, due to demographic and population changes the US labour force was set to become more heterogeneous. White males would no longer constitute the majority of the workforce; their numbers would be augmented by women, Hispanics, African Americans, and other minority groups. To ensure the US maintained economic dominance in the 21st century, the report tasked policy makers and organizations to plan for the integration and deployment of an increasingly 'diverse' workforce. With the publication of this report and the policy implications emanating from it, the understanding of 'difference' in organizations was radically shifted. For the first time, difference was seen as a positive asset to business, something which if managed and leveraged effectively could provide organizations with much needed competitive advantage. However, also evident was that to access this advantage, 'difference' within organizations would need to be managed in new and alternative ways.

A similar picture was evident in other European countries. In the UK, for example, Pearn Kandola predicted that in 2010 80% of workforce growth would be amongst women and only 20% of the workforce would consist of white, able-bodied males under the age of 45. This was a radically different workforce composition to that traditionally experienced by organizations in these countries, and how to attract, recruit, develop, and retain such a heterogeneous workforce was clearly a social policy and organizational challenge. Particularly as within the UK context, ensuring equality of opportunity has been the focus (as opposed to 'managing difference') and this has historically been located within a policy rather than a theoretical framework. This has been manifest through a framework of equality legislation originating from within the UK and increasingly through the EU, with each European Directive and Act seeking to outlaw unfair discrimination in the workplace and advance equality by extending legal protection to several social groups. The aim of this book is thus to present a comprehensive and thematic overview of the development of equality and diversity management from both research and practitioner perspectives. This will enable those studying the discipline to develop their understanding of the field and their own personal position within it as well as informing their practice as current or future diversity management professionals.

As you progress through the book you will discover the interconnected and holistic nature of the diversity management field. This is evidenced through the vast array of stakeholders, both outside and within organizations who have influenced the development of the discipline. This is also evident in respect of the strategic nature of policy intervention requiring involvement from the whole organization and not just a few targeted individuals.

Web-based content for tutors and students:

Structure of the Book

The book comprises two parts which cover the two key aspects of equality and diversity management. Part one covers chapters one to four and sets the context within which equality and diversity management have developed from outside and within organizations. Chapters one and two consider the external environmental factors shaping policy and legislation in respect of equality and diversity management. Chapters three and four adopt a theoretical focus and discuss the practical and theoretical drivers for a shift in orientation from ensuring equality of opportunity to managing diversity. In the second part of the book, from chapters five to eleven, we take a thematic perspective and consider the key equality and diversity strands from both theoretical and practical perspectives. The final chapter (twelve) provides a conclusion to the text where we draw together key issues and themes; we also look to the future and developing areas of interest.

We chose to share the writing of the all the chapters included in this book, save for Chapter two which was written by our colleague Lucy Vickers, Professor of Law at Oxford Brookes University and a qualified solicitor, and for the conclusions that we wrote jointly. We took this approach to reflect our areas of expertise and use them in a complementary way to provide students with a broader perspective of equality and diversity management issues. At the same time however, we worked in close collaboration throughout the preparation of this book to ensure a fully coherent and integrated approach and to achieve our main aim of presenting a comprehensive and thematic overview of the development of equality and diversity management. We have also made extensive use of signposts across all chapters to help students to make links between theory and practice and the different equality and diversity strands.

Chapter one (Simonetta Manfredi) is intended to help students to familiarize themselves with a range of key concepts and theories relating to equality and diversity issues in the labour market and in the workplace in order to equip them to start their intellectual journey in this subject area. It also provides an overview of the role of stakeholders like the European Union, the State, and the Social Partners to promote equality and diversity in the labour market and in the workplace.

Chapter two (Lucy Vickers) is concerned with the legislative framework in accordance with which equality and diversity policy and practice are developed. The chapter charts the origins of the UK equality framework in the 1960s and 1970s, the impact and effect of EU membership and recent developments in respect of a multi-strand approach. The chapter utilizes landmark legal cases and exercises drawn from a variety of sources to engage the reader and ensure that a complex legislative framework is presented in an accessible and engaging manner.

Chapter three (Savita Kumra) charts the rise of the diversity management perspective, causing a paradigm shift in the conceptualization and framing of difference in organizations. The chapter explains the difference between the managing diversity and equality of opportunity approaches and presents key differences and similarities between them. Alternative theoretical approaches to diversity management are presented and their contributions and shortcomings are critically assessed. The chapter concludes with a consideration of the interdependence of the two approaches, particularly at the practitioner level.

In chapter four (Savita Kumra), the implementation of diversity management is considered. To facilitate this, a change management perspective is adopted and the chapter commences with a discussion of some of the main triggers for change and the nature of the change management process. The chapter assesses the variety of approaches adopted by organizations in respect of implementing diversity management and also indicates that organizations are at differing stages in the implementation process. The chapter also considers the roles and responsibilities of key stakeholder groups such as senior managers, line managers, HR professionals, diversity practitioners, and external bodies. To conclude, the chapter considers the inherent tensions within these roles.

Chapter five (Savita Kumra) is the first chapter in part two of the book. It begins the thematic assessment of the key diversity strands. The chapter considers the issue of managing ethnic diversity in the workplace and begins with consideration of the progress made by those from black and minority ethnic communities in public and organizational life. Discussion then centres on the challenges that remain. In terms of theoretical development, the 'Ethnicity' paradigm is presented, as is the concept of 'Everyday' discrimination. The chapter concludes with an assessment of why there are so few people from black and minority ethnic backgrounds at senior positions in organizations.

Chapter six (Savita Kumra) considers the management of gender diversity. To begin, evidence of the progress women have made in key areas of public and organizational life is presented. The chapter then considers some of the key challenges remaining, with a particular focus on equal pay and the absence of women in senior organizational positions. Key concepts discussed focus on sex-role stereotyping, the Labyrinth model of leadership and the Glass Cliff phenomenon.

Chapter seven (Simonetta Manfredi) considers disability equality issues and how these can be managed in the workplace. It examines how disability has been defined and understood. Main disability models are explored including the Social Model of disability and the Affirmative Model. It also discusses evidence from research to understand how disability is actually managed by employers and considers examples of action that can be taken at an organizational level to promote disability equality.

Chapter eight (Simonetta Manfredi) examines the concept of work–life balance and discusses how work–life balance practices and policies can be developed in the workplace. It explores how the work–life balance debate has evolved in the academic literature, and how its focus has shifted from work–family issues to a more inclusive idea of work–life balance to help everybody to combine paid work with personal life. In its final section it focuses on the development and implementation of work–life balance policies and practices in the workplace and discusses the challenge to integrate company-oriented flexibility with employee-oriented flexibility.

Chapter nine (Savita Kumra) considers the management of sexual orientation and transgender within organizations. The chapter considers the approach to the issue taken by public and private sector organizations and identifies the similarities and differences between them. The concept of stigma is discussed, particularly in relation to visible and invisible stigma. The chapter concludes with a consideration of the differences in respect of key issues facing LGB people and those in the trans community.

Chapter ten (Simonetta Manfredi) examines issues around religion or belief in the workplace. It reviews some of the evidence available from research which points to the existence of discrimination on the grounds of religion or belief in the labour market, particularly in relation to certain religious faiths. It identifies and discusses principled and pragmatic reasons, based on non-religious arguments, which justify the protection of religion or belief in the workplace. The multidimensional nature of religious discrimination is also explored as well as the potential for religious freedom to come into conflict with other equality rights like gender and sexual orientation.

Chapter eleven (Simonetta Manfredi) considers age discrimination and discusses the implications of managing age diversity in the workplace. It examines the policy context that led to the introduction of protection against age discrimination and explores the main theoretical perspectives that have been used to conceptualize age equality in the workplace. It concludes with an overview of management strategies to understand how organizations need to adjust their working practices in order to manage effectively both age diversity, and an older workforce.

Chapter twelve is the final chapter of the book and considers possible future directions and challenges in the field of diversity management. Key issues discussed include the impact on diversity management of a rise in interest in corporate social responsibility. Also discussed are the emerging concepts of intersectionality and inclusion. Clear from this discussion is that the field of diversity management is and will be for some time one which presents many challenges and opportunities to theoreticians and practitioners alike.

We are conscious that many of the topics presented in this book have been the subject of much debate both in academic and practitioner-oriented literature. For reasons of space we were unable to cover all this vast body of literature and research. However, we have tried to highlight most key theories and arguments and use a selection of research findings relating to this discipline and different equality and diversity strands to equip students with sufficient knowledge and understanding to enable them to research this subject area further. We have also tried to provide several examples of equality and diversity management practices in other countries without however, losing focus on the UK.

We hope that our readers will find this book intellectually stimulating and that they will enjoy using it. Above all we hope that it will contribute to raising awareness about the importance of equality and diversity management in the workplace among current and future generations of professionals.

How to use this Book

Our aim has been to write a textbook that unravels the jargon to provide clarity on core theoretical concepts and increasingly common organizational practice. This book is also intended to appeal to diverse learning styles and objectives. For this purpose it contains a range of pedagogic features to include real-life organizational case studies, debates on topical issues, and other student activities which bring to life the reality of managing equality and diversity in the workplace. Our aim is to motivate you as readers to engage with the material included in the text and we hope your interest will be sufficiently sparked that you wish to find out more about specific topics. We very much hope we have achieved this aim. The features we have included are:

◎ Learning objectives

- Understand some of the triggers for change and the nature of the change management process.

Learning objectives

help you focus your learning, and (in conjunction with the chapter conclusions) evaluate your knowledge and understanding of each chapter.

🔑 Key terms

- **Change management:** a process through which organizations adapt to and meet the demands presented by increasingly turbulent

Key terms

at the beginning of each chapter provide clear definitions and explanations of important terms which are explored later in the chapter. Understanding these terms from the start makes the ideas and arguments more accessible.

Aversive disablism

Another form of prejudice towards disabled people is what has been defined as 'aversive disablism'

Key concepts

provide brief explanations of concepts important to developing an understanding of the key concepts included within each chapter.

➡ Student Activity 4.1

Consider each of the 'triggers' for change identified above and answer the following questions:

Student activities

are linked to the preceding text and provide you with an opportunity to think more critically about the issues and the reality of managing equality and diversity in the workplace.

◻ Case study 4.1 A Global Diversity Forum at Standard Chartered Bank

Standard Chartered Bank identified through

Case studies

focus on organizational and research examples, enabling you to link theory to practice. Each case study includes questions that help you to assess your understanding of the material covered.

Signpost to Chapter 2 An Outline of
European and UK Equality Legislation

Signposts

are used throughout the book to indicate where similar
issues are addressed in other sections in a complementary or a more extensive way.

Debate Box

Organize the class into two groups,
one for the motion and one against.
The motion is:

Debate boxes

contain questions that aim to help you become a
critical thinker and alert you to relevant debates within
a particular area. This exercise also develops your
debating skills. A motion is presented and the class split
into two groups, one for the motion and one against.

End of Chapter Case Study Telecommunications Company

The telecommunications company in this
case study

End of chapter case studies

are more substantial case studies with accompanying
discussion questions that illustrate specific issues and
learning points from the chapter. These can either be
used within the classroom for discussion or as an activity during private study.

Conclusion

In this chapter we have explored the
organizational response to implementing

Chapter conclusions

draw together themes from the chapter and can be
used to check your understanding and to link back to
the learning outcomes.

Review and discussion questions

1. What do you see as the key facilitators and barriers to the effective
implementation of diversity

Review and discussion questions

are included at the end of each chapter to provide an
opportunity to check understanding of the material
within the chapter and engage with some of the key
debates.

Further reading

CIPD (2006a) *Diversity in Business: How Much
Progress Have Employers Made? First
Findings*. Tatli, A., Ozbilgin, M., Worman, D.,

Further reading

is provided through lists of recommended reading, to
help guide you further into the literature on a particular
subject area.

References

Ahmed, S. (2007) The language of diversity.
Ethnic and Racial Studies, 30/2: 235–256.

References

contain all the sources cited in the chapter and help
broaden your understanding of the topics covered in
each chapter.

Glossary

Affirmative model of disability: this
model seeks to promote a

Glossary

provides easy access to definitions of all the principal
terms contained in the book.

How to use the Online Resource Centre

The Online Resource Centre offers to lecturers and students resources and possibilities for knowledge extension and to keep the learning package as up to date as possible.

www.oxfordtextbooks.co.uk/orc/kumra_manfredi/

Student resources

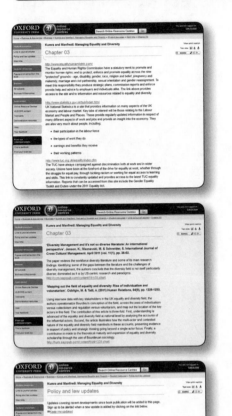

Annotated web links

direct you towards valuable sources of information.

Links to journal articles

provide a convenient way to pick out the most relevant material to complement your study. Reading and using journals is an important skill for all students, and this feature aims to make the vast array of articles available less daunting.

Policy & law updates

keep you informed of the latest developments in the field and allow you to place the chapter topics into a wider context.

Lecturer resources

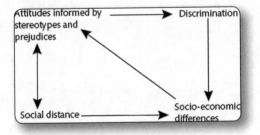

Figures and tables

from the book are available to download to use as hand-outs or to customize for your own presentations.

Part 1

Theoretical Perspectives

Equality and Diversity Issues in the Labour Market

◎ Learning objectives

- Understand the concept of equality and its different meanings
- Define disadvantage and discrimination
- Explain patterns of disadvantage and discrimination relating to different social groups
- Understand how surveys and statistical data can be used to monitor rates of labour market participation and employment patterns of different social groups and identify labour market inequalities
- Define occupational segregation and understand different theories developed to explain this phenomenon
- Explain the role of stakeholders like the European Union, the State and the Social Partners to promote equality and diversity in the labour market and in the workplace

🔑 Key terms

- **Disadvantage**: with regard to employment, disadvantage encompasses a situation where an individual, because of her personal characteristics, is not able to participate in paid work in the same way as others. An example of this is a disabled person who may not be able to work unless some adjustments are made to the working environment.

- **Discrimination**: amounts to unfavourable treatment which cannot be objectively justified.

- **Equality**: the Universal Declaration of Human Rights states that: 'All human beings are born free and equal in dignity and rights', which means that they are all equal in their humanity and moral worth and they all share an essential dignity as human beings.

- **Occupational segregation**: this relates to a situation where people from a particular social group are concentrated in certain occupations or in certain employment sectors. Occupational segregation can be horizontal (e.g. women predominantly working in administrative and clerical jobs across different sectors of employment) or vertical (e.g. women segregated in lower-status jobs and under-represented in senior jobs).

- **Social dialogue**: social dialogue is defined by the European Trade Union Confederation as 'the process of negotiation by which different actors in society (or "social partners") reach agreement to work together on policies and activities'. The social dialogue can bring together representatives of employers and employees but it can also involve government or European Union representatives.

Introduction

This first chapter is intended to help students to familiarize with a range of key concepts and theories relating to equality and diversity issues in the labour market and in the workplace in order to equip them to start their intellectual journey in this subject area. Section one starts with an exploration of the concept of equality, discusses the different meanings that have been attributed to it and how the notion of difference has helped to shape our understanding of equality. Section two explains the difference between disadvantage and discrimination and provides an overview of changing patterns of disadvantage across different social groups. Having explored key concepts such as equality, disadvantage and discrimination, the following section discusses the use of surveys and statistical analysis to monitor labour market participation trends and employment patterns of different social groups. It shows how surveys and statistical analysis can help to identify labour market inequalities and patterns of both 'vertical' and 'horizontal' occupational segregation. A range of theories are then examined which seek to explain the causes of occupational segregation. The chapter concludes with an overview of the role of stakeholders like the European Union, the state and the social partners to promote equality and diversity in the labour market and in the workplace.

Equal or diverse?

Equality and diversity may sound as a contradiction in terms but in practice these two terms are often used together, such as, for example, in the title chosen for this book, or even used interchangeably. These two terms reflect different concepts which have evolved as part of the equality discourse: some would argue that they are complementary while others would disagree with this view. This debate is fully explored in Chapter 3 and in this section we limit our discussion to define the broad meaning of equality and to show how the notion of diversity has helped to shape the idea of equality.

Signpost to Chapter 3 From Equal Opportunities to Managing Diversity for an in-depth discussion about how equality and diversity have been theorized with reference to the workplace.

From an historical perspective the concept of equality in western societies is rooted in the Enlightenment, an intellectual and philosophical movement that influenced thinking across Europe and North America in the eighteenth century. The idea of equality was at the core of the 1776 United States Declaration of Independence, which states that 'all men are created equal', and of the 1789 French Revolution, which predicated the principles of equality, fraternity and legality. More recently, the United Nations Declaration of Human Rights states that 'all human are born free and equal in dignity and rights'. However, what does equality actually mean to us in the twenty-first century?

The meaning of equality has been the subject of an extensive academic debate and much has been written about this subject. Exploring the concept of equality and its different interpretations could be the subject of an entire book. However, for reasons of space, in this chapter we shall limit ourselves to provide an overview of some of the different meanings of equality developed within legal theory.

The most intuitive meaning of equality is that everybody should be treated equally; in other words, according to the Aristotelian maxim, 'likes are treated alike'. This is referred to as formal equality (Vickers, 2011), which is achieved through the application of a symmetrical approach to the principle of equal treatment. However, in practice the application of this approach can be problematic. An old fable written by Aesop, who lived in ancient Greece (*c.* 620–560 BC), can help us to understand the difficulties of conceptualizing equality as a symmetrical relationship.

The fox and the stork

Once upon a time a fox invited a stork to dinner and provided a meal that consisted of soup in a large flat dish. The fox was able to lap this soup up very easily, while the stork, unable to take a mouthful with her long narrow bill, was as angry at the end of the dinner as she was when she began.

When it was the stork's turn to invite the fox for dinner, she provided a meal contained in a narrow-necked vessel down which the stork easily thrust her long bill, while the fox was obliged to content himself with licking the neck of the jar. As a result the fox was unable to satisfy his hunger.

What lessons can be drawn from this fable? The first point to note is that the fox and the stork are not alike. Therefore, if we apply a symmetrical approach to equality we would need to set a standard to measure equality based either on the characteristics of the fox or of the stork. However, if we set the standard either on the fox or on the stork, inevitably one of them, as the story shows, will be disadvantaged and equal treatment will not be achieved.

This fable demonstrates that there are two main flaws with the concept of formal equality: the first one is that in reality we all have different characteristics and different needs, while the second one is that in order to take a symmetrical approach to equal treatment it is necessary to choose a 'comparator' against whom to measure equal treatment. This raises a fundamental question, which is 'who should be compared against whom?' Fredman (2001: 30) suggests that the concept of a comparator is based on the premise that there is a 'universal individual' against whom to set equality standards, but she suggests that this idea is 'highly deceptive'. She argues that this apparently abstract construct of a 'universal individual' is likely to have all the relevant characteristics and 'the attributes of the dominant culture, religion, or ethnicity' which leaves no room for accommodating people's diversity. Thus the importance of recognizing and understanding people's different characteristics and attributes has led legal theorists to reconceptualize equality and shift from a formal idea of equality to a more substantive one.

At least three more substantive models of equality can be identified that can help to understand this concept: equality as dignity; equality and disadvantage; and equality and inclusion (Vickers, 2011).

- **Equality as dignity**: as mentioned above, the Universal Declaration of Human Rights states that 'All human beings are born free and equal in dignity and rights', which means that they are all equal in their humanity and moral worth and they all share an essential dignity as human beings. In other words, although individuals may present different characteristics, they are all equal in their human worth. Thus equality, underpinned by dignity, offers a broader conceptual framework which goes beyond the formal notion that everybody should be treated in the same way, but it recognizes and values different identities and, consequently, allows for the accommodation of differences. Equality as dignity is discussed in more depth in Chapter 10 on managing religion or belief in the workplace. In that chapter it is argued that this view of equality can help us to understand why religion or belief should be protected in the workplace, since religion and/or belief are an important part of an individual's self-identity and therefore they should be respected and valued by society.

- **Equality and disadvantage:** this model uses disadvantage as an underlying concept of equality and treats grounds such as sex, ethnicity, disability, religion or belief, sexual orientation and age as 'proxies' for disadvantage. As highlighted by Vickers (2011), this approach sees the wrong of discrimination as being the way it causes disadvantage, rather than its lack of recognition of different identities. However, a critique of this approach points to the fact that different grounds of equality may not necessarily be proxies for disadvantage. For example, there may be significant differences in disadvantage between gay women and black straight women; between Christian men who have high rates of employment and Muslim men who have higher rates of unemployment. Furthermore, different grounds of equality can interact with one another, making it even more difficult to identify where the disadvantage lies.

- **Equality and inclusion**: this model is based on the concept of inclusion, which promotes the idea of dignity for all as well as the need to tackle disadvantage through equality, thus encompassing both equality as dignity and equality and disadvantage. This is achieved through encouraging respect for the equal dignity of all and participation in civic life of all different social groups. Greater participation in civic life of all different social groups will give them a voice within the communities in which they live and help to combat social exclusion and disadvantage, which will lead to a more equal society both in terms of economic distribution and social cohesion (Fredman, 2002; Collins, 2003; Vickers, 2011).

Understanding disadvantage and discrimination

It is important to understand the difference between disadvantage and discrimination as well as the relationship between these two concepts. Broadly speaking, with regard to employment, disadvantage encompasses those situations where people in some social groups, because of their characteristics, are not able to participate in paid work in the same way as other people. For example, disabled people may not be able to work in some environments unless some adjustments are made. Likewise, people with caring responsibilities may not be able to take up full-time employment. This means that people in these groups, unlike others, may face some barriers to participating in paid work because of their characteristics (e.g. disability or being a carer).

Discrimination may be experienced by people belonging to a particular social group because of employers' discriminatory decisions which cannot be objectively justified. These decisions may be the result of an employer's prejudice or negative stereotyping against certain groups. For example, employers may not want to hire older workers because they think that they are less productive; women with caring responsibilities may be less likely to be promoted because they are considered to be less committed to their job. In both of these examples employers' decisions are influenced by negative stereotypes. Stereotypes can be 'regarded as a model of probability, not a statement of certainty' and the implications are that an employer whose judgement is influenced by stereotypes may discriminate against a job applicant if 'she feels that there is a degree of likelihood that the worst predictions of the stereotype may be fulfilled' (Jenkins, 1986: 92–97). Furthermore, all decision-making processes involve a certain degree of subjectivity in the decisions of employers when recruiting staff. It has been argued that the judgements of those involved in the recruitment of staff may be shaped by 'informal criteria ... heavily circumscribed by selectors' evaluation of the extent to which a candidate either contrasts, compares or identifies with their own experience or perception of themselves, they almost inevitably reproduce the prevailing employment profile' (Collinson et al., 1990: 67). Thus a job applicant who does not fit the prevailing employment profile in a particular workplace (e.g. an ethnic minority candidate applying for a job in a predominantly white environment or a woman applying for a job in a predominantly male employment sector) may be discriminated against either consciously or unconsciously.

However, in order to gain a deeper understanding of how disadvantage and discrimination interact, it is useful to refer to the theoretical framework developed by Makkonen (2002). This author argues that there is a causal connection between people's attitudes, which can be informed by prejudice, and their behaviour. Prejudice is defined as 'unfairly or unreasonably formed opinions and feelings against a group of people' (ibid.: 7). In other words, it can be said that prejudices are based on assumptions that are not substantiated either by facts or evidence but are formed on the basis of an individual's opinions, feelings, or broad generalizations. When people's attitudes are informed by prejudice, their behaviour can lead to discrimination. However, it is not automatic that attitudes informed by prejudice will result in a discriminatory behaviour because some people, in spite of their prejudices, may act fairly. For example, an employer may be prejudiced against older workers, but she may be careful not to discriminate against them to avoid legal challenges.

Also, behaviour patterns such as social distance between different social groups who have little or no voluntary interaction with each other, can create or reinforce prejudices which in turn can lead to discriminatory behaviour. This is defined by Makkonen (2002) as the 'vicious circle' of discrimination, as illustrated in Figure 1.1.

In summary, it can be observed that people's attitudes, informed by prejudice or stereotypes, can both influence behaviour and create discrimination, but can also create or reinforce social distance. Discrimination in turn can fuel prejudice as well as create or reinforce social distance. Thus discrimination can lead to socio-economic differences and these can

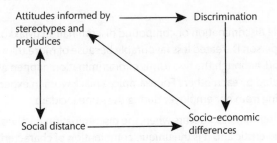

Figure 1.1 The 'vicious circle' of discrimination (Makkonen, 2002: 9)

lead to stereotype and prejudice. This demonstrates the existence of a relationship of reciprocity that interlinks these two factors and can lock people from certain social groups into a 'vicious circle' of disadvantage and discrimination which can be difficult to break. Anti-discrimination legislation can help to modify behaviours but other interventions, for example education, are also needed to tackle prejudice, break this 'vicious circle' and reduce social distance which can continue to fuel prejudice and discrimination.

◉ Case study 1.1   Cutteslowe Walls

The Cutteslowe Walls in Oxford, built in 1934, were over two metres high and topped with lethal spikes. They divide the City Council's Cutteslowe Estate, which offered rented accommodation to people on low income, from a private housing estate. The dividing walls were constructed by the developer who built the private estate. He did this because he was afraid that his houses would not sell if the so-called 'slum dwellers' were going to be neighbours, so the walls were built to separate them. The walls were eventually demolished in 1959 by the Oxford City Council.

For more information see: http://www.bbc.co.uk/oxford/content/articles/2009/03/26/cutteslowe_feature.shtml
Follow the link on the online resources and watch the short video about the Cutteslowe Walls.

....

Case study question

Use the Makkonen 'vicious circle' of discrimination model to explore the impact of the construction of the Cutteslowe Walls on the people who lived on that estate.

Multiple and intersectional discrimination

Discrimination tends to be understood as a one-dimensional issue (e.g. either sex or ethnicity or other protected characteristics), but it has been advocated that anti-discrimination law should take a more holistic approach in order to capture multiple dimensions of discrimination (Fredman and Szyszczak, 1992). For example, a woman may be discriminated against because of her sex, her age and her ethnicity. Likewise, a man may be discriminated against because of his age and because of his sexual orientation. Thus different forms of discrimination can interact with one another and result in three main types of dynamic which have been described as (Government Equalities Office, 2009: 10–11):

- Multiple discrimination occurs when a person 'is treated less favourably because of more than one protected characteristic, but each type of discrimination occurs in separate occasions'.

- Additive multiple discrimination or compound discrimination (Makkonen, 2002) occurs when 'a person is treated less favourably because of more than one protected characteristic and, although the two forms of discrimination happen at the same time, they are not related by each other'. For example, a black woman experiences both racism and sexist bullying from her employer during the same incident.

- Intersectional discrimination occurs when 'the discrimination involves more than one protected characteristic and it is the unique combination of characteristics that results in discrimination, in such a way that they are completely inseparable'.

Historically, the concept of intersectional discrimination emerged from the experience of black women in the United States. In the 1980s, the Courts began to acknowledge that black women could experience discrimination in a way that neither black men nor white women experienced it. It was recognized that 'when two bases for discrimination exist, they cannot be neatly reduced to distinct components because an attempt to bisect a person's identity at the intersection of race and gender often distorts or ignores the particular nature of their experiences' (Lam v University of Hawaii, cited in Solanke, 2010: 16).

The UK 2010 Equality Act was intended to contain provisions to tackle multiple discrimination. This would have allowed claims to be brought on the grounds of two legally protected characteristics, such as, for example, age and sex. These provisions were quite controversial from the start and in particular they were met with much opposition from the business lobby. In the face of this opposition, the Labour government at the time decided to limit possible claims of multiple discrimination to the combination of only two grounds of discrimination (Hepple, 2010: 16). However, the current UK Coalition government has decided not to enact the multiple discrimination provisions in the Act, and this represents a significant drawback and a missed opportunity for the law to start tackling multiple discrimination (Hepple, 2010: 16).

In the next section we provide an overview of patterns of disadvantage and discrimination.

Signpost to Chapter 2 An Outline of European and UK Equality Legislation

Debate Box

Organize the class into two groups, one for the motion and one against.

The BBC TV presenter Miriam O'Reilly sued her employer, the BBC, for age and sex discrimination after she was replaced in her job as a TV presenter by a younger woman. The employment tribunal found that she had been discriminated against because of her age but it rejected her claim for sex discrimination.

The motion is:

Women are more likely to be discriminated against because of their sex and age in a way that men are not likely to experience.

Stages in the debate: (each stage is given with timings, the overall time for the activity is 55 minutes – allowing a few minutes for change over of presenters, etc.)

- Each group has 20 minutes to prepare their arguments either for or against the motion.

- Each group is given five minutes to present their opening statement (10 minutes in total).

- Groups reconvene for 10 minutes to prepare rebuttal arguments.

- Each group has two minutes to present rebuttal arguments.

A vote is taken and the winners of the debate announced; the casting vote goes to impartial observers, tutors, audience members not involved in the debate, or observers.

Changing patterns of disadvantage and discrimination

Patterns of disadvantage and discrimination in relation to different social groups are not statics and they evolve as a result of socio-economic and political changes in society. While some groups that have been subjected to disadvantage and discrimination in the labour market but eventually improve their position, other groups emerge as being in a position of disadvantage and are likely to be discriminated against. Patterns of disadvantage and discrimination vary not just between different social groups but also within the groups themselves. For reasons of space, in the sections below we review briefly the situation of some groups. In particular we concentrate on migrants and issues around social class and the so-called 'working poor'. A comprehensive view about patterns of disadvantage and discrimination relating to other groups is provided in the second part of this book.

Gender

Signpost to
Chapter 6
Managing
Gender
Diversity in the
Workplace

The role of women, particularly, in western societies has changed significantly over several decades. Their level of education has increased and in several countries surpassed that of men. For example, in Britain girls outperform boys in their education attainment at age 5, 16 and at degree level (Equality and Human Rights Commission, 2010). Equally, their participation in the labour market has increased and the traditional model of family dependent on the male breadwinner has been replaced by dual earning couples or single-parent families. In spite of these achievements, as discussed in Chapter 6, patterns of disadvantage and discrimination persist with regard to women.

Many boys are performing less well in education compared to girls and this is cause for concern in some countries, e.g., the UK (ibid.). The role of men as fathers and expectations about their involvement in caring responsibilities are also changing. Several countries have introduced special leave arrangements for fathers but, as discussed in Chapter 6, workplace norms and expectations about male workers may act as a barrier for them to access these measures.

Ethnicity

Patterns of disadvantage and discrimination in relation to ethnic minorities have also evolved as some groups are no longer 'newcomers'. These groups have settled in their host country, and acquired citizenship and the right to political participation, which has helped them to integrate (Sen, 2000). For example, the occupational structure of the labour market in Britain shows positive changes for some ethnic groups, as Indian and Chinese people in Britain are twice as likely to be employed as professionals than white British people (Equality and Human Rights Commission, 2010). However, if some ethnic groups by and large appear to be well integrated, others are still in a position of disadvantage and are likely to be discriminated against either because of their ethnicity or because of their religious affiliation, or both. For example, Muslim people in Britain have the lowest rate of employment of any religious group. Only 47 per cent of Muslim men and 24 per cent of Muslim women are employed and figures suggest that 42 per cent of young Muslim people are classified as 'NEET', which means that they are neither in employment, in education, nor in training (ibid.). Issues around race and

Signpost to
Chapter 5
Managing
Ethnic
Diversity in the
Workplace

ethnicity, and religion or belief, and the management of these diversities in the workplace are explored respectively in Chapters 5 and 10.

Migrant workers

International migration is a trend shared by many European countries and it plays an important role in population growth. This is particularly important as the population of many countries is ageing against a fall in birth rates. This means that the population is below replacement levels. Migrant workers can be defined as non-nationals living in a foreign country. This definition includes non-nationals from another country within the European Union (EU) or from a country which is outside the EU. There is a significant difference between these two groups since non-nationals, from another EU country, are entitled to be treated as nationals of the host country. For example, they do not need a work permit to take up a job or set up a business, and they have access to education on the same terms as the country's nationals. Conversely, the non-nationals from a country outside the EU need a permit from the host country to take up work and they may be subject to other restrictions imposed by national immigration policies. Comparative studies about working conditions of migrants across the EU (Ambrosini and Barone (2007), and Vandenbrande et al. (2006)) have highlighted that migrants, particularly those from a non-western background, are more likely than nationals to be in a disadvantaged position in the labour market in all of the EU member states. In particular, these studies have pointed to three main sources of inequalities for migrants which are interrelated. These are: a significant pay gap compared to nationals; lack of opportunities for upward occupational mobility; and work-related health and safety issues. These sources of inequalities are determined by the fact that many migrant workers tend to be employed in low-paid and low-skills occupations.

It appears that so far, in most countries government policies have paid little attention to promoting equality of opportunity for migrant workers. Rather, policy makers tend to focus on dealing with illegal immigration. However, as the findings from the studies discussed above demonstrate, there are serious equality issues that need to be tackled by both policy makers and employers in relation to migrant workers.

Social class and working poor

Another major source of inequality is social class. The French sociologist Pierre Bourdieu (1984) highlights how differences in people's income and other material possessions, compounded with their lifestyle, mark their belonging to a particular social class. These differences become entrenched in a society as people from more affluent classes are able to provide better education and other opportunities for their children, thus facilitating their success in life and helping them to secure their place within the middle or upper classes. While the middle and upper classes maintain their position of privilege in society through this 'virtuous circle', people with low income and low levels of education find themselves caught in a 'vicious circle' since they are unable to provide opportunities for their children to move up the social ladder. As a result, they remain trapped in a position of poverty and with low social status. Wilkinson and Pickett (2010: 159–161), in their book *The Spirit Level*, discuss empirical evidence which shows a strong correlation between income inequality and social mobility. They use findings from a longitudinal study by Blanden et al. (2005), which compares international data on intergenerational social mobility in eight western countries: the USA, the UK, Germany, Canada, Denmark, Finland, Sweden, and Norway. This study looked at the correlation between fathers' incomes at the time when their sons were born and sons' income at the age of 30. It concluded that those countries with bigger income differences, such as the USA and the UK (Germany and Canada are positioned in the middle), tend to have lower social mobility compared to those with less income differences, such as the Scandinavian countries. In other words, those born in low-income families in societies where there are marked income differences are more likely to remain on low income throughout their lives. Another important finding of this study is that higher public spending on education has a significant impact on social differences in accessing higher education, which has a key role in facilitating social mobility. Most equal societies spend more on education, for example Norway, where 97.8 per cent of spending on education comes from public funding, compared to the USA where only 68.2 per cent of money spent on education comes from public funding.

Debate Box

The poorest pupils are 55 times less likely to go to Oxford.

It is feared that rising tuition fees (of up to £9,000 a year to attend university in England) will seriously reduce opportunities for social mobility.

Organize the class into two groups, one for the motion and one against, and follow the stages outlined in the previous Debate box.

The motion is:

Higher Education should not to be subsidized by the taxpayers.

Source: http://www.bbc.co.uk/news/education-12048629

Furthermore, it has been estimated that in 2007 eight per cent of the population within the European Union fell in the category of the so-called 'working poor', who are people with an income which is below 60 per cent of the national median (Hanzl-Weibss and Vidovic, 2010). In the UK, for example, one in five people live in households with less than 60 per cent of the median income, and this rises to one in three for Bangladeshi-headed households (Equality and Human Rights Commission, 2010). Overall the risk of being among the working poor, a category that tends to include people with a low level of education, migrants and single-parent families, appears to be greater in southern Europe and in some eastern European countries. However, younger people are more at risk of in-work poverty in northern European countries, while in southern Europe older people are more at risk of in-work poverty.

Monitoring labour market participation trends and employment patterns of different social groups

The purpose of this section is to help students to understand the importance of using surveys and statistical analysis to monitor levels of labour market participation and the employment patterns of different social groups. Labour market surveys are routinely collected by international organizations such as the International Labour Organization and the European Union as well as by individual countries. These are usually easily accessible online. Throughout this book we have used extracts from relevant statistics where appropriate to provide an indication of labour market trends and employment patterns. Although statistical data become out of date very quickly, the results are unlikely to change significantly from one year to the next and, even if they are not entirely up to date, they can still provide a good indication of marketplace trends and patterns. Web-links to labour market statistics produced by the organizations mentioned above and to the Labour Force Survey, produced by the UK Office for National Statistics, are included in the online resources which are made available with this text.

The use of surveys and statistical data in the study of equality and diversity in the labour market can serve two purposes. First, they enable us to observe how different social groups fare in the labour market. Second, they can be used to assess the impact of policy and legislation to address inequalities relating to different social groups. Third, they can measure the impact of economic downturns on these groups.

The significance of statistical analysis in the study of equality and diversity issues in the labour market can be best understood from an historical perspective with reference to the work undertaken in the 1970s by the French sociologist Evelyn Sullerot on Women, Society and Change. Through a longitudinal statistical analysis she showed how the life of women in the 1970s had changed, compared to previous decades, and highlighted that not only were many more women engaged in paid work, but also that a large proportion of them continued to work while they were married. Overall, their 'working curve', in other words the time spent in paid work, was becoming similar to that of men. This analysis also indicated that the expansion of jobs both in services and in the public sector attracted many women to work in these areas, although at the same time this had the effect of concentrating women's employment in these sectors, thus creating occupational segregation (ibid., 27–30). This work was fundamental in showing how women's lives had changed over time, but also in bringing these changes to the attention of policy makers within the European Union and in developing policies and legislation to support women's participation in the labour market.

If we take a look at current statistics about women's employment rates, we can see that in 27 EU countries this mounts to 59.1 per cent, which is still considerably lower compared to men's employment rates, which is 72.8 per cent. Furthermore, there are significant differences between the rate of employment of men and women across member states: higher rates of female employment (above 70 per cent) can be observed in northern European countries such as Denmark, Sweden, and the Netherland, while in southern European countries female employment rates are well below the EU average, with Malta being one of the lowest at 37.4 per cent, followed by Italy at 47.2 per cent, and Greece at 48.7 per cent, as outlined by Figure 1.2.

Disaggregated data by sex on employment rates show that there are still marked differences between men and women's levels of participation in the labour market. However, this kind of statistic does not shed any light on the possible reasons for the existence of these differences. Therefore it is necessary to gain a better understanding of women's life experiences to find explanations for these differences. Thus statisticians have shifted from producing 'statistics on women' to producing statistics about 'women and men'. This approach is underpinned by a conceptual shift that distinguishes between biological characteristics, which define sex, and the notion of gender. This concept has been adopted by social scientists to refer to the

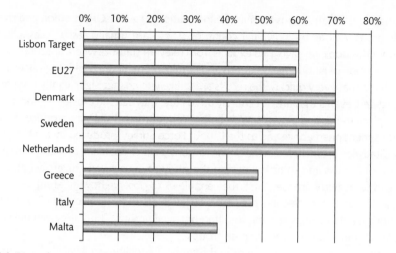

Figure 1.2 Rates of women's employment across the EU (Eurostat, 2010)

'culturally and sociologically constructed representation of women and men, such as psychological characteristics, activities, social role and status' (Nicot and Houtman, 2007: 2). When applied to statistical analysis, the concept helps us to gain a better understanding of the different experiences of men and women, at a deeper level from that offered by sex-disaggregated data, and it shows, for example, that in more egalitarian societies, in countries like Sweden and Finland, which offer better provisions to encourage a more equal distribution between men and women of childcare responsibilities, women have higher rates of employment (as shown in Figure 1.2 above). In southern European societies, however, where men and women are expected to perform different roles, namely with women taking prime responsibility for childcare and the family and men being the family provider, women's rates of employment are significantly lower.

While extensive statistical data about men and women in the labour market is available both at an international and national level, the same cannot be said about ethnic minorities. From an international perspective it would be virtually impossible to make meaningful comparisons because the profile of ethnic minorities varies from one country to another. Besides, sometimes it can be difficult to find information about these groups at a national level. The reason for this is that ethnicity can be a very sensitive subject in some countries, where for example, for political reasons, ethnic minorities may not wish to be identified as such and singled out from the general population. The UK is a highly diverse country where a wide range of different ethnic groups have settled. The Office for National Statistics monitors labour market participation and rates of employment for the main different ethnic groups who live in the UK. Table 1.1 shows an example of the percentage of economic activity within ethnic groups. Furthermore, by cross-referencing statistical data about the rate of participation of ethnic minority groups with participation rates by religious affiliation, it has been possible to identify labour market inequalities for certain groups which suggests the existence of discrimination on religious grounds.

As well as rates of economic activity by different social groups, surveys can show the distribution of different types of jobs in different sectors among men and women and among ethnic minorities

Signpost to Chapter 10 Managing Religion or Belief in the Workplace for further discussion about religious discrimination in the workplace

Table 1.1 Percentage of economic activity within ethnic groups, October to December 2009

	Employment (%)	Unemployment (%)	Inactivity (%)
All ethnic groups	72.60	6.20	21.20
White	74.30	5.80	19.90
White British	74.40	5.90	19.70
Other white	75.50	4.80	19.50
All ethnic minority groups	59.90	9.20	30.90
Mixed	61.50	10.10	28.40
Asian or Asian British	60.40	7.90	22.70
Indian	70.90	6.40	22.70
Pakistani	46.50	10	43.50
Bangladeshi	44.70	10.80	44.50
Other Asian	66.40	6.60	27
Black or black British	59.20	13.20	27.60
Black Caribbean	65.30	13.50	21.20
Black African	55.20	12.30	32.50
Other black	53.40	21	25.60
Other, including Chinese	58.90	7	34.10

Source: Barrett, 2010

or other social groups, depending how much information is available in the country under investigation. The snapshot below, which relates to the UK, shows that people from certain groups tend to be concentrated in certain types of occupation. This phenomenon is called occupational segregation. Occupational segregation can manifest itself either horizontally or vertically. Examples of horizontal occupational segregation are, as shown by the box below, the over-representation of women working in administrative and secretarial posts across all employment sectors, as well as a disproportionate representation of Pakistani men in the occupation of taxi drivers.

- One in four Pakistani men in Britain are taxi drivers or similar.
- In Britain, women occupy 77 per cent of administration and secretarial posts but only 6 per cent of engineering and 14 per cent of architects, planners and surveyors. 83 per cent of people employed in personal services are women.
- In Britain, 40 per cent of female jobs are in the public sector compared to 15 per cent of male jobs.

Source: Equality and Human Rights Commission, 2010

Vertical occupational segregation occurs when people from certain social groups are disproportionately under-represented in senior jobs, as shown by the examples in the box below.

- Women hold one in three managerial jobs in Britain.
- Bangladeshi and Pakistani women in Britain are more likely to be employed as professionals than Bangladeshi and Pakistani men.
- Indian and Chinese people in Britain are twice as likely to be employed as professionals as white British people and the trend is upwards.

- Muslim men are as likely to be in managerial or professional jobs as elementary ones; Jewish men are 13 times more likely to be in managerial or professional jobs than elementary ones.

Source: Equality and Human Rights Commission, 2010

Finally, as mentioned earlier, surveys and statistical analysis are important for monitoring the impact of legislation, but also of economic recessions on different social groups. For example, findings from the Equality and Human Rights Commission (2010) in the UK show that the latest economic recession has hit some groups harder than others. According to this analysis, men have been more adversely affected than women and young people more than older people.

Although surveys and statistical analysis are extremely important in the study of equality and diversity in order to understand how different social groups fare in the labour market, they cannot provide adequate explanations for the causes of occupational segregation. In the next section, we review a range of theories which have been developed to explain the causes of occupational segregation and labour market inequalities.

Student Activity 1.1

Look at the International Labour Organization's key indicators of the labour market (weblink available on the supporting Online Resource Centre) and compare and contrast rates of labour market participation of men and women in two or more different countries. In particular, examine the following:

- Select two different age groups for both men and women, for example age 25–54 and age 55–64, and look at their rates of labour market participation over the last three decades, 1989–1999–2009.

- Highlight any significant changes relating to gender and age over those three decades within the selected countries.

- Think of reasons that may justify any significant differences.

You may present the results of your statistical analysis in a PowerPoint presentation.

Explanations for the causes of labour market inequalities and occupational segregation

In this section we provide a summary of some of the main theories developed within academic literature to explain the causes of labour market inequalities and occupational segregation. These can be divided into two broad groups: neo-liberal theories that focus on the labour-supply side and take the individual as a basic unit of analysis, which include the human capital theory; and theories that focus on the demand-side and the structure and functioning of the labour market which include dual labour market theory (Doeringer and Priore, 1971) and segmented labour market theory (Watts and Rich, 1993: 160).

Neo-classical labour market theory predicates that the allocation of jobs and resources in a free labour market economy is determined by supply and demand. The implications of this are that discrimination based on prejudice and stereotypes against certain social groups is irrational and has no place within the functioning of a rational and efficient market since it would be uncompetitive. Therefore, according to this theory, any irrational discrimination against workers over time would be eliminated by competitive mechanisms because employers evaluate workers in terms of their individual characteristics as they seek to maximize profit (Arrow, cited in Reich et al., 1982). However, the persistence of discrimination and inequalities among workers in the marketplace has led neo-classical economists to search for a different explanation and develop the human capital theory. According to this theory, people's position in the labour market depends on how much they are prepared to invest in their education and training. For example, women may chose to invest less in their human capital because they are likely to take time out of the labour market to bring up a family. Also from this perspective, marketplace inequalities in relation to ethnic minorities are explained by the fact that they have lower levels of education, ability and skills (Shultz, 1961). Similarly, the human capital theory has been used to explain discrimination against older workers, suggesting that they are to blame for their disadvantaged position in the labour market because they tend to fail to keep their skills up to date and thus maintain themselves as sufficiently competitive workers (Wood et al., 2008).

There is no doubt that there is some validity in this theory. However, it also presents a number of flaws. First, it ignores socio-economic constraints which limit an individual's ability to invest in her human capital. Second, it does not recognize that sometimes discriminatory attitudes and stereotypes tend to be reproduced at the level of the workplace by those who are involved in making decisions about the selection and recruitment of staff (Collinson et al., 1990). For example, older workers may be discriminated against by employers, even if they have kept their skills up to date, because of negative stereotypes. These might include the belief that older workers are less productive, less adaptable and/or less willing to accept change, or more likely to take time off for sickness. Third, it fails to explain the persistence of the pay gap between men and women. A longitudinal study about graduate career paths in the UK over a period of seven years shows that men and women with the same educational capital, namely a higher education degree, start their careers with different level of earnings (Purcell and Elias, 2004). In particular, this study has highlighted the existence of a gender pay gap of 10.5 per cent between male and female graduates when they access their first job.

Another theory developed to explain occupational segregation is the so-called 'preference theory', which argues that patterns of labour market participation and employment are the results of different lifestyle preferences and values of men and women (Hakim, 2000).

What all these theories have in common is that they tend to exonerate employers from inequalities in the labour market and instead focus on individual workers' circumstances in order to explain their position of disadvantage. Thus, from this perspective, the explanation for the occupational segregation of certain social groups lies in the labour-supply side rather than in the actual functioning of the labour market. For example, as suggested by Beechey (1986: 103), women's disadvantage in the workplace is often attributed to their individual characteristics, such as their nature, capabilities, or temperament, rather than social structures. By implication, the same can be said about other social groups, such as ethnic minorities, groups with a particular religious affiliation, or older workers who may be discriminated against because of prejudice or stereotypical views that employers have about them.

Institutionalists and Marxist political economists have instead focused on the demand-side and functioning of the labour market to explain marketplace inequalities and occupational segregation of certain groups. The dual labour market theory and the labour market segmentation theory have been developed from these perspectives. According to the dual labour market theory (Doeringer and Priore, 1971), the labour market is divided into a primary and a secondary market. The primary labour market includes more skilled, secure and better-paid jobs, usually organized in an

Signpost to Chapter 6 Managing Gender Diversity in the Workforce for an in-depth discussion of the 'preference theory'

hierarchical structure to offer opportunities for career progression. The secondary labour market includes low-skilled, low-paid and insecure jobs with poor opportunities for career progression. This theory is used to explain occupational segregation of certain groups by pointing to the fact that white men are more likely to be employed in the primary labour market, as opposed to women and ethnic minorities who are more likely to be employed in the secondary one (Anker, 1997). Although this explanation provides some insight into the process of vertical occupational segregation, since it shows the existence of an hierarchical organization of work, it does not explain horizontal occupational segregation (Beechey, 1986). For example, we have seen earlier that 40 per cent of women in the UK are employed in the public sector, where many jobs, such as teachers and nurses, have primary labour market characteristics. (It is important to be clear that the distinction between primary and secondary labour market does relate to employers. For instance, public sector employers, which are usually quite large, provide a wide range of jobs which can be located both in the primary and in the secondary labour market.) Another flaw of this theory is that not all jobs fit easily within one category or the other. Jobs in the manufacturing industry, for example, require skills that are often acquired on the job; they are not necessarily insecure jobs, but nonetheless they do not fit within the category of primary labour market. However, in spite of its shortfalls, the dual labour market theory had provided scope for developing further analysis of the labour market and has led to the argument that the labour market is divided into segments.

The labour market segmentation theory builds on the dual labour market school of thought and predicates that throughout the history of capitalism 'political economic forces have encouraged the division of the labour market into separate submarkets, or segments, distinguished by different labour market characteristics and behavioral rules' (Reich et al., 1982: 359). According to this theory, the primary labour market is segmented between 'subordinate' and 'independent' jobs. The first category includes service types of job (e.g. office work) and manufacturing jobs, while the second category includes professional types of job that requires a certain degree of autonomy, creativity and problem-solving ability. The secondary labour market is segmented into low skills and poorly paid jobs where turn over is high. This theory is based on a more nuanced and thus more realistic distinction of jobs in different segments within the primary and secondary markets and offers a better explanation for both vertical and horizontal occupational segregation. It argues that certain jobs are segmented by 'race', and although workers from ethnic minorities are present in the secondary labour market as well as in both the subordinate and independent primary labour market, they still tend to be found in 'race-typed' jobs as a result of prejudice and stereotype (ibid.: 360). The same can be said about women who may be present in all the different segments of both the secondary and primary labour market, but they tend to be in 'gender typed' jobs, for example those in education and health, which can be seen as an extension of women's caring role. Also, it has been suggested that when new technology is introduced in the workplace it might already be gendered by the activities and expectations of its manufacturers and owners: 'it may even be ergonomically sex specific, scaled for the average height or anticipated strength of the sex that is to use it' (Cockburn, 1991: 38). Drew and Emerek (1998) also draw attention to gender-based segregation and flexibility as a high proportion of women, compared to men, are concentrated in part-time jobs in whatever segment of either the primary or secondary labour market.

Marxists argue that it is in the interest of employers to keep the labour force segmented into sub-labour markets as in this way workers can be better controlled, and employers can rely on a cheap and flexible supply of labour. From this perspective, discrimination serves the purpose of maintaining the economic status quo and of ensuring that organizations continue to maximize their profit. Although this analysis may provide a credible explanation for the persistence of labour market inequalities and occupational segregation, it may not pay sufficient attention to other factors, such as social class and nationality, which, as discussed previously can be sources of disadvantage as well as historical factors and migration patterns.

In the last section of this chapter we consider the role of the stakeholders, namely the European Union, the state, the social partners (i.e. trade unions and employers' organizations) in tackling inequality in the labour market and in the workplace.

The role of stakeholders in promoting equality and diversity

In this section we consider the role of stakeholders such as the European Union, the state and social partners in promoting equality and diversity in the labour market and in the workplace.

⬛ Case study 1.2   Jessica Taylor, electrician

When Jessica Taylor's son was born she needed a job. Her ex-boyfriend told her 'why don't you do beauty therapy' – 'and I thought, that sounds alright'. By the time she was 18, Jessica's son was three. She was working part-time as a beauty therapist and earning £200 per week. 'I was struggling to make ends meet', she says.

Her life turned around after she attended an equal opportunities workshop run by the YWCA in Wolverhampton. She was asked to rank a range of careers in order of the best to the worst paid. 'I noticed that electricians were quite high up', she recalls.

'It got me thinking: why can't I be an electrician, why do I have to work in a bar or a beauty salon?'

'I started to say to people that I wanted to be an electrician and they'd say "you can't be an electrician", and I'd say "why", and they'd say "because you're a girl". So I thought I'm going to prove you wrong and that I can do it.'

Once she decided to retrain as an electrician, she enrolled at a local college. She passed her preliminary exams and applied for jobs. After putting out 15 CVs she got an interview with Doncaster Council.

'Within 15 minutes of walking out of the interview I got a call to say that I had got the job out of the 200 people that applied. I was over the moon.'

'The atmosphere where I work is very loud and dirty. I have to climb through lofts and under floor ducts. I've seen rats and lots of huge spiders. I really do enjoy being an electrician. It's opened so many doors for when I am qualified.'

Now aged 23, Jessica is in her forth and final year before becoming fully qualified. Her ambition is to learn her trade before setting up her own electrician's business catering for female customers. She thinks more girls should follow her example, but warns: 'You have got to be prepared to work hard and put a lot of effort into it – you have to do the same as the men. But it's worth it. It also means that now I've got savings – I've gone abroad on holiday, I can buy new clothes and things for Kieran, I've bought a car, and I'm doing up my house. All that wouldn't have been possible if I hadn't changed my career.'

Source: Adapted from Equality and Human Rights Commission (2010) How fair is Britain? Full link available from the Online Resource Centre.

Case study questions

Explain Jessica's experience within the labour market by referring to the theories and arguments discussed in this section. In particular, address the following questions:

- Why was Jessica initially discouraged from becoming an electrician?
- Why do you think Jessica's boyfriend suggested that she become a beauty therapist?
- Jessica's experience of working as a beauty therapist seems to suggest that beauty therapists earn considerably less than electricians. In your view, which of the theories and arguments discussed in this section can better explain such a difference?
- Consider through a 'gendered lens' Jessica's comment that to become an electrician 'you have to do the same as the men' and what this implies for women.

The European Union

The European Union has played a key role in tackling inequalities in the labour market by developing a framework of legislation and policies that have been applied across all of its member states. Equality and social cohesion have been fundamental commitments for the EU as

> key political leaders, such as Delors, sought the creation of a single market and a distinctive kind of capitalism, different from that of the US or Japan. ... Part of the distinctiveness of the EU capitalism was a commitment to social cohesion, which was unlike the US. Equal opportunities policies are part of this commitment to social cohesion and to a model of capitalism in which efficiency and equity go together, in which a degree of equity is seen to help the overall efficiency of the society. (Walby, 2000: 118–119)

Equal opportunities policies were identified at the Luxembourg summit in 1997 as one of the four pillars of European employment policies (Goetschy, 2001). In 2000, the European Council, at the meeting in Lisbon, established new goals for the following decade. Its 'Lisbon Strategy' set a target of 60 per cent for women's employment in all member states and, among other things, stressed the importance for economic growth of offering better quality jobs and promoting social inclusion through employment. Equality of opportunities for all in relation to access and participation in the labour market continues to be at the core of the 2020 European employment strategy (European Commission, 2011). Its targets include:

- 75 per cent of people aged between 20 and 64 in work.
- Reducing school drop-out rates in the member states to below 10 per cent, and aiming for at least 40 per cent of 30–40 year olds completing third-level education.
- At least 20 million fewer people in or at risk of poverty and social exclusion.

In order to achieve its objectives with regard to equality of opportunities and social inclusion, the EU has been using a series of measures that include legislation and special funding to support the adoption of targeted action.

The EU can legislate in the form of Directives which are legally binding on the member states. Examples are the EU Equality Directive (2000/78) and the Race Equality Directive (2000/43) as well as others. Member states are obliged to transpose these Directives into national legislation and if they do not comply with their obligations or if the content of their national legislation is not in line with that of the EU Directives, the European Commission can take action against them and compel them to amend their national legislation.

The main source of funding to promote equality in the workplace is the Structural Fund that was set up to reduce differences in economic prosperity and standards within the member states. The European Social Fund (ESF) is part of this funding stream and it is especially devoted to promote employment and support the achievement of equal opportunities and social inclusion in the labour market. This fund has been used for about 50 years and between 2007 and 2013 it will have distributed 75 billions of Euros among member states. The type of projects funded include training, job creation and improved access to the labour market for disadvantaged groups (European Commission, 2011b).

Student Activity 1.2

Extract the following information on two or more countries:

- Their socio-economic employment situation;
- Their ESF priorities, especially those aimed at promoting equality and diversity in the labour market;
- Examples of country-specific ESF past projects.

Prepare a report or a PowerPoint presentation that compares and contrasts the situation in the member states selected and in particular highlight the main challenges faced by these countries in terms of promoting equality and social inclusion.

Visit the Online Resource Centre for a link to the ESF website.

The role of social partners and the social dialogue

Social dialogue is defined by the European Trade Union Confederation (2011) as:

> the process of negotiation by which different actors in society (or 'social partners') reach agreement to work together on policies and activities. Social dialogue can take place at a national and sectoral level as well as a European level. 'Bipartite' social dialogue brings together workers and employers, whereas 'tripartite' social dialogue also involves government or EU representatives.

online resource centre

For a link to the Businesseurope website visit our Online Resource Centre

At a European level, national trade unions are represented by the European Trade Union Confederation while employers are represented by Businesseurope, which includes small, medium and large companies. One of the most important ways in which the Social Partners can promote equality and diversity in the workplace is through the achievement of Framework Agreements which are negotiated autonomously between representatives of employers and employees at the European level. Once a Framework Agreement has been concluded between the Social Partners it can be implemented in two different ways: through EU legislation or by the Social Partners themselves, who take direct responsibility for implementing such agreements at a national, sectoral and enterprise level.

In the first instance, a Framework Agreement becomes a Council Directive which is legally bindings on all member states. Examples of these agreements are the Council Directives on parental leave (1996), the text of which was revised in 2008, part-time work (1997), and fixed-term contracts (1999). In the second instance, a Framework Agreement is known as an 'autonomous agreement'.

So far four of these types of agreement have been negotiated – in the areas of telework (2002), work-related stress (2004), harassment and violence at work (2007), and inclusive labour markets (2010).

A similar process can take place at the national level between trade unions, representing workers, and representatives of employers, and this is called collective bargaining. This is used to agree working terms and conditions and levels of pay and it can be used to promote equality and diversity in the workplace. It has been argued that historically the process of collective bargaining has not been very supportive of the needs and interests of either women or ethnic minorities. This was probably due to the fact that trade unions used to be male-dominated and thus focused on the interests of white men who where seen as the main family earner, the 'breadwinner', while women's position in the labour market and earnings were considered of secondary importance (Williams and Adam-Smith, 2006). However, from the 1970s, trade unions have started to engage more with equality and diversity issues in the workplace and used collective bargaining to advance equality in the workplace (for an in-depth and critical discussion about equality and diversity bargaining see Kirton and Greene, 2010: Chapter 7).

Another approach that has been adopted by employers and trade unions, particularly in the UK, to advance equality in the workplace is that of working in partnership to develop policies and practice at an organizational level to pursue equality and diversity goals. For an example of this approach, see the case study at the end of Chapter 6 and the online resources.

The role of the state

The state has an important role to play through policy and legislation to promote equality and diversity in the workplace. Member states within the European Union are bound, as discussed earlier, to follow European employment policies and transpose European Directives into their national legislation. This creates a common framework of employment rights across member states, which include anti-discrimination legislation and other measures to promote equality of opportunities in the workplace and social inclusion, which contribute towards the achievement of the common goals set by European employment policies. However, it is important to point out that in spite of this common framework of employment rights, member states can have very different approaches to employment relations which are influenced by their economic and political agenda. For example, the UK is characterized by a liberal market economy which favours a deregulated labour market. This means keeping employment legislation to the minimum and, more generally, limiting state intervention in the economy. An example of how this can translate in practice is the tendency of the UK government to take a 'minimalist' approach to the implementation of European Directives on maternity and parental leave (McColgan, 2000). This is unlike the approach taken by other member states, for example Germany, which are characterized by 'coordinated market economies' where there is a robust national framework of employment legislation and a centralized system of collective bargaining (Williams and Adam-Smith, 2006).

In almost any country, the state is also an employer, to a greater or lesser degree, as it provides services to its citizens (e.g. education, health, local administration. etc.). In this capacity it can promote equality and diversity goals through public sector employers.

Equally, the state has a significant purchasing power as it buys goods and services from the private sector and, as discussed in Chapter 2, public sector employers can use procurement processes to enhance equality. This involves requiring private contractors providing goods

Signpost to Chapter 10 Managing Religion or Belief in the Workplace for further discussion on the role of public sector employers in promoting equality and diversity.

and services purchased by the public sector to adopt equality and diversity policies. An example of how this can work in practice is illustrated in the case study below.

⬤ **End of Chapter Case Study** Using procurement to promote equality and diversity: the case of Transport for London and EnterpriseMouchel

This case study is based on an interview carried out by one of the authors of this book with representatives from Transport for London (TfL) and from EnterpriseMouchel. It shows how a public organization (TfL) can use its services purchasing power to require contractors to adopt equality and diversity standards.

TfL is responsible for the operation of London's transport infrastructure, which includes the underground, London rail and surface transport (e.g. buses, taxis, traffic signals, and others). It operates in one of the most diverse cities in the world, where it is projected that by 2031 39 per cent of the population will be from Black, Asian and Minority Ethnic (BAME) groups (Lulham, 2011). TfL has included equality and diversity in its tendering process and this means that private contractors who wish to bid for work from TfL have to satisfy the following:

- They need to respond to an initial Pre-qualification Questionnaire that includes questions on equality and diversity (E&D).

- Bidders who have successfully responded to the questionnaire take part in the invitation to tender. A three-envelope approach is taken at this stage. One of these envelopes needs to contain information on E&D while the other two respectively relate to quality and to price. The E&D envelope is based on a pass or fail approach.

- Those bidders who have passed E&D have to demonstrate their commitment to E&D by producing an action plan. This must address four key components: a strategic E&D plan; an E&D training plan; a supplier diversity plan; and a communication plan.

EnterpriseMouchel is a national highway maintenance company employing 220 full-time staff and, at peak times, over 400 people, including staff in their supply chain on the Transport for London contract. When in 2007 they bid for work from TfL they had to engage with the process described above and satisfy E&D requirements. They had never been requested to do this before and their initial reaction of having to comply with TfL requirements was 'to scratch their heads' because E&D was a new field for the new highways construction industry. However, they were able to develop their action plan with support from TfL and from a parent company that had already had experience of developing E&D policies and practices.

The main challenges for EnterpriseMouchel in implementing their E&D plan were, first, to raise their staff awareness about the importance of E&D and ensure that they bought into this idea, and second, to ensure that their subcontractors in the supply chain complied with E&D requirements.

Their workforce is made up primarily of blue collar workers who are predominantly white and male, so they needed to make sure that this group appreciated the relevance of the E&D agenda, for themselves as much as for other groups. For this reason the company put a lot of emphasis on inclusivity and developed a programme called RESPECT. This stresses the importance of responsible behaviour, both individually and as a company, health and safety issues, and respect in the workplace, since these are values which relate to all people. As part of this initiative, emphasis was placed up-skilling the workforce, increasing skills and developing education levels, setting up an apprenticeship programme, providing local employment, and engaging with the community.

Engaging contractors in the supply chain was also a major challenge given that some of these companies are rather small and lack the capacity to manage an E&D development process. EnterpriseMouchel helped these small businesses by sharing policies and practices with them, and by inviting TfL to explain directly to them the importance of engaging with E&D. As a result of such action, these small businesses are now in a better position to compete for public work where E&D requirements are included in the bidding process. EnterpriseMouchel has derived a number of advantages from developing an E&D approach. These include:

- A responsible procurement policy which takes into account the values of E&D, health and safety, environmental sustainability and ethical procurement, favouring and supporting SMEs.

- An improved working environment that supports their staff's needs which has resulted in lower staff turnover, recruitment costs, and increased the education level of staff.

- Greater engagement with the community through an Engagement Schools and Community annual programme and the offer of apprenticeships, work placements, and work experiences for the disadvantaged.

As a result of their effort and initiatives to promote E&D, they have won the Excellence Award 2010 for their approach to Corporate Social Responsibility.

Case study questions

Why do you think that it is important for TfL to require its contractors to develop E&D policies and practices?

What were the main challenges for EntrepriseMouchel in developing E&D policies?

How did they address them?

How important is the law on procurement to ensure that companies like EntrepriseMouchel apply E&D standards to their policies and practices?

online resource centre

The full interview can be accessed on our Online Resource Centre

Conclusion

We have explored in this first chapter the different meanings of the concept of equality and how the notion of diversity has helped us to shift from a formal approach to equality to a more substantive one. Equality and inclusion appear to be the most helpful model of substantive equality as they encompass both the idea of equality as dignity and as disadvantage.

We have also examined the concept of disadvantage and discrimination and seen how the dynamics between these two elements can create 'a vicious circle' which can lead to social distance and reinforce prejudice. Furthermore, it is important to understand that discrimination is not a one-dimensional issue, but that it can present multiple dimensions. Although, for clarity, in the second part of this book we focus on the separate strands of equality, we have nevertheless discussed here examples of multiple and intersectional discrimination.

Extensive patterns of disadvantage and discrimination still exists in the labour market. These, however, are not static and change as society evolves. Labour market surveys and statistical analysis are key tools for monitoring rates of labour market participation and employment patterns of different groups, and for identifying inequalities in the marketplace.

In the next chapters in this part of the book we focus on equality legislation and on theoretical approaches to equality and diversity and the implementation of diversity management. In the second part of the book we take a thematic approach and discuss theory and practice relating to different equality strands.

Review and discussion questions

1. How can the concept of equality be defined?

2. What is the difference between disadvantage and discrimination? Explain the concept of the 'vicious circle' of discrimination by providing examples.

3. What are the main patterns of disadvantage and inequalities affecting different social groups?

4. How can surveys and statistical analysis help with the study of equality and diversity issues in the labour market and in the workplace?

5. What does occupational segregation mean and what theories have been developed to explain this phenomenon?

6. How important is the social dialogue in advancing equality in the workplace?

For additional material on the content of this chapter please visit the supporting Online Resource Centre at **www.oxfordtextbooks.co.uk/orc/kumra_manfredi/**

Further reading

Barrett, R. (2010) Disadvantaged groups in the labour market. *Economic and Labour Market Review,* **Office for National Statistics.**

Equality and Human Rights Commission (2010) *How fair is Britain?* **Manchester: EHRC.**

Fredman, S. (2001) Equality a new generation? *Industrial Law Journal,* **30/2: 145–168.**

Office for National Statistics (2010) Disadvantaged groups in the labour market. *Economic and Labour Market Review* **4/6: 18–24.**

References

Ambrosini, M. and Barone, C. (2007) *Employment and working conditions of migrant workers.* European Foundation for the Improvement of Living and Working Condition. Luxembourg: Office for Official Publications of the European Communities.

Anker, R. (1997) Theories of occupational segregation by sex: an overview. *International Labour Review,* 136/7: 315–340.

Barrett, R. (2010) Disadvantaged groups in the labour market. *Economic and Labour Market Review,* Office for National Statistics 4/6: 18–24.

Beechey, V. (1986) Women's employment in contemporary Britain, in Beechey, V. and Whitegg, E. (eds), *Women in Britain Today.* Milton Keynes: Open University Press.

Blanden, J., Gregg, P. and Machin, S. (2005) *Intergenerational mobility in Europe and North America.* London: Centre for Economic Performance, London School of Economics.

Bourdieu, P. (1984) *Distinction: A Social Critique of the Judgment of Taste.* London: Routledge.

Cockburn, C. (1991) In the Way of Women: Men's Resistance to Sex Equality in Organizations. Basingstoke: Macmillan.

Collinson, D., Knights, D., and Collinson, M. (1990) *Managing to Discriminate.* London: Routledge.

Drew, E. and Emerek, R. (1998) Employment, flexibility and gender, in Drew, E., Emerek, R., and Mahon, E. (eds), *Women, Work and the Family in Europe.* London: Routledge.

Doeringer, P. and Piore, M. (1971) *Internal Labour Markets and Manpower Analysis.* Lexington, MA: DC Heath and Co.

Equality and Human Rights Commission (2010), *How fair is Britain?* Manchester: EHRC. Available at http://www.equalityhumanrights.com/ key-projects/triennial-review/full-report-and-evidence-downloads/

European Commission (2011a) *European Employment Strategy.* Available at http://ec.europa.eu/social/ main.jsp?catId=102&langId=en

European Commission (2011b) *European Social Fund.* Available at http://ec.europa.eu/ employment_social/esf/index_en.htm

European Trade Union Confederation (2011) *What is social dialogue?* Available at http://www.etuc. org/a/104

Eurostat (2010) Report on equality between men and women. Brussels: European Commission.

Fredman, S. (2001) Equality a new generation?, *Industrial Law Journal,* 30/2: 145–168.

Fredman, S. (2002) *Discrimination Law.* Oxford: Oxford University Press.

Fredman, S. and Szyszczak, E. (1992) The intersection of race and gender, in Hepple, B. and Szyszczak, E (eds), *Discrimination: The Limits of the Law.* London: Mansell.

Goetschy, J. (2001) The European employment strategy from Amsterdam to Stockholm: has it reached its cruising speed, *Industrial Relations*, 32/5: 401–418.

Government Equalities Office (2009) *Explaining the Equality Bill: Dual Discrimination.* Available at http://webarchive.nationalarchives.gov.uk/20110608160754.

Hakim, C. (2000) *Work-Lifestyle Choices in the 21st Century.* Oxford: Oxford University Press.

Hanzl-Weibss(beta), D. and Vidovic, H. (2010) *Working Poor in Europe, European working Conditions Observatory.* Available at http://eurofound.europa.eu/ewco/studies/tn0910026s/tn0910026s.htm

Hepple, B. (2010) The new single equality act in Britain. *The Equal Rights Review*, 5: 11–24.

Hoskyns, C. (1996) *Integrating Gender: Women, Law and Politics in the European Union.* London: Verso.

Jenkins, R. (1986) *Racism and recruitment: Managers, organisations and equal opportunities in the labour market.* Cambridge: Cambridge University Press.

Kirkton, G. and Greene, A.-M. (2010) *The dynamics of managing diversity. A critical approach.* 3rd ed. Oxford: Butterworth-Heinemann.

Lulham, J. (2011) Transport for London's approach to equality and supplier diversity through procurement. *International Journal of Discrimination and the Law*, 11, 1/2: 99–104.

Makkonen, T. (2002) Multiple, Compound and Intersectional Discrimination: Bringing the Experience of the Most Marginalized to the Fore. Abo, Finland: Institute of Human Rights.

McColgan, A. (2000) *Discrimination: Text, Cases and Materials.* 1st ed. Oxford: Hart.

Nicot, A. M. and Houtman, I. (2007) *Gender Mainstreaming in Survey, European Foundation for the Improvement of Living and Working Conditions.* Luxembourg: Office for Official Publications of the European Communities.

Purcell, K. and Elias, P. (2004) *Seven Years On: Graduate Careers in a Changing Labour Market.* The Higher Education Career Services Unit. Available at http://ww2.prospects.ac.uk/downloads/csdesk/members/reports/seven_years_on.pdf

Reich, M., Gordon, D.M., and Edwards, R.C. (1982) Dual labour markets: a theory of labour market segmentation. *The Journal of Human Resources*, 17/3: 359–365.

Schultz, T. W. (1961) Investments in human capital. *American Economic Review*, 51/1: 1–17.

Sen, A. (2000) *Social exclusion: concept, application, and scrutiny.* Social Development Papers No.1, Manila, Philippines: Office of Environment and Social Development.

Solanke, I. (2010) Multiple discrimination in Britain: immutability and its alternative. Paper presented at Current Reflections on EU Anti-Discrimination Law, Academy of European Law, Trier 13–14 September.

Sullerot, E. (1971) *Women, Society and Change.* London: Wiedenfeld.

Vandenbrande, T., Coppin, L. and van der Hallen, P. (2006) *Mobility in Europe.* Foundation for the Improvement of Living and Working Conditions. Luxembourg: Office for Official Publications of the European Communities.

Vickers, L. (2011) The expanded public sector duty: Age, religion and sexual orientation *International Journal of Discrimination and the law*, 11/1–2: 43–58.

Walby, S. (2000) *Globalisation, women and work: Global contexts for policy options for gender equity. Re-definitions of women's relationship to employment.* ESRC Seminar Series: Women, Work and Trade Unions. Oxford: The Oxford Women Studies Network.

Watts, M. and Rich, J. (1993) Occupational sex segregation in Britain, 1979–1989: the persistence of sexual stereotyping. *Cambridge Journal of Economics*, 17: 159–177.

Wilkinson, R. and Pickett, K. (2010) *The Spirit Level: Why Equality is Better for Everyone.* Harmondsworth: Penguin.

Williams, S. Adam-Smith, D. (2006) *Contemporary Employment Relations: A Critical Introduction.* Oxford: Oxford University Press.

Wood, G., Wilkinson, A., and Harcourt, M. (2008) Age discrimination and working life: perspectives and contestations – a review of the contemporary literature. *International Journal of Management Reviews*, 10/4: 425–442.

An Outline of European and UK Equality Legislation

Learning objectives

- Understand the main legal provisions in the UK and EU governing diversity and equality in the workplace
- Understand the legal concepts of direct and indirect discrimination, harassment and victimization
- Define the protected characteristics which are protected under UK and EU discrimination law
- Explain the rationale for the introduction of the legislation and understand how the legislation has been implemented

Key terms

- **Direct discrimination**: less favourable treatment of a person because of a protected characteristic. Direct discrimination cannot be justified, except in the case of age and disability. Discrimination based on a stereotypical assumption made by the employer will be direct discrimination.
- **Equal pay**: the principle that men and women are entitled to equal pay for equal work. This includes doing the same or similar work or work of equal value. Pay includes basic wages and salary as well as other contractual benefits such as company cars, annual leave, and pension contributions.
- **Harassment**: unwanted conduct which has the purpose or effect of creating an intimidating, hostile, degrading, humiliating or offensive environment, or of violating dignity. Harassment can occur on the basis of any of the protected characteristics.
- **Indirect discrimination**: the application of a provision, criterion or practice to all staff equally but which puts groups with a protected characteristic at a disadvantage compared with others. For example, a requirement may be imposed on both men and women but it may put women at a disadvantage compared with men.
- **Occupational requirement**: where it is crucial to a particular job that a person be of a particular sex, race, disability, religion or belief, sexual orientation, or age, etc., then there is an occupational requirement for the job. This provides an exception to the general non-discrimination rule and allows an employer to impose a requirement that the holder of the job must have the particular characteristic. For example, for reasons of privacy it may be that a public changing room attendant should be of the same sex as those using the changing room.
- **Protected characteristic**: these are the characteristics which are protected by UK discrimination law. They are: age, disability, gender reassignment, marriage and civil partnership, pregnancy and maternity, race, religion or belief, sex, and sexual orientation.

- **Reasonable adjustment**: (applies to disability discrimination only) the duty to make reasonable adjustments to try to remove disadvantages faced by disabled workers. Examples include changing the physical environment to enable access to a building, providing specialist equipment to help disabled workers, or changing working hours to make work possible for a disabled worker.

- **Victimization**: this occurs where a person is treated badly because he or she has, in good faith, taken action or supported someone else's actions relating to an equality claim, for example, being treated badly for bringing a discrimination claim or for agreeing to give evidence in the hearing of a discrimination case.

Introduction

This chapter will examine the law on equality and diversity as it is applied in the workplace. The equality and diversity legal framework applies beyond the employment and prohibits discrimination in the provision of goods and services and in education. However, the law considered in this chapter will focus on the protection against discrimination in the work context. The aim of the chapter is to provide an introduction to the relevant legal provisions and case law. A more critical analysis of the law can be found in the suggested further reading at the end of the chapter.

Legislation exists to protect against discrimination on grounds of age, disability, gender reassignment, marriage and civil partnership, pregnancy and maternity, race, religion or belief, sex, and sexual orientation. The legislation was introduced for different grounds at different times, with sex equality and race equality law introduced at various points during the twentieth century, and discrimination on grounds of sexual orientation, age, religion and belief being introduced in 2003. Some of the legislation was introduced as a result of the requirements of EU law. Thus, the law prohibiting discrimination on grounds of age, sexual orientation, religion and belief was introduced to comply with the EU Equality Directive (2000/78). Other legislation, such as the Race Relations Act 1976, was introduced in the UK first, with the EU introducing its Race Equality Directive in 2000 (2000/43). In each case, however, the reason for introducing the protection is the fact that the workforce in the UK and the EU is very divided, with some jobs being viewed as traditionally male or female, with lower participation in employment of workers with disabilities, and with ethnic minorities being over-represented in lower skilled jobs (McColgan, 2005).

Since the introduction of equality legislation from the 1960s onwards, the amount of legislation and regulation has grown hugely, creating a number of anomalies between different grounds and making the law cumbersome to use. The decision was therefore taken to introduce a single Act to bring the legislation into one place and to introduce more consistency between different grounds. This process led to the introduction of the Equality Act 2010. Many of the cases considered in this chapter were decided under the old legislation, but as the new Act has not substantially changed the definitions used in the law, they can be used to illustrate the meaning and application of the Equality Act 2010.

Although some of the legal protection was introduced first in the UK, the area of equality law is now largely governed by EU law, a result of the implementation of a number of EU Directives on the subject. The Directives are implemented in the UK via our domestic legislation, but ultimately the interpretation of the domestic law must comply with the EU standards, as EU law takes precedence over UK law. Therefore, both the EU and the UK standards will be referred to in this chapter.

Some separate additional legislation governs equality law in Northern Ireland. In order to create a complete picture of the legal framework in the UK, the Northern Ireland provisions will be considered where they differ from the law that applies in the rest of the UK.

The law governing discrimination in the UK now prohibits discrimination in a number of areas, such as the provision of goods and services and education, but the area in which equality law is perhaps best established is in the workplace. The Equality Act 2010 covers all who work for payment, whether they are employees, self-employed and office holders, as well as those who are seeking work. It prohibits discrimination in terms of recruitment, interview arrangements, decisions to dismiss or discipline, and in other matters relating to employment, such as access to training and promotion.

The remit of the Equality Act 2010 extends beyond prohibiting discrimination at work to allowing employers to take proactive steps to promote equality. The Act provides that positive discrimination (e.g. employing a woman rather than a man in order to fulfil an equality objective) can be allowed in some situations (see below). It also imposes additional duties on public sector employers to take steps to advance equality for some protected groups and enhance good relations between different groups. The Act also allows for regulations to be made to require public sector employers to use procurement processes that enhance equality, for example by requiring those companies with whom they work to have equal opportunities policies covering their staff.

In order to understand the full extent of the duty on employers not to discriminate it is first necessary to consider the various forms of discrimination. The grounds of discrimination which are covered by the law will then be examined. Next, the chapter will look at the exceptions to the non-discrimination principle and some special provisions relating to age and disability discrimination and equal pay. The chapter ends by considering whether positive action is justified to help to promote equality and diversity at work.

Direct discrimination

Direct discrimination occurs where a person is treated less favourably because of a protected characteristic. It is prohibited under both EU and UK law. Examples of direct discrimination include a female candidate who is not given an interview even though she has better qualifications than the male candidates for the job, or a Muslim man who is not promoted because the employer does not approve of his religion.

Regarding a claim of direct discrimination, it is no defence for the employer to argue that it did not mean to discriminate. The law is not concerned with the intention of the employer, only with whether less favourable treatment has occurred *because* of the protected characteristic. If it can be shown that the protected characteristic was the cause of the less favourable treatment, then direct discrimination will have occurred. This can be illustrated by the case of *James v Eastleigh BC* (1990), which involved the provision of services rather than employment, although the principles remain the same. Here a husband and wife, both aged 61, went for a swim. Swims were free for those of pensionable age, at that time aged 60 for women and

65 for men. On this basis, Mrs James was able to swim for free but Mr James was charged. The intention of the local council was to help those on a pension, and therefore on a lower income, to have a free swim. However, this helpful motive did not prevent a finding of sex discrimination. If Mr James had been female he would have swum for free. Therefore there was direct sex discrimination. The case also established that discrimination on a ground which itself is discriminatory (here, pensionable age) is also discriminatory.

Discrimination which is based on a stereotypical assumption made by the employer will be treated as direct discrimination. For example, an employer refused a secondment to a married woman who wished to accompany her husband to work in another geographical area. The employer thought she was unlikely to return after the secondment, but this was based on the stereotypical assumption that women tend to follow their husband's careers. The refusal of a secondment was therefore directly discriminatory (*Horsey v Dyffed CC* (1982)). Employers should treat all staff as individuals: making generalized assumptions about staff on the basis of protected characteristics will amount to direct discrimination.

A statement by an employer that it will not recruit people who share a protected characteristic will amount to discrimination in respect of recruitment, even where an individual victim cannot be identified. For example, in *Centrum vorr Gelijkheid van Kansen en voor Racismebestrijding* [2008] an employer made a public statement that it would not employ Moroccans. This was direct discrimination.

Discrimination can occur on the basis of a protected characteristic even if the person discriminated against does not have that characteristic, For example, where an employer disciplined a white employee for refusing to follow an instruction to deny services to Asian customers, this amounted to direct race discrimination. The bad treatment was because of race, even though it was not based on the race of the employee (*Weathersfield* v *Sargent* (1998)). Direct discrimination can also occur on the basis of association with a person who has the protected characteristic. For example, discrimination against a woman because her husband is a Muslim would be religious discrimination. Equally, direct discrimination can occur because of a perception that a person has a protected characteristic even if that perception is wrong. For example, it will be age discrimination if a man is denied a job because he looks too young to have sufficient experience to represent a client, even though he is older than he looks and does have sufficient experience.

➡ Student Activity 2.1

Coleman v Attridge Law [2008] ICR 1128 (ECJ)

The mother of a disabled child claimed that she had been discriminated against because of disability as she was treated less favourably because her son was disabled.

Do you think that this is a valid claim of direct discrimination? Provide reasons for your answer.

It is not directly discriminatory to require men and women to wear different work uniforms. For example, a requirement that women must wear dresses and men must have short hair is not discriminatory because both men and women have a uniform, even though it is not the same. This was confirmed in *Smith* v *Safeway* (1996), where a man claimed sex discrimination because the employer required that he had short hair whereas women could have long hair as long as it was tied back. He was unsuccessful, as the tribunal held that both sexes were subject to a dress code, based on conventional dress.

One very important feature of direct discrimination is that, except in the case of age and disability, it can never be justified. Once less favourable treatment has been shown to be because of a protected characteristic, then the treatment will be found to be discriminatory, whether or not there is a good reason for the treatment. This makes the protection particularly strong.

Indirect discrimination

Indirect discrimination occurs where all staff are treated the same (i.e. the employer imposes the same requirements on all employees), but that treatment puts some groups (defined by a protected characteristic, e.g. women, older people, etc.) at a particular disadvantage compared with others. An example of indirect discrimination would be a requirement that candidates for a job must be over 1.8 metres tall. This does not exclude all women nor does it allow all men to apply, but it has a bigger impact on women than men as fewer women are over 1.8 metres tall. A uniform rule that requires that staff have no head coverings at work would indirectly discriminate against Sikh men and Muslim women, as many of them wear head coverings as part of their religious practice. Similarly, a requirement to have 20 years' experience for a job may indirectly discriminate against younger workers.

A requirement can be indirectly discriminatory, even though individuals *can* physically comply with it if, in practice, it puts them at a disadvantage. For example, if an employer were to impose a requirement that all staff must wear skirts to work, men would be put at a disadvantage, even though they can physically comply with the requirement. On this basis, it is generally accepted by the courts that requirements linked to full-time work can be indirectly discriminatory against women because, in practice, it is more usual for women to work part-time when they have children. Thus requirements to work full-time put women at a disadvantage, even though some men also take time out of their careers to care for children.

Debate Box

Organize the class into two groups, one for the motion and one against it.
   The motion is:
On the one hand, it is arguable that a decision to work part-time while children are young is a personal choice which does not need to be protected by the law and, in modern times, it is quite usual to see men bringing up children. On the other hand, it remains the case that, in practice, most child care is undertaken by women. Debate the arguments for and against treating requirements to work full-time as indirectly discriminatory against women.
   Stages in the debate: (each stage is given with timings, the overall time for the activity is 55 minutes – allowing a few minutes for change over of presenters, etc.)

- Each group has 20 minutes to prepare their arguments either for or against the motion.
- Each group is given five minutes to present their opening statement (10 minutes in total).
- Groups reconvene for 10 minutes to prepare rebuttal arguments.
- Each group has two minutes to present rebuttal arguments.

A vote is taken and the winners of the debate are announced. The casting vote goes to impartial observers: tutors, audience members not involved in the debate, and observers.

Indirect discrimination will not occur where the policy or rule can be justified on objective grounds. In many cases, requirements which disadvantage certain groups may be justified. For example, a requirement to be able to carry very heavy weights may be essential for a job as a fire fighter, even though it disadvantages women.

In order to justify an otherwise indirectly discriminatory requirement the employer must be able to show that the requirement imposed is a proportionate means of achieving a legitimate aim. A legitimate aim may refer to a business need, or be a matter of health and safety, or some other objective need of the employer. It is for the employer to prove that there was a legitimate aim.

The employer must also show that the use of the requirement to achieve that aim was *proportionate*. The definition of 'proportionality' is provided in an EU case *Bilka Kaufhaus GmbH v Weber von Hartz* (1987). In order to be proportionate the legitimate aim must correspond to a real need of the business, and the means used to achieve the aim must be appropriate and necessary. In effect, employers 'must not use a sledgehammer to crack a nut' when imposing requirements on jobs which put protected groups at a disadvantage. In *Bilka Kaufhaus*, the employer had reduced access to its occupational pension scheme for part-time workers in an attempt to encourage more workers to work full-time so that they would be able to staff their shops easily on Saturdays. However, this rule had an adverse impact on part-timers, who tended to be women, and so it had to be justified. The European Court held that in order to be proportionate, the employer would have to show that the means used to achieve the aim (denying access to the pension scheme for part-time staff in order to encouraging Saturday working) were necessary and did not create too great a disadvantage to women in comparison with the benefits to the company. In effect, if there are other less discriminatory ways to achieve the employer's aim, then the requirement will not be justified.

Whether or not indirect discrimination can be justified will therefore depend on the employer being able to show that there is a legitimate aim for the work requirement as well as being able to show that the use of the requirement to achieve that aim is proportionate. Examples of legitimate aims for indirectly discriminatory provisions include a requirement to work at weekends (which may disadvantage some religious groups) being necessary for business reasons where weekend trading is important to the business (*James v MSC Cruises* (2006)); a requirement to be fluent in English (which may disadvantage some racial groups) being necessary where there is significant interaction with the public requiring good communication skills. The following case study gives an example of how indirect discrimination can be justified.

> **Case study 2.1** *Azmi v Kirklees Metropolitan Borough Council UKEAT/0009/07/MAA*
>
> Ms Azmi was a Muslim school teaching assistant who wanted to wear the niqab or face veil when in the presence of male colleagues. She was dismissed for refusing to remove the *niqab* in classes led by a male teacher and claimed indirect discrimination. She was unsuccessful. The court held that the requirement to have her face visible to children in class was a requirement applied to all, which put her at a disadvantage because of her religion. It was thus potentially indirectly discriminatory. However, the requirement was justified. The restriction on wearing the *niqab* was proportionate given the need to uphold the interests of the children in having the best possible education. The school had investigated and found that the quality of her teaching was reduced when Azmi wore the face covering. It was therefore proportionate to impose the restriction on face coverings in class in order to achieve the legitimate aim of ensuring the best possible educational experience for the school children assisted by Ms Azmi.

Victimization

EU Directive 2000/78 and the Equality Act 2010 provide protection for those who are victimized for making use of their provisions. Victimization occurs where a person is treated less favourably for bringing proceedings or giving evidence about discrimination on any ground, or for alleging that acts of discrimination have occurred. It is broadly defined and also contains a catch-all provision that covers doing anything in connection with the Equality Act 2010. For example, if an employer decides not to promote a member of staff because she has given evidence in discrimination proceedings brought against the employer by a colleague, the individual who was refused promotion would be able to claim that she had been victimized.

Protection from victimization can be lost if false information is given in bad faith. Thus even if the allegation turns out to be false, it will still be victimization to discipline the complainant unless the allegation is also made in bad faith, for example it is deliberately made up in order to get someone into trouble.

Harassment

Harassment is defined in the EU Directive 2000/78 and the Equality Act 2010 as unwanted conduct which has the purpose or effect of creating an intimidating, hostile, degrading, humiliating or offensive environment, or of violating dignity. It can occur on any of the protected grounds. The definition recognizes that harassment can be a very significant problem at work in that conduct can poison a work atmosphere. So the definition makes clear that the creation of a hostile or offensive environment at work is legally wrong when based on a protected ground such as race, gender, sexual orientation, etc. It also protects where conduct violates dignity. Examples of harassment can include the display of pictures of nude women at work, use of racist language, homophobic bullying, or overt displays of religious intolerance. In each case, it is not necessary to have the protected characteristic in order to find the behaviour offensive, as long as an offensive,

> ⚫ **Case study** 2.2   *English v Sanderson Blinds Ltd [2008] EWCA Civ 1421*
>
> In *English v Sanderson Blinds Ltd* [2008] a man was persistently subjected to name calling and sexual innuendo by colleagues suggesting that he was homosexual. This continued despite the fact that those subjecting him to the harassment knew that he was not gay. The court accepted that the treatment could amount to harassment related to sexual orientation.

hostile, or degrading environment is created. Thus both men and women may find topless calendars offensive and gay and straight staff may find that homophobic language creates a hostile environment. Case study 2.2 is an example of how harassment can work to protect individuals even if they do not have the protected characteristic themselves.

In addition to the form of harassment defined above, the Equality Act 2010 provides two further types of sexual harassment. First, where there is unwanted conduct of a sexual nature, which has the purpose or effect of creating an intimidating, hostile, degrading, humiliating or offensive environment, or of violating dignity. Second, where a person is treated less favourably because they have submitted to or rejected sexual harassment, or harassment related to sex or gender reassignment. For example, if a manager propositions one of his female staff, and she rejects him, she would then have a claim of harassment if she is subsequently turned down for promotion because of this.

Harassment most commonly occurs as a result of a number of incidents which take place over a long period of time. However, in some cases a single incident, if it is severe enough, will be capable of creating a hostile, degrading or offensive environment.

Creating an 'intimidating', 'hostile' or 'degrading' environment suggests that fairly high levels of harm to the victim will need to be caused before harassment occurs. However, the alternative terms 'humiliating' and 'offensive' suggest a more subjective standard, and a victim could be humiliated or offended by behaviour which others may not find upsetting. Where it is not clear whether an offensive, hostile or humiliating environment has been created, the Equality Act 2010 states that the court should take into account the perception of the victim, the other circumstances of the case, and whether it is reasonable for the conduct to be viewed as offensive, degrading, etc. The objective 'reasonableness' standard should protect against unreasonable claims of harassment by hypersensitive victims.

Protected characteristics

Under the EU Directives, the following grounds are protected: race, sex, sexual orientation, religion and belief, age, and disability. Under the Equality Act 2010, the list of protected characteristics is longer: age; disability; gender reassignment; marriage and civil partnership; pregnancy and maternity; race; religion or belief; sex; sexual orientation. In addition, political opinion is also protected in Northern Ireland.

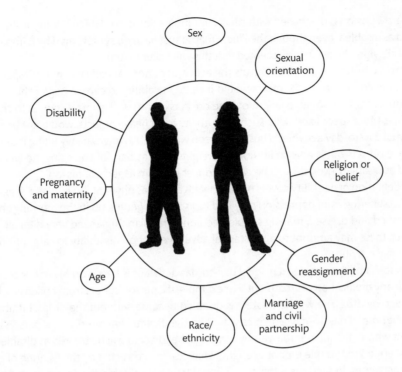

Figure 2.1 Protected characteristics

Age

Age discrimination was first prohibited in 2006 when the provisions of the EU Directive 2000/78 were implemented in the UK. There is no requirement to be of a particular age before being able to claim age discrimination. Any less favourable treatment at work because of age is prohibited. Discrimination because of perceived age is also prohibited. Discrimination can occur because of the individual's age as well as because he or she falls within a particular age range. For example, a person may be refused a job because they look too young to do the job or an employer may refuse to promote staff members aged over 50. In both cases this will amount to age discrimination.

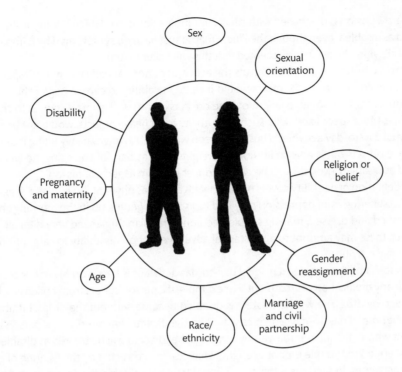

Signpost to Chapter 11 Managing Age Diversity in the Workplace

The main distinguishing feature of age discrimination is that, unlike in the case of other grounds of discrimination, direct age discrimination can be justified.

Disability

Disability discrimination was prohibited in the UK in 1995, with the EU legislation on the issue following in 2000. A person is defined as having a disability if he or she has a physical or mental impairment and the impairment has a substantial and long-term adverse effect on his or her ability to carry out normal day-to-day activities. A person's impairment is long term if it has lasted, or is likely to last for at least 12 months, or is likely to last for the whole of the person's life. Thus, a shorter illness will not be covered by the protection, but a person who is suddenly disabled in an accident will be protected from the date the disability arises, without having to wait for 12 months, if the disability is likely to last for 12 months or more.

Where a person is diagnosed with cancer, multiple sclerosis or HIV/AIDS, he or she will be treated as disabled, even though the illness may at first have no symptoms which impair day-to-day activities, because it is accepted that this will occur in future.

'Normal day-to-day activities' means the activities of normal daily life, not the specialized activities needed at work. Examples would include the ability to carry a bag of shopping, to concentrate for a reasonable length of time on a task, or to walk short distances to shops or the office. More specialized skills, such as an ability to lift heavy objects, would not be classed as normal day-to-day activities. Thus, if a person whose job involves heavy lifting is unable to lift heavy objects but is able to lift normal weights such as bags of shopping, he will not be classed as disabled, even though he can no longer perform aspects of his job.

The definition of disability covers mental health as well as physical disabilities. For example, a person suffering from depression may find tasks such as getting up in the morning and getting washed and dressed, making simple decisions, and planning ahead very difficult. Taken together, these may amount to a substantial adverse effect on his ability to carry out normal day-to-day activities.

A person's ability to perform normal day-to-day activities is based on his or her condition without any medication or treatment. For example, if a person suffers from epilepsy, which is controlled by drugs, he will be treated as disabled because, without the drugs, his ability to carry out normal day-to-day activities would be significantly impaired; and a person who is deaf but whose hearing is improved by wearing a hearing aid will be treated as disabled. The only exception to this rule is poor eyesight, which can be corrected by the wearing of glasses or contact lenses. In such cases the person is not treated as disabled.

The Equality Act 2010 and related guidance contain a significant amount of further detail about how to determine whether a person is disabled according to the definition.

Signpost to
Chapter 7
Managing
Disability in the
Workplace

Gender reassignment

Discrimination against individuals on the basis that they have undertaken or are going to undertake gender reassignment surgery has been prohibited in the UK since 1999 and under EU law since 2006 in Directive 2006/54/EC. A person has the protected characteristic of gender reassignment if the person is proposing to undergo, is undergoing, or has undergone a process (or part of a process) for the purpose of reassigning the person's sex by changing physiological or other attributes of sex.

Signpost to
Chapter 9
Managing
Sexual
Orientation and
Transgender in
the Workplace

 Student Activity 2.2

P v S and Cornwall CC Case C 13/94 ECJ
The applicant was employed as the general manager of a school, and had been employed as a male employee. In April 1992 she informed the school that she was to undergo gender reassignment. The governors of the school were informed. During the summer of 1992 P took sick leave to undergo initial surgical treatment. However, she was given notice of dismissal and was not allowed to return to the school in her female gender role. At the time of the case there was no separate 'protected characteristic' of gender reassignment. However P claimed sex discrimination.

Do you think that P had a valid claim of direct discrimination? Provide reasons for your answer.

Marriage and civil partnership

A person is protected against direct and indirect discrimination because they are married or in a civil partnership. Those who are not married or in a civil partnership are not protected. Thus single people and those who are divorced are not protected against discrimination because of this status.

Pregnancy and maternity

Discrimination because of pregnancy and maternity is covered by the Equality Act 2010. Prior to the introduction of special protection for pregnant workers, less favourable treatment because of pregnancy and maternity was treated as sex discrimination as discrimination on the basis of pregnancy and maternity only affected women. It is important to note that direct discrimination because of pregnancy and maternity cannot be justified, even on the basis of cost. The following case study provides an example discrimination on grounds of pregnancy which cannot be justified.

Protection lasts for the duration of pregnancy and the maternity leave period, and prevents any less favourable treatment, such as exclusion from training, or denying a pregnant worker an appraisal, especially if the appraisal is linked to pay via performance-related pay. However, reducing pay during a period of maternity leave does not amount to discrimination, as long as statutory maternity pay is provided.

In addition to the protection against discrimination, additional rights relating to maternity leave and maternity pay are contained in The Work and Families Act 2006 and the Employment Rights Act 1996.

Race

Race discrimination was first introduced in the UK in 1965, but was not applied to employment until 1976. Protection against race discrimination in employment was introduced in the EU in 2000 in the Racial Equality Directive 2000/43/EC.

In the Equality Act 2010, the protected characteristic of race includes colour, nationality, and ethnic or national origins, and , there is a power for the government to add caste to the list of characteristics protected under the category of race.

Case study 2.3 *Mahlburg v Land Mecklenburg-Vorpommern* (2000) European Court of Justice

Mahlburg was employed under a fixed-term contract as a nurse in a heart surgery clinic. While pregnant, she applied for a permanent contract. She was rejected because German health and safety laws relating to the protection of pregnant women from the effects of dangerous substances. The ECJ ruled that this was direct discrimination because of sex, even though she could not take up the appointment until after she returned from maternity leave.

The case does not mean that health and safety obligations can be ignored. Instead, if the pregnant woman is the best person for the job, she should be offered the job, and alternative arrangements should be made until she can take up the work.

The use of the term 'ethnic origins' is used to ensure that individuals and groups are protected against race discrimination where they may not constitute a separate racial or national group but may share a strong group identity. The question of how to define an ethnic group was considered in *Mandla v Lee* (1983), a case involving Sikhs, a group which is racially the same as other South Asians but which views itself as a separate ethnic group. The case concerned a school uniform requirement to wear a school cap. This put the complainant at a disadvantage, as he wore a turban, in accordance with his religious practice as a Sikh. Others from the same racial group (South Asians) were not affected, so the claimant could not claim discrimination because of race, and the case took place prior to the introduction of protection against religious discrimination. Thus the only way to gain protection from discrimination was to show that it was on the grounds of ethnic origin.

The court held that Sikhs were a separate ethnic group. In reaching this conclusion, they looked at a number of factors which should be present to show that there is a separate ethnic group. First was the fact that the group had a long, shared history, distinguishing it from other groups, and Sikhs are very conscious of this distinction. Second was that the group had a cultural tradition of its own, which may include a separate religious identity. Other relevant factors identifying ethnic groups are that they have a common geographical origin or a number of common ancestors, that they share a common language, not necessarily exclusive to group, that there is a common, exclusive literature, a common religion, separate from neighbouring groups, and that they share the experience of being a minority or oppressed group among the dominant group. On this basis it has also been held that gypsies (*CRE v Dutton* (1989)) and Jews (*Seide v Gillette Industries* (1980)) are ethnic groups, but that Rastafarians (*Dawkins v Department of the Environment* (1993)) and Muslims (*J H Walker v Hussein* (1996)) are not. With the introduction of protections against discrimination on grounds of religion and belief in 2003 (see below), the different treatment of these different groups had become less contentious.

Religion or belief

Discrimination on the basis of religion or belief was first prohibited in 2003 to comply with EU Directive 2000/78. Prior to this, discrimination on grounds of religion was only covered where the religious group was also a separate ethnic group, such as Sikhs and Jews. Religion and belief is now a separate prohibited characteristic and so discrimination on grounds of being Christian, Muslim, Hindu, or other religions and beliefs are also protected, including atheism and humanism.

The terms of 'religion' and 'belief' are defined as 'any religion, religious belief, or philosophical belief', and include reference to a lack of a religion or belief. Beliefs in a political party are not covered (*Kelly and others v Unison* (2010)), although belief in a political ideology may be covered (Hepple, 2011). In terms of defining religion and belief, guidance can be found in case law of the European Convention on Human Rights (ECHR), which shows that beliefs must have sufficient 'cogency, seriousness, cohesion and importance', be worthy of respect in a democratic society, be compatible with human dignity, and not conflict with the fundamental rights of others (*Campbell and Cosans v UK* (1982)).

With regard to the meaning of religion, there is no definitive list of religions. It is clear that the protection will cover well-known religions such as Christianity, Islam, Hinduism, Sikhism, Judaism, Buddhism, Jainism, Rastafarianism, Baha'i, and Zoroastrianism. However, there is no set of recognized religions in the UK, and so other religious groups will be able to claim religious discrimination if they are able to show that they have a clear and coherent set of beliefs. Groups or denominations which exist within a religion will be considered to be a religion or belief, such as Protestants and Catholics within Christianity. This means that if a Protestant discriminates against a Catholic, this will still be religious discrimination even though both are Christians.

If not accepted as religions, then the beliefs may still be protected as 'beliefs' if they meet the criteria of being sufficiently cogent, serious, cohesive, and important. There is no minimum number of adherents required to be accepted as having the religion or belief under the Equality Act 2010. Beliefs that have been accepted as covered by the legislation have been a belief in climate change (*Nicolson v Grainger*, 2009) and a belief in spiritualism (*Power v Greater Manchester Police, 2009*). However, in *Devine v Home Office* (2004), an applicant claimed he was rejected for work at the Home Office because of his sympathy for disadvantaged asylum seekers, which he said was a demonstration of the Christian virtue of charity. The tribunal held that the beliefs were too vague and ill-defined to amount to a religion or belief.

Signpost to Chapter 10 Managing Religion or Belief in the Workplace

Sex

The protected characteristic of sex means being a man or a woman, and the protection applies equally to men and women. Protection against sex discrimination was developed during the twentieth century, with Acts such as the Sex Disqualification (Removal) Act 1919, which allowed women to become solicitors, and the Sex Discrimination Act 1975, which applied to employment more generally. Within the EU, action on sex discrimination dates from the beginnings of the European Community, with the original EEC treaty containing provisions on equal pay for men and women. Since then the EU has issued a number of Directives on sex discrimination, and the European Court of Justice has decided a large number of significant judgments in sex discrimination cases which have then been applied to the UK. For example, in *Dekker* (1990) the ECJ established that pregnancy discrimination was direct sex discrimination, and therefore could not be justified.

Signpost to Chapter 6 Managing Gender Diversity in the Workplace

Sexual orientation

The protected characteristic of sexual orientation is defined as being a person's sexual orientation towards people of the same sex (i.e. the person is a gay man or a lesbian woman), towards people of the opposite sex (i.e. the person is heterosexual), or towards people of both sexes (i.e. the person is bisexual). Protection extends to those treated less favourably because of a perception that they are gay when they are not, and even to those who are subjected to homophobic harassment, even though those doing the harassing know that the person is not gay (see *English v Sanderson Blinds* (2008), above). The Equality Act 2010 would also protect against discrimination by association with a person who is gay or lesbian, for example, less favourable treatment of a person because her sister is a lesbian.

Signpost to Chapter 9 Managing Sexual Orientation and Transgender in the Workplace

Other grounds

The grounds listed above are protected in the Equality Act 2010. Some other grounds of discrimination are also protected, but the protection is found in other legislation. In Northern

Ireland only, discrimination on grounds of political opinion is prohibited. The position is currently governed by the Fair Employment and Treatment (Northern Ireland) Order 1998 (FETO).

Other legislation created in the EU and implemented in the UK prohibits less favourable treatment of part-time workers (Part-time Workers (Prevention of Less Favourable Treatment) Regulations 2000) and fixed-term workers (Fixed-term Employees (Prevention of Less Favourable Treatment) Regulations 2002). In addition, trade union members are protected in UK law against discrimination on the grounds of their union membership (Trade Union and Labour Relations (Consolidation) Act 1992).

Combined discrimination, dual characteristics

The original draft of the Equality Act 2010 also included provisions that would have made it possible to claim discrimination on the basis of a combination of two protected characteristics. Without this provision, for example, a black woman who is refused an interview might find it difficult to claim discrimination if the employer can show that it is not sex discrimination as other (white) women are employed; nor is it race discrimination as black (male) staff are employed. If those provisions had been enacted, the black woman would have been able to claim discrimination on the basis of the combination of gender and race.

Occupational requirement exception

The Equality Act 2010 contains an exception to the general principle of non-discrimination where the job for which a person is recruited has an occupational requirement for a person to be of a particular sex, race, disability, religion or belief, sexual orientation, or age, or not to be a transsexual person, married, or a civil partner. The requirement must be a genuine requirement in that it must not be a sham or pretext for discrimination. It also has to be an occupational *requirement*, meaning that it must be a defining aspect of the job, and not just one aspect of the job. In addition to being an occupational requirement, the application of the requirement must be proportionate so as to achieve a legitimate aim. The meaning of this phrase is the same as for indirect discrimination (above).

Under the old Race Relations Act 1976 and Sex Discrimination Act 1975 a set of occupational requirements was listed, and only those listed were accepted. They included authenticity for dramatic performances or in restaurants (race discrimination, e.g. a black man to play Othello, or an Indian waiter in an Indian restaurant) and for reasons of decency and privacy (for sex discrimination, e.g. a female attendant in a ladies changing room). Under the Equality Act 2010, there is no exhaustive list of legitimate occupational requirements. Instead an occupational requirement can be imposed for any legitimate aim as long as it is proportionate to do so. Although this is a more open-ended approach, it is unlikely that tribunals will allow many exceptions to the important principle of non-discrimination. The following case study provides an example of where the exception has not been accepted.

> **⊡ Case study 2.4** *Etam plc v Rowan* (1989)
>
> Mr Rowan applied for a job as a sales assistant at a women's clothes shop. He was not given the job because of his sex. In defence of the claim of sex discrimination, the employer argued that there was an occupational requirement for a woman to do the job because part of the job included personal contact with women by being present in the fitting rooms and in measuring customers. The court accepted that these aspects of the job would require a female employee, but it decided that there were enough workers in the shop to cover these duties and work could be organized so that Mr Rowan did not carry out these parts of the job. Therefore the employer was not able to rely on an occupational requirement that the employee be female.

In addition to the general occupational requirement for all protected characteristics there are some additional exceptions that relate to specific characteristics.

Occupational requirements relating to religion

Where an employer has an ethos based on religion or belief, it is lawful to discriminate in relation to work by applying a requirement to be of a particular religion or belief if having regard to that ethos of being of that religion or belief is a requirement for the work and applying the requirement is proportionate to achieve a legitimate aim. For example, if a religious group runs a publishing business, it may wish to retain its religious ethos by recruiting only those who share the religion. There must still be a requirement to be of the religion, and the requirement must still be proportionate, but in deciding if the requirement is proportionate and for a legitimate aim, a tribunal can consider the ethos of the organization. This exception allows organizations with a religious ethos to maintain their ethos, where proportionate to do so. However, it does not act as a defence if discrimination occurs on another ground. For example, an organization may require that staff be Muslim, but they cannot require that they be heterosexual or male using this provision. The following case study (2.5) is an example of an occupational requirement which was accepted by the court.

Occupational requirements relating to sex/sexual orientation, etc. in employment for an organized religion

The Equality Act 2010 contains a specific exception for employment 'for the purposes of an organized religion' allowing requirements relating to sex and sexual orientation. The

> **⊡ Case study 2.5** *Muhammed v The Leprosy Mission International* (2009)
>
> A Muslim man was refused employment as a finance administrator at the Leprosy Mission, a Christian charity. The Leprosy Mission stated that one of the selection criteria for the job was to be a practising Christian. The Employment Tribunal held that the requirement was an occupational requirement in the context of that particular place of employment, in which a Christian ethos permeated the daily life and activities of the workplace. Because of this context, it was proportionate to impose this ground of occupational requirement because otherwise the ethos of the organization would have been entirely undermined.

requirement covers a narrow range of employment, such as ministers of religion, imams, or those who carry out religious rites or who promote and represent a religion. For example, this exception allows the Catholic church to require that its priests be male. Concerns that this exception might cover staff in religious foundations such as schools, health organizations or charities were allayed in the *Amicus* (2004) case when it was confirmed that the exception does not apply to schools or other religious ethos organizations.

Disability discrimination and the duty to make reasonable adjustments

The definition of discrimination for the purposes of the protected characteristic of disability varies in a number of ways from that applying to other protected characteristics. First, discrimination on grounds of disability does not work in a symmetrical way (e.g. the Equality Act 2010 protects men and women, gay and straight, etc.). It is only discriminatory to treat disabled people less favourably: it is not discriminatory to treat disabled people more favourably than persons who are not disabled.

Second, although direct discrimination because of disability cannot be justified, an additional form of direct discrimination is provided in the Equality Act 2010, which covers discrimination arising from, or in consequence of, a disability. Such discrimination is not 'because the person is disabled' of itself (e.g. a dislike of disabled people), but for a reason arising from the disability (e.g. reduced mobility). This second type of direct discrimination will not be unlawful if it can be justified as a proportionate way of achieving a legitimate aim. This type of discrimination cannot occur if the employer does not know, and could not reasonably have known, that the person was disabled.

Third, the Equality Act 2010 contains a special form of protection for disabled people by imposing on employers a duty to make reasonable adjustments to work practices to avoid the disadvantages they may cause for disabled people. This duty helps to address the particular features of disability discrimination: in order to participate in the workplace, disabled people need some of the barriers to participation to be removed, and this may require special treatment. Thus the Equality Act 2010 puts an obligation on employers to accommodate the needs of disabled people by making reasonable adjustments to work practices and premises in order to make them accessible to disabled people. For example, the duty to make reasonable adjustments can require an employer to change working hours, to provide specialist equipment, or to make buildings accessible. Failure to comply with the duty to make reasonable adjustments is a form of discrimination and the employer can be held liable.

 Student Activity 2.3

Archibald v Fife (2004)
Ms Archibald was employed by Fife Council as a road sweeper. She became disabled and could no longer carry out her job, although she could do sedentary work. The Council arranged for her to

undertake a number of training courses to equip her with appropriate skills and she was assessed as being 'more than capable of carrying out work in an office environment'. She applied for office-based jobs in the Council, for which she was interviewed in competition with others. She claimed that a reasonable adjustment to her disability would be to redeploy her to one of the jobs without competitive interview, as she was capable of doing the job.

Do you think that she could require the employer to ignore its usual requirement for an interview, even if this means treating Ms Archibald better than other people? Provide reasons for your answer.

The duty is not an absolute duty; it is a duty to make *reasonable* adjustments. Under the Disability Discrimination Act 1995 the following factors were relevant: whether the adjustment would be effective to remove the difficulty; whether the adjustment is practicable; the extent to which other activities are disrupted by taking the step; the costs of the step; the extent of the financial resources of employer; the availability of other resources to help finance the step. Under the Equality Act 2010, it is likely that similar factors will be identified. Although excessive costs can make an adjustment unreasonable, it should be noted that this is not an overriding factor and it can depend on the resources of the employer and the availability of other resources to fund an adjustment.

Age discrimination, justification and retirement

The Equality Act 2010 contains some special provisions relating to age discrimination. First, direct age discrimination can be justified, unlike discrimination because of other protected characteristics. Less favourable treatment because of age is justified if the treatment is a proportionate means of achieving a legitimate aim. An example of treatment that may be justified could be a requirement to be under the age of 50 to start a job which requires a significant amount of training if the employer can show that the employment of a person over 50 would not allow for a sufficient length of employment before the expected retirement to warrant the expense of training.

A second special rule applying to age discrimination relates to benefits or increments paid on the basis of length of service. Such benefits can be indirectly discriminatory because those who are younger are disadvantaged, having not built up the additional years of service. The Equality Act 2010 states that additional benefits payable on the basis of length of service up to a period of five years are allowed, but that where long service benefits are built up over more than five years, they can only be justified if they fulfil a business objective, such as encouraging loyalty or motivation, or rewarding the experience, of staff. In many cases, this will mean that service-related benefits will be lawful as they are usually introduced for such purposes.

The final way in which age discrimination has differed in the past from other forms of discrimination is in the provision of separate rules relating to retirement. However, from October 2011, the retirement age has been abolished. A requirement that staff retire will therefore have to be justified in the same way as any other age discrimination, and only if the treatment is a proportionate means of achieving a legitimate aim.

> ### ➜ Student Activity 2.4
>
> Consider the following job description.
>
> A sales executive is required to work in this vibrant and exciting retail outlet. We are looking for an enthusiastic individual with at least five years' retail experience, who is not afraid of hard work, and is willing to work flexibly to meet the needs of the business. The job will involve occasional evening and weekend work, attending social events and hosting drinks receptions on behalf of the company. There are also exciting opportunities for overseas travel. We offer a competitive pay package, with the following benefits:
>
> - 4 weeks annual leave, rising to 5 weeks after 3 years' service
> - Subsidized nursery places for female workers with children under 5
>
> Consider what impact the criteria in the job description may have on people with various protected characteristics. If you think the criteria are potentially indirectly discriminatory, consider whether the criteria can be justified.

Interaction of different rights

Some people have been concerned that there may be a potential for clashes between some forms of discrimination, particularly between discrimination on grounds of religion and belief and discrimination on grounds of sex and sexual orientation. For example, individuals may have religious objections to homosexuality and could claim that a request to respect sexual orientation equality discriminates against them on religious grounds. However, a claim that a requirement to abide by an equality code discriminates on grounds of religion or belief is unlikely to succeed. A requirement to abide by an equality policy and to treat all staff and clients without discrimination would be perfectly justifiable: it serves the legitimate aim of promoting equality and diversity at work, and is it is likely to be proportionate to impose it on staff in order to achieve this aim.

> ### ➜ Student Activity 2.5
>
> Look at the following two cases and then answer the discussion questions which follow.
>
> *Apelogun-Gabriels v London Borough of Lambeth* (2006)
>
> A Christian was dismissed for distributing 'biblical extracts', which included a range of quotes that his employers considered homophobic, to members of a work-based prayer group and 'interested parties'. The tribunal found that the reason for the dismissal was not the applicant's religious beliefs in and of themselves, but his conduct in distributing homophobic literature at work.
>
> *Ladele v London Borough of Islington* (2009)
>
> Ladele claimed she was discriminated against for refusing, on religious grounds, to carry out civil partnerships as part of her job as a registrar of marriages and civil partnerships. When she was appointed, Ladele was not required to perform civil partnership ceremonies, but this changed when

the law was changed in 2004 to allow civil partnerships, and she was designated by her employer as a civil partnership registrar. She was disciplined for refusing to perform civil partnerships and claimed that this discriminated against her because of her religion. The court held that this was no direct discrimination: the discrimination was not because of her religion, but was because of her refusal to carry out the civil partnership ceremonies. This amounted to indirect religious discrimination but it could be justified as it was a proportionate way to achieve the legitimate aim of upholding Islington Borough's 'Dignity For All' equality policy.

Questions for discussion

1. In what circumstances should religious individuals be able to express religious views at work?

2. Should it make a difference to Ladele's case that when she was originally appointed to the job she was not required to carry out civil partnerships?

3. Other local authorities have allowed Christians to opt out of performing civil partnerships by not designating staff as civil partnership registrars against their wishes. If some employers are happy to accommodate religious views in this way, does it mean that it is disproportionate for Islington to refuse to do so?

Equal pay

The right to equal pay for men and women is covered by the Equality Act 2010, replacing the Equal Pay Act 1970. The principle of equal pay for equal work was enshrined in the original Treaty of Rome when the EU was founded and is an important principle of EU law.

The principle of equal pay works by implying into every contract of employment a clause which ensures that employment terms are equal between men and women. If a woman has less favourable pay than a man, then she will have a claim under the Equality Act 2010. Pay, for these purposes, includes money, pension benefits, and other contractual benefits such as company car or leave entitlements. Claims are made on the basis of a comparison between the claimant's job and that of a person of the opposite sex. The claim can be that pay should

⊙ Case study 2.6   Examples of like work or work of equal value

Capper Pass Ltd v Lawton (1977)
A woman worked as a cook preparing meals for the directors' dining room. She worked 40 hours a week preparing meals for around 10–20 people a day. She claimed that she should be paid the same hourly rate as two assistant chefs who worked as part of a team providing 350 meals a day in several sittings in the works canteen. Although there were differences between the jobs, the court accepted that they were broadly similar in terms of the skills and experience needed to perform the job, and the differences were not of practical importance. They were therefore treated as 'like work'.
Hayward v Cammell Laird (1984)
A cook in a shipyard compared her pay with that of painters, insulation engineers, and joiners working in at the same yard. An expert appointed by the court found that although the work was different, it was of equal value.

be equal because they both do 'like work' (work of a broadly similar nature), 'work rated as equivalent' (where there has been a job evaluation undertaken), or 'work of equal value' (where the jobs are different but they are of equal value in terms of factors such as effort, skill and decision-making). Case study 2.6 provides examples of how jobs which are not exactly the same can be treated as like work or work of equal value.

In each case, the claimant must be able to identify a person of the opposite sex doing the same or an equal value job and who works for the same or an associated employer. Each term of the contract is considered separately, and so if one person is paid more, but the other gets more annual leave, an equal pay claim can still be made with respect to the unequal pay rate.

Even if a female employee is able to show that she is paid less than a man for equal work, the employer may have a defence. The defence arises where the employer can show that the difference in pay is due to a difference between the two cases, based on a material factor, as long as that factor is not the difference of sex. For example, the man may have additional qualifications which justify the different pay rates.

In some cases, the factor may not be one of sex, but may have the effect of indirectly dis-criminating on the basis of sex. Where this is the case, the factor can only be relied on if it is a proportionate means of achieving a legitimate aim. For example, different pay rates may apply for evening work, as it is difficult to staff the evening shift, even though the work under-taken is of equal value in terms of effort and skill. To pay more for this work may indirectly discriminate against women, as they may find it more difficult to work evenings for childcare reasons. However, if there is a legitimate aim, such as the need to staff the organization in the evenings, it may be proportionate to pay at a higher rate for the unsocial hours.

Some of the factors which courts have allowed to justify unequal pay are 'red circling' or pay protection, where a reorganization has led someone to be moved to a different job but with their pay protected for a period of time. The additional pay has a legitimate aim of easing the transition to the new job for the person who has been moved. The additional pay will need to be proportionate, and so it may be that pay protection should be time-limited, so that unequal pay in terms of gender is not perpetuated indefinitely.

The most contentious factor that may justify unequal pay is the use of 'market forces' to explain differences in pay. For example, can an employer justify paying a recent recruit more than exist-ing staff because the new recruit negotiated a higher pay rate? In *Rainey v Greater Glasgow Health Board* (1987), the House of Lords accepted a defence based on market forces and this approach was confirmed by the European Court of Justice in *Enderby v Frenchay Health Authority* (1993). In both of these cases it was accepted that market forces may indirectly discriminate against women, but that the defence could still be relied upon as long as the reason could be justified.

The right to equal pay also applies to pensions and the Equality Act 2010 implies into pen-sion schemes a rule ensuring equal terms for men and women.

Debate Box

Organize the class into two groups, one for the motion and one against it.
 The motion is:
Market forces should be able to justify unequal pay for men and women.
Please follow the process for the debate as indicated in the previous debate box.

Proving discrimination

Proving discrimination can be very problematic in practice, particularly at the point of recruitment, as it can be very difficult for individuals to find out why they have not been selected. The Equality Act 2010 addresses this issue by ensuring that the burden of proof in discrimination cases is placed on the employer, rather than using the usual rule of requiring that those making a claim should be able to provide proof. In discrimination cases, as long as the person claiming discrimination can show facts which, in the absence of any other explanation, indicate less favourable treatment, then the onus shifts to the employer to prove that there was no discrimination. In the absence of such proof, the person claiming discrimination will be successful. Courts can take into account that it is difficult to prove discrimination, and that clear evidence of discrimination may well not be available.

The claimant does not have to show that it is 'beyond reasonable doubt' that there was discrimination: the level of proof is that 'on the balance of probabilities' there was discrimination. For example, a woman may apply for promotion at work and may not get an interview. She may find that a man, who has less experience than her, was given the job. If she brings a claim of sex discrimination, it will not be down to her to prove that there was sex discrimination. She will merely have to show that that there are facts that, in the absence of any other explanation, suggest discrimination has occurred. In effect, this means that she does not need to address and disprove the possible explanations the employer may give. It is for the employer to provide the explanation. The legal procedures provide that the claimant can send a questionnaire asking questions about the process. For example, how many applicants were there of each gender and how many shortlisted? What qualifications did the successful claimant have? What equal opportunities policies and training does the employer have? Inferences can be drawn from the answers to these questions, and, for example, a lack of equal opportunities policies could in some circumstances give rise to an inference of discrimination on the part of an employer who does not have a clear and objective explanation for its recruitment decision.

Positive action and advancing equality

Positive action

In most cases the discrimination protection provided by the Equality Act 2010 acts in a symmetrical way, protecting men and women, gay and straight, black and white, young and old, etc. This means that measures taken to promote groups with a protected characteristic are generally unlawful—measures to promote female workers will discriminate against men, measures to help gay workers will discriminate against those who are straight, and so on. Exceptions are only allowed where there is a work-related requirement to be of a particular sex, race, religion, etc. (see Occupational requirements, above). In addition, under the earlier legislation, limited exceptions were allowed in terms of advertising jobs in order to encourage applications from an under-represented group. However, reserving jobs for members of a protected group or expressing preferences for certain characteristics when making recruitment decisions is unlawful.

The Equality Act 2010 contains new provisions which allow for more proactive positive action to become lawful. The provisions apply where those sharing a protected characteristic are disadvantaged, or where their participation at work is disproportionately low. They allow for the employer to take steps to overcome the disadvantage or to increase participation. With regard to recruitment and promotion, positive action is allowed where the person with the protected characteristic is as qualified as persons without the characteristic. In effect, if an employer has two equally qualified candidates, one male and one female, then it would be lawful to employ the woman in order to increase female participation at work, if the employer reasonably believes that women are under-represented. Such steps are only lawful as long as the employer does not have a policy of treating persons who share the protected characteristic more favourably in connection with recruitment or promotion, and as long as the more favourable treatment is a proportionate means of achieving the aim of increasing participation or overcoming disadvantage. There is no requirement on employers to take such action; the Equality Act 2010 merely allows employers to do this should they wish to.

These provisions are controversial. On the one hand, it is argued that after around 40 years of equality protection we still do not have an equal society, and so more active steps are needed to achieve equality. On the other hand, it is argued that it is not fair to try to achieve equality and diversity by discriminating against other groups.

Under EU law such measures can be lawful as long as there is no automatic preference for the disadvantaged group, and that each person's application is considered objectively. For example, in the German case of *Kalanke* [1995], a law had been passed that gave priority to women in promotion and appointment to official posts as long as they had equal qualifications to the men who applied. The preference was to be given to women until they accounted for 50 per cent of the workforce in the sector. This was ruled unlawful by the European Court of Justice because it gave absolute and unconditional priority to women over men. In contrast, in *Marschall v Land Nordrhein-Westfalen* (1997), a scheme that gave priority to women in an application process, where all else was equal between the candidates, was found to be lawful as long as, before the appointment was made, any reasons specific to the male applicants were considered, in case those reasons would tip the balance in favour of appointing the man. Thus, although priority might be given to women, this was not absolute.

Public sector duties

Public sector equality duties are duties imposed on public sector organizations to take steps to eliminate discrimination and to promote equality and good relations between different groups. The aim is to make the promotion of equality central to the work of public authorities, and means that public authorities must take account of equality issues in their day-to-day work of policy making, service delivery, employment practice, and other functions.

The first equality duty was introduced in Great Britain in 2000 for the grounds of race, although such duties already existed in Northern Ireland. Similar duties were introduced to promote equality on grounds of disability in 2006 and on grounds of gender in 2007. The Equality Act 2010 extends these duties to cover age, religion and belief, gender reassignment, pregnancy and maternity, and sexual orientation. What these duties will involve is not yet clear, but they will at least require that public sector employers will need to provide equality training for managers and staff, and have clear equality policies, which involve measures to promote equality as well as commitments not to discriminate.

Public procurement

The Equality Act 2010 provides for further regulations to be made to require public sector employers to use procurement processes to enhance equality. This can include ensuring that contracts they make with external bodies (including private sector businesses) must themselves comply with equality standards. For example, a hospital can require that any private sector catering company that wants to tender for a contract to provide catering for patients must abide by minimum standards with regard to equality, by having an equal opportunities policy and evidence that it is enforced.

 ## Conclusion

This chapter has examined the main provisions of the Equality Act 2010 as it applies to equality and diversity in the workplace. It introduced the main types of discrimination (direct and indirect discrimination, harassment, and victimization) and explained the various protected characteristics. It also explored the various mechanisms used to advance equality, such as positive action and public sector duties.

 ## Review and discussion questions

1. Explain the difference between direct and indirect discrimination.

2. In what circumstances can indirect discrimination be justified? Identify some examples of factors which may justify indirect discrimination, and some factors which cannot justify discrimination.

3. Give an example of an occupational requirement which might allow an employer to discriminate because of a protected characteristic.

4. Consider the list of protected characteristics. Why have these characteristics been protected in the law? Are there other characteristics which you think should also be protected?

5. Consider the arguments for and against using positive discrimination.

 For additional material on the content of this chapter please visit the supporting Online Resource Centre at **www.oxfordtextbooks.co.uk/orc/kumra_manfredi/**

Further reading

ACAS (2009) Delivering *Equality and Diversity* (Advisory booklet). London: Advisory, Conciliation and Arbitration Service.

Fredman, S. (2001) *Discrimination Law.* Oxford: Oxford University Press.

McColgan, A. (2005) *Discrimination Law: Text, Cases and Materials.* Oxford: Hart Publishing.

Pitt, G. (2007) *Employment Law.* London: Sweet and Maxwell,

References

Hepple, B. (2011) *Equality the New Legal Framework.* Oxford: Hart Publishing.

McColgan, A. (2005) *Discrimination Law: Text, Cases and Materials.* Oxford: Hart Publishing.

Cases:

Age Concern Case, R (on the application of the Incorporated Trustees of the National Council on Ageing) v Secretary of State for Business, Enterprise and Regulatory Reform Case C-388/07 ECJ

Amicus v Secretary of State for Trade and Industry [2004] EWHC 860 (Admin)

Apelogun-Gabriels v London Borough of Lambeth 2301976/05 (5016/62) February 2006

Archibald v Fife (2004) UKHL 32

Azmi v Kirklees Metropolitan Borough Council UKEAT/0009/07/MAA

Bilka-Kaufhaus GmbH v Weber von Hartz (1987) ICR 110 ECJ Case 170/84

Campbell and Cosans v UK (1982) 4 EHRR 293

Capper Pass Ltd v Lawton (1977) QB 852

Centrum vorr Gelijkheid van Kansen en voor Racismebestrijding v Firma Feryn NV [2008] C - 54/07

Coleman v Attridge Law (2008) ICR 1128 (ECJ)

Council on Ageing (Age Concern England) v Secretary of State for Business, Enterprise and Regulatory Reform ECJ 5 Mar 2009

CRE v Dutton (1989) IRLR 8

Dawkins v Department of the Environment, sub nom Crown Suppliers PSA (1993) IRLR 284

Dekker v Stichtin Vormingscentrum voor Jonge Votwassen Case C-17/88 ECJ

Devine v Home Office, 9 August 2004, case no. 2302061/2004

Enderby v Frenchay Health Authority (1993) IRLR 591

English v Sanderson Blinds Ltd [2008] EWCA Civ 1421

Etam plc v Rowan (1989) IRLR 150

Hayward v Cammell Laird [1988] AC 894

Horsey v Dyffedd CC [1982] ICR 755

James v Eastleigh BC [1990] 2 AC 751

James v MSC Cruises 12 April 2006; case no. 2203173/05

J H Walker v Hussein (1996) IRLR 11

Kalanke (1995) ECR I-3051

Kelly and others v Unison 28 Jan 2010, ET/2203854-57/08

Ladele v London Borough of Islington (2009) EWCA Civ 1357

Mahlburg v Land Mecklenburg-Vorpommern Case C-207/98 ECJ

Mandla v Lee (1983) IRLR 209

Marschall v Land Nordrhein-Westfalen (1997) ECR I-6363

Muhammed v The Leprosy Mission International (2009) 16 December 2009, ET/2303459/09

Nicolson v Grainger [2010] ICR 360

P v S and Cornwall CC Case C 13/94 ECJ

Power v Greater Manchester Police UKEAT/0434/09 DA, 2009

Rainey v Greater Glasgow Health Board (1987) AC 224

Seide v Gillette Industries (1980) IRLR 427

Smith v Safeway [1996] ICR 868

Weathersfield v Sargent [1999] ICR 425

From Equal Opportunities to Managing Diversity

◎ Learning objectives

- Understand the necessity for a paradigm shift in the conceptualization and framing of difference in organizations
- Explain the differences between managing diversity and equal opportunities approaches
- Explain the contributions of key theoretical approaches to diversity management and critically assess their shortcomings
- Explore the interdependence of managing diversity and equal opportunities approaches

🔐 Key terms

- **Business case:** a set of arguments which for the first time promoted the diversity evident within organizations in respect of the demographic make-up of employees as a positive asset to business; something which, if managed and leveraged effectively, could provide organizations with much needed competitive advantage.
- **Discrimination:** unjust or prejudicial treatment of different groups of people.
- **Diversity :** being different or varied.
- **Equality:** being equal in status, rights and opportunities.
- **Positive action:** measures to promote equality based on a recognition that for some disadvantaged groups there may be a need to 'catch up', in terms of their access to skills development and education. Within Codes of Practice issued by the Equal Opportunities Commission and Race Relations Board (now both merged into the Equality and Human Rights Commission), recommendations are made in respect of policy initiatives which enable this to be done, for example, implementing management development programmes targeted only at members of ethnic minorities, to increase the number of ethnic minority managers.

Introduction

In this chapter we explore the paradigm shift from an equality of opportunity approach, enforced through legislation, to one based on the recognition and valuing of organizational diversity. This is a much researched topic and the centre of much academic and practitioner attention. In examining the theoretical and conceptual development of the two approaches and how practice has responded to the shift in emphasis and approach, we find that there are a number of competing opinions on the meaning and impact of diversity management on organizational life, and also a number of competing opinions on which approach best advances the protection of disadvantaged societal groups and the eradication of discrimination. We explore several of these views and seek to understand what the key arguments are in respect of this shift in perspective and whether, in practice, this has been achieved. We begin with an analysis of the key contextual factors that contribute to the necessity of considering diversity within organizations in a fundamentally different way. Key among these are demographic changes predicted within the labour market, the saturation of key market segments, and the need to access and develop new consumer markets. These have led to the development of business-based arguments focusing on equality of opportunity and a move away from those situated within morality or social justice.

We thus see a fundamental shift in thinking in respect of equality. For the first time organizations are seeing the management of difference as a potential source of competitive advantage rather than a regulatory framework that has to be complied with. Also critical within the diversity paradigm is a focus on and celebration of difference, as opposed to the more traditional equal opportunities approach of ensuring 'sameness'.

In this chapter we discuss the business case arguments for diversity management and contrast these with the philosophy underpinning the equal opportunities approach. We examine the alternative perspectives on equality of opportunity, contrasting liberal and radical positions, and then move on to a discussion of key theoretical frameworks that have been developed to enhance our understanding of the diversity management perspective. Here we look at the work of Jackson et al. (1992), Kandola and Fullerton (1994), and Dass and Parker (1999).

The chapter concludes with a critique of the diversity management perspective, focusing on three key areas of concern. The first considers whether diversity management and equality of opportunity are actually theoretically and practically separable. The second raises concern over the managerial nature of the diversity management perspective and the implications this has for changes in organizational power structures. And the third considers whether the focus within diversity management on difference in all its forms may actually prove detrimental to eliminating discrimination within organizations.

The business case for diversity management: a paradigm shift in understanding difference?

The term 'diversity' is usually thought to have evolved in the mid 1980s in the United States. A report was published by the Hudson Institute (Johnston and Packer, 1987) entitled *Workforce 2000* and it showed that by 2000 the US labour force was set to become more heterogeneous. Due to demographic and population changes, white males would no longer represent the majority of the workforce; their numbers would be augmented by women, Hispanics, African Americans and other minority groups. To ensure the USA maintained economic dominance in the twenty-first century, the report tasked policy makers and organizations to plan for the integration and deployment of an increasingly 'diverse' workforce. With the publication of this report and the policy implications emanating from it, the understanding of 'difference' in organizations radically shifted. For the first time, difference was seen as a positive asset to business, something which, if managed and leveraged effectively, could provide organizations with much needed competitive advantage (Boxenbaum, 2006; Kelly and Dobbin, 1998; Robinson and Dechant, 1997).

A similar picture was evident in the UK, where Pearn Kandola (2000) predicted that in 2010 80 per cent of workforce growth would be among women and only 20 per cent of the workforce would consist of white, able-bodied, males under the age of 45. This was a radically different workforce composition from that traditionally experienced by organizations in these countries, and how to attract, recruit, develop, and retain such a heterogeneous workforce was clearly a managerial challenge.

For those able to rise to the challenge, the rewards would be high. According to the resource-based view of the firm (Barney, 1995), which connects organizations' human resources to their ability to obtain and retain sustainable competitive advantage. To achieve this, consideration of four key factors is required: value; rarity; inimitability; and organization.

Value

Organizations need to identify and articulate the ways in which their HR function can create value. For the HR function to be considered a 'strategic partner', it will need to know which human resources contribute most to its sustainable competitive advantage in the business. To do this, some fundamental questions will need to be asked. For example:

- On what basis is the firm seeking to distinguish itself from its competitors?
- Where in the value chain is the greatest opportunity for leverage and achieving differentiation?
- Which employees provide the greatest potential to differentiate the firm from its competitors?

The value of the organizations resources alone is insufficient for sustainable competitive advantage; because other organizations can access and possess the same value, it will only provide competitive parity. To move towards competitive advantage, consideration needs to be given to rarity.

Rarity

HR managers need to consider ways to develop and exploit rare characteristics of the firm's human resources to gain competitive advantage. For example, retailer Nordstrom focused on their salespeople as a key source of its competitive advantage. Rather than hiring low-skilled employees at low pay, as per the industry norm, the organization invested in attracting and retaining young university-educated people interested in a career in retailing. It provided an incentive-based compensation system (up to twice the industry average) and encouraged employees to make a 'heroic effort' when attending to customers' needs. Nordstrom have thus taken a relatively homogeneous labour pool and exploited rare characteristics to gain competitive advantage.

Inimitability

Here the emphasis is on the development and cultivation of characteristics that cannot be easily imitated by competitors. This requires assessing the organization's unique history and culture which can be used to identify unique practices and behaviours which can be leveraged for competitive edge. These factors may be in the form of reputation, brand, cultural or gender diversity of employees, influence of national culture – factors which, by their very nature, are difficult if not impossible to imitate. SW Airlines exemplify the role that socially complex phenomena such as culture can play in gaining competitive advantage. Top management attribute the company's success to its 'personality', creating a culture of 'fun' and 'trust'. This empowers employees to act autonomously, to do what it takes to meet customers' needs. The culture is created and perpetuated through targeted and focused selection and socialization processes. So through the HR strategy, a resource is created for the organization which is rare and virtually inimitable.

Organization

To ensure competitive advantage is sustainable, the framework requires organizations to ensure they are 'organized' to capitalize on adding value and ensuring ongoing rarity and inimitability. This requires a focus on HR policies and practices which are integrated and coherent; as opposed to *ad hoc* and piecemeal. This will enable employees to reach their potential and organizations to meet their objectives. It is thus important to ensure that key aspects of HR strategy (e.g. performance management, training and development, diversity management), are not considered in isolation, but rather as integral parts of the whole HRM strategy such that each part of the function endorses and supports the key aims and objectives of the other. This is called 'horizontal alignment', so for example, the recruitment and selection strategy needs to be supported by the performance management strategy, which in turn is supported by the development strategy, and all endorse and support the key aims and intentions of the diversity strategy.

Student Activity 3.1

Take the four key factors considered in the resource-based view of the firm, namely:

- Value
- Rarity
- Inimitability
- Organization

Choose three organizations: one from the public sector, one from the private sector, and one from the voluntary sector. Research each organization, finding out as much as you can about their people management strategy and objectives. Contrast each organization's approach in respect of their people, and answer the following questions:

1. What are the similarities in approach?
2. What are the differences?

3. Have all three organizations satisfied the four factors? If not, where does attention need to be focused?
4. Do any of the organizations place workforce diversity at the centre of their approach to gaining and retaining competitive advantage?

Among the first to seek to operationalize what competitive advantage arising from diversity management actually looked like, were Taylor Cox and Stacy Blake (1991). In their view, in order to achieve cultural diversity, organizations would have to undertake wholesale and radical change. The change management process would begin with the need to ascertain a deep understanding of the nature of the organization's culture, which would require an internal review process. The key organizational processes that would need to be examined would include assessing how diversity is perceived in the organization, establishing the impact of heterogeneity, and ensuring that HR systems are free of bias and supportive of an overall culture of valuing differences and cultural inclusion. For those organizations successfully undertaking this change process, and aligning their internal operations with their diversity objectives, the rewards can be high. Cox and Blake (1991) identify six key aspects of potential competitive advantage to organizations successfully harnessing and utilizing their cultural diversity. These are:

- **Cost:** as the diversity of employees increases, so too does the cost associated with poor integration. For example, if communication does not occur effectively between diverse members of a team, productivity can be lost through misunderstanding and errors. Organizations which manage integration processes well will thus create a cost advantage in comparison with those that don't.

- **Resource acquisition:** organizations who manage diversity well get a reputation for doing so. These organizations will gain an advantage over others in the labour market when it comes to competing for resources. This becomes particularly important when searching for rare skills and talent.

- **Marketing:** for organizations operating globally, the cultural insight and sensitivity that culturally diverse employees can bring to culturally diverse marketplaces can improve access to and understanding of new and developing markets. This logic will also apply when marketing to sub-populations within domestic markets.

- **Creativity:** with increased diversity comes a diversity of perspectives and the potential to challenge traditional and accepted ways of working. Through constructive challenge can come innovative and creative insights in respect of new products, new work processes, and new markets.

- **Problem-solving:** the more diverse the group, the greater the potential for improvements in decision-making processes – through greater debate, and a more critical analysis of the issue.

- **System-flexibility:** the main thrust of the diversity argument is that with greater heterogeneity, comes a greater questioning and challenge of traditional and accepted ways of doing things. Organizations thus have the potential to move from deterministic and standardized approaches to more fluid and flexible methods, enabling improved reaction to and interaction with the environment.

These points were picked up by Lew Platt, former CEO of Hewlett-Packard, as he set out the business case for diversity. He said:

I see three main points to stress when making the business case for diversity:

1. A talent shortage that requires us to seek out and use the full capabilities of all our employees.
2. The need to be like our customers, including the need to understand and communicate with them in terms that reflect their concerns.
3. Diverse teams produce better results.

(Lew Platt, to the Diversity Research Network, Stanford Business School, 18 March 1998)

Student Activity 3.2

Looking at Cox and Blake's (1991) explanation of the competitive advantage to be gained from diversity management, answer the following questions:

1. How persuaded are you by their arguments?
2. What circumstances would need to be in place for organizations to fully embrace the approach described?
3. What are the advantages of their approach?
4. What in your view are some of the potential limitations?
5. What suggestions would you make to overcome these limitations?

Liberal/radical approaches to equality of opportunity

Signpost to Chapter 2 An Outline of European and UK Equality Legislation

In the UK, the equal opportunities approach has historically been located within a policy rather than a theoretical framework (Liff and Wajcman, 1996). This has been manifest through a number of Equal Opportunities Acts, each seeking to outlaw differential treatment in employment between the general population and those in legally protected groups.

Such an approach stems from a 'liberal' conceptualization of society, of the individual, and the role of the state (Jewson and Mason, 1986). This can be contrasted with the 'radical' approach, which sees the role and interaction between the above forces in an entirely different way. Each is described below.

In the liberal approach, equality is seen to exist when circumstances are arranged such that all individuals can compete equally, freely, and fairly for social rewards. In ensuring this occurs, the role of the policy maker is to act rather as an umpire or referee, to put in place rules and procedures that ensure equal outcome for all participants. The role of the policy maker is not to determine those who win or lose in society, but rather to ensure that the social mechanisms through which winners and losers are determined are based on principles of fairness and justice (Jewson and Mason, 1986). The logical outcome of such an approach is the design of equal opportunities policies which ensure fair procedures designed on the basis of rational-legality and bureaucratic impartiality. The resultant equality of opportunity policies thus ensure equality through a just process.

Such a view of equal opportunities policies has its roots in theories of classical liberalism or liberal democracy (Arblaster, 1984; Salvadori, 1977). For liberals, the idea of privilege, self-perpetuating elites, and unnecessary social restraints are the bases of inequality in society and need to be tackled. Liberals believe benefits and rewards in society should be allocated to those with natural talents and abilities. These are randomly distributed throughout society and do not rest in the hands of a ruling elite. Thus to ensure that those with natural talent and ability across society are fairly rewarded, the state has to intervene to remove any unnecessary social barriers and thus ensure the maximum possible levels of freedom and liberty for all (Jewson and Mason, 1986).

The radical approach differs in that, unlike the liberal approach which looks for action in respect of justice and equality at the state level, it locates intervention at the level of the workplace. Thus the radical approach focuses on the outcomes of the contest, rather than the rules of the game; fairness of distribution of rewards rather than fairness of the application of process. In the radical view, though, it is recognized that discrimination has a negative impact at the individual level. It is argued that it can only be detected and identified at the level of the group (Jewson and Mason, 1986). From this perspective, it is clear that women and those from ethnic minority groups are undoubtedly the equals of men and those from the ethnic majority. The distribution of occupational rewards should reflect this fact. We cannot claim to have reached a position of equality until the distribution of those from all social groups across the various occupations in society is consistent with their representation within society as a whole (Jewson and Mason, 1986). The very fact that we can observe an unfair distribution is *de facto* evidence of inequality in society. The radical view does not therefore look for a solution to inequality through market processes and state intervention, but rather through independent standards of human dignity and moral worth, derived from ideologies such as Marxism, Feminism, or Black Power.

A further point of departure between the two approaches is in relation to their conceptualization of talent and ability. The radical approach makes a direct attack upon liberal notions of individual talent or ability. This is done on the grounds that these terms are not as politically or morally neutral as they are presented. They do in fact contain within them a series of value judgements such that those behaviours deemed worthy of the label 'talent' or 'ability' are invariably determined by the ruling class or ruling elite. What is deemed 'talent' or 'ability' is defined by those in positions of power, and teachers and examiners institutionalize these notions of ability into educational curricular and in measures of educational attainment (Jewson and Mason, 1986). It is thus questioned whether the educational attainments demanded of many occupations are actually required as evidence of an ability to do the job, or whether they are in fact used as an apparently neutral screening device to ensure the most desirable sections of the labour market are preserved for the sons and daughters of the ruling elite (Ashton, 1982; Berg, 1970; Maguire and Ashton, 1981). From the radical viewpoint, it is thus completely acceptable, and indeed necessary, to address previous imbalance, for example by waiving entry requirements for members of hitherto under-represented groups in particular occupations or organizations.

Debate Box

Organize the class into two groups, one for the motion and one against.

The motion is:

This house believes the 'liberal' approach to achieving equality of opportunity has failed to sufficiently produce the observable outcomes in employment opportunity for socially disadvantaged groups it promised. It is thus proposed that a 'radical' approach should be adopted on this issue to bring about much needed social change.

Stages in the debate: (each stage is given with timings, the overall time for the activity is 55 minutes – allowing a few minutes for change over of presenters, etc.)

- Each group has 20 minutes to prepare their arguments either for or against the motion.
- Each group is given 5 minutes to present their opening statement (10 minutes in total).
- Groups reconvene for 10 minutes to prepare rebuttal arguments.
- Each group has 2 minutes to present rebuttal arguments.

A vote is taken and the winners of the debate announced; the casting vote goes to impartial observers: tutors, audience members not involved in the debate, or observers.

The concept of equal treatment

The aim of early legislation was 'equal treatment', emanating from the liberal legal tradition of treating like as like. The legislation is based on the protection of particular social groups viewed as disadvantaged in relation to workplace opportunities, and provides the right, on an individual basis, for the same treatment in the same circumstances as an individual from another social group or category (Liff and Wajcman, 1996). Early anti-discrimination legislation was focused on equal treatment based solely on the requirements of the job and not on the personal characteristics of members of particular social groups, for example, by race or gender. In practice, organizations have sought to ensure their policies and processes apply equally to all and are neutral in their effect on individuals, regardless of which group in society they belong to. Processes coming under particular scrutiny have been recruitment and selection, psychometric testing, and review of payment structures (Liff and Wajcman, 1996).

However, there have been criticisms of this approach. In the UK, the method by which these criticisms were addressed was for the then Equal Opportunities Commission (EOC) and Commission for Racial Equality (CRE) (now amalgamated within the Equality and Human Rights Commission – EHRC) to issue Codes of Practice. These provided guidance to employers not only on how to eliminate discrimination, but also on ways in which they could actively promote equality (Liff, 1996). Measures to promote equality (called 'positive action' in the UK) recognize that for some disadvantaged groups there may be a need to 'catch up' in terms of their access to skill development and education. Within the Codes, recommendations are made in respect of policy initiatives which enable this to be done, for example, implementing management development programmes targeted only at members of ethnic minorities to increase the number of ethnic minority managers. Another example might be to initiate a programme of talks in girls' schools to encourage more girls into careers in science and engineering. However, it is important to note that the Codes only made recommendations; there was no legal requirement for organizations to adopt the measures.

> ### ⬛ Case study 3.1 Positive action at BT
>
> Recognizing the lack of women in management positions, BT initiated a series of women's development programmes aimed at developing talented women at key levels in the organization, with a view to helping them progress. The programme focuses on increasing women's confidence and helping them to network and shows BT's commitment to them. In this way the programmes are intended to assist in maximizing the contribution of women to the business, to enhance their leadership development, and to increase their representation in applications for senior posts. By retaining and enhancing women's leadership skills, BT benefits from their creativity and highly developed communication skills, characteristics highly desirable for the global business environment (adapted from Liff, 1999: 69).
>
> The description above provides an example of a positive action initiative at BT. Having read the excerpt, answer the following questions:
>
> 1. In your view, what are the advantages and disadvantages of a positive action approach?
>
> 2. Does positive action support the concept of 'equal treatment' and are there any ways in which the concept is undermined by such initiatives?
>
> 3. What do you think the advantages of the women's programme described above are for:
>
>   - the women who attend
>
>   - BT
>
>   - the cause of equality of opportunity in the organization.

A further issue is identified by Young (1990), who concurs that the general approach to ensuring equality of opportunity in relation to acquiring jobs is to ensure that all applicants are treated equally and that they should not be asked about their domestic situation, as this is seen as an irrelevant issue when assessing candidates' suitability to do the job. This policy results in there being no consideration of whether candidates possess the characteristics typically associated with successful applicants. So, for example, when looking at a managerial job which frequently requires the ability to work long and unpredictable hours, to travel with little notice, to possess an uninterrupted career history, etc., no account is taken of an individual's domestic circumstances and caring responsibilities. This profile is typically associated with those who have the level of domestic support more usually enjoyed by men than women. Thus within this context, organizations can continue to feel that their processes are fair, meritocratic, and open to anyone who can meet the objective requirements of the job. Anyone who is unable to meet the requirements is in some way inadequate, lacking talent, drive, or initiative, while those in need of 'extra help' through equality initiatives are in some way deficient.

The combined effect of such an approach is that the responsibility for inequality is shifted squarely from collectively based organizational approaches to equality levers and drivers and on to the shoulders of individuals, who are made to feel it is their fault if they cannot compete on the same basis as others against objectively based and fairly applied job-related criteria.

This will also mean that women and other organizationally disadvantaged groups will continue to be presented with impossible choices if they want a career. They will have to take on the burden of 'fitting in' to the prevailing model of career success by not having children, and if they do have children, they are required to make domestic arrangements that mean their domestic life impinges as little as possible on their work life (Young, 1990).

Thus, the focus on sameness has resulted in women, members of the ethnic minorities, disabled, and gay and lesbian employees etc., having to deny or seek to minimize their difference from the 'norm' (generally perceived to be white, able-bodied, heterosexual men) as the price they have to pay for equality. The approach ignores the fact that there are differences inherent in all these groups; men and women are different, able-bodied and disabled employees are different, and those from the ethnic minorities are different from the majority population. Each group experiences its own different educational opportunities and different responsibilities in the domestic sphere and in society in general. When we assess 'sameness', the benchmarks are male characteristics and behaviour (Liff and Wajcman, 1996). Thus the equality of opportunity framework based on a liberal/legal-rational system, which seeks to ensure 'sameness' and 'equal treatment', has been assessed as being overly simplistic in respect of both the issue of inequality (viewing it as simply a managerial failure to treat like as like) and in the solution (equality will be achieved if we treat everyone the same) (Liff and Wajcman, 1996).

The approach has also been critiqued for its allusion to 'sameness' while simultaneously recognizing and allowing for the potential for differential treatment. This occurs through the concept of 'indirect' discrimination embedded within legislation in respect of both sex and race. 'Indirect' discrimination occurs when equal treatment is given to all but the result of this 'equal' treatment disproportionately disadvantages members of a protected group (Liff and Wajcman, 1996). This is unlawful unless it can be shown to be a genuine occupational requirement. For example, the requirement for all applicants for a particular post to be over six feet tall is applied to all equally but the ability of women to comply with this requirement is significantly more difficult than men, who are on average taller. The inclusion of the concept of 'indirect' discrimination within legislation primarily formulated to ensure equality through 'sameness' highlights the ambiguities inherent in the approach. More (1993) and Westen (1982) argue that the legal definition of equality is ambiguous in its very nature, as it does not indicate the boundaries within which likeness is to be determined. We have seen through case law that characteristics, including length of service and hours of work, can be examples of indirect discrimination, thus indicating that simple divisions between 'social' and 'work-related' criteria cannot be made (Liff and Wajcman, 1996).

Further critique has centred on the procedural nature of the approach. Manifested as it is in the formulation of objective, job-related criteria and focused as it is on ensuring individuals are fairly and identically assessed against these criteria, so that factors such as gender and race play no part in decision-making, means that though compliance may be gained for the approach and observable changes in behaviour may be evident, values and attitudes remain untouched (Liff, 1999). There is little attempt in the approach to increase broader understanding of the issues contributing to the observable disadvantage evident within the labour market, and little to encourage commitment to its solution. At best, the approach can engender consent obtained through senior management commitment, and at worst it can be viewed in organizations as coercion monitored by process-driven checks on the behaviour of those involved in activities such as recruitment, promotion, and appraisal (Liff, 1999).

> **→ Student Activity 3.3**
>
> Write a briefing paper to the diversity director of an organization you are familiar with (or one you know through secondary research) to assess the key contributions and key drawbacks of the liberal/legal-rational approach to equality of opportunity. Key points to include would be:
>
> - What indicators would you use to assess whether the approach has been successful?
> - What data might it be useful to collect?
> - What are the key stakeholder groups you would consult with?

Managing diversity: a paradigm shift?

When assessing the literature in relation to diversity management, it becomes apparent that it is an approach representing a collection of ideas rather than a uniform approach through which diversity is to be achieved within organizations. Diversity management, as the name implies, is a 'management strategy'. It is primarily applied in a top-down manner and the aim of the approach is to enhance the productivity and effectiveness of organizations (Fischer, 2007). The key point of departure between the diversity management approach and that of equal opportunities is that the equal opportunities approach is based on a liberal/legal-rational model predicated upon sameness (as discussed above), while the diversity management approach sees benefit to be gained (at the organizational level) through recognizing, valuing, promoting, and leveraging diversity, where diversity represents the multitude of differences that exist between individuals (Fischer, 2007).

As Tomlinson and Schwabenland (2010) indicate, the arrival of diversity management as an alternative approach to equality of opportunity provided a powerful and persuasive set of arguments, re-energizing management interest in protecting the needs of minority groups. Diversity management was to succeed where an equality of opportunity approach was perceived to have failed, that is in the achievement of greater organizational inclusion of minority groups (Ahmed, 2007). The managing diversity approach is articulated as a strategic response to key changes in the labour market, for example, demographic shifts and increasing customer diversity. It was, from its inception, differentiated from the equal opportunities approach through a shift in focus for organizational intervention, from the group to the individual. An additional key differentiator was to position the diversity management approach as focusing on a broad range of differences, not just those traditionally associated with disadvantage or protected by legislation (Tomlinson and Schwabenland, 2010). Thus the appeal of diversity management is that it has a broader scope and reach. It covers differences applying to everyone, and not just to those organizational members who can situate themselves in minority or disadvantaged categories.

In practice, we see that the focus of diversity management policy and practice continues to be differences emanating from discrimination. In respect of how differences are approached, Liff (1999) identifies two distinct but competing versions. The 'dissolving' differences approach accepts that organizations need to find ways to meet the needs of diverse employees, but advocates that this should be done on an individual basis and should not be based on an employee's membership of a particular social group. In contrast, the 'valuing' differences approach recognizes social group membership, and appreciates the need for the organization to find ways of accommodating group members' needs. By valuing differences, organizations are able to widen opportunities and access the broadest talent pool, thereby enabling them to attract and retain the 'best' employees regardless of their age, ethnicity, etc. Recruiting a workforce that closely matches the demographic composition of likely customers increases the organization's ability to attract customers from diverse groups and respond to their diverse needs. Liff (1999) also adds a further two approaches: accommodating and utilizing differences. These are viewed as closely aligned with equal opportunity approaches as initiatives are developed and targeted to assist specific groups, but they are also available to all organizational members. Within these perspectives, talent is recognized and accessed despite social differences, and it is achieved by accepting alternative qualifications from the norm for particular roles in the organization, and also recognizing different types of experience than has traditionally been the case.

With its focus on difference, it is argued that diversity in the workforce can contribute to organizational innovation and renewal. Established practices can be challenged and new approaches developed from employees able to offer new and alternative perspectives to traditional and accepted ways of working (Due Billing and Sundin, 2006; Kamp and Hagedorn-Rasmussen, 2004). However, care needs to be taken as it is argued that rather than breaking down group stereotypes and valuing individual difference, the managing diversity approach may in fact reinforce group-based stereotypes, as it relies upon utilizing group-based characteristics as a source of competitive advantage for the organization (Young, 1990). For example, it is argued that those from ethnic minority communities can use their knowledge as 'insiders' of these communities to provide their organizations with ideas and detailed knowledge in respect of new products and services that can be targeted at their communities, thus opening up new business avenues. However, what this does is to value the individual solely on the basis of their group membership and not as an individual who can bring all sorts of new ways of thinking and innovative ideas to the organization. The only contributions the organization is interested in are those based on the individual's membership of particular social groups (Thomas and Ely, 1996).

Thus, in defining diversity management, Kandola and Fullerton (1994), key proponents of the approach in the UK, define it as follows:

> The basic concept of managing diversity accepts that the workforce consists of a diverse population of people. The diversity consists of visible and non-visible differences which will include factors such as sex, age, background, race, disability, personality and work style. It is founded on the premise that harnessing these differences will create a productive environment in which everybody feels valued, where their talents are being fully utilized and in which organizational goals are met. (Kandola and Fullerton, 1994: 8)

Other definitions place greater emphasis on the organizational rationale for managing diversity (i.e. the link with greater productivity or profitability), the idea of the importance of appreciating and valuing differences, or the value and importance of creating an inclusive environment. Thus Bartz et al. (1990: 321) define diversity management as:

> ...understanding that there are differences among employees and that these differences, if properly managed, are an asset to work being done more efficiently and effectively.

Diversity management as a concept has also been embraced at the organizational level, and here we see that while some organizations define diversity with an emphasis on visible difference, others imply that everyone is different. For employers, the way diversity is conceptualized in their organization will inevitably impact how they manage it. For example, Astra Zeneca's website (www.astrazeneca.com/diversity) states:

> We want to draw upon the widest possible pool of talent, and to be the employer of choice for people already employed within the company, as well as for potential recruits. We will widen the range of people AstraZeneca employs and ensure that the diversity of their backgrounds, experiences and abilities is fully recognised and developed.

Such a public statement sets out the rationale for diversity management and goals for its achievement, as well as the means by which it will be done. It can be seen that there is an intention to value diversity – there is not an expectation that all differences should be assimilated to the norms – and there is a promise of recognition and development. An alternative emphasis is cited by Opportunity Now (www.opportunitynow.co.uk/diversity) who state:

> ...being an employer of choice requires respect for the talents of all individuals regardless of gender, race, disability, age or sexual orientation. It means being fair to all in recruitment, promotion and development of people and capitalising on the added value that diversity brings.

Student Activity 3.4

Look at the definitions of diversity management presented above and answer the following questions:

1. What are the common themes between them?
2. Where are the points of departure?
3. In what ways do they differ from the equality of opportunity approach?
4. Where are the following stakeholders located within the approach:
   a. The individual
   b. The group
   c. The organization
   d. Society as a whole

Differing theoretical approaches

Diversity management has been conceptualized in a number of different theoretical approaches. It is not possible to discuss all of these within this chapter. However, a number of the key approaches are discussed to provide a deeper understanding of the concept.

Jackson et al. (1992) propose a framework of diversity which focuses on changing organizational culture to achieve diversity management outcomes. Through achievement of a number of levels and stages, the organization moves from an 'exclusionary' organization to a 'multicultural' organization. These levels and stages are as follows:

Level 1, Stage 1: The Exclusionary Organization

This type of organization seeks to perpetuate the position of dominant organizational groups and to exclude others.

Level 1, Stage 2: The Club

Here, particular groups are still excluded but the manner by which this is achieved is less direct and obvious. Some members of previously excluded groups are able to become part of the organization as long as they are willing to conform to existing norms and behaviours.

Level 2, Stage 3: The Compliance Organization

Though aware that there are other perspectives, the compliance organization does not want to change current and accepted ways of doing things for fear of 'rocking the boat'. Though minority employees may be actively recruited, they are generally to be found at the lower levels in the organization occupying largely 'token' positions.

Level 2, Stage 4: The Affirmative Action Organization

In this type of organization commitment is made to eradicating discrimination and employees are challenged to examine their attitudes and encouraged to think in new and different ways. Minority employees are not only evident in the organization, but their development is strongly and actively supported.

Level 3, Stage 5: The Redefining Organization

In this organization the focus is on moving beyond simply avoiding discrimination to actively achieving a redistribution of power among key groups. This is achieved by close examination of all the organization does and its culture to assess the impact on the diverse groups within it. Policies and procedures are then changed and realigned to bring about the desired shifts in power.

Level 3, Stage 6: The Multicultural Organization

This organization can be said to have achieved true diversity. It is an organization that values every individual in it, and is a place where all individuals can feel that their contributions and interests are understood and valued. All organizational members are able to fully participate in organizational life and not only is internal diversity achieved, there is a broader social responsibility agenda in operation which seeks to educate those external to the organization in an effort to contribute to a society in which oppression is abhorred and actively tackled.

Key proponents of diversity management in the UK are Kandola and Fullerton (1994). They believe that a number of pressures combined to require an alternative approach to the management of equality in organizations. These included a growing emphasis on business-focused arguments to underpin the equality agenda, and a broader range of groups facing disadvantage in the labour market, who at the time were not protected by legislation (e.g. older workers and those from the lesbian, gay, bisexual, and trans communities). (We have, of course, since had legislation to protect all these groups. For further details see Chapters 2, 9, and 11.) There was also greater concern at the time with ethics and ethical organizational behaviour, which included equality. In light of these factors, Kandola and Fullerton (1994) asserted that the time was right for a reorientation in the approach to equality and advocated a focus on managing diversity as an alternative and more appropriate response to meet changing environmental circumstances.

Their approach, like many others, seeks culture change as the best way to achieve diversity. Their vision summarizes the key mechanisms by which this objective is to be reached through the acronym 'MOSAIC':

'**M**' = Mission and values
'**O**' = Objective and fair processes
'**S**' = Skilled workforce
'**A**' = Aware and fair
'**I**' = Individual focus
'**C**' = Culture that empowers

The approach is thus clearly based upon a programme of organizational cultural change and learning; ensuring that all individuals within the organization are able to contribute and reach their full potential without being held back by their membership of any particular group.

The approach is very much located within the rhetoric of business benefit and supports the shift from collective approaches to bringing about equality of opportunity (i.e. through legislation) to an individualistic approach (based upon business advantage and management action). This is clearly an approach which requires a major change in culture within the organization and is unlikely to leave much of the functioning of the organization untouched. It is also a top-down approach, and one which moves the responsibility for the management of equality and diversity within the organization out of the hands of professionals (i.e. personnel and HR specialists) and into the hands of management. The advantage of this is perceived to be that the management of diversity becomes the responsibility of everyone and not just a few people in the organization. The concern over such an approach is that it becomes very top-down and there is little opportunity for 'bottom-up' concerns or priorities to be heard.

Debate Box

Organize the class into two groups, one for the motion and one against.

The motion is:
The objective of achieving true 'multiculturalism' within an organization is unrealistic and cannot be delivered in practice.
Please follow the process for the debate as indicated in the debate box above.

In assessing organizational responses to diversity management, Dass and Parker (1999) identify four main approaches. These are: resistance; discrimination and fairness; access and legitimacy; and learning. Each is now discussed in turn.

Resistance: this approach is located within the 1950s and 1960s, and is characterized by a time when increasing numbers of women and members of ethnic minorities began entering the workforce. Their presence was met with resistance by the established majority, who perceived these groups to threaten their future employment prospects. Those seeking to enter organizations in any significant numbers were viewed with suspicion and were seen as different and 'not like us'. The organizational response at this time was to work to protect the status quo, with advertisements frequently claiming openly that those from ethnic minority groups or women were not to apply. The times were particularly fraught in terms of race relations, and were marked by events such as the 'Keep Britain White' campaign and the Nottingham and Notting Hill riots of 1958.

Discrimination and Fairness: moving out of the 1960s and into the 1970s, legislation began to appear to protect particular social groups in the labour market. In 1970 the first Equal Pay Act was passed. This was followed in 1975 by the Sex Discrimination Act and in 1976 by the Race Relations Act. In response to this legislative framework, organizations switched to the 'discrimination and fairness' perspective, and sought to level the playing field for previously socially disadvantaged groups (Dass and Parker, 1999). Typical interventions to endorse the approach included audits and monitoring of the access and progress of disadvantaged groups into the organization and through the ranks. They also focused on positive action programmes and initiatives directed at specific groups, designed to redress past imbalances (Thomas, 1996; Gooch and Cornelius, 1999). Examples of such initiatives in the UK, include Opportunity 2000 (relabelled Opportunity Now, after 2000), which aimed to increase the number of women in all positions in the workforce, particularly managerial positions (Garnsey and Rees, 1998), and 'Race for Opportunity', which was launched in 1995 and aimed to build mutually beneficial partnerships between ethnic minority communities and corporations in key areas of commercial activity, e.g. marketing, purchasing, and employment (Lorbiecki, 2001).

Access and legitimacy: here the focus is on accepting, acknowledging, and appreciating the wide range of 'differences' within the labour market. These include race, culture, ethnicity, age, able-bodiedness, gender, class, and ways of working (Thomas and Ely, 1996; Dass and Parker, 1999). The aim is to create an organizational culture within which all these differences can be recognized, valued, and leveraged for organizational success. The main motivation of the access and legitimacy paradigm is:

> We are living in an increasingly multicultural country, and new ethnic groups are quickly gaining consumer power. Our company needs a demographically more diverse group to help us gain access to these differentiated segments. We need employees with multi-lingual skills in order to gain legitimacy with them. Diversity isn't just fair; it makes business sense. (Thomas and Ely, 1996: 83)

Under this perspective, the people who make up a diverse workforce are referred to as 'human resources' or 'assets', and they are valuable not only for their job-related skills and experience, but also for their personal characteristics and membership of particular social groups (Lorbiecki, 2001).

Learning and effectiveness: both Dass and Parker (1999) and Thomas and Ely (1996) indicate that there are some weaknesses in the access and legitimacy approach. Approaching diversity through an equal opportunities or a valuing differences perspective raises problems. Those entering organizations from disadvantaged social groups are either exhorted to 'fit in' and not be different, or they are 'ghettoized' precisely for their differences into particular organizational roles which value them for their background, for example where they work mainly or exclusively with people from their own identity background (Thomas and Ely, 1996).

Organizations wishing to move beyond the access and legitimacy perspective and overcome these issues can adopt the 'learning perspective'. This has been explained by Dass and Parker (1999) as an approach which links diversity management strategically to the core objectives of the organization and seeks to ensure that it is work that gets diversified and not just that a few new market segments are exploited. This will only happen if organizations are willing to undergo significant cultural and structural transformation. However, in practice this may prove problematic as evidence shows that diversity initiatives tend to be isolated and episodic in nature (Lorbiecki, 2001).

Within the learning and effectiveness perspective, the focus of attention will not be members of socially disadvantaged groups (e.g. a workshop for minorities so they can learn the 'rules of the game' and succeed) or sensitizing programmes for managers so they can appreciate the diverse talents of their staff; it will take a much more systemic and systematic form. Dass and Parker (1999) provide suggestions in respect of how this can be achieved, advocating whole-organization change management processes, such as action research, total quality management, re-engineering, and organization development.

The key advantages of the approach are that it focuses on the need to diversify work rather than people, and thus brings diversity to the core of organizational processes. However, like the other perspectives outlined, there is little evidence on how the approach would work in practice (Lorbiecki, 2001).

➤ Student Activity 3.5

Read the following diversity statements and answer the questions that follow.

Diversity and Inclusion at British Gas (www.britishgas.com/diversity)
We are committed to pursuing equality and diversity in all our activities and we continue to support initiatives to provide employment opportunities for people from minority groups in the community, including people with a disability, carers and lone parents. We work with a number of partner organizations on diversity, enabling us to share best practice and tackle key issues. OFSTED has commended our efforts to recruit from under-represented groups, with female trainees accounting for almost 13% of all those recruited in 2007.

We also promote activity across the company that enables us to understand, reflect and serve the breadth of diversity in the communities in which we operate.

Diversity at the Environment Agency (www.environmentagency.gov/diversity)
The environment surrounds us all and our mission to create a better place takes us everywhere. From rivers to coastlines; from farmland to parks; from waste dumps to water treatment plants;

from town to country; from big cities to tiny villages. All our people – all 13,000 of them – are as diverse as the environment we protect and the communities we serve. That's because the work we do calls for a huge variety of skills and people from all kinds of background. So whether you're a technical specialist, an engineer, an environmentalist, a policy maker or a data monitor; we'll hire and promote you strictly on the basis of what you can do, not who you are.

When you join us, you'll find that a culture of fairness, mutual respect and equal opportunities are not just tired old clichés, but real values that are very much alive in everything we do. You'll see how much we value your contribution by the efforts we make to help you balance work, life and family commitments. And you'll have the same access to training, development and opportunity that's available to every individual in any role at every level.

So no matter which country, county, continent or culture you're from, if you've got something to give, we'd like to meet you. We've got work to do together.

1. Where are each of these organizations in relation to the four approaches outlined by Dass and Parker (1999)?

2. How do they discuss equality and diversity – separately or synonymously? How do you know?

3. Of the two, whose approach to diversity management do you identify with most? Why?

Critiquing diversity management

In assessing the key critiques of diversity management, it is evident that three main criticisms are most frequently discussed by researchers and analysts of the diversity management paradigm. Each of these is discussed below.

Are equal opportunities and diversity management conceptually separable?

One of the key criticisms of the diversity management approach is that it is not as distinct from the equality of opportunity approach that some might suggest. Studies indicate that UK employers place 'traditional' equal opportunities policies and practices within a diversity management framework, and that many practitioners use the terms interchangeably (Kirton, 2002). For example, in their study of diversity practitioners in West Yorkshire, Ford et al. (2009) found that practitioners had difficulty distinguishing between the terms. In their study, practitioners tended to use one term at the expense of the other (usually equality at the expense of diversity) and showed little understanding of the differences and potentially positive complementary nature of the terms. Foster and Harris (2005) found that employers and employees reported confusion in respect of the concepts and particularly with the simultaneous focus on equality, favouring similarity and the valorization of difference for competitive advantage. There was also a questioning of whether diversity actually offered something distinct as an approach to equality, or whether it simply represented a repackaging of old-style equal opportunities.

Thus, although diversity rhetoric advocates that it as an approach that is different and separate from the equality of opportunity approach, in practice we see that the concepts are frequently related and used interchangeably (Tomlinson and Schwabenland, 2010). Thus rather than presenting these as oppositional concepts, what seems to be happening is that diversity is seen as building upon the equality of opportunity approach, and the diversity agenda has the potential to be used to support and justify equality initiatives (Dickens, 1999). The approach can also be used to support action in respect of a wider range of employees than has traditionally been the case. For example, through a 'diversity' lens, groups other than those subsumed within anti-discrimination legislation can be accessed and assisted (Liff, 1999).

The diversity management perspective is 'too' managerialist

A further criticism of the diversity management approach is that though a moral commitment to equality is not entirely absent from the approach, it is also not central (Kirton and Greene, 2010). The approach is underpinned by the business case and as such is predicated upon a focus on organizational self interest rather than wider societal principles and values based upon justice, fairness, and equality. This has serious implications for disadvantaged groups within society. Unless policy action is taken to directly challenge and overcome discriminatory process and practice, progress will not be made in respect of the position of disadvantaged groups in society. As Dickens (1999) has indicated, the business case is unapologetically selective, partial, and contingent, and as such cannot and will not benefit all women at all times. Focusing as it does entirely on the employers perspective, the rhetoric of diversity management can in all possibility be used to justify limited action on inequalities, focusing solely on legal compliance (Kirton and Greene, 2010).

The arguments supporting a business case for diversity claim that a workforce that is more representative of the wide range of socio-demographic categories found in the general population will provide organizational advantage. However, this raises a tension between this type of utilitarian (business-based) argument and one based on human rights and social justice – a more morally based set of arguments (Tomlinson and Schwabenland, 2010). Some see these two positions in opposition with one another, arguing that the debate is politically charged, with business case arguments emanating from an unashamedly functionalist paradigm, privileging and supporting managerial interests (Noon, 2007; Sinclair, 2006). As Litvin (2006: 85–86) states, business case arguments are based in a 'normalized Mega-Discourse that enshrines the achievement of organizational economic goals as the ultimate guiding principle and explanatory device for people in organizations'. Others contend that the two approaches can co-exist side by side to produce a case for diversity that provides not just business benefit, but also enhanced social equality (Barmes and Ashtiany, 2003; Maxwell, 2004). As Kamp and Hagedorn-Rasmussen (2004: 532) explain, managing diversity was positioned as 'a story of how to obtain both equality and business success; it depicts a win-win situation where these two perspectives are united'. However, Noon (2007) disagrees. The argument in his view is fundamentally flawed because it rests upon contingent thinking. An approach based upon the exploitation of the business benefits of diversity risks short-term economic challenges (Barmes and Ashtiany, 2003) such that where it can be proved that policies targeted at the achievement of equality and inclusiveness are not economically justifiable, such policy interventions may be rejected on economic grounds (Tomlinson and Schwabenland, 2010).

A focus on individual difference can mean group-based discrimination is overlooked

Kirton and Greene (2010) examine whether a shift from equality of opportunity to diversity management has proven to be advantageous for the societal advancement of socially disadvantaged groups. Focusing on women, they argue that diversity, with its emphasis on ensuring equal treatment for everyone, engenders less hostility to groups previously perceived to be receiving 'special treatment', such as women (Sinclair, 2000). This is particularly relevant in a context when fewer people (in the UK at least) believe gender equality for women to be an issue requiring special attention or action (Howard and Tibballs, 2003). Diversity management, emphasizing as it does 'corporate image building' rather than the progression of equality goals, is more likely to fit with the dominant ideology of meritocratic individualism generally subscribed to by most managers, and thus less likely to challenge prevailing organizational systems and processes (Webb, 1997).

However, on closer inspection it becomes apparent that a key attraction of diversity management can become problematic. In a time when increasing relevance and discussion is centring on the multiple and intersecting nature of identity (Lorbiecki and Jack, 2000), the diversity management approach, focusing as it does on difference in all shapes and forms and moving away from 'pigeon-holing' individuals into specific social groups labelled either 'advantaged' or 'disadvantaged', holds promise. It enables a move from a position where all members of disadvantaged groups are viewed as homogeneous, experiencing the same issues and needing the same interventions to improve their position in the labour market, to one which recognizes the heterogeneity within groups and the notion of intersecting disadvantage (Kirton and Greene, 2010). We thus see that not all members of ethnic minorities experience the same disadvantage within the labour market. Some ethnic minorities fare better than others and a uniform approach to meeting their needs will not be effective. In respect of women, we see here too that not all women face the same disadvantage within the labour market. Some are doubly and triply marginalized (i.e. through the intersection of gender, disability, and ethnicity). However, the problem arises when, through the diversity management approach, the policy framework becomes sufficiently loose so as to ensure that all 'difference' is recognized, but it becomes meaningless in terms of policy aims and objectives. The focus of the diversity management approach is to 'dissolve' differences, but in order to achieve this, there can be no clear policy focus and the most salient differences for career chances within a particular function or department (e.g. gender, age, disability, etc.) becomes subsumed with all other differences and is lost (Kirton and Greene, 2006). Thus the concern is that the rhetoric of valuing differences could easily be the basis for a case that argues that there are no gender-based problems within an organization, only gender based differences. If we are all different, and we all have different needs, what is the issue with different women achieving different career outcomes? Following this logic, unequal career outcomes can be reconstructed as neither unequal nor discriminatory, simply different (Kirton, 2008).

⊙ End of Chapter Case Study   Study Civil Service diversity policy

In November 2005, the Cabinet Office launched a 10-point plan to increase diversity in the Civil Service by recruiting more women, people from ethnic minorities, and disabled people. In July 2007, Bill Jeffrey, Civil Service diversity champion and Permanent Secretary at the Ministry of Defence, was interviewed by Lucy Philips for an article in *People Management* (2007) to discuss key priorities and the progress made to date.

The 10-point plan comprises:

1. Departmental targets.

2. Six-monthly measurement and evaluation.

3. Allocation of diversity champions to each department, and six-monthly diversity champions meetings.

4. Visible leadership commitment.

5. Positive action in recruitment.

6. Diversity development schemes.

7. A zero-tolerance policy on discrimination.

8. Ensuring the Civil Service efficiency plans do not affect diverse representation.

9. 'Mainstreaming' diversity.

10. Effective communication strategy.

The key driving force for the initiative was so that the department could better reflect the population it serves. The biggest challenge was identified as being ensuring that diversity is present not just in junior ranks, but all the way up the organization.

In respect of how the plan is being implemented, Mr Jeffrey explained that each department has its own dedicated diversity champion and associated action plan. Diversity champions meet quarterly and undertake a process of review against the action plan to monitor progress and identify any areas where further work is required. Key policy initiatives have been the introduction of a scheme which supports those with promise from under-represented groups so that they can be encouraged and supported to meet their full potential. Recruitment advertising is also being used, and here the focus is on attracting candidates from under-represented groups. For senior positions, search consultants have been instructed to provide 'diverse' shortlists, and shortlists comprising only white males are not acceptable.

In terms of ensuring the programme remains a policy priority and not just a short-term activity, Mr Jeffrey was clear that while it is important to improve the diversity of the senior team, as a visible outcome of the programme, and to sustain the momentum and effort, it is also important to create a culture in which everyone in the organization feels comfortable and respected. Thus the challenge for the future will be that once targets are achieved, the organization moves forward to identify the next set of diversity challenges rather than feeling that the end point has been reached.

Case study questions

- Is the diversity plan outlined above indicative of a diversity management or an equality of opportunities approach? How do you know?

- Which type of organizational response does the Civil Service 10-point plan represent according to Dass and Parker's (1999) typology?

- How useful do you think the diversity champions' meetings are? What can be achieved by the peer-review process?

- Do you think the rejection of all-white male shortlists for senior positions is an example of 'positive' action or positive discrimination?

- What additional action would you recommend that the Civil Service take to ensure diversity targets are met and a change in approach is sustained?

Conclusion

In this chapter we have explored the shift in the management of equality in organizations from an approach based upon ensuring equality of opportunity to one which focuses on the management of diversity. We have seen that this is a much researched topic and concerns inequality of opportunity within organizations and the implications of this not only for individuals and organizations, but also for society as a whole. A number of competing perspectives have been discussed in respect of the meaning and impact of enhanced diversity in organizational life, and consideration has also been given to competing opinions on how best to tackle the issue. The chapter has discussed the underlying philosophies of both the equality of opportunity approach and also that of managing diversity, focusing not only on differences, but also highlighting similarities and potential synergies. Alternative theoretical models of both approaches have been presented and discussed to aid understanding of both concepts and indicate their theoretical development.

From this discussion, it is evident that while some would agree that diversity management has indeed shifted the emphasis of the equality of opportunity agenda from an externally imposed legal and compliance necessity to an issue wholly consistent with a managerially driven agenda of enhanced competitive advantage, others remain to be convinced. We thus see that key criticisms of the diversity management perspective are that it is neither theoretically nor empirically separable from the equality of opportunities approach it seeks to distance itself from, and that this is a good thing rather than a bad one. We have also considered concerns that the diversity management agenda is too managerialist in focus, and this may be detrimental to the furtherance of an equality agenda. There are also worries that through a focus on an increasingly broad definition of 'difference', the cause of socially disadvantaged groups may be hindered rather than helped.

 ## Review and discussion questions

- How persuaded are you by the business case for diversity management? Assess its merits and analyze the areas of weakness within this approach.

- Looking at Dass and Parker's (1999) model of organizational approaches to diversity management, what policy recommendations would you make to move an organization from an approach focused on 'access and legitimacy' to one promoting 'learning and effectiveness'?

- Who would you identify as the key stakeholders in achieving diversity management in an organization? What are the key contributions of each stakeholder?

- Of the three theoretical perspectives presented to achieve diversity management (i.e. Jackson et al., 1992; Kandola and Fullerton, 1994: and Dass and Parker, 1999), which are you most persuaded by and why?

- If you saw advertisements for both a 'diversity manager' and an 'equal opportunities manager', which one would you apply for and why?

For additional material on the content of this chapter please visit the supporting Online Resource Centre at **www.oxfordtextbooks.co.uk/orc/kumra_manfredi/**

Further reading

Cox, T.H. (1991) The multicultural organization. *Academy of Management Executive,* 5: 34–47.

Cox, T.H. (2001) *Creating the Multicultural Organization: A Strategy for Capturing the Power of Diversity.* San Francisco: Jossey-Bass.

Dass, P. and Parker, B. (1999) Strategies for managing human resource diversity: from resistance to learning. *Academy of Management Executive*, 13/2: 68–80.

Harvard Business Review (2002) *Harvard Business Review on Managing Diversity*. Boston, MA: Harvard Business School Publishing Corporation.

Liff, S. (1996) Two routes to managing diversity: individual differences or social group characteristics. *Employee Relations*, 19/1: 11–26.

References

Ahmed, S. (2007) The language of diversity. *Ethnic and Racial Studies*, 30/2: 235–256.

Arblaster, A. (1984) *The Rise and Decline of Western Liberalism*. Oxford: Blackwell.

Ashton, D. (1982) *Youth in the Labour Market*. Research Paper No. 34. London: Department of Employment.

Barmes, L. and Ashtiany, S. (2003) The diversity approach to achieving equality: problems and pitfalls. *International Law Journal*, 32/4: 274–296.

Barney, J.B. (1995) Looking inside for competitive advantage. *Academy of Management Executive*, 17/10: 99–120.

Bartz, D., Hillman, L., Lehrer, S., and Mayburgh, G. (1990) A model for managing workforce diversity. *Management, Education & Development*, 21/5: 321–326.

Berg, I. (1970) *Education for Jobs: The Great Training Robbery*. Harmondsworth: Penguin.

Boxenbaum, E. (2006) Lost in translation: the making of Danish diversity management. *American Behavioral Scientist*, 49: 939–948.

Cox, T.H. (1991) The multicultural organization. *Academy of Management Executive*, 5: 34–47.

Cox, T.H. and Blake, S. (1991) Managing cultural diversity: implications for organizational competitiveness. *Academy of Management Executive*, 5: 45–56.

Dass, P. and Parker, B. (1999) Strategies for managing human resource diversity: from resistance to learning. *Academy of Management Executive*, 13/2: 68–80.

Due Billing, Y. and Sundin, E. (2006) From managing equality to managing diversity: a critical Scandinavian perspective on gender and workplace diversity, in Prasad, P., Pringle, J., and Konrad, A. (eds), *Handbook of Workplace Diversity*. London: Sage, pp. 95–120.

Dickens, L. (1999) Beyond the business case: a three-pronged approach to equality action. *Human Resource Management Journal*, 9/1: 9–19.

Fischer, M. (2007) Diversity management and the business case. Research Paper 3-11, HWWI Research Programme, Migration Research Group.

Ford, J., Tomlinson, J., Sommerlad, H., and Gold, J. (2009) 'Just don't call it diversity': developing a programme for the business case for diversity in West Yorkshire. Working paper presented to the Gender in HRD track, UFHRD Conference, June 2009.

Foster, C. and Harris, L. (2005) Easy to say, difficult to do: diversity management in retail. *Human Resource Management Journal*, 15/3: 4–17.

Garnsey, E. and Rees, B. (1998) Discourse and enactment: gender inequality in text and context. *Human Relations*, 49/2: 1041–1064.

Gooch, L. and Cornelius, N. (1999) Recruitment, selection and induction in a diverse and competitive environment, in Gooch, L. (ed.), *Human Resource Management: A Managerial Perspective*. London: Thompson.

Howard, M. and Tibballs, S. (2003) *Talking Equality: What Men and Women Think about Equality in Britain Today*. London and Manchester: Future Foundation/Equal Opportunities Commission.

Jackson, S. et al. (1992) *Diversity in the Workplace: Human Resource Initiative*. New York: Guilford Press.

Jewson, N. and Mason, D. (1984/85) Equal opportunities policies at the workplace and the concept of monitoring. *New Community*, 12/1.

Jewson, N. and Mason, D. (1986) The theory and practice of equal opportunities policies: liberal and radical approaches. *Sociological Review*, 34/2: 307–334.

Johnston, W.B. and Packer, A.H. (1987) *Workforce 2000: Work and Workers in the 21st Century*. Indianapolis, IN: Hudson Institute.

Kamp, A. and Hagedorn-Rasmussen, P. (2004) Diversity management in a Danish context: towards a multicultural or segregated working life? *Economic and Industrial Democracy*, 25/4: 525–554.

Kandola, R. and Fullerton, J. (1994) *Managing the Mosaic: Diversity in Action*. London: Institute of Personnel and Development.

Kelly, E. and Dobbin, F. (1998) How affirmative action became diversity management. *American Behavioral Scientist*, 4/7: 960–984.

Kirton, G. (2002) What is diversity?, in Johnstone, S. (ed.), *Managing Diversity in the Workplace*. London: LexisNexis, pp. 1–23.

Kirton, G. (2008) Managing multi-culturally in organizations in a diverse society, in Clegg, S. and Cooper, C. (eds), *Sage Handbook of Macro-Organizational Behaviour*. London: Sage, pp. 309–322.

Kirton, G. and Greene, A.M. (2006) The discourse of diversity in unionized contexts: views from trade union equality officers. *Personnel Review*, 35/4: 431–448.

Kirton, G. and Greene, A.M. (2010) What does diversity management mean for the gender equality project in the United Kingdom? Views and experiences of organizational actors. *Canadian Journal of Administrative Sciences*, 27/3: 249–262.

Liff, S. (1996) 'Two Routes to Managing Diversity: Individual Differences or Social Group Characteristics', Employee Relations, 19(1), pp. 11–26.

Liff, S. (1999) Diversity and equal opportunities: room for a constructive compromise? *Human Resource Management Journal*, 9/1: 65–75.

Liff, S. and Wajcman, J. (1996) Sameness and difference revisited: which way forward to equal opportunity initiatives? *Journal of Management Studies*, 33/1: 73–94.

Litvin, D. (2006) Diversity: making space for a better case?, in Konrad, A., Prasad, P., and Pringle, J. (eds), *Handbook of Workplace Diversity*. London: Sage, pp. 75–94.

Lorbiecki, A. (2001) Changing view on diversity management: the rise of the learning perspective and the need to recognize social and political contradictions. *Management Learning*, 32/3: 345–360.

Lorbiecki, A. and Jack, G. (2000) Critical turns in the evolution of diversity management. *British Journal of Management*, 11: s17–s31.

Maguire, M. and Ashton, D. (1981) Employers' perceptions and use of educational qualifications. *Educational Analysis*, 3/2.

Maxwell, G. (2004) Minority report: taking the initiative in managing diversity at BBC Scotland. *Employee Relations*, 26/2: 182–202.

More, G. (1993) 'Equal treatment' of the sexes in European Community law: what does 'equal' mean? *Feminist Legal Studies*, 1/1: 45–74.

Noon, M. (2007) The fatal flaws of diversity and the business case for ethnic minorities. *Work, Employment and Society*, 21/4: 773–784.

Pearn Kandola (2000) *A Declaration on Learning: A Call to Action*. Oxford: Learning Development Group, Pearn Kandola.

Philips, L. (2007) Will the civil service meet its workforce diversity targets? *People Management*, 26 July.

Platt, L. (1998) Address to the Diversity Research Network, Stanford Business School, 18 March.

Robinson, G. and Dechant, K. (1997) Building a business case for diversity. *Academy of Management Executive*, 11/3: 21–31.

Salvadori, M. (1977) *The Liberal Heresy*. London: Macmillan.

Sinclair, A. (2000) Women within diversity: risks and possibilities. *Women in Management Review*, 15(5/6): 237–245.

Sinclair, A. (2006) Critical diversity management practice in Australia: romanced or co-opted?, in Konrad, A., Prasad, P., and Pringle, J. (eds), *Handbook of Workplace Diversity*. London: Sage, pp. 511–553.

Thomas, R. Jr. (1996) *Redefining Diversity*. New York: Amacom.

Thomas, R. Jr. and Ely, R. (1996) Making differences matter: a new paradigm for managing diversity. *Harvard Business Review*, September/October: 79–90.

Tomlinson, F. and Schwabenland, C. (2010) Reconciling competing discourses of diversity? The UK non-profit sector between social justice and the business case. *Organization*, 17/1: 101–121.

Webb, J. (1997) The politics of equal opportunity. *Gender, Work and Organization*, 4/3: 159–169.

Westen, P. (1982) The empty idea of equality. *Harvard Law Review*, 95: 537–596.

Young, I. (1990) *Justice and the Politics of Difference*. Princeton, NJ: Princeton University Press.

4 Implementing Diversity Management

Learning objectives

- Understand some of the triggers for change and the nature of the change management process
- Appreciate the variety of approaches adopted by organizations in respect of diversity management implementation
- Be aware that organizations are at different stages in their implementation of diversity management
- Critically analyze where progress has been made in respect of diversity management implementation and where future attention is required
- Understand the roles and responsibilities of key stakeholder groups, such as senior managers, line managers, HR managers, diversity practitioners, and external bodies (e.g. Opportunity Now) in respect of diversity management implementation and the inherent tensions within these roles

Key terms

- **Change management:** a process through which organizations adapt to and meet the demands presented by increasingly turbulent and volatile markets.
- **Diversity champion:** an individual, usually senior within the organization, who is given the role of communicating the key aims, objectives, and policy initiatives in respect of diversity management both inside and outside the organization.
- **Diversity Council:** body charged with developing and then implementing the local response to strategic objectives in respect of diversity management emanating from the Global Diversity Forum.
- **Employee networks:** groups formed, usually by employees themselves, at which issues of common interest to members of the group can be debated, discussed, and explored.
- **Global Diversity Forum:** a decision and policy-making body that works through key actors within the organization's diversity structure to provide information from both outside and inside the organization on which decisions in respect of future directions for diversity strategy can be based.
- **Stakeholder:** an individual or representative of a group of individuals with an interest in the processes, practices, and outcomes of the organization. Stakeholders can be both inside (e.g. employees, managers, etc.) and outside (e.g. shareholders, consumers, customers) the organization.

Introduction

In this chapter, we explore the way in which diversity management has been implemented within organizations. It is clear from an examination of the literature that the implementation of diversity management is part of a fundamental change management process, requiring organizations to shift paradigms in the way in which concepts such as equality, disadvantage, prejudice, and difference are constructed, and the approach adopted to dealing with these issues. In moving from an 'equal' opportunities perspective to one of 'diversity management', organizations are required to set aside a liberal/legal framework based upon social justice and 'sameness', and focus instead on business-based arguments which indicate the organizational benefits to be derived from recognizing 'difference'. How organizations have responded to this challenge is the focus of the chapter.

Utilizing the eight-stage change management process proposed by Kotter and Cohen (2002), we assess how diversity management has been implemented in organizations. From this assessment it can be seen that organizations are at various stages in their development in respect of implementing diversity management, with some having introduced highly sophisticated structures and frameworks to support the development of key strategic priorities, underpinned by appropriate mechanisms to ensure their implementation and achievement. Roles and responsibilities in the delivery of diversity management are clearly assigned and these organizations are seeking to make diversity a part of day-to-day working life rather than an issue that is only considered when taking part in a training course. Other organizations are at a much earlier stage in their development and have not moved much beyond ensuring they comply with equality legislation.

In assessing the progress made so far, data are presented from a number of Chartered Institute of Personnel and Development (CIPD) reports on the approach towards diversity management implementation adopted in 285 UK companies. We also present findings from a study by Kirton and Greene (2009) on the experiences of diversity management practitioners, and case studies are presented from Standard Chartered Bank, IBM, and a large telecommunications organization. Taken together, this information provides a comprehensive picture of the current situation in respect of diversity management implementation as well as enabling us to assess lessons learnt and areas for future attention.

Delivering diversity management: the change agenda

In today's increasingly volatile and dynamic business environment, it can be argued that the only constant is change. Organizations, if they are to survive, let alone grow and prosper, need to learn to adapt to their internal and external environment. Triggers for change come from a variety of sources, key among them are the following:

- **Globalization and fierce world competition.** Organizations are seeing competition from a variety of sources, which change radically and regularly. Such competition can emerge from deregulated markets for resources, such as capital and labour, or come in the form of technological advancements which impact cost, flexibility, and innovation. In terms of where competition comes from, it is increasingly likely to emerge not just from economies at similar stages of economic development, but also from emerging and developing economies, representing new and formidable players in the global marketplace.

- **Legislation and government policy**. As governments change, so too do their priorities. Organizations are constantly required to be aware of the shifting emphasis of government activity and the likely legislative changes emanating from government policy. The previous UK government bought in a number of legislative changes in the area of equality and diversity management, and it is likely that these will be augmented by additional initiatives by the current and future governments. However, it is not sufficient for organizations simply to be mindful of the legislative agenda in their own countries. European Union member states will be directly impacted by EU regulations in respect of employment. Legislative changes in one country can directly impact others, for example, deregulation of labour markets in India and China has directly impacted employers in the UK, the USA, and beyond.

Signpost to Chapter 2 An Outline of European and UK Equality Legislation

- **Demands for quality and customer satisfaction**. The global marketplace has also brought with it a much more informed and discerning customer base. Customers who once had to content themselves with the products and services on offer in their local marketplace, even if these did not entirely meet their requirements in terms of quality, price or functionality, no longer need to compromise. Through developments such as online shopping and greater cross-border mergers and alliances, customers have access to an increasingly wide range of options and they are using this new found muscle in the marketplace to make demands on their suppliers, who in the current much tighter trading climate are having to up their game and not just satisfy their customers, but delight them.

- **Flexibility in organizational structures**. A further set of changes we have seen in recent times has been increasing flexibility not just in terms of how work is done, but also in terms of how organizations are structured. Organizations are constantly required to effectively and efficiently manage their cost base, and for many this has meant changes in the way they work. We have seen some implementing change to more effectively utilize their premises, with extended opening hours. Examples here would be retailers and call centres who now offer extended hours of operation and thus more effectively utilize their fixed capital resources in the form of buildings and equipment. Others have sought to streamline their use of fixed capital resources, and streamline operations such that they can divest themselves of costly premises and free up much needed capital. Such changes can be bought about by the more efficient use of fewer buildings, and practices such as home working, 'hot-desking', and relocation to less expensive areas have also been deployed.

Signpost to Chapter 8 Managing Work–Life Balance

Student Activity 4.1

Consider each of the 'triggers' for change identified above and answer the following questions:

1. For each of the factors identified explain how it has contributed to the drive within organizations to move from an equal opportunities approach to a focus on managing diversity.

2. Which, in your view, has been the most important 'trigger'? Justify your answer.

3. Are there any key triggers which have not been listed above? If so, what additional factors would you add?

In respect of how organizations adapt to and meet the demands presented by increasingly .urbulent and volatile markets, many have turned to models and frameworks of change man-.gement to assist them. And those implementing diversity management initiatives in their organizations are no different. One of the most enduring and influential change management frameworks is presented by Kurt Lewin (1951). He presents a three-stage model to bring about behaviour modification in an organizational setting. Each stage is discussed below.

Stage 1: Unfreezing: in this stage in the framework, action is taken to reduce those forces within the organization which maintain behaviour in its current form. The emphasis here is on a communication process to promote recognition within the organization of the need to change.

Stage 2: Movement: in this stage, action is taken to develop new attitudes and behaviour which will facilitate and support the change in behaviour required.

Stage 3: Refreezing: in this third and final stage, action is taken to stabilize and cement change at the new level. Reinforcement of the new behaviours is achieved through supporting mechanisms such as performance management systems and reward management processes.

Lewin's original model has been built upon and developed further by a number of authors. These authors have taken the original three-stage model and developed it to present a more detailed framework for managers to adopt and, where necessary, adapt when implementing change within their organizations. One such model is that developed by Kotter and Cohen (2002), who present an eight-stage process for securing effective change. This model will be utilized throughout this chapter to provide an analytical framework for the assessment of the organizational approach to implementing diversity initiatives.

The eight stages in the Kotter and Cohen (2002) model are:

1. Create a sense of urgency
2. Build a guiding team
3. Create a vision
4. Communicate the vision
5. Empower action
6. Produce short-term wins
7. Don't let up
8. Make change stick

In considering organizational responses to implementing diversity management, we will utilize the stages in Kotter and Cohen's (2002) framework. This will be done not to assess the implementation strategy of any organization in particular, but rather as an analytical mechanism through which the array of organizational responses can be discussed.

Signpost to
Chapter 3
From Equal
Opportunities
to Managing
Diversity

Create a sense of urgency

In relation to diversity management, there is little doubt that there is a sense of urgency. This has been primarily promoted through business case arguments and increased competition.

> ### ⮞ Student Activity 4.2
>
> Consider the following questions in relation to business case arguments for diversity management (you may need to refer back to Chapter 3 to help you with these questions):
>
> 1. What are the main business case arguments for diversity management?
>
> 2. Which of the arguments advanced over the last 20 years or so has not proven to be as much of an issue as originally anticipated?
>
> 3. Have there been factors which were not included in business case arguments which are in fact directly relevant to a diversity management agenda?

In 2006, the CIPD commissioned a survey to assess the extent to which employers have understood and taken action in respect of the business case for diversity. The effect of action in relation to diversity was also examined, as were the attitudes of those tasked with implementing change within organizations. The survey was conducted among UK organizations with 285 taking part.

Findings revealed that in respect of key drivers for diversity in organizations, the main factors were legal pressures, cited by 68 per cent of respondents; recruitment and retention of talent, cited by 64 per cent of respondents; corporate social responsibility, cited by 62 per cent of respondents; a wish to be seen as an 'employer of choice', cited by 62 per cent of respondents; and because it makes business sense, cited by 60 per cent of respondents. Sixty per cent of respondents take action on diversity because they believe it to be morally right, 48 per cent do so to improve business performance, and 43 per cent do so to improve customer relations. Forty-three per cent of respondents believe that taking action on diversity will enable them to improve their creativity and innovation and 40 per cent that it will assist them in reaching diverse markets.

However, when asked to rank the most significant factor, legal compliance is the most important reason businesses have taken action in respect of diversity management; the business case is behind, with only 17 per cent of organizations citing this as the most important driver for managing diversity. The moral case also slips in employers' priorities, with only 13 per cent citing this as their main driver.

As discussed in Chapter 3, the key differentiator between diversity management and the equal opportunities approach is the more inclusive nature of the diversity management perspective which seeks to emphasize and celebrate difference. The findings are encouraging, as 93 per cent of organizations surveyed have a diversity policy. However, when asked what the policy covers, it becomes evident that the majority of organizations are specifically targeting the protected groups who are the focus of legislation. Thus most organizations cover disability (170 of the 285), ethnicity/race (166 of the 285), and gender/sex (165 of the 285). Religion is covered by 160 organizations, sexual orientation by 159, and age by 130. However, only 47 organizations look at social and economic background, 57 look at all forms of difference, and just seven consider accent.

These findings support empirical research which has shown that the implementation of diversity management is context-specific (Janssens and Zanoni, 2005; Kamp and Hagedorn-Rasmussen, 2004) and the weight given to purely business-based arguments will vary significantly across organizations (Tomlinson and Schwabenland, 2010). The focus on business-case arguments implies that managers will be unlikely to oppose a case for diversity based upon economic factors and material benefit to the organization. To argue the alternative to the business case, i.e. from an equality and social justice perspective with a moral rather than a utilitarian foundation, may have less resonance with managers. However, there is some evidence that the approaches are not mutually exclusive, and they are often presented alongside one another in 'creating a sense of urgency'.

For example, Kamp and Hagedorn-Rasmussen (2004) explain in their study of the implementation of diversity management in a Danish Municipal Authority that the inclusion of 'moral' arguments, drawing on principles of social justice, and positioning the organization as a socially responsible enterprise strengthened the case for the programme at the strategic level. Barmes and Ashtiany (2003) showed though the prime motivation for diversity management was framed in business-case arguments in a study of UK investment banks, the 'moral' benefits were seen as serendipitous side-effects. Ahmed (2007) reported that practitioners within Australian universities switched the focus of the their justifications for diversity management from a business model to a social justice model depending on which arguments they felt would most appeal to particular audiences.

However, the question remains as to the compatibility of these two approaches in creating a sense of urgency in respect of action with regard to diversity management. Are arguments based on morality and social justice merely added to business-based arguments to widen their appeal, implying that a deeper commitment to the principles of morality reflected in the arguments is absent in the organization. If this is the case, then, for some, the very nature of the arguments has been undermined and obscured. Sinclair (2006) and Noon (2007) both argue that morality-based arguments are ends in themselves and cannot be deployed when based on a contingent argument predicated upon potential organizational benefit. Noon (2007: 781) contends that an organization's commitment to diversity management should emanate from the fact that equal opportunity 'is a human right based in moral legitimacy (social justice) rather than economic circumstances'. How committed an organization is to these principles is evidenced by their pursuit of diversity objectives without reference to the potential benefit that may accrue to the organization. Indeed, it is evidenced by the extent to which the organization is willing to continue to work towards these ends even if doing so is economically disadvantageous. Within this formulation, we see a fundamental incompatibility between business interests and social justice objectives.

Debate Box

Organize the class into two groups, one for the motion and one against.
    The motion is:

This house believes that the business case for diversity and arguments emanating from a social justice/equality perspective are mutually exclusive.

Stages in the debate: (each stage is given with timings, the overall time for the activity is 55 minutes – allowing a few minutes for change over of presenters, etc.)

- Each group has 20 minutes to prepare their arguments either for or against the motion.
- Each group is given 5 minutes to present their opening statement (10 minutes in total).
- Groups reconvene for 10 minutes to prepare rebuttal arguments.
- Each group has 2 minutes to present rebuttal arguments.

A vote is taken and the winners of the debate announced; the casting vote goes to impartial observers: tutors, audience members not involved in the debate, or observers.

When assessing the broad organizational approach to 'creating a sense of urgency' for attention and action to be given to diversity management, we see that a pragmatic approach has been adopted. It is evident that the majority of organizations are building their case for attention to the diversity agenda on business-case arguments. Legal compliance is the main driver and remains the principle focus of organizational policy and practice. However, 60 per cent of organizations endorse the view that they are pursuing a diversity agenda because 'it is the morally right thing to do'. This figure drops to only 13 per cent when organizations are asked to state their primary driver. There is also evidence that only a minority of organizations are embracing the 'celebrating differences' ethos advocated by the diversity management perspective. For example, only 47 of the 285 organizations in the study (CIPD, 2006a) are looking at social and economic background as an issue, and even fewer – just seven – are considering the impact that accent may have on employees' treatment in the workplace. These findings lead us to question how much of a departure we have seen from the equality of opportunity approach, with its clear focus on legal compliance and ensuring equal treatment for all employees.

Build a guiding team

Organizations will differ in the way they set up the mechanisms through which the diversity management agenda will be delivered, with some opting for a relatively loose structure where everyone has a responsibility for diversity to much tighter frameworks in which roles and responsibilities are clearly identified. However, despite this, it is evident from the literature that there is widespread agreement that the commitment and support of one group of people, senior managers, is a critical success factor. It is also clear that without this support diversity commitment at lower levels will be compromised and it is possible initiatives will not progress at the rate hoped for or, indeed, that they may fail altogether.

In terms of evidence in respect of senior management support and commitment for diversity initiatives, the figures are not encouraging. In 2007, the CIPD published a further report on the findings from their study of the diversity practices of 285 UK organizations (Tatli et al., 2007). They found that only 42 per cent of their respondents felt their senior management encouraged diversity in the organization, and only 16 per cent were positive about the amount of support they received from senior management.

Discouraging though these findings are, it is apparent that organizations do not rely solely on top management commitment to advance the diversity agenda. Empirical evidence suggests that organizations have established structures in which diversity strategy can be debated and discussed. There are then mechanisms through which agreed objectives can be cascaded throughout the organization and diversity values are communicated to all (Michielsens et al., 2008). A typical structure could look like that shown in Figure 4.1, for example.

Figure 4.1 shows a formal structure established to enable the organization to set its strategic objectives in relation to diversity management and the mechanisms through which the strategic objectives are cascaded through the organization.

Global Diversity Forum. The process begins with the establishment of a Global Diversity Forum, at which senior managers meet and discuss current and future priorities in respect of diversity management across the business and assess progress against previously set and agreed objectives. The Global Diversity Forum tends to be a decision and policy making body which depends upon input from key actors within the formal diversity structure to provide data on

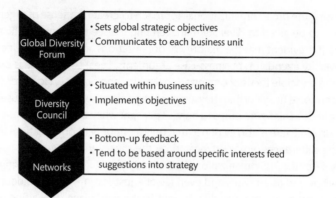

Figure 4.1 Simple structure of diversity management implementation process

progress with objectives and evidence from research and analysis, both within and external to the organization, on which decisions in respect of future directions for diversity strategy can be based.

Looking at diversity from a global perspective enables organizations to identify key issues which impact the organization across all its operations and enables action to be taken collaboratively to address the issue.

⊙ Case study 4.1   A Global Diversity Forum at Standard Chartered Bank

Standard Chartered Bank identified through their diversity forum that the issue of gender diversity was a key area of concern for them. This was an issue that was impacting them not just in a single country or region, but was having an impact globally. As a consequence, the bank formed a Global Women's Council to focus on the issue of gender diversity, with the aim of furthering the Bank's strategic objective of enabling women to achieve their full potential through personal development and integrated supportive practices implemented in an engaging and inclusive workplace. The Global Women's Council was launched in 2007 with an event at which a number of the Bank's most talented women employees gathered. They met in Dubai for two days to discuss topics relating to women in the workplace, women in the community, and women as customers.

Joanna Fielding, Chair, commented: 'Standard Chartered's strength is the diversity of our people – mirroring our customers and the communities we operate in. We believe that we also have the potential to lead the way on gender diversity. This event is an opportunity to showcase our progress and to inspire our female talent to take their careers to new heights'.

The event was sponsored by Peter Sands, Group Chief Executive of Standard Chartered Bank, and gave participants the opportunity to hear from some outstanding role models and inspirational leaders. The sessions covered a number of issues, some in relation to personal and professional development, others concerning the Bank's involvement in community projects to help women across the world, and further sessions were directed towards opportunities for the Bank to develop products and services aimed specifically at their women customers.

Source: Adapted from posting on AME.com, 22 May 2007.

Case study questions

1. In your view, what are the costs and benefits of an event of this kind?

2. What does it tell you about Standard Chartered Bank's approach to diversity management that the two-day event covered sessions not just on personal development for the women involved, but also for communities and customers?

Diversity Council. Once strategic global objectives have been determined, they are then cascaded down to locally-based Diversity Councils. This is often achieved through the mechanism of a 'diversity champion', a senior individual within the local business unit charged with communicating and promoting the diversity agenda and focusing action and resources in respect of key diversity objectives. Other members of the Council would typically be a specialist diversity manager operating either within a business unit or across a number of business units, line management representatives from key functions in the unit, and employee representatives or representatives of the trade union (where these are present). Action in respect of key diversity targets would be assessed within the business unit, and progress and results presented back to the Global Diversity Forum.

Employee networks. Bottom-up mechanisms in respect of diversity management tend to take the form of employee-led networks and special interest groups. These groups are usually formed by employees themselves and are established as a forum where issues of common interest to members of the group can be debated, discussed, and explored. They are also forums where issues can be identified for inclusion in the overall strategic direction of the organization in respect of diversity management, establishing a feedback loop.

It becomes apparent that for diversity management to succeed and become embedded within the organization, clear lines of authority, accountability, and responsibility need to be

---

⬛ **Case study 4.2** Employee networks at IBM

An organization which has used its diversity networks to great effect is IBM, which currently has 190 networks globally. The initiative grew from grassroots activity which was employee-driven and broader in scope than existing mechanisms and structures. Communication within the networks is conducted either electronically or face to face, and enables discussion of issues of relevance to particular constituencies (Thomas, 2004). So, for example, the key areas of concern for the Asian Network are stereotyping, networking and mentoring, and employee development and talent pipelines. For the People with Disabilities Network, the key areas of concern are recruitment, target advertising and marketing, benefits review, and New World HQ (accessibility issues). For the White Men's Network, the key areas of concern are executive accountability, education and awareness, ageing and work–life balance. We thus see that by having a number of networks for key constituents, individuals are able to discuss with like-minded others issues of concern to them as a group (Thomas, 2004).

IBM has also set up mechanisms for the networks to communicate with one another and work collectively where issues are of common concern. Such issues identified at IBM were development, promotion, senior management's commitment to diversity, and the need to focus on recruiting a diverse pool of employees, especially in engineering and science-related positions. The identification of these issues from the grassroots level is particularly useful for the organization as it can then go on to form the focus of future policy. Once identified, the issues can be fed back to the Global Diversity Forum, via the Diversity Councils, providing an agenda for action. They can then be discussed, prioritized and fed into strategic decision-making.

There is also evidence to suggest that employee-led networks not only provide benefits to the individuals who are part of them, but also provide tangible organizational benefits. In the IBM case, the organization broadened its efforts to develop its client base among women-owned businesses to include a focus on Asian, Black, Hispanic and Native American markets. Their Market Development organization has, as a consequence, grown revenue in their Small and Medium Size Business Sales and Marketing organization from $10 million in 1998 to hundreds of millions of dollars in 2003 (Thomas, 2004).

established. Also necessary are organizational mechanisms to support the determination of strategic directions and mechanisms situated throughout the organization to implement those policies.

Research evidence suggests that building a guiding team is the most effective way to ensure that diversity management achieves key outcomes. In their study of the effectiveness and efficacy of diversity programmes across a number of organizations, Kalev et al. (2006: 611) concluded:

> Broadly speaking, our findings suggest that although inequality in attainment at work may be rooted in managerial bias and the social isolation of women and minorities, the best hope for remedying it may lie in practices that assign organizational responsibility for change. ... Structures that embed accountability, authority and expertise (affirmative action plans, diversity committees and taskforces, diversity managers and departments) are the most effective means of increasing the proportions of white women, black women and black men in private sector management. ... Affirmative action plans and diversity staff both centralize authority over and accountability for workforce composition, diversity committees locate authority and accountability in an interdepartmental task force and may work by causing people from different parts of the organization to take responsibility for pursuing the goal of integration.

Thus we see that through a structured approach to the issue and action directed at different levels within the organizational hierarchy change can be achieved.

Create a vision

The purpose of building a guiding team is to put in place an organizational framework through which a vision for the management of diversity can be created and promulgated throughout the entire organization. A typical facilitative structure has been presented in Figure 4.1. In this section we turn our attention to how likely it is that such a structure will be implemented in practice.

Pitts (2007) notes research into policy implementation which indicates that the more specific and coherent a policy is, the greater the likelihood that it will be appropriately implemented. Diversity management programmes are frequently typified by a vast array of components which often do not seem to have a central core or guiding set of principles. As a consequence, diversity management strategy can become rather muddled, with the result that the outcomes required of its component parts are wildly at odds with each other. It is thus critical from the outset that those charged with formulating diversity strategy ensure they understand the vision and the key objectives the organization is seeking to achieve. This needs to be underpinned by guiding principles that support the achievement of the vision and key targets or measures so that, as an organization, it is clear when achievement in respect of the vision has been attained.

In its study of the diversity processes and practices of 285 organizations, the CIPD (2006a) looked at the content of organizations' diversity policies, a public statement of the vision of these organizations, and an indication of the weight and emphasis they give to particular diversity issues. They found that organizations were most likely to include action and resources in respect of legally protected groups. The survey revealed that 170 of the 285 respondents had policies covering disability in the workplace, 166 had policies covering ethnicity/race, 165 covered gender/sex, 160 included religion in their policy statements, and 159 included sexual orientation. Of the responding organizations, 138 extended their policies to cover nationality, and 130 covered age. Only 87 covered parental status, 47 had regulations in respect of social and economic background, 31 covered physical appearance, and nine covered weight.

It is thus apparent that organizations do not appear to have extended their vision much beyond compliance with legal regulation in respect of equality of opportunity. It is also clear that 115 organizations (of the 285 in the sample) either do not have a diversity policy at all or do not include any of the categories mentioned in the study – those legally protected or otherwise. This indicates a very patchy and unstructured response to diversity management.

Of those groups protected by diversity management policy statements, the majority are also those protected by law. In terms of the broader diversity agenda, we see that very few organizations are looking more broadly to the valuing of difference, with only a small minority focusing on issues concerning those in categories beyond legally protected groups. So, for example, only 31 of the 285 organizations in the sample have policy in respect of physical appearance and only nine are looking at the issue of weight. Also of interest is the fact that some of the legally protected groups are being overlooked by organizations. For example, less than half of the organizations (130) have policy objectives in respect of age and none in the sample seem to have objectives in respect of protection for the trans community; a legally protected group since 1999, with amendments to those protections in 2008. This indicates the complexity of the legislation in the area and the fact that many organizations are still finding it difficult to formulate their response to all of the equality strands covered by legislation. It also indicates that this is an area in which formulation of a vision for diversity management and development of strategic objectives in respect of that vision is a process that many organizations are not yet engaging with to any great extent.

In their follow-up report in 2007, the CIPD further noted that over two-thirds of the diversity professionals in the study (70 per cent) admitted that they do not have formally set objectives against which diversity is measured and advanced. This once again indicates that diversity management is not considered at the strategic level, and that action in relation to diversity management remains at a piecemeal and superficial level.

Signpost to Chapter 2 An Outline of European and UK Equality Legislation

Student Activity 4.3

Considering the evidence above from the CIPD study, answer the following questions:

1. Why do you think organizations struggle to identify a vision for their diversity management programme?

2. Why do you think that 115 of the 285 organizations in the study either have no formal diversity policy or, if they do, it doesn't appear to cover any of the legally protected employee groups?

3. In your view, why have organizations not moved towards a 'valuing difference' approach in any significant way?

These findings are disappointing for those wishing to see the progression of the diversity management agenda at the strategic level within organizations being fully integrated with business objectives. However, there is no shortage of advice on how diversity strategy 'should' be developed. For example, Ted Childs, one of the architects of the IBM diversity strategy who now runs his own diversity consultancy, providing guidance to organizations on how to manage their diversity strategy and policy, recommends four main goals of a diversity strategy, which apply globally or locally. These are (Childs, 2007):

1. Identify, attract, and retain the best people no matter what group they come from.
2. Create an organization where that talent can perform to the best of its ability without any hindrance to respond to customers and enhance shareholder value.
3. Ensure that you understand the diversity in your customer base and that you are responding to customers as they are and not as you would wish them to be. It is important that they can see themselves in your vision, actions, and workplace.
4. Use your external relationships and connections to overcome disadvantage and increase the diversity of candidates in the talent pool, now and in the future.

In a study by Michielsens et al. (2008) of the implementation of diversity management by four case study organizations operating in different sectors, they concluded that workplace diversity is defined in a number of ways and organizations will vary in their approach to the issue in line with the maturity of their ideas, their business strategy, and market sector. For some, it is important to stress the international dimension of the diversity agenda; for others, the equal opportunities dimension is more important. However, it was clear from the study that despite their differences all four organizations clearly linked diversity with the concept of 'inclusion'.

In the professional services company in the study, they claimed that The company's vision is to create an environment 'in which people can be themselves, but at the same time be an inclusive workplace where talented individuals are treated with respect, have choices in their working patterns and in their development' (Michielsens et al., 2008: 12). The telecommunications company also referenced the concept of inclusion, but linked this more clearly to arguments regarding equality and legal compliance: 'We continue to work to create an inclusive working environment in which employees can thrive regardless of their race, sex, religion/beliefs, disability, marital or civil partnership status, age, sexual orientation, gender identity, gender expression, or caring responsibilities' (ibid.).

From this, we see that for those organizations with the resource and the will, creating a vision for diversity management is possible. It would appear that for the majority, this concerted strategic approach remains an aspiration rather than a reality.

Communicate the vision

In this section we consider the organizational approach to communicating the vision for diversity management. As discussed in the section above, few organizations have the coherent strategic approach recommended by Pitts (2007) as a requirement for successful implementation. However, what is clear from a reading of the literature is that this does not mean there is no activity in respect of diversity management. There is in fact a great deal of activity and key aspects of this will be discussed. But what needs to be borne in mind is that the activity is tending to be directed at the solution of locally identified issues rather than in pursuit of a wider strategic change agenda. In this section, then, we consider communication of the vision through equal opportunities and Diversity policy and diversity training.

Equal opportunities and diversity policy

A key mechanism through which an organization communicates its commitment to equality and diversity is through policy. These still tend to take the form of Equal Opportunities (EO) policies whose purpose is to ensure equality of access to employment opportunities by eliminating differential treatment based upon membership of a particular social group (Walsh, 2007). Although EO policies have the same intent, in practice they take a variety of forms and vary in their nature and scope. As indicated by Liff (2003), EO policies can be simple statements of intent or much more fully articulated visions of the aims of the policy, the groups it seeks to protect, and the mechanisms through which this will be done. The Workplace Employee Relations Survey 2004 (WERS) is a large study of the working practices of British workplaces and includes data on the coverage and scope of EO practices in the period 1998–2004. Findings show clear evidence that there has been an increase in the number of organizations with formal, written EO policies, or policies in respect of managing diversity (Walsh, 2007). In 2004, almost three-quarters of workplaces (73 per cent) with ten or more employees had a formal written EO policy. This compares with less than two-thirds (64 per cent) in 1998. There is also evidence that the scope of these policies has increased, with policies extending beyond the more usual areas of gender, race, and disability to include the newer equality strands of age, religion/belief, and sexual orientation.

The findings indicate that larger workplaces were more likely to have an EO policy, particularly those with more than 100 employees. Equal Opportunities policies are also more likely in the public sector (with an almost universal presence) than in the private sector (Walsh, 2007). In workplaces with an HR specialist, there was a much higher likelihood of a formal EO policy – 92 per cent for organizations with an HR specialist compared with only 48 per cent for those without.

➔ Student Activity 4.4

Pick an organization you are familiar with and obtain a copy of their EO/diversity policy. If you do not have access to a policy, do some research and identify a company's EO/diversity policy.

- What is covered by the policy?
- What is left out?
- Does the policy go beyond measures to ensure compliance with legal provision in respect of legally protected groups?
- What would you like to see included in the policy?
- What recommendations could you make to senior management in respect of making the policy more effective?

Diversity training

In terms of the nature and focus of diversity policy, it would appear that much of it takes the form of some kind of training intervention. Michielsens et al. (2008) found that in order to effectively promote the diversity agenda and foster an environment in which diversity is not just tolerated but actively valued required awareness-raising through daily communication, complemented by targeted diversity awareness training. In their four case study organizations, they found differences in the targets of these programmes, but all the firms engaged in diversity awareness training. In some organizations, all employees received diversity awareness training during the induction programme, although this took place online rather than face to face. Managers responsible for recruitment are also frequently singled out for diversity awareness training, but training for all line managers is not the norm. In the telecommunications company and professional services organization in their study, there appeared to be growing recognition that all line managers may need such training, though this was not evident in the other two organizations they studied.

At the financial services company global diversity awareness training had been available for all staff since 2004. For the 13,000 employees, a diversity webcast formed part of their induction programme. Networks and business units were also able to organize their own diversity awareness initiatives to endorse and support corporate programmes. In terms of the content of such programmes, the telecommunications company made it a policy issue not to target specific under-represented groups in the awareness programme. Rather, the approach was to ensure an awareness of diversity issues across all equality strands and to create an environment in which issues could be fully discussed and reflected upon (Michielsens et al., 2008).

However, evidence suggests that such programmes are largely ineffective. This derives not just from the ineffectiveness of the programmes themselves, but also from a lack of understanding of the scope of the issue, a focus only on issues of legal compliance, and a lack of buy-in from senior leadership (Nancheria, 2008). These shortcomings are worrying enough, but evidence from social psychologists indicates that diversity training can actually create bias, which is clearly contrary to the original intent. As a consequence of such training interventions, rather than ignoring or celebrating differences, individuals may become much more aware of them and subconsciously begin to act on them. 'Irresistible' stereotypes and prejudices are likely to be deeply ingrained in individuals and thus not easily cancelled out by a two-hour (frequently online) session (Nancheria, 2008). These findings are supported by Kalev et al. (2006: 611), who conclude in their study on the effectiveness and efficacy of a variety of corporate diversity initiatives that 'Practices that target managerial bias through ... education (diversity training) show virtually no effect. ... They show modest positive effects when responsibility structures are also in place.'

Debate Box

Organize the class into two groups, one for the motion and one against.
  The motion is:

Diversity training has failed. Organizations are now going to have to look to alternative approaches to advance the diversity management agenda.
  Please follow the process for the debate as indicated in the debate box above.

Empower action

A key feature of change management is to enable those tasked with bringing change initiatives to fruition to achieve their objectives. This requires clarity of objectives, support from key constituencies within the organization (particularly from senior management), resources to achieve the objectives, and authority to make decisions and enforce non-performance. In this section we assess whether this has occurred in respect of diversity management.

In the subsequent report of their 2006 survey, the CIPD asked the 285 participating organizations at what level their diversity specialists are located in the organizational hierarchy. Only 6 per cent of the 280 respondents had diversity specialists at Board level, 37 per cent of diversity specialists were located at the senior management level, and 41 per cent were located at the middle management level. Only 10 per cent of diversity specialists were to be found at the supervisor level and only 4 per cent at a junior level (CIPD, 200x). We thus see that the majority of diversity specialists are to be found in middle management positions, although those located in senior management positions are not far behind (37 per cent compared to 41 per cent). Those least likely to take ownership of diversity are at Board level, with only 6 per cent of the organizations in the survey reporting their diversity specialist resides here, and junior staff with only 4 per cent representation.

However, when asked how strongly it is perceived that senior management support diversity, the results are not quite as encouraging. Only 16 per cent of respondents strongly agreed with the statement that 'Those in senior management encourage diversity'; 27 per cent agreed; 21 per cent either strongly disagreed or disagreed; and 36 per cent of respondents were neutral. In response to the statement 'It's very important for my diversity role to know the names and faces of senior staff and to be able to approach them easily', 89 per cent either agreed or strongly agreed to this statement, with only 2 per cent disagreeing and 9 per cent remaining neutral. Only 11 per cent of respondents strongly agreed to the statement 'My organization aims to make sure that diversity and equality are at the heart of everything it does'. Twenty-seven per cent agreed with the statement, 25 per cent disagreed, 4 per cent strongly disagreed, and 33 per cent of respondents were neutral on this question.

These figures show that while diversity specialists in organizations know and understand that senior management support is essential to the achievement of their role, only a minority feel they receive this support. In response to the statement 'senior managers encourage diversity', only 16 per cent strongly agree and 27 per cent agree. However, over one-third of respondents neither agree nor disagree, and 21 per cent disagree or strongly disagree. Having this support, and feeling able to rely on it, is clearly important to respondents as 89 per cent of them either agree or strongly agree with the statement that it is important to their role in diversity to know senior managers personally and to feel they can approach them on these matters when necessary. In terms of the final question, just over one-third of respondents (38 per cent) felt able to agree or strongly agree that their organization seeks to ensure diversity and equality are at the heart of everything it does. However, 29 per cent either disagreed or strongly disagreed and 33 per cent did not feel able to answer the question definitively.

In terms of who diversity practitioners are, what their background is and how they perceive their role, the work of Kirton and Greene (2009) is instructive. In their study, they interviewed

41 diversity specialists from a variety of organizations across the public and private sectors. They were particularly interested to find whether diversity practitioners are qualitatively different from their organizational predecessors, equality of opportunities managers/officers. This was expected to be the case given that the emphasis of the Equal Opportunities practitioner's role was the protection and advancement of socially disadvantaged groups (Cockburn, 1991; Jewson and Mason, 1986). Diversity practitioners, on the other hand, are required to advance the equality agenda based upon a business case which is in line with strategic and business objectives. The key constituency through which this is to be achieved is managers. They are thus tasked with using language based on business objectives, linking activity to the strategic plan, and ensuring that actions taken in respect of diversity are connected with issues which are important to managers to secure ownership and commitment (Johnstone, 2002).

This shifts the position of diversity practitioners away from that of equality specialists, whose role was clearly to ensure the organization met its legal responsibilities, and who were working to achieve this from either an HR background or one rooted in political activism. However, regardless of the background of the individual, at the heart of the role was a concern with social justice outcomes, which in turn was linked with the advancement of disadvantaged social groups within the workplace. Equality practitioners may have had a challenging role within the organization, but there was clarity and purpose to their role. Diversity practitioners, by contrast, find themselves in a less clear-cut position. They are 'outsiders-within' (Lorbiecki, 2001) as they are the people in the organization who view part of their role as to speak out against discrimination and disadvantage. Yet at the same time they are tasked with ensuring the achievement of the organization's business objectives. This suggests there is an inherent tension in the role. For example, we see evidence that those in diversity practitioner roles often find it difficult to fit in with the prevailing culture within the organization (Lawrence, 2000; Lorbiecki, 2001). They may also find themselves in a position where they have to compromise their own personal beliefs and values in order to undertake their role (Kirton et al., 2007).

In the findings of their study, Kirton and Greene (2009) identified diversity practitioners as being more likely to be drawn from managerial ranks, with business and operational backgrounds, rather than have experience of political activism. Those from HR were likely to have come from either generalist roles or other HR specialisms; they were not likely to have had an equality background. Diversity practitioners were also likely to have been with the organization for some time, which implied that they 'understood the business'. Most of the diversity specialists were located within HR, but a minority either worked in stand-alone units or were to be found in the corporate social responsibility area. In terms of support, this varied hugely. Many of the specialists interviewed were the only person working on diversity in their organization. More commonly, those specialists at a senior level had between one and two assistants. Sizeable units were evident, but this was only in the public sector, where one local authority specialist was in charge of a team of 40. Many of the practitioners from both the private and public sectors were supported in their role by a management decision-making committee (either a diversity council or diversity forum) at which management and (sometimes) non-management representatives were present (Kirton and Greene, 2009).

Interviewees reported that they did not feel the sense of isolation identified in previous studies. The support of external networks was particularly helpful here, as was the seniority of the individual, which meant they were already embedded within the business and had existing contacts and networks to draw upon when issues needed to be discussed.

Sinclair (2006: 517) has described diversity practitioners as being on the 'edge of managerial legitimacy' because she believes diversity work to be a marginal activity regardless of the claims of diversity practitioners and the organizations themselves of its centrality. However, this was not found to be the perception among the interviewees in the study. It could be this was because most of them were white, senior, high earners who had generally come from the managerial ranks and thus had already achieved tangible success and legitimacy. An additional factor supporting their perception of a lack of marginalization was the support they felt they received from senior management, often the CEO, and through this relationship they could enhance not only their own authority, but also the credibility and centrality of the diversity policy (Kirton and Greene, 2009).

The study also identified a number of opportunities emanating from the shift from equal opportunities to diversity. Many of the interviewees in the study believed they enjoyed higher status than their equal opportunities predecessors. The seniority of the practitioners themselves meant they did not have to worry about many of the potential costs associated with diversity work that might be experienced by those lower in the management hierarchy. Many practitioners had come from operational management positions and they generally had good experience of the organization, so many felt they had credibility and authority. Through senior management commitment to diversity, the work of the diversity practitioner is enhanced and the agenda is more likely to be advanced. This point was supported by many in the study who indicated that they were further supported in their roles by diversity and equality decision-making structures within their organizations.

Alongside these opportunities, a note of caution needs to be sounded (Kirton and Greene, 2009). If diversity practitioners continue to over-identify with management interests, the change that is achieved within the organization may serve to support organizational objectives. However, this narrow focus may mean that the need to improve working lives is not prioritized and progress may not be made. This is an area where future work is needed as the solution to this tension is clearly an important issue.

➤ Student Activity 4.5

You can see above two quite different accounts from diversity practitioners of their organizational experience. The CIPD (2007) study indicates some issues for concern with the role, whereas the Kirton and Greene (2009) study, while also raising a number of issues of concern, does present some optimistic findings. Consider both accounts and answer the following questions:

1. What are the similarities and differences between the two accounts of the role of diversity practitioners presented above?

2. Why do you think these differences have occurred?

3. When we see such differences in research study outcomes, does one have to be right and the other wrong or are there ways in which it is possible for both to be accurate?

Produce short-term wins and don't let up

Introducing diversity management into an organization is like any culture change programme: if it is to work, it will take time and needs constant attention and consistent action. One of the main ways in which organizations keep themselves on track and ensure that they don't lose heart or interest is through producing short-term or 'quick' wins. These are boosts to the programme and the organizational effort which recognize achievement in one or more areas of activity and help those in the organization tasked with the achievement of the diversity agenda to maintain the attention of key organizational stakeholders. A visible and very popular way of producing 'quick' wins is to put the organization forward for one of the many diversity awards that have proliferated in the marketplace. Usually sponsored by a body which campaigns for the furtherance of diversity management issues, or publications with diversity management at their heart; these awards provide a focus for activity and a much needed motivational boost during the lengthy change process.

Signpost to
Chapter 6
Managing
Gender
Diversity in the
Workplace

An organization whose awards are particularly renowned in the gender diversity arena is Opportunity Now (www.opportunitynow/awards), and we have featured some of their previous winners and their stories in other chapters of this book.

The aim of the Opportunity Now award scheme is to celebrate outstanding examples of best practice and innovation at the organizational level as well as individual achievement. The awards have been running for 16 years and are seen as the most prestigious awards for recognizing achievements in the advancement of women in the workplace. Those considered for awards nominate themselves and entry is welcomed across all economic sectors. In terms of the judging criteria, three main areas are considered:

- Motivate: this looks at nominees' commitment to gender equality, diversity, and inclusion to support organizational engagement and facilitate the involvement of people across the organization in positive action.

- Act: here evidence is needed that equality, diversity, and inclusion are integrated into day-to-day organizational life.

- Impact: explores organizational processes designed to ensure that the impact of action is monitored and measured. This is reported to appropriate bodies within the organization and action is taken on the basis of the information.

The awards are growing, with new categories added as time goes on and the issue matures. There are now eight categories or award and these are:

The Advancing Women in the Workplace Award

The Agile Organization Award

The Champion Award

Directing Diverse Talent Award

Diverse Women Award

Global Award

Inclusive Culture Award

The Santander Award: Inspiring the Workplace of the Future

> **Student Activity** 4.6
>
> Imagine you are working in the diversity function of a medium-sized organization (approximately 700 employees) which has put a lot of effort into advancing gender diversity. Write a briefing paper to your manager, who is Head of Diversity in the organization, on the advantages and disadvantages of self-nominating for one of the Opportunity Now Awards. The paper should propose your recommendation as to whether you should proceed or not, and provide a justification for the decision.

In respect of needing to continue to pay attention to enhancing increased diversity in the labour market, data from WERS (2004) are clear. The findings indicate that regarding gender diversity the incidence of horizontal job segregation has fallen, with the number of people stating their job is done equally well by men and women rising from 30 per cent in 1998 to 38 per cent in 2004 (Walsh, 2007). Vertical segregation, on the other hand, seems a much more entrenched issue and little movement is evident in this respect. Women's presence in senior management grades has not progressed to any significant extent over the six-year period. Women were under-represented in management in 71 per cent of organizations in 1998 and in 69 per cent of organizations in 2004. The sectors showing the greatest disparity were financial and business services workplaces (Walsh, 2007).

The ethnicity findings show that although only 6 per cent of the workforce is from an ethnic minority, nearly half of all workplaces (44 per cent) employ at least one ethnic minority employee. There was, however, a clear difference across sectors, with hotels, restaurants, and the financial services employing a higher proportion than others, such as construction. Employees with a disability are employed by 19 per cent of organizations. Organizations in public administration, electricity, and gas are more likely to employ someone who is long-term disabled than other workplaces, for example the hotel and restaurant sectors (Walsh, 2007). Thus it is evident that there is some diversity across sectors in terms of basic characteristics such as gender, ethnicity, and disability, although it is also clear from this picture that there is still some way to go and as such organizations cannot 'let up' on their diversity efforts.

Make change stick

There is an old organizational adage that 'what gets measured, gets done', and it is no different in respect of diversity management. However, when it comes to measuring diversity outcomes many organizations baulk at the task for fear that it will be seen as affirmative action or positive discrimination, which is generally illegal within equality legislation. In the absence of measurement, diversity policies and initiatives can lack drive, and direction, and as a consequence organizations may lose focus. It is also evident that organizations are constantly tackling a number of competing priorities at any given time, and to have one aspect of work which is neither monitored nor measured may mean that this is the activity which is sacrificed when time and resources are scarce. For these reasons, the CIPD, in their report on *Managing Diversity* (2006b), recommend that success in respect of diversity is actively measured and recorded. In their study with a number of diversity specialists drawn from a broad spectrum of business sectors and organizations of various sizes, they identified several factors which endorse the importance of measurement and provide suggestions on how success might be measured. Some of these are as follows:

- Track progress from where you began rather than where you wish to end up. In this way, effort, time, and success are recognized and not lost.

- A broad set of measures enables success to be tracked across a number of dimensions and enables understanding of the broader impact of diversity management initiatives.

- Use the eyes and ears of those who have participated in diversity initiatives to track change and report on how training activities are being translated into day-to-day changes in behaviour.

- Where possible, use hard measures to support the business case for diversity, such as employee retention rates, the financial benefit of new business opportunities identified through accessing new segments of the market, or the costs of legal suits to the organization in equality based court cases. These costs can be tangible, in the amount of money spent on the case, for example, but also intangible in the loss of reputation and goodwill.

Park (2008) also believes measurement to lie at the heart of implementing effective diversity management. In his view, it is important to ensure that everyone is involved in the diversity agenda and accountability is shared across the business and does not simply reside with diversity practitioners and specialists. He advocates including in the performance reviews of all managers, from senior managers down, a criterion related to 'Creating value through inclusion'. This can be translated into the language of the appraisee's business unit and tailored to the context of their responsibilities. So an HR manager might be tasked with increasing the number of high-potential women across the organization, while those in sales and marketing could be tasked with increasing the organization's market share of gay and lesbian consumers.

In terms of whether the advice is being taken by business and translated into action, the findings of the CIPD (2007) survey are useful. They developed a scale based on 146 variables which were included in their questionnaire and which they have called the 'sophistication' scale. Organizations scoring high on the scale are evidencing a high rate of take-up and integration of diversity management policies and processes into their everyday organizational working. Those scoring lower have some way to go.

The results are probably somewhat unsurprising given the preceding discussion. With a sample size of 285 organizations, only one had a sophistication score of 122 and five had a score of zero. Size seemed to impact on how 'sophisticated' an organization is in respect of diversity management, with larger organizations scoring higher on the sophistication measure. Of large organizations (those with 1,000 or more employees), 38 were in the top 20 percentile, compared with only 11 medium-sized organizations (those with between 250 and 999 employees) and three small firms (those with 250 or less employees).

The public sector were by far the most likely to have sophisticated diversity practices, with 34 public sector organizations in the top 20 percentile, compared with only seven in the private sector and 18 in the voluntary sector. It is interesting to note that despite the strong business case rhetoric emanating from the private sector, those organizations at the vanguard of sophistication in diversity management are most likely to be found in the public sector, followed by the voluntary sector and, coming some way behind, the private sector.

⬛ End of Chapter Case Study Telecommunications Company

The telecommunications company in this case study is a large private sector company with 92,000 employees and a turnover of £20 billion. It has four main business divisions organized across its key lines of service. These are wholesale, retail, infrastructure/maintenance, and global services. The organization operates in 170 countries, but its main activities still take place in the UK, where corporate and wholesale customers generate the most revenue. The organization has a large number of employees with an engineering profile (mainly in their infrastructure/maintenance division) and a strong customer services adviser profile (located in the retail division).

Twenty-two per cent of employees are female, 9 per cent are from ethnic minority backgrounds, and 2 per cent have a declared disability. However, there is great variation within the divisions. For example, in retail, 32 per cent are women, whereas this figure falls to 6.7 per cent in infrastructure/maintenance.

In terms of the way in which it has implemented its diversity management practices, the organization is considered to be an example of best practice within the ICT sector. Once in the public sector, the organization retains a public service ethos and a commitment to ensuring that services are equally accessible to all in the UK, and that equality of opportunity is evident within the organization. Diversity in the organization has both moral and business case dimensions.

Diversity strategy is delivered through a Global Diversity Forum which cascades down through a variety of Diversity Steering Groups, Diversity Forums and employee-led networks. Both the top-down and bottom-up communication emanating from these groups are linked with the organization's operational and organizational responsibilities. Locally, policy is implemented through Diversity Steering Groups, which are chaired by the most senior person in the Division, and have HR representation to ensure that activities dovetail with central initiatives and priorities. Divisional teams are supported by 'Diversity Champions' and 'Diversity Ambassadors' who ensure that the message of the decisions taken and the reason for them are communicated both internally and externally to main stakeholders.

Key performance indicators in respect of diversity are built into every employee's appraisal and the main successes are logged, for example being a Diversity Ambassador. This information is then used within formal appraisal processes and for internal promotion. In this way, diversity management communication and activity becomes part of what individuals do everyday rather than being seen as something separate that they have to pay attention to on a periodic basis. Communication of the diversity agenda is comprehensive and employees are frequently reminded of the values underpinning this activity. Awareness-building occurs through formally held awareness training for all employees, as well as diversity-related publications, an intranet news site, and sections in the employee attitude survey. Managers are also provided with briefing materials so that they can communicate this further.

Source: Adapted from: Michielsens et al. 2008: 7 and 14.

Case study questions

1. How does the approach to implementation of diversity management at this telecommunications company map out against the eight stages of a change management programme discussed above?

2. In what areas is the organization strongest?

3. Where do you think improvements could be made?

4. What might the priorities be for this company going forward?

Conclusion

In this chapter we have explored the organizational response to implementing diversity management. We have seen that this is a topic in which research is very much at the stage of reporting practice, process, and progress regarding organizational activity in implementing diversity management. We have explored several views on the approach adopted in implementing diversity management, and have seen that the organizational response varies in respect of the centrality of the issue for policy making and the overall impact on business. Some organizations are in the very early stages of developing their response to the diversity management agenda and have not moved much beyond ensuring that they comply with the relevant legislation and possibly run a few diversity awareness training courses for employees. Others have implemented highly sophisticated structures and frameworks, with support mechanisms located all around the organization, and in this way they have not only focused on action, but also in mainstreaming that activity, where diversity has moved from a stand-alone activity to being part of day-to-day working.

This chapter has utilized a change management framework, as presented by Kotter and Cohen (2002), and through this it has been possible to see where progress has been made and where gaps remain in the implementation of diversity management. A critical area for attention is at the strategic level. It is evident that a few, well-researched and frequently quoted organizations have whole-heartedly embraced the approach, and have a coherent and well-structured strategic focus on the issue. For the majority, however, we see an approach which is dominated by activity but which does not have at its core either vision or clear direction. In such a situation, the diversity management agenda becomes unfocused and muddled, and those within the organization begin to resent the time and attention they are required to pay to it.

In the chapter we have also discussed the shift from an equality agenda underpinned by concepts of social justice and a liberal/legal paradigm based on 'sameness' to one that is aligned with business interests and focused on difference. Kirton and Greene's (2009) study on diversity practitioners indicates that such a shift is indeed beginning to take place. The findings show the profile of diversity practitioners differs from that of equal opportunities managers, with diversity management practitioners being far more likely to be drawn from the ranks of operational management. If they are from an HR background, they do not come from an equality background, they are likely to be at senior levels within the organization and are less likely to feel isolated or unsupported in their roles than their equal opportunity predecessors. Gone is the emphasis on a political activist past or close association or alignment with the values of social justice.

The chapter concludes with a case study considering the implementation of diversity management in a large telecommunications company which has embraced the approach. It provides an example of leading-edge practice in the area.

 Review and discussion questions

1. What do you see as the key facilitators and barriers to the effective implementation of diversity management?

2. Why do you think that 'creating a vision' for diversity management has proven so challenging for many organizations?

3. Do you think an emphasis on equality of opportunity and managing diversity are mutually exclusive or two sides of the same coin?

4. How would you advise an organization at the early stages of diversity management implementation to undertake the activity? What frameworks or structures would you suggest they need to implement to support the activity?

5. Assess the usefulness of 'best practice' examples in respect of diversity management implementation.

 For additional material on the content of this chapter please visit the supporting Online Resource Centre at **www.oxfordtextbooks.co.uk/orc/kumra_manfredi/**

Further reading

CIPD (2006a) *Diversity in Business: How Much Progress Have Employers Made? First Findings.* Tatli, A., Ozbilgin, M., Worman, D., and Price, E.

CIPD (2006b) *Managing Diversity: Learning by Doing.* Tatli, A. Ozbilgin, M., Worman, D., and Price, E.

CIPD (2006c) *Managing Diversity: Measuring Success.* Tatli, A., Ozbilgin, M., Worman, D., and Price, E.

Michielsens, E., Bingham, C., Clarke, L., Miller, S., Urwin, P., Siara, B., and Karuk, V. (2008) *Implementing Diversity Employment Policies: Examples from Large London Companies.* London: Westminster Business School.

Thomas, D. (2004) Diversity as Strategy. *Harvard Business Review*, 82/September: 98–108

References

Ahmed, S. (2007) The language of diversity. *Ethnic and Racial Studies*, 30/2: 235–256.

Barmes, L. and Ashtiany, S. (2003) The diversity approach to achieving equality: problems and pitfalls. *International Law Journal*, 32/4: 274–296.

Childs, J.T. (2007) Diversity: why we're not nearly there yet. *Associations Now*, August: xxx–xxx.

CIPD (2006a) *Diversity in Business: How Much Progress Have Employers Made? First Findings.* Tatli, A., Ozbilgin, M., Worman, D., and Price, E.

CIPD (2006b) *Managing Diversity: Linking Theory and Practice to Business Performance.* Ozbilgin, M., Mulholland, G., and Worman, D.

CIPD (2007) *Diversity in Business: A Focus for Progress.* Tatli, A., Ozbilgin, M., Worman, D., and Price, E.

Cockburn, C. (1991) *In the Way of Women.* Basingstoke: Macmillan.

Janssens, M. and Zanoni, P. (2005) Many diversities for many services: theorizing diversity (management) in service companies. *Human Relations*, 58/3: 311–340.

Jewson, N. and Mason, D. (1986) The theory and practice of equal opportunities policies: liberal and radical approaches. *Sociological Review*, 34/2: 307–334.

Johnstone, S. (ed.) (2002) *Managing Diversity in the Workplace.* London: Eclipse/IRS.

Kalev, A., Dobbin, F., and Kelly, E. (2006) Best practices or best guesses? Assessing the efficacy of corporate affirmative action and diversity policies. *American Sociological Review*, 71/3: 589–616.

Kamp, A. and Hagedorn-Rasmussen, P. (2004) Diversity management in a Danish context: towards a multicultural or segregated working life? *Economic and Industrial Democracy*, 25/4: 525–554.

Kirton, G. and Greene, A.-M. (2009) The costs and opportunities of doing diversity work in mainstream organizations. *Human Resource Management Journal*, 19/2: 159–175.

Kirton, G., Greene, A.-M., and Dean, D. (2007) British diversity professionals as change agents – radicals, tempered radicals or liberal reformers? *International Journal of Human Resource Management*, 18/11: 1979–1994.

Kotter, J.P. and Cohen, D.S. (2002) *The Heart of Change.* Boston, MA: Harvard Business School Press.

Lawrence, E. (2000) Equal opportunities officers and managing equality changes. *Personnel Review*, 29/3: 381–401.

Lewin, K. (1951) *Field Theory in Social Science.* New York: Harper & Row.

Liff, S. (2003) Two routes to managing diversity: individual differences or social group characteristics. *Employee Relations*, 19/1: 11–26.

Lorbiecki, A. (2001) Opening and Burdens for Women and Minority Ethnics Being Diversity Vanguards in Britain. Stoke-on-Trent, UK: Gender, Work and Organization, Keele University.

Michielsens, E., Bingham, C., Clarke, L., Miller, S., Urwin, P., Siara, B., and Karuk, V. (2008) *Implementing Diversity Employment Policies: Examples from Large London Companies.* London: Westminster Business School.

Nancheria, A. (2008) Company diversity programs often pick fluff over substance. *Training & Development*, November: 53–58.

Noon, M. (2007) The fatal flaws of diversity and the business case for ethnic minorities. *Work, Employment and Society*, 21/4: 773–784.

Park, A. (2008) Making diversity a business advantage. *Harvard Management Update*, April.

Pitts, D. (2007) Implementation of diversity management programs in public organizations: lessons from policy implementation research. *International Journal of Public Administration*, 30/3: 1573–1590.

Sinclair, A. (2006) Critical diversity management practice in Australia: romanced or co-opted?, in Prasad, P., Pringle, J., and Konrad, A. (eds), *Handbook of Workplace Diversity*. London: Sage, pp. 511–530.

Thomas, D. (2004) Diversity as strategy. *Harvard Business Review*, 82/September: 98–108.

Tomlinson, F. and Schwabenland, C. (2010) Reconciling competing discourses of diversity? The UK non-profit sector between social justice and the business case. *Organization*, 17/1: 101–121.

Walsh, J. (2007) Equality and diversity in British workplaces: the 2004 Workplace Employment Relations Survey. *Industrial Relations Journal*, 38/4: 303–319.

Part 2

Equality and Diversity in Practice

Managing Ethnic Diversity in the Workplace

Learning objectives

- Appreciate the progress those from black and minority ethnic (BME) communities have made in public and organizational life
- Be aware of some of the key challenges that remain
- Understand the 'ethnicity paradigm' and the concept of 'everyday discrimination', and comment on their causes and consequences
- Understand competing debates to explain the absence of those from BME communities in senior organizational positions

Key terms

- **BME:** stands for black and minority ethnic, a term coined to encompass a number of minority groups within society.
- **Ethnicity paradigm:** within the ethnicity paradigm key areas of study are immigration and the social patterns and experiences of usually European immigrants (Omi and Winant, 1986). The debate within the paradigm has focused on two opposing themes: assimilation versus cultural pluralism, namely incorporation or separation of ethnic groups.
- **'Everyday' racism:** this is defined as 'those subtle and pervasive manifestations of racism faced by Blacks on a daily basis in the workplace' (Essed, 1991, in Deitch et al., 2003: 1300).
- **Institutional racism:** defined in the Macpherson report as: 'The collective failure of an organization to provide an appropriate and professional service to people because of their colour, culture, or ethnic origin. It can be seen or detected in processes, attitudes and behaviour which amount to discrimination through unwitting prejudice, ignorance, thoughtlessness and racist stereotyping which disadvantage minority ethnic people' (Macpherson, 1999: para. 6.34).
- **Race relations cycle:** developed by Park (1950 [1939]), the 'race relations cycle' has four key stages: contact, competition, accommodation, and eventual assimilation. For Park, the cycle is progressive and irreversible, though he does acknowledge that any particular stage may be prolonged. At the heart of Park's work is the view that assimilation is the logical and natural antidote to racism and ethnocentrism.

Introduction

In this chapter we explore the issue of discrimination in respect of individuals from Black and Minority Ethnic (BME) communities. This is a research topic which many have observed requires further examination, concerning as it does inequality in opportunity for those from BME communities. A number of competing opinions on the meaning and impact of ethnic diversity in and on organizational life are discussed, as are alternative views on how best to tackle the issue. In this chapter we explore several of these views and seek to understand where progress has been made and how this has been achieved, but we also focus on the areas where there is still work to be done. In terms of progress made, we look at how high-achieving women from BME communities have attained their power and position from their own perspective. We also comment on progress made in respect of education and entrepreneurship. However, we continue to see a picture of those from BME communities gaining access and entry to organizations, but once in them not progressing at the rate that their qualifications and number would suggest should be the case. We thus turn to explanations as to why this might be. We look at the work of Ogbonna and Harris (2006), who discuss the concept of 'everyday' racism in relation to work in an inner-city bakery, and who document in detail the causes and consequences of these actions.

We also explore the experience of BME entrepreneurs, focusing on factors contributing to their decision to become self-employed and the challenges they face in leading their own enterprises. We conclude with examples of organizational responses to the issue, focusing on 'institutional racism' and the impact this has had on work practices in the Home Office. We also look at organizational interventions from a 'business case' perspective, examining an initiative undertaken by Lloyds TSB to better serve and meet the needs of their BME business customers.

UK general election 2010: position and progress of ethnic minority candidates in the UK Parliament

In an article published in *The Guardian* on 27 April 2010, leading up to the general election in that year, Afua Hirsch, *The Guardian*'s legal correspondent, presented her analysis of the stance of the three main political parties to BME candidates. In total, the three main parties fielded 119 BME candidates (44 Conservative, 32 Labour, and 43 Liberal Democrat). Labour, traditionally viewed as the party most in tune with the issues and concerns within BME communities and currently with the largest number of BME MPs (13 of the 15 elected at the 2005 election), fielded a lower number of candidates than their two key rivals. Also of interest is that although the previous Labour government introduced some of the most far-reaching equalities legislation in recent times, their manifesto contained no further future proposals.

The Liberal Democrats, with no BME MPs, fielded 43 BME candidates. They were seeking to improve on their current position and are the party which, unlike the other two parties, highlights their focus on racial diversity in manifesto policy and pledges. They pledged to reduce the time that records are held on the DNA database (on which people from BME communities are substantially over-represented), and they included radical proposals on immigration rules and race discrimination in employment.

The Conservative party focused considerable energy on improving their record in relation to candidates from BME communities. They fielded the highest number in the election (44) and accessed media aimed at BME communities in an unprecedented manner. They provided specialist BME publications with access to David Cameron, something the party had not previously done. Those in BME media publications have mixed views as to the motives of these changes. Some comment that the moves are simply a cynical way to access BME communities to seek their votes, with little in substance changing in key policy areas. Others see this as progress: the fact that BME publications and media are being targeted and manipulated in the same way as mainstream media is a sign of integration and progress. However, when assessing whether policy is evident to support key issues of relevance to BME communities, the Conservative party manifesto shows there is little in respect of planned policy. There is reference to civil partnerships, marriage, and assistance for the disabled, but nothing on race equality or discrimination.

The outcome of the election was reported by Afua Hirsch in *The Guardian* on 7 May 2010. Of the 119 candidates fielded, 27 were elected – 16 Labour and 11 Conservative. The Liberal Democrats remain the only main party to have no BME MPs. A number of firsts were also observed in this election: Shabhana Mahmood is the first female British Muslim to be elected, Helen Grant is the first black woman to represent the Conservative party at Westminster, Chi Onwurah (Labour) became the first African woman to be an MP, and Priti Patel, a Conservative, became the first Asian female MP.

> **Student Activity 5.1**
>
> 1. In your view, does it matter that BME communities are represented in Parliament?
> 2. What do you think are the key benefits of such representation?
> 3. Do you foresee any drawbacks?
> 4. What further developments would you like to see?

BME participation in key institutions

Those from ethnic minority communities represent a small but growing presence in the UK working population. Although over one in ten of the British population is from an ethnic minority group, those from BME communities represent only 8.5 per cent of those employed. BME employees represent just 6.5 per cent of managers and the number at director level is so small that measuring it accurately is not possible (Race for Opportunity, 2010a).

In terms of education, those from BME communities are taking up university places in increasing numbers, though their representation at elite universities does not mirror their presence in the general population. We thus see a position where one in six university places is taken up by a BME student, but less than half of those universities making up the Russell Group (the group which represents the UK's top universities) have representative numbers of BME students (Race for Opportunity, 2010b). There is also evidence that although BME students are gaining access to higher education, their outcomes are not keeping pace with the majority white population. For example, the likelihood of a Pakistani student being awarded a good degree, such as a 2:1 or First, were only 43 per cent of those of a white student in 1997. By 2009 this had fallen to 39 per cent. For those from a Chinese background the figures were 67 per cent to 55 per cent, and for those from the 'black other' group (excluding African and black Caribbean) 43 per cent to 33 per cent respectively (Richardson, 2009).

When it comes to employment rates, we see that three sectors account for 80 per cent of ethnic minority workers in management positions. These are public administration, education, and health (BITC, 2007). BME women are more than twice as likely to be unemployed as women from the white population (Equal Opportunities Commission (EOC), 2004). Those in work also report difficulties. EOC research shows that 30–40 per cent of BME women say they have personally experienced racism or sexism (EOC, 2004). Twenty per cent of Pakistani and Bangladeshi women have heard derogatory comments about their religious dress at work, and 80 per cent of those from the Black Caribbean community believe they have to work harder to get to the top of their organizations and decide that they cannot apply for certain jobs because of their ethnicity (Opportunity Now, 2010).

Employers recognize that those from BME communities face difficulties. Half of employers agree that BME women face difficulties in employment because of presentation, personal characteristics, and family/caring responsibilities (EOC, 2006). Thirty-eight per cent of private sector and 13 per cent of public sector organizations have no BME women employees at all (Opportunity Now, 2010). Interestingly, and possibly as a consequence of these factors, women from BME communities are more likely to be self-employed than their white counterparts (GEM, 2004): 30 per cent of 'Other Black women', 11 per cent of Bangladeshi women, 11 per cent of Black Caribbean women, 10 per cent of 'Other Asian women', and 10 per cent of 'Mixed women' are self-employed, compared with only 4 per cent of white women (GEM, 2004).

Race discrimination in the workplace: causes and consequences

From the discussion above it is evident that those from BME communities are the subject of a number of discriminatory practices which combine to disadvantage them in the workplace. In seeking to understand the antecedents of this discriminatory practice, we turn our attention to the underlying causes of discriminatory practice and behaviour within organizational settings. As recently as 20 years ago, Cox and Nkomo (1990) observed that those studying organizations did so with a view that organizational members comprise a relatively homogeneous group. The consequence of this assumption within organizational research is to view organizations as race 'neutral'. However, this presents an inaccurate picture, as Nkomo (1992: 488) observes: '... race is one of the major bases of domination in our society and a major means through which the division of labour occurs in organizations'. She argues that race impacts every aspect of organizational life, even if it has been ignored or suppressed as an issue in organizational research.

In seeking to understand why the issue of race may have been ignored in organizational research, Nkomo (1992: xx) points to 'intellectual errors in the production of knowledge'. This arises from a basic misconception that by looking at a few people from the dominant group

(usually white males), the norm will be typified and we can draw universally applicable conclusions for the population as a whole (Minnich, 1990). That the theory which emanates from
this partial sample is limited in its application, particularly when applied to the more usual
heterogeneous groups, goes largely unacknowledged and the universality of key management theory remains uncontested (Cox and Nkomo, 1990).

Where race is directly studied, Nkomo (1992) observes that a number of paradigms have
emerged which consider the impact of race on various aspects of organizational life. These
paradigms reflect the nature of race relations evident within any historical period (Omi and
Winant, 1986) and it is observed that a particular paradigm dominates particular historical
periods despite the presence of a number of alternatives (Blanton, 1987). The dominant theory provides society and scholars with a framework through which they can understand race
relations and guides the questions asked and the types of study undertaken. The paradigm
which dominates for interpreting race and its impact in organizations is the ethnicity paradigm (Blanton, 1987; Omi and Winant, 1986; Thompson, 1989).

Within the ethnicity paradigm, key areas of study are immigration and the social patterns
and experiences of (usually) European immigrants (Omi and Winant, 1986). The debate
within the paradigm has focused on two opposing themes: assimilation versus cultural pluralism, namely incorporation or separation of ethnic groups. Other key questions addressed
within the paradigm are ethnic identity and the impact of ethnicity on life experiences (Omi
and Winant, 1986).

One of the earliest accounts of assimilationism came from Park (1950 [1939]), in his essay
'The Nature of Race Relations'. His key focus was on European immigration into the United
States, and the issue of 'culture contact' was central to his work. Park (1950 [1939]) developed
the 'race relations cycle', and this became the foundation for the future development of assimilation theory (Gordon, 1964). The cycle has four key stages (see Figure 5.1): contact, competition, accommodation, and eventual assimilation. The cycle is progressive and irreversible,
though Park acknowledges that any particular stage may be prolonged. At the heart of Park's
work is the view that assimilation is the logical and natural antidote to racism and ethnocentrism. Through assimilation, groups learn to understand one another's way of thinking, senti-
ments, and attitudes, leading to a fusion of cultures (Park, 1950 [1939]). It is from Park's original
work that the still popular 'melting pot' approach to cultural assimilation emanates (Omi and
Winant, 1986).

At the *contact* stage, a new ethnic group is introduced into a majority population. This may
be for a variety of reasons, for example, widespread immigration due to strife at home, demand within the host country for immigrant labour, or a wish from the immigrant population
to improve their economic condition. At the contact stage, the majority population seeks to
understand the key attributes and characteristics of the immigrant minority, and vice versa.
Each looks to confirm or refute prevailing thoughts and ideas they have about one another
based on perceived knowledge rather than personal contact.

In the *conflict* stage, each community seeks to assert its rights. The majority population is
keen to impress upon the immigrant minority they are no longer in their own country, and to
live amicably some of their ways will need to alter. For their part, the immigrant minority seek
to impress upon the majority population that although they have left their home country,
they have not abandoned their culture. Adherence to home culture will be manifest through
an unwillingness to alter language, diet, religion, etc. merely to fit in with those from the

Figure 5.1 Park's (1950 [1939]) Race relations cycle

majority culture. Each culture will stand its ground; conflict will occur from an unwillingness to accept the cultural norms and behaviours of the host culture and preferring to retain one's home culture.

As time passes, each group will begin to understand the other's culture more fully. Children will be born into the host culture, and will be the conduits between the two cultures. Those from the immigrant culture will begin to form friendships with and gain a deeper understanding of those from the host culture, and through this begin to value some of the practices and traditions of the host culture. At the *accommodation* stage, we thus see a coming together of cultures through joint appreciation, knowledge, and understanding.

The final stage is *assimilation*. Here Park (1950 [1939]) argues that the immigrant community is assimilated into the host culture. Those from the immigrant culture begin to accept and adapt to the ways of their host country, while those from the majority culture learn to appreciate the richness of the immigrant community culture. Neither culture has yielded to the other; each has informed and contributed to the other in ways which are valuable to all.

The race relations cycle has drawn a number of critics. The nature of the unilinear evolutionary process is challenged (Barth and Noel, 1972) as it does not accord with actual evolutionary patterns observed across a number of societies. Barth and Noel cite cases from the American context and contend that rather than advancing through the four-stage process as indicated by Park, initial contact has in fact led to annihilation or mass expulsion. In other cases, a temporary period of accommodation has led to a further period of competition which in turn has led to a new form of accommodation. The example is given of black workers from the colonies. They were reduced to the status of slaves after originally being granted the status of bondsmen (Palmer, 1966). Barth and Noel (1972) thus conclude that it is more likely that rather than moving smoothly and unilinearly through the stages of the cycle, it is more likely that accommodation is temporary and unstable, with a move back to competition before a more permanent accommodation can be established. They also assert that assimilation is not the only ultimate and stable outcome available. In their view, there are five possibilities:

1. Exclusion: including expulsion and annihilation.

2. Symbiosis: a stable exchange relationship of relatively equal benefit between those of two distinct sociopolitical systems.

3. Ethnic stratification: this involves the subordination of one group to another within a single political system.

4. Pluralism: an integration between distinct ethnic groups which yields equal status to each group within a common political and economic system.

5. Assimilation: the fusion of distinct groups through which a new and ethnically undifferentiated society is created.

Student Activity 5.2

1. Which of the views do you agree with most: that of Park (1950 [1939]) and his race eelations cycle or that of Barth and Noel (1972)? What are your reasons for your choice?

2. Can you think of any ethnic groups in the UK that are at the 'contact stage'? How do you know this? What are the defining characteristics?

3. Can you think of any ethnic groups in the UK that are at the 'conflict' stage'? How do you know this? What are the defining characteristics?

4. What kinds of accommodation do you see in UK society? Do you think these are temporary/unstable or stable? How have you made your decision?

From the assimilation framework it is concluded that the most appropriate action to overcome racial discrimination takes the form of legal remedies such as legislation aimed at removing barriers to ensure that those from BME communities encounter the same organizational conditions as those from the dominant ethnic group (Thompson, 1989).

The alternative to the assimilation paradigm is cultural pluralism. Here, the possibility is mooted that rather than assimilate, cultures can remain distinct, with each retaining cultural identity. However, proponents of cultural pluralism maintain that a supposedly 'normal' (understood to mean superior) majority culture exists, against which other groups are juxtaposed (Omi and Winant, 1986). In this view, the separation of ethnic and racial groups is natural and immutable. However, Steinberg (1981) asserts that in a society in which inequality exists, cultural pluralism is not a viable option as cultural pluralism is based upon equality between and among groups, not on the subservice of many groups to a dominant one. Cultural pluralism has often been seen as an opportunity to 'celebrate difference' (Yinger, 1986), an approach reflected in much of the managing diversity discourse (Thomas, 1990).

Debate Box

Organize the class into two groups, one for the motion and one against.
  The motion is:
This house believes that the best way to overcome issues of race discrimination within organizations is for those from BME communities to assimilate with the dominant ethnic group. Stages in the debate: (each stage is given with timings, the overall time for the activity is 55 minutes – allowing a few minutes for change over of presenters, etc.)

- Each group has 20 minutes to prepare their arguments either for or against the motion.
- Each group is given 5 minutes to present their opening statement (10 minutes in total).
- Groups reconvene for 10 minutes to prepare rebuttal arguments.
- Each group has 2 minutes to present rebuttal arguments.

A vote is taken and the winners of the debate announced; the casting vote goes to impartial observers: tutors, audience members not involved in the debate, or observers.

The ethnicity paradigm discussed above is an example of a key sociological approach to understanding race within organizations. However, conceptualizations of the issue vary across disciplines. Social psychology, for example, looks at how prejudice is expressed at the individual level from the perspective of social identity theory and social categorization theory (Dovidio and Gaertner, 1986), and social attribution theory (Hewstone, 1989). We begin with an examination of the social identity and social categorization theories.

These posit that the construction of an individual's identity will depend on the social groups of which they are members and from which they receive positive social identity (Tajfel, 1969, 1970; Tajfel and Turner, 1979, 1986). We understand the status and standing of those within our own group through value-laden comparisons of attributes and characteristics of those in other reference groups. This is the basic mechanism through which we determine our social identity. The comparisons require individuals to identify similarities between people belonging to the same group and contrast this with differences between people belonging to key reference groups (Tajfel, 1981). It follows that where categorizations are based upon criterion relating to membership of a particular racial or ethnic group, it is likely that the process accounts in part for the prejudice found between different groups, particularly when it is recognized that key criteria upon which such categorizations are made include power, status, and material interdependence (Tajfel, 1981).

Social attribution theory refers to 'how members of different social groups explain the behaviour and social condition of members of their own group (in-group) and other social groups (out-groups)' (Hewstone, 1989: 25). Within this paradigm, the focus of research is explaining the behaviour of those who are members or who are viewed as representatives of social groups. A key explanatory concept within this framework is what Pettigrew (1979) has called the 'fundamental attribution error'. This is the notion that when explaining the behaviour of others, we tend to focus on internal factors rather than situational factors (Oudenhaven and Willemsen, 1989). In the most extreme manifestation of the 'ultimate attribution error', we find prejudice, defined by Pettigrew as 'a systematic patterning of intergroup misattributions shaped in part by prejudice' (1979: 464). Thus when those from BME groups behave in a way perceived to be negative, those from the majority group, particularly those who are prejudiced, will likely attribute the behaviour to all members of the BME group. When an individual from a BME group behaves in a way perceived to be positive, prejudiced majority group members will explain this behaviour by saying it is that of a 'special' individual within the group but unrepresentative of the behaviour of the group as a whole. The individual was lucky or had access to some special advantage which is viewed as unfair, or the individual was exceptionally highly motivated, or that the context had in some way been manipulated (Pettigrew, 1979). This enables the in-group majority to retain their negative assessments of the out-group minority despite evidence to the contrary.

➡ Student Activity 5.3

Look at the except below. Nkomo (1992: 506) has constructed a list of research questions asked from an ethnicity perspective which she sees as the dominant paradigm for understanding race in organizations, and a number of questions she believes have been silenced as they emanate from alternative (less socially desirable) paradigms.

Asked and unasked questions about race

Research questions from ethnicity paradigm

- Does discrimination exist in recruitment, selection etc.?
- Can the [BME candidate] be an effective executive?
- Do blacks identify with the traditional work ethic?
- Do blacks' and whites' problem-solving styles differ?
- How can blacks/minorities be assimilated into organizations?

Silenced research questions from alternative paradigms

- How are societal race relations reproduced in the workplace?
- How did white males come to dominant management positions?
- To what extent is race built into the definition of a 'manager'?
- What are the implications of racial identity for organization theories based on individual identities?

1. How can you tell that the questions from the ethnicity perspective are reflective of the paradigm?
2. Why do you think the questions in the second list may be considered more problematic and are thus in Nkomo's view 'silenced'?
3. Can you think of questions that you would like to see asked in respect of race within organizations that are not to your knowledge being addressed?

Recent research developments

The work cited above comprises some of the seminal work in the area of race discrimination and has formed the bedrock for much of our understanding of the issues involved. In terms of recent research in the area of race discrimination, we see work that seeks to analyze race at the micro level. The focus here is at the individual and single-firm level, with studies looking at 'everyday' discrimination and the impact this has on the workplaces in which this occurs, and the effect on those experiencing it. Recent studies have also sought to segment the BME community and consider how race impacts specific groups. Examples here include work which has sought to understand the experience of BME women in the labour market and which has assessed the challenges faced by BME entrepreneurs. Each of these issues will be considered in this section.

'Everyday' race discrimination

Deitch et al. (2003) observe that it is only recently that research has focused on the experience of those on the receiving end of discrimination and stigmatization in society, particularly in the workplace. Focusing on the experience of black Americans, these authors assess the impact of what they term 'everyday' discrimination. This is defined as 'those subtle and pervasive mani-festations of racism faced by Blacks on a daily basis in the workplace' (Essed, 1991, in Deitch et al., 2003: 1300). In a departure from previous literature, which has focused on unusual but extremely serious acts of discrimination, the study examines 'everyday' discrimination – the subtle yet pervasive acts of mistreatment which are experienced disproportionately by mem-bers of BME groups. Arguing that there is evidence to suggest that the more direct and overt forms of racism are declining (e.g. Bobo, 1998), Deitch et al. (2003) assert that this has been replaced by new and less obvious forms of discrimination. Examples include 'modern racism' (McConahay, 1986), or 'ambivalent racism' (Katz and Hass, 1988). These perspectives enable those holding racist views to position them within a broader more positive discourse (e.g. mobility, opportunity, etc.) which is not racist, thus exonerating themselves from the negative, but more accurate, racist label. People with these views are likely to engage in 'microaggres-sions' (Pettigrew and Martin, 1987), for example, the avoidance of black people, closed and unwelcoming verbal and non-verbal communication patterns, and an unwillingness to pro-vide help and assistance.

In their study, Ogbonna and Harris (2006) explored this theme further. They found evi-dence of 'everyday' discrimination in a medium-sized organization 'Harmony Bakeries', lo-cated in a vibrant and ethnically diverse inner city in the UK. The workforce is highly ethnically diverse and the researchers found evidence of 'everyday' discrimination in relation to two key issues: religion, and language and communication.

In respect of religion, the high ethnic diversity within the workforce has had some work-based implications. A high proportion of staff are practising Muslims, with strong outward signs of their religion (e.g. headwear) and practices (e.g. strict prayer routines). When inter-twined with culture, the effect on the working environment has been highly impactful. For example, there was evidence of some male/female segregation, and of tensions in respect of diverse religious groups, for example, between Hindus and Muslims.

Language and communication was also an issue in the organization. A number of lan-guages were spoken and there was evidence that this became a key method by which indi-viduals identified their similarity with others. On the shop floor, affiliations and friendships tended to develop around the two main languages spoken: Arabic and Urdu. Those in friend-ship groups sought to work on shift together and also tended to take their breaks together. However, language also became a defining feature of 'in-groups' and 'out-groups' (Hambrick et al., 1998; Palich and Gomez-Mejia, 1999), with out-groups becoming the target of criticism. However, Ogbonna and Harris (2006) observed that inadequacy in speaking English came to be construed by different groups in different ways. For some, such as those in supervisory positions, the lack of proficiency in English became a genuine barrier, hindering immigrant employees from effective communication. However, English-speaking shop-floor workers were not quite so convinced. They blamed those from BME communities for their inadequacy with English and believed they should try harder to master language skills more effectively.

Others believed that the lack of proficiency in English was merely a device used by BME workers to avoid work, and they also felt that this placed an unfair burden on fluent English speakers. These views resulted in a number of consequences within the working environment, which Ogbonna and Harris (2006) have identified as conflict, discrimination, and organizational issues.

Conflict

The analysis indicated a high level of religiously motivated conflict within the organization. There was evidence of a number of religiously motivated physical clashes between groups, consisting of arguments in most cases, but in a more serious instance there was a physical fight between two Muslim sects. The police were called and both men were dismissed. Interestingly, we see 'everyday' discrimination occurring not just between those from BME and the majority white community, but also between and among various BME communities. An extreme outcome of this situation was to avoid friction, shifts were organized so that Indian and Pakistani workers did not meet (Ogbonna and Harris, 2006).

However, the majority of conflict occurred between white employees and their BME colleagues. This resulted in little communication between white workers and those from other BME groups and led to misperceptions on both sides. White employees resented their BME colleagues for perceived latitude shown to them when they broke company rules (e.g. health and safety requirements), while those from BME communities resented their white colleagues for their perceived lack of respect towards them.

Discrimination

Though 'direct' discrimination was hard to determine, evidence of 'everyday' discrimination in respect of attitudes and behaviour was apparent. For example, it was clear that those with limited language skills would be unlikely to advance within the organization to 'premium' posts (e.g. supervisor) as it was felt they would be unable to cope with the challenges presented at the higher level. There was also evidence of racially based derogatory language (e.g. 'coloured') being widely used in the organization but remaining unchallenged and unchecked by managers (Ogbonna and Harris, 2006).

Organizational issues

Relationships were clearly affected as a consequence of the above account of working practices within the organization. However, an organization-wide issue that was particularly evident was the impact on health and safety policy and practice (Ogbonna and Harris, 2006).

More specifically, concern was voiced over the number of potential health and safety breaches of which the organization may be culpable. These systems breaches were rationalized within the organization as a language issue. For those with limited English, understanding the detailed written instructions in respect of health and safety codes and guidelines would be problematic. However, what seemed to remain relatively unrecognized was that the organization was failing to comply with legislation in the area, allowing employees who clearly did not understand the health and safety regulations to operate machinery which could potentially harm not just themselves but others around them.

Thus we see in this study confirmation of Deitch et al.'s (2003) assertion that while overt forms of discrimination are declining, there is evidence that they are being replaced by subtle and more pervasive forms of 'everyday' discrimination. Interviewees in the study (Ogbonna and Harris, 2006) were keen to distance themselves from discrimination on grounds of skin colour, gender, and disability. However, they had no qualms in voicing their frustration with and lack of sympathy for those with limited ability to speak English. There was also free admission within the organization that those with limited English would not be promoted, even when the promotion necessitated no greater grasp of English than the individual's current role. Thus those from BME communities experienced not just horizontal discrimination (i.e. that from their work colleagues), but also vertical discrimination (that from their superiors).

Student Activity 5.4

Write a briefing paper to the diversity director of an organization you are familiar with (or one you know through secondary research) to assess how you could identify and tackle 'everyday' discrimination. You will need to address the following questions:

- What indicators would you use to assess whether 'everyday' discrimination exists within the workplace?
- What data might it be useful to collect?
- With which key stakeholder groups would you consult?
- What would be your key strategic objectives to address the issues identified?
- How will you know whether your approach is successful?

BME entrepreneurs

Entrepreneurial activity is increasing across all business sectors (Office for National Statistics, 2008), with the increase more evident in London (Government Office for London, 2007). BME communities comprise 46 per cent of the working population in London (ibid.), and there is evidence to suggest that many of those from such communities have opted to start and run their own businesses rather than seek employment in existing organizations. However, research has shown that those from BME communities may turn to entrepreneurial activity because of an absence of employment opportunities rather than a burning desire to be entrepreneurs, and there is also evidence that once in self-employment those from BME communities may encounter a number of barriers to their success which would not be the case for their white counterparts.

In terms of participation rates, we find in the UK that 20 per cent of the Turkish and Turkish Cypriot community are self-employed, as are 19 per cent of Bangladeshis and Pakistanis, 18 per cent of Chinese, and 15 per cent of Indians. The figure for white entrepreneurs is 12 per cent (Basu and Altinay, 2002; ONS, 2001), which would indicate higher participation rates for those from BME communities than those from the white majority. Quite why these figures are so high may be revealed by studies which explore the driving forces for BME entrepreneurial activity. Here we find that many first-generation entrepreneurs enter such activity as a consequence of 'push' factors: there is an absence of alternatives, thus making self-employment almost the only option (Chavan and Agrawal, 2000). Such 'push' factors include difficulties entering the labour market and, once there, discrimination in the workplace. Key reasons for discrimination centred on a lack of educational qualifications, a lack of experience in the host country labour market, language barriers (as indicated by Ogbonna and Harris, 2006), social exclusion, and poor knowledge of local culture (Levent et al., 2003; Volery, 2005). Entrepreneurship in this situation is seen as an alternative to unemployment rather than as an opportunity to succeed.

Thus rather than approaching entrepreneurial activity as a first choice, many from BME communities are 'pushed' into starting up their own businesses because of disadvantage and discrimination faced in the access to, and advancement within, the labour market. However, once the decision has been taken to start a business, there is evidence that BME entrepreneurs experience further barriers in the establishment and growth of their enterprises. It is clear that all business start-ups face barriers to their growth and development. These can include the ability to differentiate the product, gaining and leveraging economies of scale, legal barriers, the possibility of competitor retaliation, accessing distribution channels, and high-cost capital requirements (Levent et al., 2003). However, research clearly shows that these barriers pose much more of a challenge to entrepreneurs from BME communities. Levent et al. (2003) conclude that these fall into two clear areas: administrative, and regulatory barriers. In respect of administrative barriers, it is likely that those from BME communities who have language difficulties will find it extremely difficult to access and understand administrative regulations pertaining to the establishment and running of a business. They will also face particular issues in respect of finance due to a lack of sufficient capital to invest in the business and an inability to access credit through the 'normal' channels. There is evidence that to overcome these barriers BME entrepreneurs gain finance to start their businesses from community-based cooperatives, family, or informal loans (Cooney and Flynn, 2008). Obtaining finance seems to be most difficult for those from the African/Caribbean community, and family and community-based cooperatives as a source of funding seems to be most available to those of Asian origin (Cooney and Flynn, 2008; Smallbone et al., 2003).

There is also evidence to suggest that BME entrepreneurs face particular problems when seeking to access influential business networking groups which are not ethnically based, which in turn creates a barrier to business opportunities. It is also frequently very difficult to gain trust from local communities as BME entrepreneurs are often in direct competition with mainstream businesses (Cooney and Flynn, 2008). BME entrepreneurs also find it difficult to access social capital in the mainstream business environment. Social capital is extremely important in the formation of any business as it comprises resources such as relationships with suppliers and customers, valuable information on trends and potential business opportunities, and leads and access to influential networks (Baker, 2000). In the absence of access to the mainstream business community, some ethnic minority entrepreneurs rely solely on their own ethnic community. However, this overdependence brings its own disadvantages. As businesses grow and develop, they need access to new markets and new customers. Where a business has sole reliance on a single community, with a uniform conceptualization of the way in which the business should operate, such growth and development becomes problematic (Cooney and Flynn, 2008).

Another key barrier faced by BME entrepreneurs is their concentration in marginal, low value-added economic sectors. BME entrepreneurs concentrate in the service sector, for example, restaurants, small-scale retailing, personal services, and manufacturing (Cooney and Flynn, 2008; Masurel et al., 2002). These sectors are particularly attractive to those from BME communities because they have low barriers to entry in terms of capital investment, education, and business skills. However, with such large numbers entering these sectors, competition is high and the ability to make large profits is consequently limited (Hjerm, 2004). Diversifying may not be an easy option, as though the rewards are higher, so too are the barriers to entry.

Debate Box

The following excerpts have been adapted from an article on www.growthbusiness.co.uk by Kathleen Hall on 6 May 2009.

In the article she discusses prominent BME entrepreneurs, such as Saira Khan and Tim Campbell, both from TV's *The Apprentice*, who are involved in activities to encourage people from BME communities to set up and run their own businesses. Tim Campbell has founded The Bright Ideas Trust, a social enterprise charity which aims to support and encourage those from BME communities to start their own enterprises. In his view, a key imperative to encouraging those from BME communities to become entrepreneurs is not just a socially responsible one, but also an economic imperative. With their international connections, BME entrepreneurs are ideally placed to engage internationally and in doing so enable the UK to further its aim of internationalization.

Jay Patel, entrepreneur and founder of investment firm Sparks Ventures, agrees. In his view, it is a key challenge to engage those from the BME communities in establishing their own enterprises. He has established a 'shadow an entrepreneur' scheme which enables those from BME communities who may be thinking about setting up their own businesses but have no idea of where to start to shadow an entrepreneur for a period of time to get a hands on, experience-based feel of what is involved. Nineteen-year-old Sonia Abboussad Sugar participated in the programme and feels that she has benefitted from the experience. 'There aren't enough culturally diverse role models, but I think schemes like this one help. To see someone being successful in practice makes the idea of going into business much more tangible.' Abboussad Sugar commented that she had always known she would be an entrepreneur. Participating in the scheme simply provided more focus and made her even more determined to achieve her ambition.

Organize the class into two groups, one for the motion and one against.
The motion is:
This house believes that BME entrepreneurial activity may only serve to marginalize these groups further, rather than bring about much needed social integration.
Follow stages for the debate as given above.

BME women in the workforce

BME women are more likely to be found in the public sector – 33.6 per cent compared with 16.7 per cent for BME men (HM Government Equality Office, 2007). There are at present 168 BME female councillors in England, representing 0.9 per cent of all councillors, despite the fact that BME women make up 4.6 per cent of the adult population (National Census, 2006; ONS, 2006). Women comprise 35.5 per cent of chairs of local NHS boards, with 3.8 per cent of them coming from BME communities. Of non-executive directors on these Boards, 39.2 per cent are women, but only 5 per cent of these are from BME communities (Women and Equality Unit, 2007). There are no BME judges in either the House of Lords or the Court of Appeal (Fawcett Society, 2005). In the business world, of the 961 directors of FTSE 100 companies, only eight are of non-European descent and all are non-executives (Female FTSE Report, 2007).

In a study by the Government Equalities Office, *Ethnic Minority Women: Routes to Power* (Gervais, 2008), an understanding of why black and minority ethnic women remain under-represented in positions of power and decision-making was examined through an analysis of the career experiences of 23 women who have succeeded in reaching positions of power. In discussing their motivations and professional career trajectories, the participants in the study expressed their view that organizational discrimination is manifesting itself in new forms. This echoes the discussion above in relation to 'everyday' discrimination and the work of Deitch et al. (2003) and Ogbonna and Harris (2006). Interviewees in the study commented that while race and sex discrimination legislation has succeeded in ending the most blatant forms of sex and race discrimination, putting diversity and inclusion on to organizational agendas and creating increased opportunities for women from BME communities, the legislation has not fully succeeded in 'changing hearts and minds'. What the legislation has actually done is create new kinds of discrimination and two key practices were discussed: tokenism and typecasting.

Tokenism

This is the use of BME women as 'tokens' to prove that the organization 'values diversity'. The following quote illustrates this view (Gervais, 2008: 42):

> 'Because I am the only one at that level in the organization, they always use me for events and recruitment fairs and for attracting ethnic minority business.'

Though at times unintended, the result is an undervaluing of BME women because there is an assumption that they have not attained their positions as a result of their own merit and abilities, but rather as a consequence of their ethnicity and gender. The following quote illustrates this point (ibid., 2008: 43):

> 'Initially I had a very hard time because people assumed that I was there because of some sort of privilege. They were there on merit, of course, but I was there because of political correctness!'

The assumption that BME women are merely tokens can also be evidenced in others' expectations that they are present only to 'represent' other minorities, as opposed to contributing in the same way as any other professional. The following quote sums this up (ibid., 2008: 43–44):

> 'It was my first day and I came across this man who said to me: "Are you part of the UK delegation?" When I responded yes, his reply was: "I heard the appointments for this mandate were politically correct!" "Really", I responded, "are you representing white men over fifty?!".'

It was clear how deeply affected by the charge of tokenism the group were. Despite a sample comprising a number of OBEs, CBEs, peerages, and the recipients of professional awards and public recognition, a large proportion of the women in the sample felt the need to establish that they had earned their achievements based on their merit. They were at pains to point out that they had not benefitted from any advantage because of their BME status or gender, and had in no way 'cut corners'. Thus we see how disempowering and undermining an effect tokenism can have. If women at this level of power and achievement feel the need to distance themselves from claims that they have enjoyed special advantage, then is any minority group attaining beyond expectations able to be immune from such feelings?

A further consequence of tokenism was the assertion from many women that they felt they constantly had to prove their competence over and over through hard work and dedication to the task. The following quote illustrates this point (ibid., 2008: 45):

> 'You have to keep on demonstrating how brilliant you are. Ethnic Minority women at every level have got to work harder and to be better qualified to really demonstrate many times over that they can do the job.'

Typecasting

BME women are not given full freedom to achieve their potential as they are constantly steered towards specializing in BME or gender issues. Where this is in fact what the individual wishes to do, this poses no problem; rather, it enables the individual to specialize in her chosen field and make a strong contribution to the furtherance of the issue. However, when a role is imposed on an individual because of others' assumptions about the limits of what they can do, then this is problematic. Typecasting is closely aligned with stereotyping. In a climate where organizations are expected to promote diversity, BME women have been provided with opportunities to be advocates, champions, and role models in respect of these objectives. For many women in the study, this is a role they have embraced and welcomed, as they are deeply committed to values of equality, social justice, and empowerment. They also frequently feel that they are ideally placed and have a particular understanding of issues of discrimination. However, many of the women in the study felt that they had been limited in the development of their full range of skills because of constant demands on them by their organizations and other groups to focus on issues of gender and ethnicity. The following quote is indicative of the comments made (ibid., 2008: 46):

> 'Invariably I get asked to chair this or that equality or diversity group. You get pigeon-holed and stereotyped that somehow you know a lot about the subject matter when this is not necessarily your area of expertise.'

Most women in the sample said that at some stage in their career they had faced the dilemma of whether they should become involved in equality and diversity issues. Only a few women decided they would not be involved, and one woman explained her decision as follows (ibid., 2008: 47):

> 'I refused to be the token ethnic minority leader in ethnic minority work. But it's been difficult to resist being pigeon-holed in a tiny little corner and not be able to use your real professional skills and talent.'

Tokenism and typecasting is most prevalent within the public sector and politics, though there is some evidence that these practices also occur in the private and voluntary sectors.

Key contributions of BME women

The Government Equalities Office study (Gervais, 2008) identified a number of key contributions that women in the sample felt they were able to bring their organizations.

Making a difference

Women in the study felt that through their persistence and achievement, they make a difference in their organizations. One way they do this is by having a different approach to power. For the women in the sample, it was clear that attaining power is a means to achieve a specific end – the ability to make a difference. Power provides influence, access to resources, and skills which enable greater and faster social change. The BME women in the study see themselves as change agents, activists, and agitators. This was true across the sample, regardless of position or sector. The following quote summarizes this view (ibid., 2008: 68–69):

> 'My role is to get a point of view across, to try and convince others to come in, to chase the resources, to highlight deficiencies and opportunities whenever I can. I'm an activist.'

The strong values orientation BME women bring to their work and organizations is a key contribution. Irrespective of their field, and the types of organizations they work for, an emphasis on equality, social justice, and empowerment are central to the contribution and approach of BME women. The following quote illustrates this point (ibid., 2008: 69):

> 'What makes me different? The experience of struggle, of inequality, of having to prove ourselves against the odds.'

This drive to make a difference and strong values-orientation displayed by BME women would seem to emanate from a deep knowledge of their communities and an awareness, if not first-hand experience, of exclusion and deprivation. As one woman commented (ibid., 2008: 70):

> 'I suppose I bring a sense of realism to the job. I'm far more credible with young people, black people and women than a lot of others [in the organization] because I am still one of them in a way and I understand their struggles.'

Reflexivity

The women in the sample also showed a remarkable capacity for reflexivity. As a group, they were highly self-aware and understood precisely their skills and limitations, and how others were likely to perceive them. They also showed a deep knowledge of how social structures determine individual experiences and that the way in which power is distributed will be to the advantage of some groups and the detriment of others. This reflexivity arises, they believe, from the experience of minority status. It is also a valuable skill which enables them to be more enlightened, inclusive, and consultative leaders. The following quote illustrates this point (ibid., 2008: 70):

> 'If you're a white man who's always worked with white men and who has always been in a position of power, you've got no reference points and you've never had the need to take the perspective of other people into account. But that's a really important people skill to have which people in minority groups are more likely to have.'

Cross-cultural competence

A final skill BME women in the sample indicated they have is a unique understanding of community life, combined with their experience of reaching positions of power. This combination provides them with a unique skill-set, enabling them to successfully straddle two diverse worlds, that of ethnic minority communities and mainstream white British society. The following quote illustrates this point:

> 'We have that additional skill that we are equally at ease in the corridors of power as we are working with deprived youth in run-down community centres.'

Thus we see that a move away from treating everyone from BME communities as a homogeneous group, and an emphasis on understanding the heterogeneity within and among these groups, provides us with a greater understanding of not only the challenges they face, but also the contributions they can bring.

Organizational interventions to address racial diversity

Signpost to
Chapter 3
From Equal
Opportunities
to Managing
Diversity

In the final section of this chapter, we turn to the practical actions that organizations have taken to address many of the issues we have discussed. These stem from two types of motivation. Businesses have sought to improve diversity within their organizations based upon either an interest in doing the legally and morally 'right' thing, or from a more self-interested position in which diversity management is undertaken on the basis of 'business case' arguments, the underlying rationale being one of financial benefit to the organization. In this section we will consider organizational interventions based upon each of these perspectives.

Legal and moral intervention: institutional racism

> ### ⊙ Case study 5.1   Tackling institutional racism at the Home Office
>
> In 1999 an inquiry headed by Lord Macpherson was undertaken into the failure of the Metropolitan Police to fully investigate the murder of black teenager, Stephen Lawrence. The report introduced into the lexicon of race relations in the UK the term 'institutional racism', defined by Lord Macpherson as:
>
>> The collective failure of an organization to provide an appropriate and professional service to people because of their colour, culture or ethnic origin. It can be seen or detected in processes, attitudes and behaviour which amount to discrimination through unwitting prejudice, ignorance, thoughtlessness and racist stereotyping which disadvantage minority ethnic people. (Macpherson, 1999: para. 6.34)
>
> The term was needed as no specifically racist acts could be evidenced as having taken place in the inquiry. Institutional racism remains a relatively unrecognized concept in the private sector, but in the public sector it is a driver for policy and debate in areas as diverse as housing and the Home Office. Institutional racism comprises a number of indirect and largely invisible processes and practices which can be compared with homosocial reproduction and the 'glass ceiling'. It

refers to the often unintentional barriers embedded within key processes, such as selection and promotion, which serve to disadvantage members of ethnic minority groups. In terms of policy to address institutional racism and also satisfy their obligations under the Race Relations (Amendment) Act 2000, in which a general duty has been placed on all public authorities to promote race equality, the Home Office, with the then Home Secretary Jack Straw, were, not surprisingly, in the vanguard of seeking to implement the findings. A change programme was established to create equal opportunities for everyone. The first step in the programme was to introduce targets for the recruitment, retention, and promotion of ethnic minorities within the Home Office and all its services, including the police, the fire service, and the prison service. In some areas of the Directorate, progress is good. For example, the Immigration and Nationality Directorate has 20 per cent ethnic minority staff. However this is not the picture across the Department. When looking at senior grades in the fire service, there is a significant drop, where the number of people from BME communities holding such positions is below 2 per cent. The aim is to get overall recruitment to the national average for ethnic minorities at about 7 per cent, and to set higher targets in areas where those from BME communities comprise a larger proportion of the population, for example, in London.

The targets are set for implementation over a 10-year period, with key milestones to monitor progress along the way. Recruitment is addressed, but attention is also placed on retention of able BME employees so that barriers to their advancement are eliminated. A key aspect of the programme is that these are targets and not quotas. Quotas are illegal, and opposed by most BME communities. Special privileges or favouritism are not being sought, people simply want an equal chance. Managers are charged with delivering the targets, and if they are unable to meet their targets, they will have to explain why, as they would with any other organizational target. Their performance will be judged on their ability to deliver.

A key group advising policy in the Home Office has been the Home Secretary's Race Relations Forum. This was established in 1997 with a view to bringing in people from the ethnic minorities to advise government. The knowledge and experience of forum members is being used to the full, and their diverse backgrounds provide a valuable resource in developing strategic thinking on the best way to implement policy and measure progress.

Case study questions

1. How useful is the concept of 'institutional racism' in helping us to understand the way in which less obvious forms of racism operate?

2. Are there, in your view, problems with this conceptualization? If so what do you believe these to be?

3. What do you think about the approach the Home Office has adopted to tackling 'institutional racism'? Do you think the approach will be successful and if so, why?

4. What might some of the potential drawbacks of the approach be?

5. As you can see, this programme of action was implemented over 10 years ago. Conduct your own research on the Home Office to see how things have gone. Try to answer the following questions:

   - Have they delivered on their targets?

   - How much progress has been made?

   - What have been the main successes?

   - Where does work remain to be done?

Business case arguments: BME marketing

It was expected that by 2010 BME spending power would reach £300 billion (MCC, 2007). This huge economic resource has not gone unnoticed by organizations and many are structuring their marketing plans and strategies around BME marketing. For years companies have been segmenting their markets and making distinctions in their approach and the products marketed to different groups. There is now a growing realization within organizations that a further market segment; and one whose needs may currently be unaddressed, are first- and second-generation immigrants. Ethnic marketing is the label being used to describe this realization and reflect the fact that someone born in India may not have the same tastes and needs as someone born in New Zealand.

Guion and Kent (2005) provide five key principles for ethnic marketing:

1. Recognize and value the uniqueness of your ethnically based target group.
2. Make sure that you work with members of the community to ensure clarity in establishing and then meeting the needs of the community.
3. Value cultural beliefs, symbols, and practices within the target group.
4. Value differences in language, accent, practices, and social conduct.
5. Value word of mouth and interpersonal communication because for some target groups these may be more effective means of accessing the community than previously tried-and-trusted methods.

Examples of how businesses are reaching out to communities include the following:

- Tesco launched a range of imported and own-brand products to address the needs of the growing Polish population in the UK. These products can be accessed both in-store and through a special website.
- In the USA, food giant Wal-Mart provide hitching posts so that customers from the Amish community can tie up their horses outside stores. They also launched Supermarcados de Walmart to meet the needs of the large Hispanic communities in Phoenix and Houston.

There is also growing acceptance within organizations that their BME employees are ideally placed, through their understanding of BME communities, to provide a valuable resource and a conduit for tapping into this relatively unexplored market. These concepts are illustrated in our end of chapter case study, which focuses on the experience of Lloyds TSB.

🔘 End of Chapter Case Study Lloyds TSB

Approximately 10 per cent of business start-ups are initiated by BME entrepreneurs, yet 80 per cent of UK Asians believe their banking needs are neither recognized nor properly understood. These hard-hitting but unambiguous facts confronted Lloyds TSB Business Banking, so they determined to initiate a cultural-awareness training programme for all their relationship managers to better enable them to meet the needs of the BME communities on their doorsteps.

Their aim was to attract and retain the best people from the widest applicant pool, which enabled them in turn to widen their customer base. Before implementation of the programme, the key barrier to achieving this was a lack of understanding in respect of employee and customer diversity. At the time, the workforce was primarily white and male, which was in stark contrast to the communities they were seeking to serve.

The company hired Winning Communications to design and deliver the needed change. A three-day training programme was developed (a two-day programme with a one-day follow up several weeks later). Three years later over 400 business relationship managers, business development managers, and credit and risk managers have attended the programme.

The initial two days training is based on a four-step ABCD approach:

1. Awareness of the changing make-up of the UK population

2. Building bridges, focusing on developing an understanding of cultural, ethnic, and religious differences

3. Communicating effectively with people from different cultures who will have different perspectives and values

4. Developing an agenda for improving and increasing one's 'reach' within BME communities.

Participants receive a briefing pack on key BME communities in the UK (e.g. the Chinese, Indian, and Pakistani communities), and also gain information about the communities most prevalent in their local area and how best to meet their needs. Mechanisms for establishing closer relationships are also explored, as are resources aimed at key BME segments from which information can be gained on their interests, concerns, and needs. The programme also highlights different attitudes to wealth, saving, and spending evident in particular BME communities.

In the follow-up event which takes place 3–6 months after the initial two days, delegates are able to share their learning and any best practice examples they may have encountered.

The training has certainly met many of its original aims in respect of raising cultural awareness and has also delivered tangible business results much faster than expected. Delegates have succeeded in gaining new customers and improving the service they offer to existing ones. Managers report a number of new links being forged with BME community-based groups, and participation in a variety of activities aimed at specific groups, e.g. an event for business customers in Coventry to celebrate the Chinese New Year.

Source: Pollitt (2009)

Case study questions

1. What do you think of the approach adopted by Lloyds TSB? List three things that are positive about the approach and three that you think could have been improved.

2. Do you think a training programme is the best way to tackle the challenges the Bank faced? What other options might you suggest?

3. In the national briefings, how do you think stereotyping can be avoided?

4. The programme appears to have delivered some benefits to the organization. What would you suggest as the next steps to build and develop the agenda further?

Conclusion

In this chapter we have explored the issue of race discrimination. We have seen that this is a topic in which research has been sporadic and much remains to be done. We have explored a number of competing opinions on the meaning and impact of racial diversity in society as a whole and in organizational life. We have also examined a number of competing opinions on how best to tackle the issue. We have explored some of these views and sought to understand those areas in which progress has been made, and have also analyzed and assessed where there is still work to be done. In terms of progress made, evidence has been presented in respect of a modest increase in BME representation in Parliament, and also the causes and consequences of the rise and success of BME entrepreneurs. Progress has also been noted in access to and success in education, and there have been modest gains in attaining positions of power and influence. However, when looking at senior management levels in organizations, there is little cause for optimism.

In seeking to understand this position, we explored the work of Nkomo (1992), who explains the ethnicity paradigm, the underpinning of the managing diversity agenda. We also explored the more recent focus on discrimination through the concept of 'everyday' discrimination (Deitch et al., 2003; Ogbonna and Harris, 2006).

The final section in the chapter presented key approaches to implementing ethnic diversity, with the observation that initiatives either fall in the 'morally' driven camp or emanate more from a 'business case' perspective. Case studies were presented from the Home Office to illustrate the former and from Lloyds TSB to illustrate the latter.

 ## Review and discussion questions

- Why do you think the Indian and Chinese communities fare better in respect of education and employment than those from other BME communities?

- From the assimilation framework it is concluded that the most appropriate action to overcome racial discrimination takes the form of legal remedies such as legislation aimed at removing barriers to ensure that those from BME communities encounter the same organizational conditions as those from the dominant ethnic group (Thompson, 1989). Do you agree with this approach and if so, why? Can you suggest other mechanisms which may be more effective?

- In your view, which interventions are more appropriate to bring about organizational change in respect of BME participation and representation: those which are morally based or those which are based upon a 'business case'? Discuss, developing key arguments to support your position.

- Make recommendations to your organization (or one you are familiar with) to ensure that issues of 'tokenism' and 'typecasting' are avoided in respect of BME members of staff who have attained senior organizational positions.

For additional material on the content of this chapter please visit the supporting Online Resource Centre at **www.oxfordtextbooks.co.uk/orc/kumra_manfredi/**

Further reading

Afua Hirsch, Guardian Legal Correspondent. Blog: deals primarily with human rights issues, but frequently discusses issues of race and diversity.

Business in the Community (2007) *Race to the Top Report.* London: Business in the Community.

Gervais, M.L. (2008) *Ethnic Minority Women: Routes to Power.* London: Government Equalities Office (Crown Copyright).

Nkomo, S.M. (1992) The emperor has no clothes: rewriting race in organizations. *Academy of Management Review*, 17/3: 487–513.

Ogbonna, E. and Harris, L.C. (2006) The dynamics of employee relationships in an ethnically diverse workforce. *Human Relations*, 59/3: 379–406.

References

Barth, E. A. and Noel, D.L. (1972) Conceptual frameworks for the analysis of race relations: an evaluation. *Social Forces*, 50/2: 333–348.

Basu, A. and Altinay, E. (2002) The interaction between culture and entrepreneurship in London's immigrant businesses. *International Small Business Journal*, 20: 371–393.

Blanton, M. (1987) *Racial Theories*. Cambridge: Cambridge University Press.

Bobo, L. (1998) Race, interests and beliefs about affirmative action: unanswered questions and new directions. *American Behavioral Scientist*, 41: 985–2003.

Business in the Community (2007) *Race to the Top Report*. London: Business in the Community.

Cooney, T.M. and Flynn, A. (2008) A mapping of ethnic entrepreneurship in Ireland. Report presented to Enterprise Ireland, November.

Cox, T. Jr. and Nkomo, S.M. (1990) Invisible men and women: a status report on race as a variable in organization behavior research. *Journal of Organizational Behavior*, 11: 419–431.

Deitch, E.A., Barsky, A., Butz, R.M., Chan, S., Brief, A.P., and Bradley, J.C. (2003) Subtle yet significant: the existence and impact of everyday racial discrimination in the workplace. *Human Relations*, 56/11: 1299–1324.

Dovidio, J.F. and Gaertner, S.L. (eds) (1986) *Prejudice, Discrimination and Racism*. Orlando, FL: Academic Press.

Equal Opportunities Commission (2004) *Ethnic Minority Women and Men*. Briefing. London: EOC.

Equal Opportunities Commission (2006) *Moving on up: Ethnic Minority Women and Work*. London: EOC.

Essed, P. (1991) *Understanding Everyday Racism*. Newbury Park, CA: Sage.

Fawcett Society (2005) *Black and Minority Ethnic Women in the UK*. London: Fawcett Society.

GEM (2004) Title? *Prowess Global Entrepreneurship Monitor*, January.

Gervais, M.L. (2008) *Ethnic Minority Women: Routes to Power*. London: HMSO/Government Equalities Office.

Gordon, M.M. (1964) *Assimilation in American Life: The Role of Race, Religion and National Origin*. New York: Oxford University Press.

Government Office for London (2007) *Borough Indicator Profiler*. London: Government Office for London, August.

Guion, L.A. and Kent, H. (2005) Ethnic Marketing: A Strategy for Marketing Programs to Diverse Audience. Working Paper Series. Gainesville, FL: University of Florida.

Hambrick, D.C., Davison, S.C., Snell, S.A., and Snow, C.C. (1998) When groups consist of multiple nationalities: towards a new understanding of the implications. *Organization Studies*, 19: 181–205.

Hewstone, M. (1989) Intergroup attribution: some implications for the study of ethnic prejudice, in Van Oudenhaven, J.P. and Williemsen, T.M. (eds), *Ethnic Minorities: Social Psychological Perspectives*. Amsterdam: Sivets & Zeitlinger, pp. 25–42.

Hirsch, A. (2010a) General election 2010: if Britain is really post-racial, why is the election so white? *The Guardian*, 27 April.

Hirsch, A. (2010b) UK election results: number of minority ethnic MPs almost doubles. *The Guardian*, 7 May.

Hjerm, M. (2004) Immigrant entrepreneurship in the Swedish welfare state. *Sociology*, 38: 739–756.

Katz, I. and Hass, R.G. (1988) Racial ambivalence and American value conflict: correlational and priming studies of dual cognitive structures. *Journal of Personality and Social Psychology*, 55: 893–905.

Levent, B.T., Masurel, E., and Nijkamp, P. (2003) Diversity in entrepreneurship: ethnic and female roles in urban economic life. *International Journal of Social Economics*, 30/11: 1131–1161.

Macpherson, Lord (1999) The Stephen Lawrence Enquiry. London: HMSO.

Masurel, E., Nijkamp, P., Tastan, M., and Vindigni, G. (2002) Motivations and performance conditions for ethnic entrepreneurship. *Growth and Change*, 33/2: 238–260.

McConahay, J.B. (1986) Modern racism, ambivalence and the Modern Racism Scale, in Dovidio, J.F. and Gaertner, S.L. (eds), *Prejudice, Discrimination and Racism*. San Diego, CA: Academic Press, pp. 91–125.

Minnich, E.K. (1990) *Transforming Knowledge*. Philadelphia, PA: Temple University Press.

Nkomo, S.M. (1992) The emperor has no clothes: rewriting race in organizations. *Academy of Management Review*, 17/3: 487–513.

Ogbonna, E. and Harris, L. C. (2006) The dynamics of employee relationships in an ethnically diverse workforce. *Human Relations*, 59/3: 379–406.

Omi, M. and Winant, H. (1986) *Racial Formation in the United States from the 1960s to the 1980s*. New York: Routledge and Kegan Paul.

Opportunity Now (2002) *Sticky Floors and Cement Ceilings: Women in Non-managerial Roles in the UK*.

Opportunity Now (2010) *Black and Minority Ethnic Women*. Opportunity Now Factsheet.

Oudenhaven, J.P. and Williemsen, T.M. (eds) (1989) *Ethnic Minorities: Social Psychological Perspectives*. Amsterdam: Sivets & Zeitlinger.

Palich, L.E. and Gomez-Mejia, A. (1999) A theory of global and firm efficiencies: considering the effects of cultural diversity. *Journal of Management*, 25: 587–606.

Palmer, P.C. (1966) Servant into slave: the evolution of the legal status of the Negro laborer in colonial Virginia. *South Atlantic Quarterly*, 65/3: 355–370.

Park, R.E. (1950 [1939]) *Race and Culture*. Glencoe, IL: Free Press.

Pettigrew, T.F. (1979) The ultimate attribution error: extending Allport's cognitive analysis of prejudice. *Personality and Social Psychology Bulletin*, 5: 461–476.

Pettigrew, T.F. and Martin, J. (1987) Shaping the organizational context for Black American inclusion. *Journal of Social Issues*, 43: 41–78.

Pollitt, D. (2009) Diversity pays dividends for Lloyds TSB. *Human Resource International Digest*, 17(5).

Race for Opportunity (2010a) *Race and the Professions: Aspirations and Frustration*. Place: Publisher.

Race for Opportunity (2010b) *Race into Higher Education: Today's Diverse Generation into Tomorrow's Workforce*.

Richardson, J. (2009) *Degree Attainment, Ethnicity and Gender*. Place: Higher Education Academy and Equality Challenge Unit.

Smallbone, D., Ram, M., Deakins, D., and Alcock, R. (2003) Access to finance by ethnic minority businesses in the UK. *International Small Business Journal*, 21: 291–314.

Steinberg, S. (1981) *The Ethnic Myth*. New York: Atheneum.

Stone, E.F., Stone, D.L., and Dipboye, R.I. Stigmas in organizations: race, handicaps and physical unattractiveness, in Kelley, K. (ed.), *Issues, Theory and Research in Industrial/Organizational Psychology: Advances in Psychology* (Vol. 82). Amsterdam: North-Holland, pp. 385–457.

Tajfel, H. (1969) Cognitive aspects of prejudice. *Journal of Social Issues*, 25/4: 79–97.

Tajfel, H. (1970) Experiments in intergroup discrimination. *Scientific American*, 223/5: 96–102.

Tajfel, H. (1981) *Human Groups and Social Categories*. Cambridge: Cambridge University Press.

Tajfel, H. and Turner, J.C. (1979) *An Integrative Theory of Intergroup Conflict: The Social Psychology of Intergroup Relations*. Monterey, CA: Brooks/Cole.

Tajfel, H. and Turner, J.C. (1986) The social identity theory of intergroup behaviour, in Worchel, S. and Austin, W. (eds), *Psychology of Intergroup Relations*. Chicago, IL: Nelson Hall, pp. 7–24.

Thomas, R.R. (1990) From affirmative action to affirming diversity. *Harvard Business Review*, 58/2: 107–117.

Thompson, R.H. (1989) *Theories of Ethnicity: A Critical Appraisal*. New York: Greenwood Press.

Volery, T. (2005) Ethnic entrepreneurship: a theoretical framework, in Dana, L.P. (ed.), *Handbook of Research on Ethnic Minority Entrepreneurship*. Cheltenham: Edward Elgar, pp. 30–41.

Yinger, J.M. (1986) Intersecting strands in the theorization of race and ethnic relations, in Rex, J. and Mason, D. (eds), *Theories of Ethnic Relations*. Cambridge: Cambridge University Press, pp. 20–41,

Managing Gender Diversity in the Workplace

Learning objectives

- Appreciate the progress women have made in areas of public and organizational life
- Be aware of some of the key challenges that remain
- Understand the concept of equal pay for equal work and engage with some of the main explanations as to why this has not been achieved despite 40 years of equal pay legislation
- Understand competing debates to explain women's absence in senior organizational positions

Key terms

- **Glass ceiling:** one of the most dominant metaphors used to explain women's absence in senior organizational positions. The glass ceiling has been defined as 'a barrier so subtle that it is transparent, yet so strong that it prevents women and minorities from moving up in the management hierarchy' (Morrison and von Glinow, 1990: 200).

- **Glass cliff:** a term coined by Ryan and Haslam (2007) to explain the higher than average number of women being appointed to the boards of organizations experiencing under-performance and financial difficulty. The 'glass cliff' is a term used to denote the precarious nature of the positions and the gendered processes embedded within their allocation to women.

- **Labyrinth model of women's leadership:** the labyrinth, a term coined by Eagly and Carli (2007), which symbolizes a complex journey towards a goal of value to the individual. To negotiate a labyrinth is not a simple or direct endeavour; it requires persistence, an understanding of progress, and careful analysis of the challenges that lie ahead. It is this message they seek to give to women as they aspire to leadership positions. There are routes to the top, but there are many twists and turns that have to be negotiated along the way – both expected and unexpected – but because all labyrinths have a route through them, the ultimate goal is attainable.

- **Preference theory:** emanating from longitudinal research conducted in the USA and Europe which charts lifestyle preferences and values as key determinants of the employment decisions men and women make, the assertion of preference theory is that it advances a new explanation for labour market participation and employment outcomes, particularly for women.

- **Sex-role stereotyping:** research evidence that supports the contention that there are distinct characteristics, attitudes, and temperaments that can be attributed to men and others which can be attributed to women.

Introduction

In this chapter we explore the issue of gender discrimination. This is a much researched topic and concerns inequalities in opportunity between the genders. As with all the main topics we discuss in this book, there are a number of competing opinions on the meaning and impact of gender diversity on organizational life, and also a number of competing opinions on how best to tackle the issue. In this chapter we explore some of these views and seek to understand where progress has been made and how this has been achieved. We also focus on the areas where there is still work to be done. In terms of progress made, we look at women's increased participation in key areas of public and organizational life, with particular progress noted in access to and success in education, managerial work, and the professions.

However, what we continue to see is a picture of women gaining access and entry to organizations, but once in them not progressing at the rate that their qualifications and numbers would suggest should be the case. We thus turn to explanations as to why this might be. We look at the work of Catherine Hakim, who, with her advancement of preference theory, believes that the 'choice' for their advancement or otherwise in the world of work lies squarely in the hands of individual women. She argues that advances in modern society mean there is no reason for women to be disadvantaged in relation to men in terms of their career choices and, most significantly, outcomes.

This view has been challenged by several writers. Key among those who examine the concept of the 'glass ceiling', and the more recent articulation of key barriers to women's advancement and leadership, are Eagly and Carli (2007), with their 'labyrinth model'. We also discuss the continuing issue of unequal pay between the genders, analyzing some of the explanations for the prevalence of this form of inequality despite 40 years of legislation.

'Women in the developed world have never had it so good'

This was the motion presented in a recent (19–20 January 2010) *Economist* debate. The debate was run along the classic format developed at the Oxford Union, with Richard Donkin, author of *The Future of Work* (2010), defending the motion, and Terry O'Neill, President of the National Organization for Women (NOW), against the motion. Donkin's arguments for the motion included the great change women have seen to their lives compared to women from past generations. These include access to the vote, access to contraception, and relatively easy access to divorce. He points to census data from the USA which reveal that the percentage of married couples where women out-earn their male partners has increased from 15.9 per cent in 1988 to 26.2 per cent in 2008. However, he argues that access to these forces for 'liberation' have bought problems of their own. For example, working women still carry the greatest responsibility for domestic work and family life, while simultaneously pursuing careers. He further concedes that to argue that women have never had it so good is not to say they cannot have it better. In terms of where progress remains to be made, he specifically mentions access to senior organizational positions and equal pay. Both of these issues will be dealt with in this chapter. In summing up, Donkin asserts: 'The most convincing of all the points that support the motion we are debating here must be that women today have choices they never enjoyed in the past. It is not up to me or anyone else to suggest what they do with those choices' (Donkin, 2010).

Arguing against the motion, Terry O'Neill addresses the issue of equal pay. She points out that in the USA the gender pay gap has reduced by less than half a cent per year since 1963, with women earning only 77 cents for every dollar earned by a man. She argues that as women age, the wage gap grows. Men earn more as they advance in age and in their careers, but women who try to negotiate for higher pay are perceived negatively. Only 38 per cent of managerial jobs in the USA are held by women (and when we look at the top of organizations, only 3 per cent of Chief Executives in the Fortune 500 are women). Several indicators would support the view that women are faring well in education (see below), but O'Neill counters this with evidence which demonstrates that while it is true that women are earning more degrees across a number of disciplines, they continue to bump into what she terms 'the ivy covered brick wall' when it comes to the still male-dominated domains of mathematics, engineering, information technology, and the hard sciences. Just over one quarter of full-tenured US professors are women and in the 50 most prestigious research universities in the USA, there are no women in higher academic positions. It is clear from this analysis that while progress has been made, there remains some way to go.

Debate Box

Organize the class into two groups, one for the motion and one against.
   The motion is:

This house believes that women in the western world have never had it so good.

   Stages in the debate: (each stage is given with timings, the overall time for the activity is 55 minutes – allowing a few minutes for change over of presenters, etc.)

- Each group has 20 minutes to prepare their arguments either for or against the motion.
- Each group is given 5 minutes to present their opening statement (10 minutes in total).
- Groups reconvene for 10 minutes to prepare rebuttal arguments.
- Each group has 2 minutes to present rebuttal arguments.

A vote is taken and the winners of the debate announced; the casting vote goes to impartial observers: tutors, audience members not involved in the debate, or observers.

Women's participation in organizational life: room for improvement?

As can be seen from the debate above, the issue of gender diversity remains a topical issue. The interest sparked by the debate and the level of engagement and emotion displayed on both sides indicates the importance of the issue and its relevance for contemporary society and the organizations within them. It is clear that great strides have been made. In the UK, 63.4 per cent of girls (compared with 53.8 per cent of boys) achieve five or more GCSEs grades A*–C, women now earn more degrees than men, and are the recipients of 56.6 per cent of first-class degrees (Office for National Statistics, 2007). In 2008, 14.3 million women were in the workforce, compared with 16.9 million men (Office for National Statistics, 2008). In the 2008 'Sex and Power Report' published by the Equality and Human Rights Commission (EHRC), we see that in the UK women comprised 19.3 per cent of Members of Parliament in 2008 compared with 18.1 per cent in 2003. They constitute 26.1 per cent of members of Cabinet, compared with 23.8 per cent in 2003. In business, 11 per cent of directors (executive and non-executive) in FTSE 100 companies were women, up from 8.6 per cent in 2003, and 13.6 per cent of editors of national newspapers were women in 2008, compared with 9.1 per cent in 2003. Progress has also been made in public appointments, with women comprising 26.6 per cent of top management in the Civil Service in 2008, compared with 22.9 per cent in 2003, and 9.6 per cent of senior judiciary (high court judge and above) in 2008, rising from 6.8 per cent in 2003. There has been an improvement in the numbers of women in senior positions in education, with women constituting 14.4 per cent of university vice-chancellors in 2008, up from 12.4 per cent in 2003. Women also represented 36.9 per cent of health service chief executives in 2008, compared with 28.6 per cent in 2003.

It is also evident that increasing numbers of women are attracted to careers in the professional services, which include law, accountancy, management consultancy, and investment banking. As Bolton and Muzio (2008: 282) note: 'There seems little doubt that women have made huge progress, numerically dominating areas of the labour market and entering and succeeding in previously male-dominated occupations and professional groups.' For example, in the past 30 years, women's participation in the legal profession has increased by a phenomenal 1800 per cent (SRU, 2006a) and women represent over 40 per cent of practising solicitors (SRU, 2006b). It is also clear that this is a trend likely to continue. In 2006 more than 60 per cent of new trainees, new law graduates, and acceptances on university law degree programmes were women (SRU, 2006b). A similar trend is evident in accounting where women comprise 42 per cent of all Institute of Chartered Accountants in England and Wales. In management consulting firms, women typically represent between 30 and 40 per cent of the intake, and similar numbers are evident in investment banking.

However, optimistic forecasts that the rise in women's participation in the professional services would translate into gender equality at the senior levels are somewhat challenged by figures which show at the partner level (the most senior position in such firms) only 23.2 per cent are women (SRU, 2006b). The 'Sex and Power Report' (EHRC, 2008) indicates that although progress has been made, the rate of that progress is cause for concern. At current rates, it will take 73 years to gain gender equality in FTSE 100 companies at Board level, 27 years to achieve equality in top management in the Civil Service, 55 years to achieve an equal number of women in the senior judiciary and, perhaps most worryingly of all, 200 years to achieve an equal number of women in Parliament (EHRC, 2008). Internationally, the UK does not compare well; it currently ranks 70th in the world in terms of women's representation in Parliament, behind countries such as Rwanda, Afghanistan, and Iraq (Inter-parliamentary Union, 2008).

The report notes that it is important to understand these findings in respect of the impact they have on women, but also in the broader context of what effects this failure to tap into the talent of women will have on the economy and the country overall. Old-fashioned and inflexible ways of working are preventing us from identifying and maximizing the talent which comes in a variety of forms and can be found in a number of places. The nature of the world is changing and so is the nature of our economy, and the way in which work is done. It is time for employers to catch up. Some key indicators of these changes are provided in the report. They are that:

- between 2009 and 2014 for every 10 newly created jobs in the UK, five will go to women (Wilson et al., 2006)

- by 2020, 40 per cent of the working population will be aged 45 and over (Madouros, 2006).

→ Student Activity 6.1

Find a picture of any group meeting of Heads of State, for example, G20 meetings, EU gatherings, summits on climate change, etc. What do you notice about them?

- If there were a greater number of women among the Heads of State, do you think this would impact on the issues that are discussed and the manner in which they are discussed? Explain how.

- How do you think working in such a male-dominated environment impacts on those few women who are executive Heads of State?

While the issue of the under-representation of women in key areas of public life has been studied, the absence of men in certain occupations has also received attention. Here the focus has been on the organizational and personal experiences of men in female-dominated occupations, and the occupations that have been studied have included male nurses, primary school teachers, and cabin crew (Simpson, 2004). Researchers in this area believe it may actually be easier for women to make their way in male-dominated occupations, as this will usually enhance their status and potentially increase their pay. A man moving into a female-dominated occupation, by contrast; disrupts the gender assumptions associated with the particular type of work (e.g. nursing as a 'caring' profession), sometimes resulting in him no longer being viewed as a 'real man' (Williams, 1993).

There is evidence that once in these occupations men find themselves in a 'double-bind'. On the one hand, because they are men they are imbued with the positive aspects of their masculine status and are seen as possessing enhanced leadership abilities and having a more 'careerist' attitude to work (Floge and Merrill, 1989; Heikes, 1992). We thus see that male nurses often have a quicker ascent up the hierarchy than their female counterparts and they are over-represented in positions of power (Bradley, 1993; Williams, 1993). On the other hand, female-dominated occupations, such as nursing, primary school teaching, and social work, may be deemed as requiring special abilities that only women are seen to possess (Hochschild, 1983). This can be problematical for men as it can call into question their suitability and competence for these jobs if they behave in traditionally masculine ways, yet invite challenges to their masculinity and sexuality if they adopt the more 'feminine' and accepted approach. Strategies that have been observed to negotiate the 'double-bind' have been a reconstruction of the job to minimize its non-masculine associations, for example, male primary school teachers tending to take charge of PE (Lupton, 2000).

Gender discrimination in the workplace: the equal pay gap

Signpost to Chapter 2 An Outline of European and UK Equality Legislation

The gender pay gap persists in the UK and across many countries in the developed and developing world, despite decades of legislation taking a variety of forms to address it. It is the persistence and complexity of the issue which has prompted Vladimir Spidia, the EU's Equal Opportunities Commissioner to comment: 'The gender pay gap has multiple causes and needs multiple solutions. Tackling it requires action at all levels and a commitment from everyone concerned, from employers and trade unions to national authorities and every citizen' (speech on 3 March 2009 at the launch of a campaign to address the issue of pay inequality in the EU).

What is the extent of the problem?

From Table 6.1 we can see the nature of the gender pay gap across Europe. It averages 17.4 per cent across the EU as a whole, and is highest in Estonia (30.3 per cent) and lowest in Italy (4.4 per cent).

Figures from the European Commission on member countries' gender pay gaps – the percentages by which women's compensation, on average, lags behind men's – show a considerable spread. A pay gap usually reflects the working patterns of women in a given country. In most countries with a low female employment rate, the pay gap is lower than average, possibly reflecting a small proportion of low-skilled or unskilled women in the workforce. A high pay gap is usually characteristic of a highly segregated labour market or where a significant proportion of women work part-time.

Table 6.1 The gender-based pay gap across Europe

Country	Pay gap (%)	Country	Pay gap (%)	Country	Pay gap (%)
Estonia	30.3	Lithuania	20.0	Bulgaria	12.7
Austria	25.5	Finland	20.0	Romania	12.7
Czech Republic	23.6	Sweden	17.9	Luxembourg	10.0
Netherlands	23.6	Denmark	17.7	Belgium	9.1
Slovakia	23.6	Spain	17.6	Portugal	8.3
Cyprus	23.1	Ireland	17.1	Slovenia	8.3
Germany	23.0	Hungary	16.3	Poland	7.5
UK	21.1	France	15.8	Malta	5.2
Greece	20.7	Latvia	15.4	Italy	4.4

Source: European Commission – (2009)

⬤ **Case study 6.1**   Speech and language therapists

Pamela Enderby, a speech and language therapist, challenged the way the professionals in her female-dominated work area were valued and financially rewarded. Speech and language therapists are highly trained and skilled to help patients who cannot communicate following an accident or illness, such as a stroke, and children who do not develop speech and language normally, but they were not paid as highly as male-dominated professions requiring a similar level of skill, such as psychologists and pharmacists. Pamela argued that the salaries of speech and language therapists were lower because they were mostly women. Her case took 14 years, but she won, going all the way to the European Court.

Source: Fawcett Society (2008).

Case study questions

1. Why do you think the gender pay gap has occurred in this case?

2. Why do you think the case has taken 14 years to conclude?

3. Write a briefing paper to the HR manager in Pamela's organization outlining your recommendations on how these issues can be overcome.

What are the causes of the pay gap?

In analyzing the reasons why we continue to see a pay gap between men and women, it is, as Vladimir Spidla observes, a complex issue. However, there does seem to be agreement across various sources that the pay gap exists for two main reasons. These are:

- **Undervaluing of women's work.** While we have seen a decline in 'direct discrimination' in respect of gender pay differences, we still see an undervaluing of the work that women do. The sectors women work in are, on average, paid less than those where men dominate (Deschenaux, 2009). Women tend to dominate areas covering the five 'Cs' (Fawcett Society, 2008) – caring, cleaning, catering, clerical work, and cashiering. Women doing such work are generally viewed to be working for 'pin money' (i.e. money for optional extras in the household), not for money that is critical to the household budget, and so women are very firmly placed in the role of second earners. Women take these jobs because they tend to be flexible and they are able to fit the job around their other responsibilities, and they also tend to be local.

- **Lack of transparency.** The second main reason given for a continuing gender pay gap is that of a lack of transparency surrounding information in respect of pay. Transparency is critical if we are to uncover the complex variables that combine to produce the inequality of pay between the genders that we observe, but it is also essential if women are to be able to make a claim at all. At present, the equal pay legislation in the UK puts the onus on the individual to seek redress, as indicated by Pamela Enderby's case above. However, how can women do this if they do not have the information available to them about what they earn in comparison to their peers and to other occupations considered as 'like work' with their own. Many workplaces are shrouded in secrecy on this issue, with some making it a sackable offence to disclose details of pay and bonus packages to colleagues.

> ### ⊡ Case study 6.2   BT Group
>
> BT's initial pay audit in 1998 revealed a gap largely due to the over-representation of women in lower paid clerical and call centre roles, and men in technical or management roles. BT's last pay review in 2008 allocated 0.5 per cent of the pay budget to address equal pay issues, with £5.53 million spent on 17.8 per cent of employees. The underlying principle was to address employees receiving low pay within a range for no justifiable reason and was based on comparison with market rates across organizations, rather than basic salary within the organization.
>
> *Source:* Fawcett Society (2009).
>
> Case study questions
>
> **1.** Do you think this is a positive step on BT's part?
>
> **2.** What other action(s) do you think they could have taken?

> ### → Student Activity 6.2
>
> In January 2010 the Equality and Human Rights Commission announced that firms which first check and then make public any differences in pay between their male and female staff will receive immunity from further investigation. A spokesperson for the Equality and Human Rights Commission explained that the move, which is unprecedented in the UK, has been developed to encourage organizations to take voluntary measures to address the issue of persistent and continuing gender-based pay inequalities.
>
> Women are still paid 20 per cent less per hour than their male counterparts and this worsens to 25 per cent in private sector firms. This is despite 40 years of equal pay legislation in the form of the Equal Pay Act 2010.
>
> In a study commissioned by the Equality and Human Rights Commission, half of workers see tackling pay inequalities as a top priority for organizations. However, when it comes to publishing data in respect of the gender pay gap, only one firm in ten does this.
>
> 1. What do you think about the proposal from the EHRC?
>
> 2. Do you think it will contribute to transparency?
>
> 3. What do you think about the CBI's position? Why do you think they oppose these proposals?

Other action employers can take includes ensuring the better application of existing legislation, promoting equal pay as an issue related to social responsibility, and supporting the exchange of best practice across EU countries (Deschenaux, 2009).

Gender discrimination in the workplace: the glass ceiling

From the preceding discussion it is clear that progress has been made in women's representation in organizations, although what is also clear is that there is much room for improvement. Gaining access to organizations is no longer the issue, as has been shown in the number of women managers and the number of women entering professional service organizations, where in some cases, such as law, they outnumber men. However, significant progress remains to be made at the most senior levels of the organization and it is to an analysis of the causes and consequences of an absence of women in senior organizational positions that attention now turns.

One of the most dominant metaphors used to explain women's absence in senior organizational positions has been that of the 'glass ceiling'. This has been defined as 'a barrier so subtle that it is transparent, yet so strong that it prevents women and minorities from moving up in the management hierarchy' (Morrison and von Glinow, 1990: 200). An analysis of the literature on women's absence in senior positions shows that studies are segmented into two key areas (Kumra, 2003). The first examines individual characteristics required for advancement, with a view to assessing whether women possess such characteristics and whether those charged with making promotional decisions believe women to be in possession of such characteristics. The second concentrates on the determinants of managerial career success. Here studies vary in the approach they adopt, with some looking at objective measures to explain individual and organizational requirements, while others include subjective measures which contend that advancement is not purely an objective process. Each of these areas is examined in turn.

Influence of gender on advancement: a focus on individual characteristics

In this section we consider the individual and the personal characteristics that are likely to influence career success. The premise adopted is that women will be less likely to possess the personal attributes generally associated with managerial advancement, or that those assessing candidates for future advancement will perceive women as being less likely to possess the required personal attributes.

There is clear research evidence to indicate the strong influencing role of sex-role stereotypes on both men and women's occupational aspirations and expectations. One of the first studies to explore the relationship between sex, managerial stereotypes, and gender stereotypes was conducted by Schein (1973, 1975). Schein built on previous work into sex-role stereotypes (Anastasi and Foley, 1949; Maccoby, 1966; Rosenkrantz et al., 1968) which suggested that there were distinct characteristics, attitudes, and temperaments which can be attributed to men and others which can be attributed to women. She argued that sex-role stereotypes could create a barrier to the advancement of one gender where an occupation is 'sex-typed', i.e. a large majority of individuals in it are of one sex, and there is an associated normative expectation that this is how it should be. Writing in the early 1970s, Schein viewed management as a sex-typed occupation due to the high ratio of men in managerial positions. If this were the case, she hypothesized that the managerial position would require personal attributes thought to be more characteristic of men than of women (Schein, 1973: 95).

In order to test this hypothesis, she developed Schein's Descriptive Index (SDI), consisting of 92 items that described characteristics typical of males and females. Schein tested the SDI on a sample of 300 male middle line managers of various departments within nine insurance companies located in the USA (Schein, 1973). The sample was split randomly into three equal groups, and each was presented with a different form of the SDI containing the same descriptive terms and instructions. However, one form asked for a description of women in general, one for a description of men in general, and one for a description of successful middle managers. In a second study (Schein, 1975), a sample composed of 167 female managers in the insurance sector, who matched as closely as possible the male sample from the previous study, were asked to complete the same task.

The results showed that there was a significant group effect for 86 out of the 92 items. As regards the results for male managers, 'a large and significant resemblance between the ratings of Men and Managers and a near zero non-significant resemblance between the ratings of Women and Managers' were found (Schein, 1975). For female managers, a 'large and significant resemblance between Men and Manager' was computed and the resemblance that existed between Women and Managers was significantly less than between Men and Managers (ibid.). In her discussion of the results Schein writes that, other things being equal, the perceived similarity between the characteristics of managers and men is most likely to increase a male manager's chances to be chosen for a managerial position to the detriment of his female colleagues: 'A woman, by virtue of her gender alone, was viewed as less qualified than her counterpart' (ibid.: 42).

Further research replicating Schein's experiment has tended to produce the same results from men, although women no longer sex-type the managerial job (e.g. Brenner et al., 1989; Heilman et al., 1989; Schein et al., 1989; Schein and Mueller, 1992; Schein et al., 1996). Heilman et al. (1989) expanded Schein's original research by asking 268 male managers to rate one of seven target groups against Schein's original 92 descriptors:

- Men in general
- Men as managers
- Men as successful managers
- Women in general
- Women as managers
- Women as successful managers
- Successful middle managers.

The results from this study were similar to Schein's original findings in relation to ratings of men and women in general and as managers. However, they also discovered that the correlation between descriptions of women and successful managers strengthens when women are depicted as managers, and is very strong when women are depicted as successful managers (Heilman et al.,1989). The authors point out that although these findings might suggest a demise in stereotypical thinking about women and their capabilities to be effective managers, the characteristics on which there are perceived dissimilarities could be seen to be pivotal to effective managerial performance.

The importance of this work cannot be understated. Taken together, the studies highlight the strength of stereotypical views of what is, and is not, 'women's work' and the way in which such views become embedded in organizational processes which superficially appear 'objective'. If being female is viewed as being inconsistent with managerial work, and the criteria or characteristics sought of future managers are drawn from a predominantly male managerial population, entering such positions is undoubtedly challenging for women. However, even more challenging is progression within male sex-typed occupations, resulting in what is termed a 'double-bind' (i.e. a double hurdle) – women clear one hurdle only to be presented with another.

> ### ⊙ Student Activity 6.3
>
> Below is a list of sex-role stereotypical characteristics collated from training and marketing materials (Fawcett Society, 2009).
>
> | | |
> |---|---|
> | Emotional | Dominant |
> | Affectionate | Aggressive |
> | Mild | Rational |
> | Sentimental | Goal-oriented |
> | Multi-tasker | Problem-solver |
> | Carer | Decision-maker |
> | Feeling | Analytical, logical, linear, focused |
> | Tend and befriend | Fight or flight |
> | Interest in people | Interest in things |
> | Motivated by empathy | Motivated by self-interest |
> | Survival through relationships | Survival through hierarchy |
> | Connection | Competition |
> | Empathize | Systemize |
> | Pursuit of the aesthetic | Pursuit of order |
>
> The lists above show sex-role stereotypical characteristics. Looking at them, consider the following:
>
> 1. Which list do you think are characteristics typical of men?
> 2. How do you know this?
> 3. Consider the characteristics typical of the opposite gender from yourself (i.e. if you are female, look at the male list). Are any of these characteristics in your view typical of your own behaviour? Or that of your friends of the same gender?
> 4. How useful is the concept of sex-role stereotyping? What are the potential problems of such an approach?

Determinants of managerial career advancement: a gendered perspective

In this area of the literature, researchers have sought to determine what leads to success at the individual and organizational level for both men and women. For example, Ragins and Sundstrom (1989) viewed women's advancement to senior organizational positions as arising from the interaction of several key factors. These were organizational influences such as access to training and selection for high-visibility projects; interpersonal influences, where the presence of powerful networks and mentors is significant; and individual influences, where personality aspects, such as self-confidence, early experiences, and non-work roles have an impact. Adopting a similar person-centred perspective, Fagenson (1990) also proposed the interaction of three sets of factors as being useful in explaining female advancement: gender as an internal trait; the employing organization in its provision of structural opportunities; and institutional systems, and how these are manifested through practices and beliefs. Thus, the paucity of women in managerial positions arises from the interaction of socialization, organizational structural issues, such as fewer women present at senior hierarchical positions, and negative organizationally-endorsed beliefs about women and their suitability for managerial positions.

Moving away from a comparison between men and women to looking at successful women only, Mainiero (1994) interviewed senior female executives to determine the factors contributing to their success. In her analysis, she found that women achieving senior organizational positions shared a number of key organizational experiences. They acquired supervisory experience early on in their careers, and this continued throughout their careers; they held positions with line management responsibility as opposed to positions that were more advisory in nature; they had time spent at company headquarters; they had time spent either assisting a senior manager or forming part of a high-profile task force; and later in their careers, they acquired general management experience that was crucial in making the move into executive positions.

A recent body of work has augmented these findings, and also extended the glass ceiling metaphor. Ryan and Haslam (2007) have introduced the concept of the 'glass cliff'. Through a number of experimental studies and archival analysis, they have found that women are far more likely than men to be placed into highly risky leadership positions where the chances of failure are high. Ryan and Haslam were responding to an article by Judge (2003), which argued that corporations needed to be careful in promoting women into senior Board positions because his analysis showed that of the ten companies with the highest number of women at Board level, six were under-performing relative to the mean performance of the FTSE 100, whereas the five companies with the lowest number of women at Board level (i.e. male only boards) were performing better than the FTSE 100 average.

Ryan and Haslam (2007) sought to analyze these findings further. They found that the companies had been under-performing before women had been appointed to Board positions. Indeed, it was their precarious organizational performance that had prompted these corporations to hire women. They provide systematic evidence to support their assertion. In crisis situations, organizations may find it useful to move away from the old adage 'think manager, think male' and to consider an alternative – 'think crisis, think female'. To support this contention, they cite evidence from Schein's original studies (1973, 1975), which indicated that some of the traits that correlated with management success were viewed by participants as being more typical of women in general than of men in general. 'These included being understanding, helpful, sophisticated, aware of the feeling of others, intuitive, creative and cheerful' (Ryan and Haslam, 2007: 553). It is not unlikely that many of these characteristics would also be viewed as highly desirable in times of crisis.

In a study in which participants were asked to describe those managers who were best suited to manage successful companies and those who were best suited to manage unsuccessful companies, the 'think manager, think male' association held for successful companies. But when considering unsuccessful companies, there was a very strong correlation with the female stereotype (Ryan et al., 2007). These findings also held for a number of other experimental studies conducted by the authors across a number of sectoral settings, for example in the business sector and in the legal profession. The authors were able to conclude: 'it is sufficient to emphasize that these experimental studies suggest that the processes that contribute to the selection of women for glass cliff appointments are not isolated to a particular context or participant group' (Ryan et al., 2007: 554).

Such findings draw attention to two issues emerging from the glass cliff phenomenon. First, those offering women such opportunities will believe they are treating women favourably, as they are providing them access to challenging and stretching assignments. The women themselves may feel they are being given a favourable opportunity and thus feel unable to decline. Those in senior positions can deny any charges that they are not advancing women in their organizations, even though the opportunities they are providing are of limited value as they are highly precarious, with a high likelihood of failure, and there is little real opportunity for challenge and growth. They thus achieve a double advantage: the organization is able to appear to be advancing the position of women; there is little chance that gender hierarchies will actually be challenged or altered (Ryan and Haslam, 2007).

The second issue concerns group dynamics and in-group favouritism. The 'glass cliff' phenomenon may be evidence that largely male power elites in organizations will reserve the safer and more attractive positions for their fellow in-group members (i.e. jobs for the boys: see Balls, 1992; Gallagher, 1994; Powell and Butterfield, 2002), leaving out-group members to undertake any remaining positions. Organizational decision-makers may be willing to appoint women to 'glass cliff' positions because they see them as being more expendable and, indeed, more attractive for such positions as they make obvious scapegoats when things (inevitably) go wrong.

In this area of the literature, we are able to identify a body of evidence identifying many of the key determinants to managerial advancement; we have also discussed the way in which person and situational factors combine to inhibit women in their attainment of them.

Debate Box: The Unshattered Glass Ceiling

The standard explanation [for the glass ceiling] is that women have babies and that this arrests their career development. Improvement in maternity provisions seem to have exacerbated this trend. Paid maternity leave has now been extended to a full year, but it is available to the mother only. This has, perversely, entrenched women in the traditional role of wife and mother because the man is unable to take the same parental leave to share the child care. The Government should change the law to allow couples to choose which of them wants to take the year off.

But there is more to the problem than that, which is why women who do not have children – a quarter of the female workforce at age 40 – suffer from the same discrimination and disadvantage. The trouble is that the attitudes and habits of the British workplace were forged in an era when breadwinner dads and stay-at-home mums were the norm. That mindset persists. It is a macho culture of long working hours where, even if the boys' network is not what it was, the boys go out for a beer with the boss after work. And – despite the fact that girls now outperform boys at school and at university – there continues to be a subliminal consensus that women are less capable or strategically able than men. (*The Independent*, 5 September 2008)

Organize the class into two groups, one for the motion and one against.
   The motion is:

This house believes that the glass ceiling is simply a convenient excuse given by women who are not as successful in their careers as they would like to be.

   Follow stages for the debate as given above.

Critiquing the glass ceiling

As can be seen from the preceding discussion, the glass ceiling metaphor has had a widespread and enduring impact on the analysis of women and their organizational advancement. However, it is important to note that not all agree with the notion of a 'glass ceiling' as the explanation for women's lack of parity in senior organizational positions. Other explanations have been advanced, and two will be discussed here. One, Hakim's preference theory (2000), lays responsibility for women's careers squarely in the hands of individual women, arguing that a number of macro-economic factors have combined to place women in a position where they have 'unfettered choice' and how they opt to use this choice is a matter for the individual. The other is a model of women's leadership advanced by US social psychologists, Eagly and Carli (2007). They argue that the metaphor of the glass ceiling is misleading for several reasons and seek to replace it with the 'labyrinth model'. In their view, this metaphor is more indicative of the barriers women face in forging their way to leadership positions. Each of these approaches is discussed in turn.

Preference theory

In advancing the case for preference theory, Hakim (2000) asserts that it is an approach which departs from the sociological tradition, where the main focus is on social, structural, and institutional factors. It is also a perspective which rejects the economist tradition, where the assumption of stable and homogeneous preferences is seen to preclude direct empirical investigation. Preference theory emanates from the research findings of longitudinal studies conducted in the USA and Europe which chart lifestyle preferences and values as key determinants of the employment decisions of men and women. The assertion is that preference theory advances a new explanation for labour market participation and employment outcomes, particularly for women.

At the centre of preference theory is the view that when given genuine choices, women choose between three lifestyles: home-centred, work-centred, or adaptive (Hakim, 2000). This variety in preferences is to be found at all educational levels and across all social classes. Table 6.2 provides a classification of each of these groups. Adaptive women prefer to combine paid employment and family work, giving neither a fixed priority but flexing between the two as circumstances require. Adaptive women constitute the largest group and can be found in most occupations. Home-centred women, on marriage, prefer to prioritize home and family life. They tend to have larger families and prefer to avoid paid work after marriage, although under financial strain they will engage with it. Home-centred women are not less likely to invest in qualifications, as the educational system can function as a marriage market as well as a training institution (Hakim, 2000: 193–222). The third category is work-centred women. These are a minority, despite the growing numbers of women going into higher education and gaining entry to the professions and all aspects of working life in the past four decades. Those in the work-centred category (men and women) have as their focus competitive activities in all aspects of the public sphere, e.g. career, sport, politics, or the arts. Family life fits around work, and many of the women in this category choose to remain childless, even when married. It is contended that the majority of men are work-centred, while only a minority of women qualify for this category (typically between 10 and

Table 6.2 Classification of women's work lifestyle preferences in the twenty-first century (Hakim, 2000: 6, by permission of the Oxford University Press)

Home-centred	Adaptive	Work-centred
20% of women; varies between 10 and 30%	60% of women; varies between 40 and 80%	20% of women; varies between 10 and 30%
Family life and children are the main priorities throughout life	This group is most diverse and includes women who want to combine work and family, plus drifters with unplanned careers	Childless women are concentrated here. The main priority in life is employment or equivalent activities in the public arena, e.g. politics, sport, etc.
Qualifications obtained for intellectual dowry	Qualifications obtained with the intention of working	Large investment in qualifications or training for employment or other activities
Responsive to societal and family policies	Very responsive to all policies	Responsive to employment policies

Signpost to Chapter 8 Managing Work–Life Balance

30 per cent). 'Preference theory predicts that men will retain their dominance in the labour market, politics, and other competitive activities because only a minority of women are prepared to prioritise their jobs (or other activities in the public sphere) in the same way as men' (Hakim, 2000: 15).

Critiquing preference theory

Hakim's preference theory has, not surprisingly, sparked much comment and debate. Criticism has been drawn from a range of sources and covered almost every aspect of the theory. Crompton and Lyonette (2005) query the notion of 'voluntarism' implied throughout Hakim's argument, stating that through an emphasis on the central significance of individual 'choice', no allowance is made for the impact of societal and structural constraints. They further contend that feminists have consistently argued that differences and inequalities between men and women are not naturally occurring issues but are socially constructed. Thus, Hakim (2000), by reaffirming the 'naturalness' of gender differences and consigning this to 'choice', reaffirms the inequalities which arise and thus legitimizes the differences themselves.

McRae (1993) is particularly concerned that preference theory fails to recognize women who have essentially the same preferences in wishing to combine work and family but who can in fact experience very different outcomes because they make choices within their personal situations – as women, wives, mothers, and workers. She believes that Hakim's linkage of 'genuine' choice to outcomes (behaviour) is too simplistic an approach which may result in the production of trivial and ultimately misleading conclusions being drawn. Women face many constraints as they 'choose' how they will balance labour market work and family work, and what priority they will give to one over the other at particular times. In terms of what those constraints might be, McRae (1993) indicates that they typically fall into two categories: normative and structural. The normative category considers women's self-identity, gender relations in the family, and the attitudes of husbands or partners. The structural category includes issues such as the availability of appropriate jobs and the cost and availability of childcare of a suitable quality.

Thus, there are a number of claims made against preference theory's central tenet (genuine and unfettered choice), and through this, the theory's ability to explain women's lifestyle preferences. Most significantly, preference theory has been criticized for ignoring social and structural issues which affect women's career prospects, including social class and its translation into qualifications, social networks, and income (McRae, 1993, 2003). To claim 'voluntary' and 'genuine' choice, as Hakim (2000) does, is to ignore the reality of women's lives, the constraints women face, and the impact of these constraints on their choices.

> ### ⊗ Student Activity 6.4
>
> - Having read the account of Hakim's preference theory, and the various critiques, would you alter any of your answers to the questions in Student Activity 6.3?
> - If you would, in what way would you do this and why?
> - If you wouldn't, why not?

Exploring women's leadership: through the labyrinth

Eagly and Carli (2007) contend that for years the problem of women's absence at senior organizational positions has been misdiagnosed, and because of this the programmes put in place to correct the issue have been misdirected. They argue that to conceptualize the lack of women at the highest organizational levels as a 'glass ceiling' is to miss the point about the disadvantage women face and contributes to the intractability of the problem. In their view, the metaphor of the glass ceiling is misleading for the following reasons:

- It conceptualizes an absolute barrier, preventing women attaining a specific senior organizational position. The fact that women have made it to the most senior positions in almost every walk of life, through public appointments and attaining chief executive positions – albeit in small numbers – gives the lie to the charge.

- The imagery of a transparent barrier implies in some way that women are misled about the possibilities available to them because they cannot see the barrier from a distance. Some of the impediments women face within organizations are not so subtle and can be seen from a great distance.

- The final criticism, and in their view the worst of all, is that the glass ceiling represents a single, unvarying obstacle. It fails to account for the complexity and variety of the challenges faced by women as they embark upon their leadership journey. The reality of women's leadership journey is not that they are rejected at the very last stage of attainment, but that they disappear at many points and for many reasons on the way up the organizational hierarchy.

That the 'glass ceiling' metaphor has been so durable and yet, in their view, so wrong matters because, through a belief in a 'glass ceiling', action is focused and directed towards certain interventions (e.g. mentoring, selecting a diversity of candidates in succession planning), none of which is counter-productive, and thus divert resources and energy from other courses of action which may be more successful at gaining the sought-after change. Eagly and Carli (2007) thus contend that a more meaningful metaphor may be that of the 'labyrinth'. It symbolizes a complex journey towards a goal of value to the individual. To negotiate a labyrinth is not a simple or direct endeavour; it requires persistence, an understanding of progress, and careful analysis of the challenges that lie ahead. It is this message they seek to give to women as they aspire to leadership positions. There are routes to the top, but there are many twists and turns that have to be negotiated along the way – both expected and unexpected. However, because all labyrinths have a route through them, the ultimate goal is attainable.

Eagly and Carli (2007) discuss the key barriers that, in their view, make up the labyrinth. These are:

- **Vestiges of prejudice:** men still out-earn women in all developed countries (as discussed above). They also have longer and uninterrupted careers and so are able to progress more rapidly in organizations. Countless studies conducted at a variety of organizational levels all conclude the same thing: the most advantaged group in employment are white, able-bodied men, and all other groups face one or more forms of discrimination.

- **Resistance to women's leadership:** we have discussed the issue of sex-role stereotyping above, and it is this issue which comes to the fore here. There is a clash of assumptions when we are confronted with a woman in a leadership or management position. Women attaining such positions are viewed as likely to be 'deceitful, pushy, selfish, and abrasive', in the absence of any further information, yet there are no such associations for men in such positions.

- **Issues of leadership style:** given this 'clash of assumptions', women often struggle to cultivate a style of leadership with which they and others are comfortable – one which reconciles the dichotomy between women possessing the qualities typically associated with women (but not leaders) and also those associated with leaders. This can lead to a lack of authenticity, where women sacrifice their preferred style too much, and though they satisfy others' views of the kind of leader they should be, this does not fit comfortably with their natural or preferred style. In terms of whether there is a typical women's style of leadership, the evidence seems to indicate that women are likely to have a more collaborative and participative leadership style than men. Interestingly, it is believed that this is not a genetic preference; rather, it is a way of leading as a woman that does not appear to be too masculine.

- **Demands of family life:** women are still likely to retain primary responsibility for family matters. They are more likely to interrupt their careers for family life, take time off when children are ill, and work part-time. As a consequence, they progress more slowly and earn less. In a study of a law firm seeking to understand why few women made it to the most senior positions in such firms, namely partners, it was found that women were constantly having to make trade-offs between work and family life, with the consequence that many left to work in the public sector or to take time out of their careers altogether. Of those who did make partner, 60 per cent were childless and the remainder had waited until they were made partner before starting a family. For women who do make arrangements to manage their work–life balance, there is evidence that they may not be able to enjoy the full benefits of their efforts. As one participant of a study of promotion in a US government agency commented, 'I mean there were two or three names [of women] in the hat, and they said, "I don't want to talk about her because she has children who are still home in these [evening] hours". Now they don't pose that thing about men on the list, many of whom also have children in that age group' (Eagly and Carli, 2007: 68).

- **Underinvestment in social capital:** perhaps one of the biggest casualty of the work–life balancing act that many women have to perform is that it leaves little or no time for socializing with colleagues and attending out-of-hours professional functions. The social capital that accrues from such activity, which is often felt to be 'non-essential', cannot be overstated. Countless studies have shown the benefits of social capital and, most particularly, the career benefits that social capital can bring. These have been articulated by Baker (2000) as information, resources, ideas, advice, etc. However, even when women are willing to engage in networking, they may find it difficult, particularly if the group is predominantly male and the networking activity is structured around typically male activities. A recent gender discrimination lawsuit against Wal-Mart provides such an example. Sam Walton, head of the company, hosted an executive retreat at his ranch that was centred on a quail hunting expedition. It was usual for middle managers' meetings to include visits to strip clubs and restaurants known to treat women in a demeaning manner. A sales conference attended by thousands of store managers had football as its focus, and a female executive received feedback that she was unlikely to advance within the organization because she didn't hunt or fish. It is unsurprising that many women faced with such networking environments, decide not to attend. That their careers are negatively affected by their absence is not in doubt.

Having articulated the key barriers in the labyrinth, Eagly and Carli (2007) conclude that once barriers are recognized, what seemed an impossible path through the labyrinth becomes more traceable. It becomes clearer to women what they must do to negotiate the labyrinth, but it also becomes clearer to leaders and policy makers within organizations where the barriers are and where action needs to be focused.

➔ Student Activity 6.5

Write a briefing paper to the diversity director of an organization you are familiar with (or one you know through secondary research) on how to tackle women's advancement to leadership in the organization. From the bulleted list below, pick the issue that you feel is most pressing in the organization and focus on the following:

1. Where are the vestiges of prejudice and how can they be tackled?

2. In what ways does resistance to women's leadership present itself in the organization and how can it be surfaced and challenged?

3. What are the dominant leadership styles in the organization and how gendered are they? What would you propose to tackle this?

4. What policy recommendations would you make to ensure that the demands of family life are taken into account when planning workloads?

5. How would you ensure that women do not miss out on opportunities to build and develop social capital?

Organizational interventions to address gender diversity

A report compiled by the Lehman's Centre for Diversity and Leadership in 2007, looked at the implementation of gender diversity across Europe. It was noted that though the report focused on the issue of gender diversity implementation, the approach suggested would be of use to the strategic implementation of diversity in general. The study focuses on the process by which 61 companies across Europe implement gender diversity. Key findings from the report are that in implementing gender diversity, four 'waves' of activity are observed.

Wave 1: Measurement and reporting

For many organizations, the starting point of gender diversity implementation has been the measurement and reporting of gender diversity. These measures are typically focused on recruitment (e.g. the gender balance of recruitment panels), induction and progression (e.g. measuring and reporting on the career development of women at key career stages), checking for gender imbalance in salaries, scrutinizing the numbers of women in senior positions, and the measurement and reporting of women's employment turnover rates (i.e. checking that greater numbers of women are not leaving the organization in comparison to men).

While it is common for organizations to track the progression of women through the organizational ranks and to check for salary parity, it is less usual for systematic monitoring to occur in respect of issues such as the numbers of women in internal and external training programmes, or the proportion of women in business critical challenging roles.

As organizations become more familiar with measuring and reporting in this first wave, some use these results to set targets to address issues identified.

Wave 2: Enabling women to be wives, mothers, and carers

A number of companies in the study reported initiatives to support women in respect of their caring responsibilities. These initiatives took the form of flexible work options, leave, and re-entry programmes. Almost all of the organizations in the study offer part-time work and just under 90 per cent of the organizations offer flexible working options. Over 75 per cent offer job share options. However, although policies are in place, there was a significant gap between policy aspirations and day-to-day practice. While flexible working options are offered by almost all the companies participating in the study, just under half of them report that less than 10 per of women managers actually take up these options, and nearly 80 per cent of executives report that less than 20 per cent of managers and senior executives work part-time. Sixty-five per cent of the companies report that less than 10 per cent of their managers are in job shares. An example of good practice is provided by the international law firm, Allen & Overy. In this organization, maternity coaching is available and career breaks of up to three years are offered, as is an emergency childcare service. Such practices combine to provide much needed support for those combining work with the care of children.

Wave 3: Creating supportive networks

The third wave of initiatives observed are those that focus on creating supportive networks for women within the organization. A range of such networks was identified and they included induction networks, professional networks, and external networks. The main aim of these networks is to facilitate the exchange of opinions and to provide support for mentoring and coaching for women. However, company policy tends to lag behind behaviour: 65 per cent of organizations report that they are actively working to create these support networks for women; they also report that 75 per cent of women are participating in such networks. It is thus evident that even where a network does not exist in their own organization, women are seeking externally organized networks to gain support.

An example of such a network is the FTSE cross-company mentoring programme. Twenty-eight Chairmen of FTSE 100 companies have volunteered to mentor senior high-potential women from an organization other than their own (and one which is not a competitor) to provide guidance and support in respect of their career development. Access to mentors of this calibre gives senior high-potential women visibility and also provides legitimation and role modelling for the mentoring of women.

Wave 4: Preparing women to be leaders

In this wave, practices and processes that prepare women to be leaders are considered. Research over the years into leadership has indicated that those who access leadership positions are generally those who have been given access to, and so have experience of, business-critical projects. They also tend to have worked on one or more overseas assignments and they have been successful in the accomplishment of a variety of 'stretching' work assignments. They also tend to have been involved in high-profile, senior leadership training programmes. The research indicates that not only does such a profile prepare individuals for leadership positions, it also provides them with legitimacy once they are within them.

The report concludes that, having reviewed all four waves of intervention, it is evident that the first three waves seem to attract the greatest organizational attention, at least at the policy level. The fourth wave, the active development of women as leaders, is least developed of all, and yet this is possibly the most important if the gender composition of organizational structures is to change. Of those organizations most likely to give attention to the fourth wave of activity, the study showed that is was those with the highest number of women.

⊡ End of Chapter Case Study IBM

This case study concerns a programme developed at IBM to address the needs of its high-potential women. The programme has been titled 'Blue Talent' and seeks to improve the organization's 'pipeline' of future women leaders capable of moving through to executive positions. The programme runs for 12–18 months and focuses on tools and techniques to equip and empower women to take charge of their careers. Key elements include education, opportunities for executive shadowing, one-to-one coaching sessions and networking activities. The programme also provides access to a number of external training opportunities to work with senior executives. For example, in one of the elements of the course the focus is on Building Relationships and Influencing, which utilizes video analysis and peer feedback to enable delegates to understand their personal influencing style. Individual career coaching with a professional coach is also available to participants.

During the course of the programme, women are able to build powerful networks whose purpose is to provide support and enable the development of insight and connectivity across the business. Delegates' progress and advancement through the organization is tracked throughout the programme and they continue to be monitored when the programme is complete. Delegates from previous programmes go on to form their own network – a powerful alumni providing continued support for the group and also for future intakes of 'Blue Talent' women.

Through a focus on the skills development, capabilities, and confidence of its women, IBM believes it is better placed to retain talent and thereby meet current and future business needs. There is little doubt that mentors, role models, and networks are key mechanisms through which organizational careers are advanced. These are integral elements of the programme design and active steps are taken to ensure that previous participants undertake these roles for future delegates. In this way, knowledge and learning are promulgated throughout the organization, and new joiners and those beginning their careers are able to gain a positive image of women in the business. IBM is keenly aware of delivering on these benefits. The programme is to be a long-term initiative, forming part of a wider cultural change initiative.

The programme also benefits from the extensive commitment and support of top leadership. The leadership team is strongly committed to and plays an active part in the executive shadowing element of the programme. The General Manager regularly hosts round-table discussions at which participants are able to debate and discuss key issues with senior organizational members and external speakers.

Access to the programme is through nomination by business leaders who show their commitment to it in terms of time (i.e. allowing participants to attend sessions over the period), but also through financial support as the cost of the programme comes from departmental budgets.

Source: Adapted from: Opportunity Now, UK Diversity Award Winners, 2009; http://www.bitc.org.uk/workplace/ diversity_and_inclusion/race/case_studies/ibm_case_study.html; http://www-05.ibm.com/employment/uk/ consulting/support_benefits/

Case study questions

1. With which 'wave' of gender diversity implementation do you think IBM is engaging in this initiative?

2. In your view, what are the likely benefits to the firm and to those participating in this scheme?

3. What do you think some of the drawbacks might be to the firm, to those participating in the scheme, and to those not chosen to participate?

4. The programme is for women only. What do you imagine the reaction from men in the organization would be to:

   a) the programme itself?

   b) women participants of the programme?

5. The case study indicates that women are chosen to participate in the programme by their business leaders who, in the majority of cases, are likely to be men. Given Eagly and Carli's caution in the labyrinth model in respect of resistance to and issues with women's leadership style, and the work of Schein on sex-role stereotyping, in your view what are the drawbacks of this selection process? What recommendations would you make to overcome these issues?

6. What further information would you like to have before judging this programme a 'success'?

Conclusion

In this chapter we have explored the issue of gender discrimination. We have seen that this is a much researched topic and concerns inequalities in opportunity between the genders. We have discussed a number of competing opinions on the meaning and impact of gender diversity on organizational life, and also a number of competing opinions on how best to tackle the issue. We have explored some of these views and sought to understand those areas in which progress has been made. We have also analyzed and assessed where there is still work to be done. In terms of progress made, evidence has been presented in respect of women's increased participation in key areas of public and organizational life, with particular progress noted in access to and success in education, managerial work, and the professions. However, when looking at senior organizational levels, there is little cause for optimism.

In seeking to understand this position, we found contrasting explanations. Hakim (2000) places the responsibility for lack of progress squarely in the hands of individual women, arguing that their 'preferences' determine their career outcomes (Hakim, 2000). Others challenge this view, with some pointing to the presence and impermeability of the glass ceiling, while others contend that the glass ceiling is a misleading metaphor. A more recent articulation of key barriers to women's advancement and leadership is advanced by Eagly and Carli (2007), who argue that their 'labyrinth model' is more appropriate for understanding the phenomenon.

Equal pay was also discussed as a persistent issue across much of the developed and developing world. Key reasons for continued pay inequality were presented, as were the changes made to reporting with the implementation of the Equality Bill in the public sector and its forthcoming implementation in the private sector.

The final section in the chapter presented key approaches to implementing gender diversity: first, by presenting the findings of the Lehman's Centre for Diversity and Leadership report (2007) and, second, by presenting the case study of IBM and their approach to women's leadership development.

 ## Review and discussion questions

- Why do you think the Government has stopped short of introducing mandatory pay audits into the Equalities Bill for both public and private sector employers? Write a report indicating the main arguments for and against mandatory pay audits, concluding with your recommendations on how best to proceed in respect of this key issue.

- Of the four explanations advanced for the prevalence of the glass ceiling, which do you find most convincing and why?

- Think about Hakim's (2000) 'work-centred' category. In your view, is it possible for women to prioritize work in the way suggested by the model? What personal, societal, and organizational factors do you think would need to be taken into account?

- Do you agree with Eagly and Carli (2007) that the metaphor of the glass ceiling is misleading and focuses attention in the wrong places? In what ways is their 'labyrinth' metaphor an improvement?

- Why do you think the fourth wave of the Lehman's study, 'Preparing Women to be Leaders', is frequently neglected by organizations? How would you persuade senior management in your organization (or in an organization with which you are familiar) to pay attention to this issue?

For additional material on the content of this chapter please visit the supporting Online Resource Centre at **www.oxfordtextbooks.co.uk/orc/kumra_manfredi/**

Further reading

Eagly, A.H. and Carli, L.C. (2007) *Through the Labyrinth: The Truth about How Women Become Leaders.* Cambridge, MA: Harvard Business School Press.

Equality and Human Rights Commission (2008) Sex and Power Report.

Fawcett Society (2009) Closing the Gap: Does Transparency Hold the Key to Unlocking Pay Equality? A Fawcett Society think piece for the Gender Equality Forum. London: Fawcett Society, November 2009. Rowena Lewis and Sharon Smee

Kumra, S. (2010 forthcoming) Exploring career 'choices' of work-centred women in a professional service firm. *Gender in Management: An International Journal.*

Ryan, M. and Haslam, A. (2007) The glass cliff: exploring the dynamics surrounding the appointment of women to precarious leadership positions. *Academy of Management Review,* 32/2: 549–572.

References

Anastasi, A. and Foley, J.P. Jr. (1949) *Differential Psychology.* New York: Macmillan.

Baker, W. (2000) *Achieving Success through Social Capital: Tapping the Hidden Resources in Your Personal and Business Networks.* San Francisco: Jossey-Bass.

Balls, E. (1992) Economics of failure: no jobs for the boys. *New Statesman and Society,* 5: 14–15.

Bolton, S. and Muzio, D. (2008) The paradoxical processes of feminization in the professions: the case of established, aspiring and semi-professions. *Work, Employment and Society,* 22/2: 281–299.

Bradley, H. (1993) Across the Great Divide, in Williams, C. (ed.), *Doing Women's Work: Men in Non-Traditional Occupations.* London: Sage, pp. 10–28.

Brenner, et al. 1989 see Ryan and Haslam?

Crompton, R. and Lyonette, C. (2005) The new gender essentialism – domestic and family 'choices' and their relation to attitudes. *The British Journal of Sociology,* 56/4: 601–620.

Deschenaux, J. (2009) Pay gaps persist throughout Europe. *HR Magazine,* June.

Donkin, R. (2010) *The Future of Work.* Basingstoke: Palgrave Macmillan.

Eagly, A.H. and Carli, L.C. (2007) *Through the Labyrinth: The Truth about How Women Become Leaders.* Cambridge, MA: Harvard Business School Press.

Equality and Human Rights Commission (2008) Sex and Power Report.

European Commission (2009) *Equality between Women and Men* (Report). Brussels: European Commission.

Fagenson, E.A. (1990) Perceived masculine and feminine attributes as a function of sex and level in the organizational hierarchy. *Journal of Applied Psychology,* 75: 204–211.

Fawcett Society (2008) *Closing the Inequality Pay Gap between Men and Women.* London: Fawcett Society.

Fawcett Society (2009) Closing the Gap: Does Transparency Hold the Key to Unlocking Pay Equality? A Fawcett Society think piece for the Gender Equality Forum. London: Fawcett Society, November. Rowena Lewis and Sharon Smee

Floge, L. and Merrill, D. (1989) Tokenism reconsidered: male nurses and female physicians in a hospital setting. *Social Forces,* 64/4: 925–947.

Gallagher, J. (1994) QUANGOS: Jobs for the boys. *New Statesman and Society,* 7: 16.

Hakim, C. (2000) *Work-Lifestyle Choices in the 21st Century.* New York: Oxford University Press.

Heikes, J. (1992) When men are in the minority: the case of men in nursing. *The Sociological Quarterly,* 32/3: 389–401.

Heilman, M.E., Block, C.J., Martell, R.F., and Simon, M.C. (1989) Has anything changed? Current characterizations of men, women and managers. *Journal of Applied Psychology,* 74: 935–942.

Hochschild, A. (1983) *The Managed Heart: Commercialisation of Feeling.* Berkeley, CA: University of California Press.

Inter-Parliamentary Union (2008) Women in national parliaments as of 31 July 2008.

Judge, E. (2003) Women on board: Help or hindrance? *The Times*, 11 November, p. 21.

Kanter, R.M. (1977) *Men and Women of the Corporation.* New York: Basic Books.

Kumra, S. (2003) The Influence of Impression Management Strategies on the Promotion to Partner Process: A Gendered Perspective. Unpublished PhD thesis, Cranfield School of Management.

Lehman's Centre for Diversity and Leadership (2007) *Inspiring Women: Corporate Best Practice in Europe.*

Lupton, B. (2000) Maintaining masculinity: men who do women's work. *British Journal of Management*, 11: S33–48.

Maccoby, E.E. (ed.) (1966) *The Development of Sex Differences.* Stanford, CA: Stanford University Press.

Madouros, V. (2006) *Labour Force Projections 2006–20.* London: Office for National Statistics.

Mainiero, L.A. (1994) Getting anointed for advancement: the case of executive Women. *Academy of Management Executive*, 8/2: 53–67.

McRae, S. (1993) Returning to work after childbirth: opportunities and inequalities. *European Sociological Review*, 9: 125–138.

Morrison, A.M. and Von Glinow, M.A. (1990) Women and minorities in Management. *American Psychologist*, 45: 200–208.

Office for National Statistics (2007) Population Estimates by Ethnic Group 2001–2005 (experimental). London: Office for National Statistics.

Office for National Statistics (2008) Labour Force Survey, Historical Quarterly Supplement – Calendar quarters. Available at [add website] (accessed 27 August 2008).

Opportunity Now (2009) Diversity Award Winners – Case Studies.

Powell, G.N. and Butterfield, D.A. (2002) Exploring the influence of decision makers' race and gender on actual promotions to top management. *Personnel Psychology*, 55: 397–428.

Ragins, B.R. and Sundstrom, E. (1989) Gender and power in organizations. *Psychological Bulletin*, 105: 51–88.

Rosenkrantz, P., Vogel, S., Bee, H., Broverman, I., and Broverman, D.M. (1968) Sex-role stereotypes and self-concepts in college students. *Journal of Consulting and Clinical Psychology*, 32: 287–295.

Ryan, M. and Haslam, A. (2007) The glass cliff: exploring the dynamics surrounding the appointment of women to precarious leadership positions. *Academy of Management Review*, 32/2: 549–572.

Schein, V.E. (1973) The relationship between sex role stereotypes and requisite management characteristics. *Journal of Applied Psychology*, 57: 95–100.

Schein, V.E. (1975) Relationships between sex role stereotypes and requisite management characteristics among female managers. *Journal of Applied Psychology*, 60/3: 340–344.

Schein, V.E. and Mueller, R. (1992) see Ryan and Haslam.

Schein, V.E. et al. (1989) see Ryan and Haslam

Schein, V.E., Mueller, R., Lituchy, T., and Liu, J. (1996) Think manager-think male: a global phenomenon? *Journal of Organizational Behaviour*, 36: 112–126.

Simpson, R. (2004) Masculinity at work: the experiences of men in female-dominated occupations. *Work, Employment & Society*, 18/2: xxx–xxx.

SRU (Law Society Strategic Research Unit) (2006a) *Trends in the Solicitors' Profession: Annual Statistical Report.* London: Law Society.

SRU (Law Society Strategic Research Unit) (2006b) *Number of Solicitors since 1950* [Fact Sheet Information Series]. London: Law Society.

Williams, C. (ed.) (1993) *Doing Women's Work: Men in Non-Traditional Occupations.* London: Sage.

Wilson, R., Homenidou, K., and Dickerson, A. (2006) *Working Futures 2004–14, National Report.* Wath on Dearne: Sector Skills Development Agency.

Managing Disability in the Workplace

Learning objectives

- Explain disability-related patterns of disadvantage and discrimination in the labour market
- Define different models of disability
- Understand the legal context relating to managing disability in the workplace, including the implications of the equality duty for public sector employers and educational institutions
- Define perceptions and manifestations of disability discrimination in the workplace
- Explain what the concept of 'reasonable adjustment' means and provide examples of how this is applied in practice

Key terms

- **Affirmative model of disability**: this model seeks to promote a positive discourse on disability by moving away from the notion that disability is a 'personal tragedy' (Swain and French, 2000). It also suggests that an impairment should be viewed as an 'ordinary characteristic' of human experience rather than as an 'extraordinary characteristic' (Cameron, 2008).
- **Disability**: this can be defined as 'a consequence of processes that exclude people from society' (Howard, 2003: 4).
- **Impairment**: this can be defined as 'problems with the function or structure of the body' (Howard, 2003: 4).
- **Medical model of disability**: a model that locates the issue of disability with an individual.
- **Reasonable adjustment**: the legal duty to make reasonable adjustments to try to remove disadvantages faced by disabled workers. Examples include changing the physical environment to enable access to a building, providing specialist equipment to help disabled workers, or to change working hours to make work possible for a disabled worker.
- **Social model of disability**: this model distinguishes between the notion of impairment and disability and, unlike the medical model, it locates the issue of disability with society. It is based on the idea that 'it is not individual limitations, of whatever kind, which are the cause of the problem, but society's failure to provide appropriate services and adequately ensure that the needs of the disabled people are fully taken into account in its social organization' (Oliver, 1996: 32).

Introduction

This chapter examines disability equality issues and how these can be managed in the workplace in order to support disabled workers. Protection against disability discrimination in the workplace was introduced relatively recently within the European Union, with the adoption of the Council Equality Directive (2000/78). Prior to this only a few member states had disability equality legislation in place and one of these was the UK. On a wider international level, the United Nation Convention on the rights of disabled people aims to achieve similar goals, and it has been signed by many countries around the world. However, in spite of these measures, disabled people are still significantly disadvantaged and discriminated against, and are more at risk of economic exclusion compared to other social groups, as highlighted by some of the evidence reviewed in this chapter.

In order to understand how disability issues are managed in the workplace it is important to discuss how disability has been defined and understood. Main disability models are explored, including the social model of disability, which has stemmed from the Disability Movement in the late 1960s and early 1970s. This model distinguishes between impairment and disability and locates the latter in the socio-structural barriers which exclude people with impairments. This way of thinking has deeply influenced contemporary perceptions of disability which are reflected in the use of terminology. For the purpose of clarity and consistency, in this chapter we define 'impairments' as 'problems with the function or structure of the body' and 'disability' as 'a consequence of processes that exclude people from society', as suggested by Howard (2003: 4). Thus throughout this chapter we have chosen to use the expression 'disabled people', which is most commonly used in the UK, and reflects the social model of disability. However, we are aware that in other countries the expression 'people with disability' is more commonly used, as reflected for example by some of the sources cited in this chapter (in the interest of accuracy we have used the expression 'people with disabilities' when used in the original source).

The rest of this chapter focuses on perceptions of disability discrimination and explores how this manifests itself in the labour market. It concludes with a section looking at managing disability in the workplace which presents a range of practical examples of action that can be taken by employers to support the full integration of disabled people in the workplace.

Policy context: disability issues and the labour market

Measuring employment rates of disabled people across the globe is not easy due to the difficulties of finding available or comparable data. However, work undertaken on an international level shows that across OECD countries only one in four disabled people have a job. Also, disabled people appear to benefit less from economic growth and to be more likely to be disadvantaged by economic crises (EU–US Seminar on Employment of Persons with Disabilities, 2009).

A study undertaken for the International Labour Office (Buckup, 2009) has highlighted that there are approximately 650 million disabled people across the world and about 80 per cent of them live in developing countries. They are more likely to suffer disadvantage and discrimination and, as a result, their opportunities to take part in paid employment and enjoy an independent life can be significantly reduced. A similar picture can be observed in developed countries where there is still a significant employment gap between disabled and non-disabled people. In the UK, for example, as shown in Table 7.1, employment and self-employment rates of disabled people are lower compared to those of non-disabled people, while rates of unemployment and of economic inactivity for disabled people are significantly higher compared to those of non-disabled people.

The exclusion of disabled people from the labour market and reduced opportunities for them in the workplace are not only against social justice, but also carry significant costs for societies. Thus a number of initiatives have been taken by international organizations and by individual states to support the integration of disabled people in the labour market. For example, the European Commission has developed a series of strategies to encourage the 'mainstreaming of disability issues'. The concept of 'mainstreaming' was first adopted by the European Commission within the context of gender equality and it has been extended to include other equality strands such as disability. In general, mainstreaming can be defined as the process of analyzing relevant policy areas from an equality perspective (e.g. gender, disability, age, etc.) to make sure that the needs of people belonging to different social groups are being taken into account when developing policies. The application of the concept of mainstreaming to disability means that the interests of disabled people will need to be taken into account when formulating employment policies to facilitate their integration in the labour market. This can be achieved by removing barriers for disabled people to access paid work, but equally by acknowledging and valuing their contribution to the economy and society as a whole. For this purpose, a series of Disability Action Plans (DAPs) have been adopted on a two-yearly basis to identify policy priorities that address disability-related inequalities. For example, the 2008–2009 DAP (2007) focused on accessibility and set out the following priorities:

- fostering accessibility of the labour market (through flexisecurity, supported employment and working with Public Employment Services)
- boosting accessibility of goods, services, and infrastructures
- consolidating the Commission's analytical capacity to support accessibility (through studies, etc.)
- facilitating the implementation of the UN Convention
- complementing the Community legislative framework of protection against discrimination.

online resource centre

For further details and a link to the EU Disability Action Plan website visit the Online Resource Centre.

Table 7.1 Employment rates for disabled and non-disabled people in the UK, 2010

	Employed (%)	Self-employed ( )	Unemployed (%)	Inactive ( )
Disabled	41.5	6.9	11	45.6
Non-disabled	67.9	9.6	7.5	16.2

Source: Office for Disability Issues, Roadmap 2025 Disability Equality Indicators, available at http://odi.dwp.gov.uk/roadmap-to-disability-equality/employment.php.

Recent economic crises have led to the reduction of social budgets and welfare benefits have been significantly cut in many countries. This in many cases has had a negative impact on measures to integrate disabled people in paid employment and support their independent living.

How is disability defined and understood?

In order to understand disability issues in the context of the workplace, it is important to review the different models and definitions of disability that have been developed, and to explore how disability has been understood and how these models have influenced policies and perceptions about disabled people.

The late 1960s and early 1970s represented a turning point in the way disability is understood within societies, as radical thinking permeated disabled people's organizations which started to question social perceptions of disability. It has been suggested that these changes were driven by an '"age of affluence" when disabled people began to organize themselves around issues of income, employment, rights and community living rather than institutional care' (Campbell and Oliver, 1996: 20–21). Until then, disability was represented as a medical problem and an issue for an individual, an approach known as the 'medical model' which focused on 'cure' (Howard, 2003: 5). However, in order to address these issues it was necessary to rethink how disability is represented and perceived within society. The first step towards a radical rethinking of what disability meant involved a debate to address the following fundamental questions (Finkelstein, 2004: 15):

- 'Whether disabled people are incapable of social functioning because of their impairments, or
- Whether society is constructed by people with capabilities for people with capabilities in such a way that it makes it difficult for people with impairments to be able to function'.

This encouraged a new way of thinking which led to a shift from understanding disability and impairments as a medical problem, and an issue for an individual, to an issue for society. In particular, it was argued that a distinction had to be drawn between impairment and disability as 'disability only exists in so far as it is socially constructed and imposed on people with impairments' (Llewellyn and Hogan, 2000: 159). This distinction became a key factor in looking at disability from a new perspective: although it acknowledges that people may have impairments, it also stresses that this does not mean that they cannot function. Following this logic, a disability is not the consequence of having an impairment, but it is the result of limitations within the environment that surrounds an individual. For example, a wheelchair user is disabled by the lack of ramps to access buildings or means of transport; a blind person is disabled by the lack of written information available in Braille. This distinction underpins what has become known as the 'social model', which, as highlighted by Oliver (1996: 32) 'it does not deny the problem of disability but locates it squarely within society. It is not individual limitations, of whatever kind, which are the cause of the problem but society's failure to provide appropriate services and adequately ensure that the needs of the disabled people are fully taken into account in its social organisation.' Thus unlike the 'medical model' which locates the issue of disability with an individual, the 'social model' locates the issue of disability with society. It is the way in which the latter is organized that creates barriers for those people who have impairments and exclude them, for example, from the labour market and other aspects of social life. In summary, it should not be assumed that because a person has an impairment that this will affect her or his ability to function (Bajekal et al., 2004).

The 'social model' of disability has been adopted by several policy makers and it has helped to focus action on the integration of disabled people in the labour market (EU–US Seminar on Employment of Persons with Disabilities, 2009). This is clearly evidenced, for example, by the UK Disability Rights Commission (DRA) (subsequently merged into the Equality and Human Rights Commission), which expressly stated in its strategic plan that:

> The DRA will be guided by the social model of disability. . . . We believe the barriers that exclude disabled people from full participation in society are the result the way the social and built environment are constructed, and society's attitudes towards disabled people, rather than just the result of individual impairments. A key part of our work will be to address, in a strategic way, those social structures and attitudes that have a disabling effect. The social model of disability is the most suitable model to adopt in our work. (Disability Rights Commission, 2001, cited in Campbell, 2002: 473)

Although the social model has been the product of radical thinking from the Disabled People's Movement in the 1970s, and it is now widely adopted by policy makers in many countries, nonetheless it has attracted criticism from some authors for neglecting the notion of impairment and the impact that this can have on an individual's life (Swain and French, 2000). Also, both the social and the medical models have been criticized since they treat a disabled person as 'a passive victim either or their condition or their social situation' (Howard, 2003: 6).

Alternative models have been proposed and these are: the 'bio-psychosocial (BPS) model' and the 'interactionist model'. According to the BPS model, both impairment and the environment can contribute to disability. It places an individual's impairment into a context which is both personal to the individual concerned, but also recognizes her social environment. In the interactionist model, the problem is located neither entirely in the individual nor entirely in society, as predicated by the medical or the social model, respectively, but it is seen as the result of a social process which involves the interaction between an individual and her environment. From this perspective, disability is also a 'dynamic' process that 'could be altered through elements of both individual and social change, and targeted where they occur' (ibid.: 5). Both of these models offer a more holistic perspective about disability which takes account of the impact of an impairment on an individual and of the existence of disabling factors within society. Table 7.2 outlines the implications of these different models when applied in practice.

Table 7.2 Implications of the different models of disability

	Medical	Social	BPS	Interactionist
Barriers/problem	Disability results from impairment	Disability results from society's failure to adapt	Disability results from impairment but also depends on psychosocial and social factors	Disability is the outcome of a social process – an individual's interaction with social and environmental systems
Bridges/solutions	Medical treatment and rehabilitation	Society has to remove barriers	Combination of health care, rehabilitation, personal effort, and the modification of social situation interactions	Removal of barriers at appropriate levels, e.g. socially created barriers, and changes to systems and individual attributes where possible
Assumptions about work	Disabled people can't work	Disabled people are excluded from work	More disabled people can work if individual, psychosocial, and systems barriers are removed	More disabled people can work if different levels of barriers are tackled and under the right conditions
Focus of intervention	Individual/supply side	Employer's demand side	Individuals, health care professionals, and employers	Individuals, employers, and systems

Source: Howard (2003: 6)

More recently, a new perspective on disability has emerged, the 'Affirmative Model of Disability'. This model seeks to move away from the idea that sees disability as a 'personal tragedy' in favour of a 'non-tragic view' of disability and impairments (Swain and French, 2000). Furthermore, as part of an evolving discussion about the Affirmative Model of Disability, it has also been suggested that an impairment should be viewed as an 'ordinary characteristic' of human experience rather than an 'extraordinary characteristic' (Cameron, 2008). In other words, this means that the chances of being born with an impairment or developing one throughout a life course are part of the human experience and therefore should not be seen as extraordinary characteristics. In particular, in the light of the increase in people's life expectancy, we are all more likely to develop impairments at some point in our life as we get older. Equally, as a result of medical and technological advances, increasingly people can either be cured from a number of impairments or the impact of these impairments on individuals may be minimized.

In the next section we take an overview of the legal framework to prevent and sanction discrimination against disabled people in the workplace, and consider how the social model of disability has influenced legislative developments.

Debate Box

Adolf Ratzka, a disabled activist from Germany, contested the use of the universal wheelchair sign and stated that: 'By using this symbol of access you do yourself a disservice, because the symbol serves as an alibi for the accepted norm of inaccessibility, emphasizing the exception rather than the rule' (Ratzka, 1998, cited in Campbell, 2002).

Organize the class into two groups, one for the motion and one against.

The motion is:
Wheelchair signs should be banned as they reinforce the idea that wheelchair access to buildings is just an exception rather than the norm.

Stages in the debate: (each stage is given with timings, the overall time for the activity is 55 minutes – allowing a few minutes for change over of presenters, etc.)

- Each group has 20 minutes to prepare their arguments either for or against the motion.
- Each group is given 5 minutes to present their opening statement (10 minutes in total).
- Groups reconvene for 10 minutes to prepare rebuttal arguments.
- Each group has 2 minutes to present rebuttal arguments.

A vote is taken and the winners of the debate announced; the casting vote goes to impartial observers: tutors, audience members not involved in the debate, and observers.

The legal context

In many countries, legal provisions to ban discrimination on the grounds of disability were introduces relatively recently, following the adoption of the European Equality Directive (2000/78) which prohibited discrimination on the grounds of age, disability, sexual orientation, and religion or belief. Prior to the adoption of this Directive only a few countries in Europe had legislation in place to protect disabled people against discrimination. One of these was the UK, which introduced the Disability Discrimination Act (DDA) in 1995. This replaced the Disabled Person (Employment) Act 1944. Under the 1944 legislation, employers employing 20 or more employees were required to adopt a quota system and reserve 3 per cent of their jobs for registered disabled people. Under these provisions employers were not allowed to employ non-disabled people if they were below this quota.

However, in the UK, for practical reasons, this system failed (Connolly, 2004) but it should be noted that quotas for employing disabled people are still used in several countries. For example, 16 out of the 27 EU countries have a quota system (EU–US Seminar on Employment of Persons with Disabilities, 2009). This system is underpinned by a 'radical approach' to equality, which is informed by the principle of fairness of distribution of rewards and resources among different social groups and focuses on equality of outcomes as opposed to equality of

Signpost to
Chapter 3
From Equal
Opportunities
to Managing
Diversity

opportunities (this approach is fully discussed in Chapter 3). However, its application to disability has been criticized because, although the aim of a quota system is to ensure that disabled people have access to jobs, it provides them with employment opportunities irrespective of their merits. As highlighted by Connolly (2004), this can raise a number of problems. First, it can reinforce negative stereotypes about disabled people and encourage the view among employers that disabled people can only do jobs which involve a low level of skills. Second, it can be viewed as a rather paternalist approach since 'it imposes a solution on disabled people rather than empowering individuals by the granting of rights' (Connolly, 2004: 426). Third, it singles out disabled people as a separate category and this appears to run counter to the social model discussed above, which locates disability within society rather than with an individual. Finally, as demonstrated by the UK experience, a quota system in practice may not be very effective. This may be due to the fact that often employers can argue and obtain exemptions from it, and because of the reluctance of the authorities to enforce it and interfere with business operations.

The DDA was adopted in the UK in 1995, following the example of other jurisdictions such as the USA and Australia. This was then extended to schools, educational authorities, and higher education. The 2005 Disability Discrimination Act broadened disability legislation to the public sector, requiring public authorities to take action to eliminate disability discrimination. This legislation has now been replaced by the 2010 Equality Act, which imposes a single public sector equality duty on public sector organizations and in higher education and covers all the protected characteristics.

The legal definition of disability has already been discussed in Chapter 2. However, it is useful to remind ourselves here that a person is defined as disabled if she has a physical or mental impairment which has a substantial and long-term adverse effect on her ability to carry out normal day-to-day activities. It is important to stress that the legal definition of disability covers both mental health (e.g. depression, schizophrenia, bipolar disorder, etc.) as well as physical disabilities. Conditions such as cancer, multiple sclerosis, or HIV/AIDS are also covered, even though these illnesses may at first have no symptoms which impair day-to-day activities. This is because it is accepted that these conditions are progressive and are likely to lead to impairments in the ability to carry out day-to-day activities. Day-to-day activities are defined as normal daily life activities, such as getting up in the morning, getting washed and dressed, walking a certain distance, carry a bag of shopping, and an ability to undertake paid work. For reasons of space, we have chosen to focus on the UK legal framework, although it is important to note that legal definitions of disability may vary in different countries as well as in the content of disability anti-discrimination legislation and the type of conditions that are covered.

A distinctive feature of the legislation to protect disabled people against discrimination in the workplace is the duty for employers to make 'reasonable adjustments' to work practices and to premises in order to remove any disadvantage that these may cause to disabled employees. Failure to comply with the duty to make reasonable adjustments amounts to discrimination, for which employers can be held liable. The content of this duty is discussed in more detail in Chapter 2, and later in this chapter, where we provide examples of some of the types of adjustments which can be made in the workplace to comply with this duty. Here it is important to highlight that in order to achieve equality for disabled people, the legislation provides for preferential treatment in the form of an obligation to make 'reasonable adjustments' to the workplace environment and/or practices. This approach reflects a substantive model of equality that recognizes the importance of acknowledging and accommodating difference in order to achieve equality for disabled people.

One of the main criticisms that has been levelled at the Equality Act with regard to its provisions relating to disability is that it is still based on a medical model of disability rather than on the social model. As highlighted by Hepple (2011), the Act focuses on an individual's impairment and whether it can be shown that this is a long-term and substantial impairment that warrants legal protection. It does not consider the types of barrier that an individual may face as a result of her impairment within society. Hepple also points out that this approach contrasts with that taken by the UN Convention on the Rights of Persons with Disabilities (2006), which was signed and ratified by the UK government in 2009. This Convention recognizes that 'disability is an evolving concept which results from the interaction between persons with impairments and attitudinal and environmental barriers that hinder their full and effective participation in society'. Hepple concludes that 'the implications of this approach are that everyone with an impairment should be protected, without requiring the effects of that impairment to be substantial or long term' (2011: 35).

It is also worth noting that it is not only the law relating to disability that continues to be based on the medical model of disability, but also the system of welfare benefits, which is of fundamental importance in upholding the right to independent living for disabled people. At the time of writing, there is public debate about the UK government's decision to cut disability benefits as part of a wider programme of cuts to the whole of the benefit system. The government claims that their reform is aimed at encouraging the greater integration of disabled people in paid employment. As a result, thousands of disability benefit claimants are being reassessed and declared fit for work, which means that they will be able to claim a reduced level of benefits. The government policy approach appears to rely entirely on a medical assessment of an individual's impairment and to ignore the difficulties and barriers that disabled people experience in society, and particularly in the labour market. This government policy is causing serious concern among disabled people, many of whom took place in an unprecedented public demonstration in London in May 2011. In an article published by *The Guardian* newspaper on 12 May 2011, one of the demonstrators neatly summarized some of the barriers faced by disabled people in the labour market by saying 'When I apply for jobs I am seen as a health and safety risk' (Guardian, 2011).

Signpost to Chapter 2 An Outline of European and UK Equality Legislation

---

⊙ Student Activity 7.1

Guess who among the following famous people was/is disabled:

- The music composer Ludwig von Beethoven
- The Nobel Prize winner Albert Einstein
- The first president of the United States, George Washington
- The actor Leonardo di Caprio
- The footballer David Beckham
- The actress Julia Roberts
- The musician and singer John Lennon

To find out the correct answers, go to the ORC resources for this chapter.

Disability discrimination

In spite of the introduction of anti-discrimination legislation there is persistent evidence that perceptions of disability discrimination are widespread. A survey carried out by the European Commission (2009: 11–12) about perceptions of discrimination across the EU shows that the majority of the respondents (53 per cent) believes that discrimination based on disability is widespread. It also highlights that there are significant variations across different European countries. For example, the countries where discrimination on the grounds of disability is perceived to be most widespread are France (74 per cent), Latvia, Hungary (both 64 per cent), Belgium, Greece (both 63 per cent), and the Netherlands (62 per cent). Those countries where this perception is least common are Ireland (35 per cent), Turkey (34 per cent), and Malta (33 per cent). The results from this survey also suggest that people who defined themselves as disabled are more likely to say that discrimination on the grounds of disability is widespread.

At the beginning of this chapter we saw that there are significant labour market inequalities between disabled and non-disabled people, and discrimination against disabled people may be one of the explanations for the existence of such marked differences. Experiences in both the UK and the USA about the application of anti-discrimination legislation on the grounds of disability suggest that the law is more likely to have a positive impact on disabled people who are already employed than on those who are out of work and are trying to get a job (EU–US Seminar on Employment of Persons with Disabilities, 2009). Negative perceptions of disability by employers and by the general public can be a significant barrier for disabled people in either securing or maintaining employment. This was clearly identified as an issue in a study undertaken in Canada with a group of 56 disabled people (Shier et al., 2009). The study reported that employers' lack of understanding about disability and a tendency to label disabled people can make it difficult for them to disclose their disability for fear of being discriminated against. As one participant in the study explained:

> I won't use the word afraid to let people know that I'm disabled, but I find that if I let them know ahead of time it might give them a set of reasons to say, 'don't bother coming for the interview, because we want someone who is more capable', for the lack of a better word. (Shier et al., 2009: 68)

The same study shows that employers' negative perceptions or lack of understanding of disability can lead them to disregard or undervalue disabled people's qualifications. Thus this study stresses in its conclusions the importance of providing employers with better education and understanding about different types of disability in order to avoid discrimination.

With regard to staff recruitment practices in relation to disabled applicants, a study undertaken on behalf of the UK Department of Work and Pensions (Thornton, 2005: 67) found that non-disabled job applicants 'were 150 per cent' more likely to receive a positive answer from employers compared to disabled applicants. Employers were also asked about the likelihood of employing single parents, long-term unemployed people, and disabled people. Their responses revealed that only 62 per cent of the employers surveyed indicated that they were prepared to employ disabled people with physical impairments, and that only 37 per cent to employ people with mental health issues (ibid.: 68).

The findings from this research highlight that disabled people are not a homogeneous group and that the nature of their impairment may also have an impact on the likelihood of them experiencing discrimination in the labour market. People with mental health issues seem to be particularly disadvantaged. For example, in the UK only 19 per cent of people with mental health issues of working age are in paid work compared to 48 per cent of disabled people in general (Sayce, 2003). Research about employers' attitudes towards workers with mental health issues in the workplace shows a mixed picture (Shaw Trust, 2010). On the positive side, it appears to indicate that there has been a general improvement in employers' understanding of mental health issues. For instance, more employers named anxiety and depression as examples of mental health issues. Moreover, it was found that the proportion of employers who acknowledged that they employed someone with mental health issues had increased significantly from 11 per cent in 2006 to 21 per cent 2010. However, on a less positive note, 42 per cent of employers still underestimate the prevalence of mental health issues in the workplace. For example, a high proportion of them, 71 per cent, still do not seem to have a policy in place to support this group. This study also concluded that overall there are still significant barriers for job applicants with mental health issues to access to jobs.

These studies suggest that people with mental health issues are more likely to be at risk of 'economic exclusion' (Pillai et al., 2007: 45). Sayce (2003) highlights how stereotyping about this group, which is reinforced by mass media portraying negative images of mental health issues, can have a profound impact about the way people in this group are perceived. Yet depression is a common condition and it has been predicted that by 2020 there will be 'a notable increase in the number of people with mental health impairments across all younger age groups' (Pillai et al., 2007: 49). However, mental health issues in many societies seem to carry a stigma. It is useful here to cross-reference to the concept of stigma, which is fully discussed in Chapter 9 in the context of sexual orientation. As highlighted in that chapter, members of stigmatized groups find themselves marginalized, the subject of negative social identities, and frequently the targets of discrimination (Crocker et al., 1998; Goffman, 1963; Ragins et al., 2007). This can apply to disabled people, and especially those with mental health issues, and it may explain, at least in part, the reasons for them being even less integrated in the labour market than disabled people in general. Also, mental health issues, unlike other types of impairment, are not visible, and the way in which these issues are stigmatized in societies can make it more difficult for those who are affected to disclose them.

Signpost to Chapter 9 Managing Sexual Orientation and Transgender in the Workplace

Recently, there has been a number of cases reported by the press of celebrities or other well-known public figures who have 'come out' and publicly revealed that they suffer with mental health issues. One of these cases is that of the actress Catherine Zeta-Jones, who revealed that she had been treated for bipolar disorder (*The Guardian*,15 April 2011). Another well-known figure who has disclosed having experienced a mental breakdown, is Alistair Campbell, the former press secretary to the former British Prime Minister Tony Blair. Campbell acts as an ambassador for an organization called Time to Change that is campaigning to change attitudes towards mental issues. In the article mentioned above, he commented about the news relating to the actress Zeta-Jones and warned there is a risk that a focus on celebrities with mental issues 'tends to get in the way' of spreading the key message about mental issues. This is that anyone may experience them at some stage in their lives. He stressed that it is important not to reinforce 'one of the myths, that mental illness hits creative, achieving people'.

> ### ➡ Student Activity 7.2
>
> Visit the Online Resource Centre. Click on the video link and answer the following questions:
>
> - What strikes you about the manager's reaction when he hears from the new employee that he has a history of depression?
> - Why do you think the manager reacted in the way he did?
> - How do you think the manager's reaction is perceived by the new employees?
> - If you had been the manager, how would you have handled this situation?

Aversive disablism

Another form of prejudice towards disabled people is what has been defined as 'aversive disablism' (Deal, 2007). This concept has been borrowed from the literature about aversive racism and it is applied to the experience of disabled people. Deal suggests that, similar to aversive racism, 'aversive disablism' can manifest itself as a subtle form of prejudice that is often unintentional but still highly damaging. Although people may not be anti-disabled individuals, nonetheless they may tend to be more pro-non-disabled individuals. This kind of attitude can influence the way employers interact with disabled people. For example, even though they have good intentions, employers may not offer disabled employees opportunities to take on additional responsibilities or undertake training as they try to 'protect' them from additional work pressure. In other words, disabled employees may be perceived as

> ### ▣ Case study 7.1   Discrimination in mental health issues: two cases
>
> Consider the actions of the employers in the two following cases:
>
> In 2001 Ms X, who worked as a customer service manager in an educational publishing company, took her employer to court after she was sacked for misconduct while she was a psychiatric in-patient. Her performance and conduct at work had been affected by a 'high' phase relating to her psychiatric condition.
>
> Ms Y was offered a job as a finger-printing officer with a police force. However, the offer was withdrawn when her employer found out that she had been diagnosed with manic depression. She challenged this decision and took the employer to court.
>
> *Source:* Sayce (2003: 630)
>
> ....
>
> #### Case study questions
>
> 1. What are the differences and similarities in both cases?
> 2. Do you think that the actions of the employers were justified?
> 3. How do you think that these cases were decided by the employment tribunal?
>
> Look on the online resources to find out how these cases were decided.

being more vulnerable compared to non-disabled employees, and this can undermine their career opportunities.

Deal (2007) has also highlighted how information technology can contribute towards aversive disablism. Although technology has had a positive impact in supporting disabled people's integration in the workplace, it can still have the unintended consequence of isolating disabled employees. Deal offers the example of an internet training course for employees with restricted mobility as an alternative to attending a course, which may be located away from the employer's premises. Although this may be more convenient for an employee with restricted mobility than having to access a different location, it may also deny her an opportunity of networking with her colleagues (ibid.: 100).

Debate Box

Organize the class into two groups, one for the motion and one against.

The motion is:
There is still a lot of prejudice against disabled people which prevents them from becoming better integrated in the workplace. The only way to overcome this problem is to follow the example of those countries which have adopted a quota system. Quotas can work if there is the political will to make them work.

Follow the stages for the debate as given above.

Managing disability in the workplace

In this section we discuss evidence from research to understand how disability is actually managed by employers and consider examples of action that can be taken at an organizational level to promote disability equality. We start by considering to what extent an Equal Opportunity (EO) approach or a Diversity Management (DM) approach can support the integration of disabled people in the workplace and tackle inequalities. These two approaches are fully discussed in Chapter 3. Here we shall only mention that an EO approach is driven by the principle of social justice, while a DM approach is driven by the 'business case'. The latter focuses on an individual's differences and the need to maximize the potential of all workers (Kandola and Fullerton, 1994a, 1994b).

A number of organizations, for example the Employer Forum on Disability in the UK, have tried to promote a 'business case' for employing disabled people. However, more recently, it has been questioned whether 'a business case can be constructed around a diverse group of people who may need very different (and perhaps) contradictory adjustments' (Howard, 2006: 81). This point is further articulated by Woodhams and Danieli (2000), who argue that it can be difficult to demonstrate that initiatives for disabled people can make good business sense. They suggest that the reason for this is the greater heterogeneity of disabled people compared to other groups. They draw a comparison with another potentially disadvantaged group, women, to show that while it can make good business sense for some organizations to adopt 'women friendly' practices, this could prove more problematic in the case of disabled people. For example, there can be a good business case for organizations, particularly if they employ a lot of women, to develop flexible working or childcare facilities since these can help female employees to combine paid work with their caring responsibilities. These initiatives can ensure greater staff retention, a reduction of absenteeism and, consequently, a return on the organization's investment.

However, Woodhams and Danieli argue that it would very difficult for organizations to put in place initiatives that could potentially benefit disabled people as a group. Because of the great heterogeneity of different types of impairment, such initiatives would require a major reorganization of the workplace. This would involve reviewing communication systems, premises, work stations, and office equipment as well as incurring in significant costs. Even if a workplace could undergo such a major reorganization, there is no guarantee that barriers for disabled people would be removed, since what may be needed for one type of impairment may not be needed for another. Another argument that is often used in support of the business case for diversity is that a diverse workforce can better reflect customer diversity. However, Woodhams and Danieli highlight that there is insufficient evidence to show that 'disabled customers are especially attracted to organizations where disabled people work' 2000: 411).

Research undertaken by Dibben et al. (2002) has also explored the link between the 'business case' and disability-related practices adopted by organizations. These authors analyzed the annual reports of 100 listed companies. They assessed the influence of the business case against a set of disability-related practices, including recruitment, training, career development, and workplace adjustment, among other things. They found that, with the exception of training, organizations with lower profitability were more likely to make reference to disability-related practices. They suggest that the concept of corporate social responsibility (CRS) appears to have a greater influence on the adoption of disability-related organizational practices. Thus interventions to support disabled people in the workplace appear to be driven by an EO approach and the concept of social justice.

Recruiting disabled people

Research discussed earlier in this chapter shows that disabled people are less likely to be successful as job applicants compared to non-disabled people, and this suggests that they may be discriminated against at the recruitment stage. This might be caused by employers' lack of awareness about disability legislation, or their unwillingness to make adjustments in their staff recruitment and selection procedures to support disabled applicants.Equally, it can be due to a possible lack of understanding of different types of disability. Research undertaken for the UK Department of Work and Pensions about the employment of disabled people, based on a sample of over a 1,000 organizations of different sizes, shows that most employers associate disability with mobility restrictions (83 per cent), while relatively few employers are aware that conditions like diabetes (14 per cent), HIV (13 per cent), or facial disfigurement (11 per cent) are disabilities (Dewson et al., 2009: 27). These conditions tend to be viewed as illnesses rather than disabilities. Moreover, this study found that larger employers are more likely to have a higher level of awareness of disability equality legislation, and a better understanding about a broader range of impairments. Also, larger organizations are more likely to make adjustments at the recruitment stage. Table 7.3 indicates the most common types of adjustment likely to be made at the recruitment stage (by establishment size).

Table 7.3 Adjustments made at the recruitment stage (by establishment size)

Number of employees	3–6 (%)	7–14 (%)	15–99 (%)	100+ (%)	Overall (%)
Provided application forms in alternative format, such as large print or Braille	14	16	22	42	17
Provided disability awareness information for staff involved in recruitment	32	44	60	76	44
Provided help with communication at interviews, e.g. a sign language interpreter	9	10	16	36	12
Checked at the interview whether an applicant would need an adjustment if appointed	30	40	53	74	40
Guaranteed disabled applicants an interview	28	35	35	43	32
Other adjustments	7	8	11	23	9

Source: Dewson et al. (2009: 45).

Although the adjustments listed in Table 7.3 may be helpful in supporting disabled applicants, they may still be not sufficient to tackle interviewers' prejudices and attitudinal barriers towards disabled people which can lead to covert discrimination. Also, the first hurdle in the selection process for a disabled applicant is to be offered an interview. As discussed earlier, disabled people's qualifications, skills, and abilities can be overlooked by employers. An example of good practice in this area is a scheme that has been developed by Jobcentre Plus in the UK to support disabled applicants (see Student Activity 7.3).

> **Student Activity 7.3** Action to improve the recruitment and integration of disabled people in the workplace: the two-ticks scheme
>
> The two-ticks symbol is a mark of the recognition given by Jobcentre Plus in the UK to employers who have agreed to take action to meet five commitments regarding the employment, retention, training, and career development of disabled employees. Employers who use the symbol have agreed that they will take action on these five commitments:
>
> - To interview all disabled applicants who meet the minimum criteria for a job vacancy and to consider them on their abilities.
> - To ensure there is a mechanism in place to discuss, at any time, but at least once a year, with disabled employees what can be done to make sure they can develop and use their abilities.
> - To make every effort when employees become disabled to make sure they stay in employment.
> - To take action to ensure that all employees develop the appropriate level of disability awareness needed to make these commitments work.
> - To review the five commitments and what has been achieved on an annual basis, plan ways to improve on them, and let employees and Jobcentre Plus know about progress and future plans (*Source*: Oxford Brookes University).

> Work in teams to prepare an action plan to enable employers to put into practice these five commitments. When preparing your plan consider the following points:
>
> ● Identify the specific steps that should be taken to action each of the five points.
>
> ● Identify who should be responsible within the organization to progress the different types of action, e.g. human resources managers, line managers, co-workers, etc.
>
> ● Describe the types of action(s) that in your view could best ensure compliance with the five commitments.
>
> ● Explain how your action plan would be communicated throughout the organization.
>
> ● Consider what mechanisms should be adopted to review achievements in relation to the five commitments.

Another example of good practice to support disabled job applicants involves providing training for interviewers. It is important to make them aware of the type of attitudinal and communication issues that could arise during the course of an interview with a disabled applicant and suggest ways of overcoming them. Table 7.4 shows an example of guidelines that have been developed for staff involved in the selection and recruitment of job applicants. These guidelines are intended to identify and address possible disability-related issues that may occur during the interviewing process.

Some disabled people may, because of the nature of their disability, find some of the following areas difficult at interview, but this is not necessarily an indication of their ability to perform a role satisfactorily. If you are aware that a candidate has a particular disability, it would be expected for the interview panel to make reasonable adjustments, as suggested below.

The crucial question that the panel should address is not whether a disabled person could do the job, but whether they could do it if a reasonable adjustment were put in place.

Table 7.4   Guidelines on the recruitment and selection of disabled job applicants

Adjustments in specific areas:

Possible difficulty	Interviewer's behaviour
Communication difficulties (e.g. people on the autistic spectrum, learning difficulties, speech difficulties)	Use simple language and rephrase if necessary. Give people time to answer.
Applicant may not be able to articulate how they reached solutions (e.g. characteristic of neurodiverse people such as those on the autistic spectrum or with dyslexia)	Focus on evidence of outcomes rather than on the process of how they were achieved.
Unusual appearance (e.g. people with facial disfigurement, obvious physical disabilities); someone with dyspraxia may appear untidy and clumsy	Be alert to unconscious prejudices. Do not make assumptions about the person's abilities on the basis of their appearance.

Table 7.4 (*continued*)

Possible difficulty	Interviewer's behaviour
Social skills, e.g. turn-taking, engaging with all panel members	Chair of panel to explain the interview structure clearly at the start, and signal transitions from one panel member to another.
Making eye contact (could be difficult for people with autism or some mental health conditions)	Be aware that some disabled applicants may not be able to sustain eye contact and interviewers should ensure they treat the person no differently as a result.
Unusual body language (this may be affected by a physical or mental disability, including a tremor or tic)	Do not draw inferences from a person's body language that are linked to their disability.
Understanding and responding appropriately to questions	Prompt the interviewee to go beyond yes/no answers.
Some people may struggle with hypothetical questions	Stop someone giving excessive detail. Consider asking more focused questions. Look for evidence of past behaviour rather than asking hypothetical questions, if this will provide the evidence you need.
Applicant appears uncomfortable with lighting, ventilation or temperature (some disabled people are hypersensitive to sensory input)	Check whether the interviewee is comfortable and adjust conditions.
Applicant fails to 'sell themselves'	Interviewer should consider evidence that person could do the role. The stress of the interview may cause the applicant to perform less well than they would in a more relaxed setting. If a disabled applicant is demonstrably stressed at interview, look to reassure and support that person and make additional efforts to help them feel at ease.
Applicant has little previous work experience. They may not recognize how evidence in a different context could be relevant, e.g. that volunteering experience could be cited if asked about teamwork	Prompt the interviewee to think about other contexts.
Speech difficulties, including speech that is slurred or difficult to understand (e.g. due to cerebral palsy or hearing impairment)	Listen for key points. Check your understanding by repetition or rephrasing. Is most communication in this role by email? Is clear spoken English required in the person specification?
An uneven pattern of skills, with very strong capabilities in some areas and weakness in others	The interviewer will have to decide whether exceptional skills in some areas outweigh weaknesses in others.

Source: Oxford Brookes University Guidance for Recruiting Disabled Staff

Another important issue to consider is that 'reasonable adjustment' should not only relate to material types of support, such as, for example, providing information in alternative formats, but it should also relate to the job criteria where appropriate. The excerpt below provides an example of how 'reasonable adjustments' can be made in relation to job criteria.

Reasonable adjustments to criteria

When considering whether a disabled person is a suitable candidate, the panel needs to decide whether they could perform the job satisfactorily, **with reasonable adjustments if needed.**
    Adjustments could relate to:

Speed – a disabled person may be slower, but more accurate in performing a task which may be of benefit in certain roles. Some disabled people are very good at doing regular, repetitive tasks, or may have a meticulous eye for detail.

Quantity – it is impossible to specify the amount of work required in most jobs. There are normal variations between people, and this applies to disabled people as well.

Performance of all duties – if a disabled person could perform most of the role, it would be reasonable to consider reassigning minor duties to another team member, asking the disabled person to take on more of the duties they could perform.

Full-time role – if a person is unable to work full-time because of their disability, explore options for part-time work and job-sharing. This is an opportunity to think creatively about opportunities for other team members or people on the redeployment list.

(Source: Oxford Brookes, *Guidance for Recruiting Disabled Staff*
http://www.brookes.ac.uk/services/hr/eod/disability/interviewing_for_managers.html)

➔ Student Activity 7.4

Consider the following hypothetical scenarios and answer the true or false questions that follow.
    A person applies for a job and asks for information in large print format because they have a visual impairment. An administrator dealing with this does not understand what they are being asked to do and is not aware of their own or their employer's duty to avoid discriminating against disabled people. She ignores their request and the applicant is unable to apply for the vacancy.

a) This is a failure to comply with the duty to make a reasonable adjustment and therefore this person could sue the company for disability discrimination. True or false?

b) In the end this person did not apply for the job and therefore has no right to legal redress. True or false?

An employer asks job applicants, when invited to come for interview, to say whether they have any disability-related requirements and states that reasonable adjustments will be made if necessary.

a) It is illegal to ask job applicants whether they have a disability. True or false?

b) It is not illegal for an employer to ask applicants whether they have any disability-related requirements so long as the employer does not use any information an applicant gives to discriminate against them. True or false?

(Adapted from Equality and Human Rights Commission, *Guidance for Employers*, available online at http://www.equalityhumanrights.com/advice-and-guidance/guidance-for-employers/)

Supporting disabled employees

Several measures can be adopted by employers to provide a more inclusive working environment that supports disabled employees or employees who may become disabled during the course of their employment. These can include general types of action such as interventions aimed at raising awareness about disability issues among managers and co-workers trough training or other initiatives. A specific form of intervention involves making 'reasonable adjustments' which are aimed at removing barriers that could impact on the ability of a disabled person to do her job effectively. Adjustments may be made at an organizational level and these can involve, for example, improving accessibility to organizational premises or other facilities. These can also include the introduction of organization-wide policies and practices, such as those on flexible working, which can benefit disabled employees as well as employees with other needs. Adjustments, however, may be of a specific nature and aimed at a particular disabled employee. Examples of these types of adjustment include making use of special technology or office equipment (e.g. a specially adapted office chair), making changes to the job role or responsibilities, or transferring a disabled employee to another job or to a different work location which may be more accessible. However, it is important to note that not all disabled employees will require 'reasonable adjustments'.

Research shows that overall employers found it easy to make adjustments for disabled staff and this has been attributed to the improved accessibility of modern buildings, the availability of special equipment and other types of aid, but also to an increase in the level of awareness of disability equality. Only a small proportion of employers reported having found it difficult to make adjustments either on the grounds of costs (6 per cent), planning constrains (5 per cent), or health and safety reasons (2 per cent) (Dewson et al., 2009: 55).

The same study highlighted that the most common types of adjustment made for disabled staff already in post tend to be:

Signpost to Chapter 8 Managing Work–Life Balance

- Transferring people with back problems or mobility restrictions into different jobs within the same organizations
- Adapting the working environment, including making use of special office chairs or other equipment
- Using flexible working arrangements, including working from home.

However, it is important to be aware that a preliminary condition for employers to support disabled people in the workplace is that they are encouraged to disclose their disability. As discussed earlier in this section, often disabled people are reluctant to disclose their disability for fear of being discriminated against. Another reason identified by the former UK Disability Rights Commission (2005) for lack of disclosure is the lack of awareness of what constitutes a disability from some of the people who may be affected. In order to fully understand the scale of disability issues in the workplace and create a supportive culture, two key elements can be identified: the importance of developing a positive culture towards disability, and the importance of monitoring disclosure. In the following case study, we consider the action taken by a large company to promote disability equality.

◉ Case study 7.2 Dow's commitment to disability initiatives

Dow connects chemistry and innovation with sustainability to help address many of the world's challenging problems, such as the need for clear water. It is based in Midland, Michigan, in the USA and it operates in 37 countries. It employs approximately 52,000 people worldwide. The company is committed to the recruitment, development, and retention of top talent, including individuals who have a disability. As part of this commitment it has developed a number of initiatives that include:

- A 16-hour Diversity and Inclusion Training Programme to equip newly-appointed leaders with skills to create an inclusive environment for disabled employees and support their professional growth.

- A disability employee network which comprises disabled employees, employees who are parents of disabled children, and other supporters to improve perceptions about disabled people and raise awareness about their contribution.

- Internship programmes to include disabled qualified students. Since the programme's inception in 2005 the company has tripled the number of disabled interns and extended opportunities for jobs across the company for disabled candidates.

Case study questions

1. Consider whether the initiatives described above could be framed as part of an Equal Opportunity or Diversity Management approach?

2. With reference to the evidence discussed in this chapter, identify the areas that should be covered by a Diversity and Inclusion Training programme to equip leaders with skills to create an inclusive environment for disabled employees.

3. What are the benefits of having a disability employee network in the workplace.

4. Given that disabled people are such a heterogeneous group, what kind of steps do you think a company like this could take to ensure that graduates with different types of impairments would have an equal opportunity to apply for an internship?

◉ End of Chapter Case Study Disability-related inequality in Cambodia

The United Nations Convention on Disability Rights states that disabled people have the same rights to be included in society as anybody else and to be respected for who they are (United Nations Enable, www.un.org/disabilities/). However, experiences and challenges faced by disabled people in countries across the world can be very different as they are shaped by country-specific socio-economic contexts. This short case study is based on research undertake by Gartrell (2010) in north-west Cambodia, which is one of the poorest nations in the world, to investigate the experience of disabled people in the labour market.

The findings from this paper show that opportunities to access work are shaped by Cambodian social hierarchy which is reflected by occupational categories. People commonly refer to 'big work' and to 'small work'. The first category includes the better jobs, while the second one includes the low-skilled and poorly paid jobs. Although Gartrell points out that no official data are available in Cambodia about disabled people's rate of participation in the labour market, her research suggests that disabled people are more likely to be employed in 'small work' and experience systematic marginalization in the labour market. Disabled people also experience marginalization in the education system as often parents and teachers do not think that they are worth educating. Other attitudinal barriers that disabled people are likely to face in Cambodia come from the prevailing belief about *karma*, as part of Buddhism. *Karma* dictates that bodily status and well-being in this life are linked to actions committed in a previous life. From this perspective, disability is seen as a form of punishment for bad actions committed in a previous life.

The Royal Cambodian Government is developing a policy framework to tackle disabled people's inequalities, but, as Gartrell highlights, broader socio-cultural changes are also needed to deliver equality for disabled people.

Source: Gartrell, (2010). Reprinted by permission of the publisher.

Case sudy questions

Analyse this case study by referring to some of the concepts and theories discussed in Chapter 1. In particular, consider the following:

- Explain the dynamics of disadvantage and discrimination for disabled people in Cambodia by referring to the 'vicious circle of discrimination' (Makkonen, 2002).

- What theoretical frameworks can be used to explain the reasons why disabled people in Cambodia are more likely to be employed in 'small work'?

- In your view which equality model should underpin the Royal Cambodian Government policy framework to tackle disabled people inequalities? Explain the reasons for your choice.

Conclusion

The social model of disability has been instrumental in changing perceptions of disability in contemporary societies since it has shifted the locus of disability from the individual to society. Thus, according to this model, any challenges experienced by disabled people within the workplace, and more generally within society, are the results of socio-structural barriers rather than of their impairments. Although, as discussed in this chapter, criticism has been levelled at the social model of disability, and alterative models have been proposed, this model has had the merit of providing a powerful tool to challenge perceptions of disability and has advanced disabled people's rights. It has also paved the way for the development of more radical thinking about disability which is expressed by the Affirmative Model. The latter promotes a more positive image of disability by moving away from the idea that disability is a 'personal tragedy' and stresses that impairments are 'ordinary' characteristics of human experience.

However, in spite of radical thinking and the technological advances that have led to changes in the way disability is understood in contemporary societies, evidence reviewed in this chapter suggests that disabled people still face significant barriers, especially in relation to access to jobs. Thus legislation and social policy have a key role to play in tackling disability inequality and in encouraging employers to develop a positive culture in the workplace that supports and enables disabled people at all stages of their working life.

Review and discussion questions

- Explain the concept of mainstreaming and how relevant this is to disability-related policy making.

- What are the key aspects of the social model of disability?

- Compare and contrast different models of disability and discuss their implications for the integration of disabled people in the workplace.

- What does 'aversive disablism' mean and how can it manifest itself?
- What are the main barriers faced by disabled people in the workplace?
- Explain the concept of 'reasonable adjustment' and provide examples of how this can be applied in practice in the workplace.

 For additional material on the content of this chapter please visit the supporting Online Resource Centre at **www.oxfordtextbooks.co.uk/orc/kumra_manfredi/**

Further reading

Campbell, J. and Oliver, M. (1996) *Disability Politics: Understanding Our Past, Changing Our Future.* London: Routledge.

Danieli, A. and Wheeler, P. (2006) Employment policies and disabled people: old wine in new glasses? *Disability and Society*, 21/5: 485–498.

Deal, M. (2007) Aversive disablism: subtle prejudice toward disabled people. *Disability and Society*, 22/1: 93–107.

Gartrell, A. (2010) 'A frog in a well': the exclusion of disabled people from work in Cambodia. *Disability and Society*, 25/3: 289–30.

Woodhams, C. and Danieli, A. (2000) Disability and diversity – a difference too far? *Personnel Review*, 29/3: 402–416.

References

Bajekal, M., Harries, T., Breman, R., and Woodfield, K. (2004) *Review of Disability Estimates and Definitions.* London: Department for Work and Pensions.

Buckup, S. (2009) *The Price of Exclusion: The Economic Consequences of Excluding People with Disabilities from the World of Work.* Employment Sector Working Paper No. 43. Geneva: ILO. Available at www.ilo.org/disability.

Cameron, C. (2008) Further towards an Affirmative Model, in Campbell, T., Foutes, F., Hemengway, L., Soarenian, A., and Till, C. (eds), *Emerging Insights and Perspectives.* Leeds: The Disability Press.

Campbell, J. (2002) Valuing diversity: the disability agenda – we've only just began. *Disability and Society*, 17/4: 471–478.

Campbell, J. and Oliver, M. (1996) *Disability Politics: Understanding Our Past, Changing Our Future.* London: Routledge.

Communication from the Commission to the Council, the European Parliament, the European Economic and Social Committee and the Committee of the regions. Situation of disabled people in the European Union: the European Action plan 2008–2009. Brussels 26 Nov 2007: Commission of the European Communities.

Connolly, M. (2004) *Townshend-Smith on Discrimination Law: Text, Cases and Materials* (2nd edition). London: Cavendish.

Crocker, J., Major, B. and Steele, C. (1998) Social stigma, in Gilbert, D., Fiske, S. and Lindzey, G. (eds), *The Handbook of Social Psychology* (4th ed.) Boston, MA: McGraw Hill, 504–53.

Deal, M. (2007) Aversive disablism: subtle prejudice toward disabled people. *Disability and Society*, 22/1: 93–107.

Dewson, S., Williams, C., Aston, J., Carta, E., Willison, R., and Martin, R. (2009) *Organisations' Response to the Disability Discrimination Act.* London: Department of Work and Pensions.

Dibben, P., James, P., Cunningham, I., and Smythe, D. (2002) Employers and employees with disabilities in the UK: an economically beneficial relationship? *International Journal of Social Economics* , 29/6: 453–467.

Disability Rights Commission Submission to the Equalities Review, December 2005. Available at http://www.leeds.ac.uk/disability-studies/archiveuk/DRC/DRC.html (Please note this Commission no longer exists, it has been merged with the other equality commission into the Equality and Human Rights Commission. Access through the archive website above.)

EU-US Seminar on Employment of People with Disabilities. Brussels: 5–6 November 2009 Report.

Eurobarometer (2009) Discrimination in the EU in 2009. Special Eurobarometer, 317. Brussels: European Commission. Available at http://ec.europa.eu/public_opinion/archives/ebs/ebs_317_sum_en.pdf

European Commission (2010) Preparation of a New EU Disability Strategy 2010–2020. Summary of the Main Outcomes of the Public Consultation. Brussels: European Commission, Employment, Social Affairs and Equal Opportunities (June).

Finkelstein, V. (2004) Representing disability, in Swain, J., French, S., Barnes, C., and Thomas, C. (eds), *Disabling Barriers – Enabling Environments* (2nd edition). London: Sage.

Gartrell, A. (2010) 'A frog in a well': the exclusion of disabled people from work in Cambodia. *Disability and Society*, 25/3: 289–301.

Goffman, E. (1974 [1963]) *Stigma: Notes on the Management of Spoiled Identities.* New York: Simon and Schuster.

Guardian (2011) Zeta Jones' disclosure of bipolar treatment will have huge impact, charities predict. *The Guardian*, 15 April.

Guardian (2011) Disabled marchers turn out in thousands for benefit protest. *The Guardian*, 12 May.

Hepple, B. (2011) *Equality. The New Legal Framework.* Oxford: Hart Publishing.

Howard, M. (2003) An 'interactionist' perspective on barriers and bridges to work for disabled people. London: Institute for Public Policy Research.

Kandola, R. and Fullerton, J. (1994a) *Managing the Mosaic.* London: Institute of Personnel Development.

Kandola, R. and Fullerton, J. (1994b) Diversity: more than just an empty slogan. *Personnel Management*, November: 46–49.

Llewellyn, A. and Hogan, K. (2000) The use and abuse of models of disability. *Disability and Society*, 15/1: 157–165.

Makkonen, T. (2002) *Multiple, Compound and Intersectional Discrimination: Bringing the Experience of the Most Marginalised to the Fore.* Abo, Finland: Institute of Human Rights.

Oliver, M. (1996) *Understanding disability.* London: Macmillan.

Pillai, R., Rankin, J., and Stanley, K., Bennett, J., Hetherington, D., Stone, L. and Withers, K. (2007) *Disability 2020: Opportunities for the Full and Equal Citizenship of Disabled People in Britain 2020.* London: Institute of Public Policy Research.

Ratzka, A. (1998) *Crip Utopia.* Stockholm: Institute on Independent Living.

Roadmap 2025. Achieving disability equality by 2025. Office for Disability Issues available at http://odi.dwp.gov.uk/roadmap-to-disability-equality/indicators.php.

Sayce, L. (2003) Beyond good intentions: making anti-discrimination strategies work. *Disability and Society*, 18/5: 625–642.

Shaw Trust (2010) *Mental Health: Still the Last Workplace Taboo?* Chippenham: Shaw Trust. Available at www.shaw-trust.org.uk.

Shier, M., Graham, J.R., and Jones, M.E. (2009) Barriers to employment as experienced by disabled people: a qualitative analysis in Calgary and Regina, Canada. *Disability and Society*, 24/1: 63–75.

Swain, J. and French, S. (2000) Towards an Affirmative Model of disability. *Disability and Society*, 15/4: 569–582.

Thornton, P. (2005) Disabled people, employment and social justice. *Social Policy and Society*, 4/1: 65–73.

Woodhams, C. and Danieli, A. (2000) Disability and diversity – a difference too far? *Personnel Review*, 29/3: 402–416.

8 Managing Work–Life Balance

 Learning objectives

- Understand the demographic changes that have led to the development of the concept of work–life balance and the approaches taken by different countries to develop work–life balance policies

- Explain how the work–life balance debate has evolved and its different dimensions relating to gender equality and equality of opportunities, and diversity management

- Define alternative discourses on work–life balance such as work–life harmonization and socially sustainable work, and understand the far-reaching implications of the work–life balance debate

- Understand the work–family border theory, and be able to define how this explains the way in which people manage their relationship with paid work and other parts of their lives

- Understand the challenges and the benefits of implementing work–life balance policies and practices in the workplace

Key terms

- **Family-friendly employment:** refers to a mix of flexible working patterns and leave arrangements, such as maternity, paternity, and parental leave, that can be made available to working parents in the workplace.

- **Socially sustainable work:** relates to the importance of considering the impact of the organization of paid work on the wider society.

- **Work–life balance:** it can be broadly defined as a set of policies and practices to help individuals to achieve a balance between the demands arising from paid work and their personal lives.

- **Work–life harmonization:** this concept has been proposed as an alternative to that of work–life balance, which implies a separation between the domain of paid work and that of personal life. It has been suggested that work–life harmonization can better capture the multiple challenges faced by individuals at different stages of their life cycle, to combine paid work with other parts of their life (Gambles et al., 2006).

Introduction

In this chapter we examine the concept of work–life balance and discuss how practices and policies can be developed in the workplace. Work–life balance can be broadly defined as a set of policies and practices to help individuals to achieve a balance between the demands arising from paid work and those arising from their personal lives.

Work–life balance has become part of the overall discourse about equality in the workplace and, although it is not a specific equality strand such as gender or race, it can be instrumental in supporting the achievement of equality in relation to other strands. An example of this can be seen in relation to gender equality, as work–life balance practices can serve the dual purpose of supporting women's participation in the labour market while at the same time facilitating a redistribution of caring responsibilities between men and women. Likewise, flexible working arrangements are important in extending working lives and in supporting the participation of disabled people in the labour market (see Chapter 7).

Signpost to Chapter 7 Managing Disability in the Workplace

This chapter starts by highlighting the main drivers which have placed work–life issues on the public policy agenda in most industrialized countries, such as women's increased participation in the labour market and other demographic changes. We then explore how the work–life balance debate has evolved in the academic literature, and how its focus has shifted from work-family issues to a more inclusive idea of work–life balance to help everybody combine paid work with their personal life. We also examine alternative discourses which conceptualize issues around paid work and personal life in terms of work–life harmonization, or as part of socially sustainable work. Subsequently, we discuss how people manage their work–life balance demands by examining the work-family border theory (Clark, 2000). This theory argues that people are border-crossers and make daily transitions between the world of work and the world of family.It explains how the borders between these two worlds are moulded by people and the environment in which they live.

Finally, we discuss the development of work–life balance polices and practices in the workplace with reference to: a 'dual agenda' strategy (Rapoport et al., 2002) that seeks to link business effectiveness with equality issues; the need to integrate company-led flexibility with employee-led flexibility; the role of line managers in implementing flexible working; and the main management capabilities which are needed to manage flexible working successfully.

Throughout this chapter we have adopted the expression 'work–life balance' since it is commonly used and widely understood internationally, although some alternative definitions have been suggested by academics and commentators.

Policy context: the development of the work–life balance agenda

Issues around reconciliation of paid employment with family life came to the attention of policy makers in the 1970s and 1980s as a result of an increased participation of women in the labour market in most industrialized countries, compounded with other significant demographic changes, such as falling birth rates and an increase in the number of single-parent families. In response to these demographic changes, the European Union started to develop a policy agenda to help working parents, and in particular women, to combine paid work with family responsibilities (Hantrais, 2000). This involved the introduction of a series of measures, including a number of legally binding Directives, to ensure the adoption of a common legislative framework across all EU member states in order to provide a platform of employment rights aimed at facilitating reconciliation of paid work with family life. These Directives provided for maternity rights; rights for part-time workers; a maximum working week of 48 hours; and a right to unpaid parental leave. More recently, work–life balance policies and practices have become an integral part of EU employment policies and the Lisbon Strategy for Growth and Employment expressly refers to the need for enabling 'people to stay in employment ... by creating structures in which they can best combine their work and non-work responsibilities' (European Foundation for the Improvement of Living and Working Conditions, 2007: 3).

Countries within and outside the European Union have taken different approaches towards the development of their work–life balance agenda. For example, the Nordic countries have used legislation to introduce leave arrangements for both parents and a right to adjust their working hours. Collective bargaining and workplace agreements have also been used to introduce greater flexibility in the workplace in the Netherlands and Germany (International Labour Office, 2009), and in Italy where a special fund was set up by the government in 2001 to encourage and support the development of flexible working arrangements, agreed by employers and trade unions within their collective bargaining framework (Natoli, 2005). Germany has introduced part-time legislation to facilitate work–life balance which has been complemented by a number of initiatives, such as the Alliance for Families, to promote family-friendly practices in the workplace, and family pacts that encourage cooperation at local level between employers, trade unions, local government, and other service providers to develop work–life balance initiatives (Hegewisch, 2009: 52).

Some countries have sought to take a more holistic approach to work and life issues by introducing provisions for all workers regardless of caring responsibilities. In Belgium, for example, a 'Time Credit' or sabbatical leave has been introduced which is open to all employees and allows them to take up to one year's leave over their working life (Hegewisch, 2009: 17). In Italy, all employees, both in the public and in the private sector, are legally entitled to take up to 11 months of unpaid leave to undertake further education or training. Furthermore, issues around work and life balance have also been addressed within the broader context of urban life, as City Councils have a positive duty to ensure that the opening hours of public services are more responsive to people's needs (Natoli, 2005) .

The UK, on the other hand, has taken a mixed approach by encouraging employers' voluntary initiatives to adopt flexible working, followed by the introduction of a legal right for working parents to request flexible working, a gradual increase in legislative provisions to improve maternity and parental leave, and the introduction of paternity leave. In 2000, the UK's Labour government launched a major work–life balance campaign that focused on the 'business case' to highlight a number of benefits that employers could gain from the adoption of work–life balance practices: improved staff recruitment and retention; reduction of absenteeism; and increased staff productivity and performance (Department of Trade and Industry, 2001) . The business case approach was largely influenced by the American model, which focused (as outlined below) on persuading employers to take action on these issues. A Challenge Fund was also set up to provide employers with consultancy services to introduce flexible working arrangements in their organizations that would support employees as well as satisfy business needs. The right to request flexible working was initially limited to working parents with young children up to the age of six, but it has been extended to parents with children up to the age of 16 and to employees who have caring responsibilities for adult dependants.

In the USA during the 1980s, demographic changes and the need for the federal government to reduce its deficit and expenditure for public and social services were the main drivers for focusing on work and family issues. This led the government to take action to persuade 'employers to assume more responsibility for the private lives of employees and their families' (Bowen, 2000: 84). A number of initiatives were taken by the federal government to debate the role of government and businesses to help employees to achieve work–family balance. Such efforts continued well in the 1990s when the Family and Medical Leave Act was introduced by the Clinton administration in 1993, requiring employers with 50 or more employees to offer up to 12 weeks' unpaid leave to their employees for either health or childcare reasons. However, a report for the Executive Office of the US President (2010) has highlighted that many firms have not yet adopted work–life balance practices.

This review shows that the concept of work–life balance has developed in most western economies, where it is now supported by legislation, government policies, and workplace practices, albeit to different degrees in various countries. However, in some developing countries, work–life issues are seen as a 'luxury' that governments, employers, and individuals cannot afford to consider until their economies 'catch up' with those in the western countries. India is a case in point, where in spite of the country's fast economic development, the existence of widespread poverty and the lack of infrastructure 'leaves no alternative but to adhere to the dominant model of capitalism that puts profit first before considering social and personal needs of workers' (Gambles et al., 2006: 15). However, work–life balance can also be a luxury in western economies, where many workers in low-paid jobs cannot afford to reduce their working hours or take periods of leave for caring responsibilities unless their countries' legislation provides for financial compensation. Furthermore, as highlighted by several commentators and academics, work intensification, long hours, and periods of economic recession can undermine work–life balance policies and practices, and make it difficult for many workers to achieve a balance between paid work and their personal lives.

Signpost to Chapter 2 An Outline of the European and UK Equality Legislation

---

Student Activity 8.1

Choose two or more countries and find out about working hours, policies, and legislation that support work–life balance. Compare and contrast them. A useful source to consult for relevant information is the European Foundation for the Improvement of Living and Working Conditions. A link to this website can be found on the Online Resource Centre.

The evolution of the work–life balance debate

This section reviews the evolution of the debate on work–life balance and discusses some of the main discourses that have emerged from the academic literature around this topic. The origins of the work–life balance debate can be traced back to an increased level of women's participation in the labour market over the last decades. Consequently, a large body of academic literature has been developed to analyze the gender dimension of work–life balance. The focus of the work–life balance debate, however, has subsequently shifted from women with dependent children and the family, to everybody's need to balance the demands arising from paid work with their personal life, thus linking it to the diversity management ideology. A more inclusive approach to work–life balance issues, compounded by a trend towards an increasing blurring of the boundaries between paid work and people's personal lives, has led a number of academics and commentators to question whether the concept of work–life balance can adequately capture the complex reality that it is trying to define. Thus alternative ideas have been articulated, such as work–life harmonization and work–life integration, among others. More recently, the concept of socially sustainable work has emerged in Europe (Lewis et al., 2007) from concerns about population sustainability as a result of ageing and falling birth rates. Within this context, work–life balance policies and practice appear to be crucial to human sustainability.

Overall, this section intends to help students to understand the far-reaching implications of the concept of work–life balance. For this purpose, we have covered some of the main dimensions of the work–life balance debate, although these by no means exhaustively represent the very rich academic literature that has been developed on this topic.

The gender dimension of work–life balance

Flexible working options and leave arrangements are key practices to support the participation in the labour market of women with family and caring responsibilities. For this reason, such arrangements are often labelled as 'family-friendly employment', and can be viewed as a form of positive action to promote gender equality in the workplace. Houston (2002: 8) points out, however, that 'family-friendly or flexible working has the potential to either deepen or eliminate the gender differences in work participation' as experiences of work–life balance remain gendered since they reflect social norms and values about gender roles within the family and at work. The need of women with caring responsibilities for family-friendly employment can reinforce gender occupational segregation both horizontally and vertically: horizontally, as many women tend to work in highly feminized sectors where flexible working arrangements are more widely available; vertically, as working reduced hours may hinder women's career prospects, as they end up in the so-called 'mummy track', and they may be overlooked for promotion opportunities (Gatrell, 2007; Lewis, 2006). Therefore, men need to be included in the debate on work–life balance in order to redistribute caring responsibilities between men and women and to achieve greater gender equality in the workplace as well as in the family.

The objective of promoting greater gender equality has led to the introduction in several European countries of paid paternity leave and non-transferable periods of parental leave targeted at fathers, and research shows a significant increase in the number of fathers taking up these arrangements, particularly if they are paid. For example, 80 per cent of fathers in Sweden take up paid paternity leave, followed by 69 per cent in Finland, 66 per cent in the Netherlands and 55 per cent in France (Moss and O'Brien, 2006), while Iceland has recorded a very high proportion, 90 per cent, of fathers taking parental leave since the introduction of generous paid statutory arrangements that include a period of three months non-transferable leave for fathers (Gíslason, 2007). However, in spite of these positive trends, men are still less likely to take up flexible working, as evidenced by comparative research in several countries (Hegewisch, 2009).

This might be partly explained by the fact that many of them are the breadwinners in their families or the higher earner in a dual-earner couple, but also by the existence of a gendered culture in the workplace. Gendered assumptions about men's role in the workplace may cause them to feel a lower 'sense of entitlement', compared to women, to modify their working patterns (Lewis, 1999; Lewis and Smithson, 2001). It has been argued that men often face 'an invisible dilemma', which means that in the case of men with dependent children, families, rather than the workplace, are expected to make adjustments (Levine, 1993: 83). Several studies have highlighted that men's choice to take up parental leave or flexible working arrangements is influenced by organizational culture and expectations about their commitment to their job (Allard et al., 2007; Haas et al., 2002; Haas and Hwang, 2007). Consequently, they may be reluctant to take time off work or work flexibly for childcare reasons as they may be concerned about sending the wrong message to their organization, thus hindering their career prospects. This demonstrates that although work–life balance policies and practices in the workplace are important to promote greater gender equality, they are, however, not enough to challenge deep-seated assumptions about gender roles in the workplace and in the family.

Debate Box

Working fathers are unhappy with their working hours

Research undertaken on behalf of Equality and Human Rights Commission in the UK found that 62% of fathers thought that, in general, fathers should spend more time caring for their children. Fathers were more likely to be unhappy with their working hours than mothers. However, many of them continue to work full-time and their partners take primary responsibility for childcare within the family.
(Equality and Human Rights Commission 2009)

Organize the class into two groups, one for the motion and one against.
The motion is:

Expectations about the role of men in the workplace and in the family makes it more difficult for them to reduce their working hours and take greater responsibility for their children.

Stages in the debate: (each stage is given with timings, the overall time for the activity is 55 minutes – allowing a few minutes for change over of presenters, etc.)

• Each group has 20 minutes to prepare their arguments either for or against the motion.

• Each group is given 5 minutes to present their opening statement (10 minutes in total).

• Groups reconvene for 10 minutes to prepare rebuttal arguments.

• Each group has 2 minutes to present rebuttal arguments.

A vote is taken and the winners of the debate announced; the casting vote goes to impartial observers: tutors, audience members not involved in the debate, or observers.

From work–family balance to work–life balance for all

The gendered dimension of work–life balance is clearly reflected by terminology such as 'reconciliation of paid work with family life', or 'work and family balance', and 'family-friendly employment', whereas the expression 'work–life balance' is more inclusive and implies that this is an issue for everybody. Doherty and Manfredi (2006: 242–243) suggest that different terminology reflects different underlying approaches which can be 'tracked back to the ideologies of equal opportunity (EO) and diversity management (DM) initiatives for tackling inequality in the workplace'. An EO approach is based on the principles of social justice and fairness, and 'family-friendly' employment can be conceptualized as a form of positive action to address issues arising from women's dual role as mothers and workers. Conversely, the notion of work–life balance implies that everybody needs to achieve a balance between paid work and personal life, whether or not they have caring responsibilities, and it can be seen as part of a DM approach which stresses the advantages of a diverse workforce, and the added value that this can bring to the workplace.

Unlike the EO approach, diversity management is not driven by the principles of social justice and fairness, but by the 'business case', and it focuses on individuals' talents and the need to maximize the potentials of all workers (Kandola and Fullerton, 1994a, 1994b). Therefore, the idea of work–life balance for all appears to best fit within a DM approach. In practice, while an EO approach tends to rely more on legislation to achieve equality in the workplace, a DM approach uses the business case to advocate its benefits for both workers and employers, and relies on employers' voluntary initiatives to develop working practices that support the needs of a diverse workforce. The advantage of using a DM approach to frame the debate on combining paid work with a personal life is that it is more inclusive. Thus it can also be argued that it avoids the risk of a backlash against working parents, since workers without caring responsibilities may feel that their needs are overlooked, while those with caring responsibilities are seen as receiving preferential treatment. Furthermore, work–life balance underpinned by a DM approach can be more appealing to employers because it stresses the business advantages that can be gained from work–life balance practices in terms of staff recruitment and retention, job satisfaction, and productivity.

However, as highlighted by Doherty (2004), the downside of a DM approach is that it is contingent on the existence of a business case for offering flexible working, which depends on a tight labour market, and this can change in times of economic recession. Moreover, research shows that there is no conclusive evidence that work–life balance practices can provide business benefits. An extensive review of the academic literature on the business case for work–life balance (Beauregard and Henry, 2009) indicates that although there is some evidence to support the claim that work–life balance practices can help staff recruitment, there is insufficient evidence to corroborate the claim that such practices can enhance organizational performance. However, research also shows that if work–life balance practices do not appear to improve performance and productivity in the workplace, neither do they seem to have an adverse impact (Hegewisch, 2009: 44).

Signpost to Chapter 3 From Equality of Opportunity to Managing Diversity

Work–life balance or work–life harmonization?

Several commentators and academics have started to question whether the concept of work–life balance can adequately capture the complexity of the relationship between paid work and other parts of people's lives that it is trying to define. The first point to note is that the notion of work–life balance seems to imply a dichotomy between paid work and the rest of an individual's life, while in fact not only is paid work part of the latter, but it is also often an important component. This is because paid work is not just a source of income, but can also be a source of self-fulfilment and personal satisfaction. The idea of such separation between paid work and people's private lives seems to be reminiscent of the industrial era, where the world of work is supposed to be entirely separate from people's private lives and 'family demands are subordinated to organizational demands' (Bowen, 2000: 83). It has also been argued that work–life balance reflects the 'corporate perspective' that prioritizes work, while from an individual's perspective, personal life comes first (Johnson, 2004: 59). Therefore, it is suggested that it would be more appropriate to refer to 'life-work balance', but we believe that changing the order of these words does not help to overcome the underlying notion of a separation between the world of paid work and people's personal lives.

One of the problems with this idea of *separation* between the domain of paid work and personal life is that it can potentially generate a conflict between these two domains and consequently become a source of stress for an individual. Academic literature that investigates the link between work-life balance initiatives and well-being has highlighted that people have multiple roles throughout the course of their life and, depending on a series of circumstances, these roles can be a source of fulfilment (Crosby, 1987), but equally a source of stress if they lead to conflict between roles and overwork (Lewis and Cooper, 1987). This suggests the importance of helping people to manage these different roles in complementary ways rather than keeping them separately.

Gambles et al. (2006: 35) have also highlighted further problems with the concept of work–life balance. They point out that not only does this concept imply a continued separation between the domain of paid work and that of personal life, which, as mentioned above, can lead to conflict, but it also ignores distinctions between paid and unpaid work, and further undervalues unpaid care work, often undertaken by women looking after children, the elderly, or adult dependants, by implying that it is just another part of the 'non-work' domain. They suggest as an alternative the use of the concept of 'harmonization', as they argue that this would better capture the multiple challenges faced by individuals at different stages of their life cycle, to combine paid work with other parts of their lives, and 'encourage wider and more radical thinking' about these issues. The notion of 'harmonization' is an interesting concept which overcomes the idea of the existence of a dichotomy between paid work and personal life and also appears to be better suited to a working environment increasingly driven by the information economy and technological advances, where the boundaries between paid work and people's personal lives are becoming blurred. At the same time, however, it is sufficiently flexible to reflect the fact that people may use different strategies at different times in their life to harmonize multiple challenges and demands.

Socially sustainable work

Most industrialized countries are facing a major demographic challenge as their population is ageing while birth rates are still falling. As a result, many people find themselves to be part of what has been defined as the 'sandwich generation', having to shoulder double

> ### ➔ Student Activity 8.2
>
> Interview half a dozen people or more (e.g. family members, friends, other students) to explore what is their experience of work–life balance and what this means to them. Try to ensure that your sample includes people of both sexes, with and without caring responsibilities, different ages, and possibly different cultures. Discuss your results with the other students by reflecting on the following questions:
>
> - To what extent do age, gender, family status, and cultural differences impact on people's experiences of work–life balance?
> - Is the reality of people's experiences better captured by the concept of work–life balance or work–life harmonization?
> - Are there any other points worth highlighting?

responsibilities, for childcare and eldercare. All these factors raise issues about population sustainability and the need to have the time to care for children and the elderly. Equally, however, they raise issues about the importance of having time and energies to become involved in community life, to undertake voluntary activities, and to take part in political life.

Pillinger (2002: 21) highlights that 'an examination of work–life balance and the politics of time directs attention to changing values associated with the division of time between work, family and leisure; between women's and men's time; and as result, the reorganisation of social and economic life at the individual, family or even city/town level'. This leads on to the question whether a work-centred organization of time where paid work is expected to take priority over other parts of an individual's life is at all sustainable in the long term. From this perspective, it has been argued that as people have become aware about environmental issues and the importance of making changes to the economy and to their lifestyles in order to promote environmental sustainability, 'the twenty-first century is beginning to grasp the dimensions of a comparable crisis, this time of human sustainability – a scarcity of conditions that nurture resilient, secure individuals, families, friendships and communities. Who has time to care for whom in the overwork culture?' (Bunting, 2004: xxi, cited in Gambles et al., 2006). These arguments take the work–life balance debate on to a new level, beyond the perspective of the individual and that of workplace, and, as pointed out by Webster (2004: 62–63, cited in Lewis et al., 2007), 'we now have to broaden our concerns to consider the impact of the organization of work on the wider sphere of life beyond paid employment – for the individual, for communities, for society at large. In other words, our concern must now be with enhancing the broader social sustainability of working life.' Thus, similarly to the concept of environmental sustainability, an equivalent idea has emerged in Europe about socially sustainable work, which focuses on the importance of considering the impact of the organization of work on the wider society.

Debate Box

Shall we be working a four-day week in the future?

It has been reported that 'State employees in Utah have already shifted to a four-day week, albeit on compressed five-day hours' (Collinson, 2009). Over time the working week has become shorter: people used to work six day a week, while now most people work five day a week. Maybe in the near future we shall all work four days a week?

Organize the class into two groups, one for the motion and one against.

The motion is:

A four-day week is simply too short. It will never become a widespread reality in the future. Please follow stages in the debate as indicated above.

How do people manage their work–life balance?

People's experiences of work–life balance can be very different as they depend on a number of variables, such as, for example, at what stage of their life they find themselves, whether they have caring and family responsibilities, their position in the labour market, and, more generally, their overall needs and aspirations. In this section we explore how individuals manage their work–life balance or harmonization by using as a theoretical framework – the work-family border theory, developed by Clark (2000) – to explore how individuals handle the relationship between paid work and personal life. This theory is based on the premise that paid work and family life became two separate domains following the Industrial Revolution, which created a clear division between the workplace and home. Clark argues that:

> People are border-crossers who make daily transitions between two worlds – the world of work and the world of family. People shape these worlds, mould the borders between them, and determine the border-crosser's relationship to that world and its members. Though people shape their environments, they are, in turn, shaped by them. It is this very contradiction of determining, and being determined, by our work and home environments that makes work/family balance one of the most challenging concepts in the study of work and the study of families. (Clark, 2000: 748)

It is suggested that the borders between the two different domains can be:

- physical (e.g. an office or a home)
- temporal (e.g. working hours)
- psychological (e.g. thinking patterns or emotions that relate to either one or the other domain)

Furthermore, it is highlighted that some of the main characteristics of these borders include:

- permeability, which relates to the extent to which elements from one domain enter the other

- flexibility, which indicates the extent to which borders may expand or contract to accommodate the demands arising from one or another domain.

When the borders between the two domains are very permeable and flexible, they allow a certain amount of 'blending' between the two. Conversely, borders that are neither very permeable nor flexible do not allow 'blending' to occur, and keep the two domains separate (Clark, 2000: 757, 758). In order to understand the way in which, in practice, people mould their borders and manage 'the border-crosser relationship', this theory is used to consider the findings from a study which looks at work–life balance issues for employees working in two new sectors of the economy: the software industry and call centres (Hyman et al., 2005). This research shows that the workers in the software sector enjoy a certain degree of autonomy over their working hours and patterns of work, which includes the choice of working from home. Their working environment appears to be 'more open to manipulation and boundary flexibility by employees' (Clark, 2000: 718). This suggests that these workers have a certain degree of control over their temporal borders (e.g. when to work), their physical borders (e.g. place of work, either the office or their home), and that autonomy enables them, to a certain extent, to make choices on how to manage 'the border-crossing relationship', which allows a certain amount of 'blending' to occur between the two domains. The downside for these employees is that they have to work 'uneven hours' to respond to the business demands of companies working over 24 hours. Thus it may be argued that while, on the one hand, technology can help workers to take control over temporal (e.g. when to work) and physical (where to work) borders, on the other hand, it may cause problems with the psychological borders as people may find it difficult to switch off from work.

Conversely, in the case of the call-centre workers, hours and patterns of work are determined and tightly controlled by their employers, making it more difficult for them to 'mould' their work–home boundary. Flexibility is entirely employer-led in this kind of company and the work border tends to expand at the expense of the home domain. These workers, unlike those in the software sector, have no control either over physical borders, as they have to carry out their work in the call centre, or on temporal borders, as their working hours can expand up to two hours a day 'to meet the business needs' (Clark, 2000: 712). Therefore, for this group of workers' lack of control over their working hours, compounded with a lack of workplace support, means that the two domains remain rigidly separate as there is little permeability between the two. As a result, they are more likely to experience conflict between paid work and personal life.

One of the key differences between these two groups of workers appears to be the degree of autonomy and control that the workers in the software sector have over their working hours. Research undertaken by the Work Foundation (2003: 11) suggests that workers' degree of autonomy and control over their working hours is a key factor in achieving a work–life balance as it gives people 'the opportunity to have some control over when, where, and how they work, so that they can pursue activities and aspirations as they wish'. According to the same study, this is further confirmed by the fact that self-employed people, in spite of the fact that they may have to work long hours, are more likely to be happy with their work–life balance compared to those who are employed, which suggests that autonomy and some degree of control over working times can contribute to making people more satisfied with their work–life balance.

Case study 8.1 The workplace of the future for the future work-force

Figure 8.1 The staff car park

A workplace of the future?

We run as a virtual firm, all our lawyers and typists/support staff are on total flexi-time and flexi-holidays. We have no offices. We get incredibly high-quality lawyers from top firms joining us because of the lifestyle they can achieve. We would never attract those lawyers to a small firm like ours without this flexibility. We have never had any issue with trust or how long people have worked, etc. Good professional people know what hours to work and don't need it enforced. (Woolley & Co, Solicitors)

Source: for photograph and above text, Equal Opportunities Commission (2007: 5)

Case study questions

1. Use the border theory to explore how the employees in this firm make their daily transition between paid work and their personal life.

2. Consider the advantages and disadvantages from an individual's perspective of working from home.

3. Would you like to work in this way and do you think that it would help you to achieve a good work–life balance?

Developing work–life balance policies and practices in the workplace

Workplaces in western countries find themselves at the centre of increased demand for work–life balance practices. These are driven by demographic and social changes, government policies and legislation, changes in employees' expectations, and by demands from the market and customers for greater flexibility in the way goods are produced and services are delivered. This is illustrated in Figure 8.2.

Developing work–life balance policies and practices in the workplace involve the adoption of a series of measures which can include:

- Mandatory leave arrangements provided by employment legislation and other statutes such as maternity, paternity, and parental leave. Employers are bound by legislation to offer these leave arrangements and have very limited or no discretion in the way they are implemented. Some employers may choose to improve minimum statutory provisions by offering more generous terms.

- Improved leave arrangements and flexible working options negotiated with trade unions through the collective bargaining process or workplace agreements.

- Policies and flexible working arrangements to enable employees to change their hours and patterns of work. In the UK, employees with caring responsibilities have a legal right to ask for flexible working. Employers should try to accommodate such requests unless there is a demonstrable business reason not to do so.

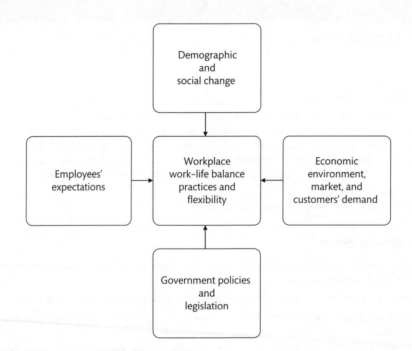

Figure 8.2 Demands on work–life balance practices

- Voluntary employers' work–life balance initiatives that can include improved leave arrangements and flexible working. In this case, employers have full discretion in designing these arrangements, which are often agreed informally between employees and managers. Small businesses (Dex and Scheibl, 2002) are more likely to use informal rather than formal work–life balance practices.

Flexible working is a key practice to enable employees to achieve a better work–life balance, and this can be defined as employee-oriented flexibility. But likewise, flexible working is a key practice for employers to respond to market and customers demands, and this can be defined as company-oriented flexibility, which can include:

- Numerical flexibility: this involves changing the size of the workforce (e.g. reducing it or increasing it) in order to respond to market demands by making use of fixed-term and temporary contracts, and/or using agency workers.

- Functional flexibility: this involves training employees to be able to perform a range of different functions so that they can be deployed to cover different areas of the business.

- Temporal flexibility: this involves the adjustment of time either during the working day (e.g. flexi-time) or over the working year (e.g. term-time only work or annualized hours) (Lewis and Roper, 2008).

Employee-oriented flexibility can include a wide range of working patterns, the most common are listed in Table 8.1.

The challenge for employers is to integrate company-oriented flexibility with employee-oriented flexibility (Lewis and Roper, 2008) as these two types of flexibility can potentially conflict with one another. For example, in the 1980s and 1990s in the UK economy, the term 'flexible working' referred predominantly, if not exclusively, to company-oriented flexibility, since flexible working was used to respond to customers' demand and maximize profit (Hogarth et al., 1999). It was in the late 1990s and the early twenty-first century that flexible working began to be associated with the work–life balance agenda. Flexible working became a key element of the UK government work–life balance campaign launched in 2000. Also, the trade unions introduced the concept of 'positive flexibility', which by and large relates to working practices that support employees' work–life balance, rather than other types of working practices, such as working long hours, which instead can undermine employees' work–life balance. In one of their publications (*Changing Times*, 2001: 2), the UK Trades Union Congress emphasized the importance of organizations negotiating 'working practices which also benefit staff, are forward looking and competitive and profitable ... [and that a] WLB [work–life balance] is central to positive flexibility ... [and] to achieve a win-win outcome for staff and management'. Thus the term *flexibility* within the context of the workplace has undergone a process of 'discursive rehabilitation', as argued by Fleetwood (2006), since it has shifted from referring to 'employer-friendly flexibility' entirely aimed at maximizing profit to 'employee friendly flexibility'. Fleetwood, however, also warns that in spite of the 'rehabilitated' discourses on flexible work, 'employee unfriendly' flexible working remains, as evidenced by the research findings discussed earlier, about work–life balance issues for workers employed in call centres. This research provides a clear example of flexible working which appears to be entirely company-oriented (or employer-friendly, to use Fleetwood's terminology) and driven by business needs, making it very difficult for employees to achieve a work–life balance.

Table 8.1 Flexible working arrangements

Part-time work	This involves working reduced hours compared to a full-time job
Job-sharing	This involves two employees sharing the duties and responsibilities of one full-time post
Flexi-time	This offers employees the opportunity to vary the time of starting or finishing work (usually outside agreed working core hours e.g. 10am–4pm)
Staggered hours	This involves employees working for the same employer having different start and finish times
Compressed hours	This enables employees to work their total number of hours over fewer days. For example, the number of hours of a full-time job which would normally be spread over five days are compressed over four days
Part-year working or term-time working	This enables employees to reduce the number of weeks they work in a year. For example, an employee may choose to work only during school term time and take time off during the school holidays
Annualized hours	This involves organizing the number of hours to be worked over a year rather than a week. From an employer's perspective, this arrangement can be particularly useful to deal with peaks and troughs of work, while it can offer an employee periods of reduced work or free time during the year
Teleworking/ homeworking	This involves working from home or other distant location either part-time, full-time, or occasionally
Shift swapping	This is when employees do shift work, they can negotiate their working time to suit their needs and/or rearrange shifts among themselves
Self-rostering	This looks at the number of staff and skills required during each working day, then allows individual employees to put forward the times when they would like to work. Shift patterns are then compiled, matching as closely as possible individuals' preferences with the agreed staffing level required
Career breaks/ sabbaticals	These involve a period of unpaid leave that an employee may take for different reasons, such as caring for small children, travel, study, or simply to have a break from paid employment

Source: Adapted from Department of Trade and Industry (2001)

However, it is also important to note that flexibility which is entirely employee-led such as, for example part-time work, which is provided by employers almost entirely 'to fit individual labour supply choices', runs the risk of being perceived by line managers as more of a source of disadvantages than advantages for the business (McRae, 1998: 102).

This discussion points to the importance for employers of integrating company-oriented and employee-oriented flexibility, but how can this be achieved in practice? An approach that can be adopted is that developed by Rapoport et al. (2002: 42) which links organizational effectiveness with opportunities for equitable work–life balance practices. They suggest that these should not be pursued as separate strategies but as a 'dual agenda' since they believe that organizations can serve their own ends by addressing equality and work–life balance issues. The way in which the 'dual agenda' approach can achieve this objective is through a collaboration between employers and employees, or their representatives (e.g. trade unions), where assumptions about how work is done are questioned and consideration is given to how these assumptions may impact on both work effectiveness and employees' work–life balance. Through this process, innovative approaches to work can be developed that 'meet the dual agenda' (Lewis et al., 2007: 370).

For example, by looking at working practices through a 'dual agenda' lens, one can find a way of accommodating the need of some employees to work part-time, while fulfilling at the same time the requirements of a full-time job. This can be achieved by allowing those employees who cannot comply with the requirements of full-time employment to job-share, while ensuring that the level of cover and continuity of a full-time post is retained. Furthermore, employees who job-share can offer additional cover for each other during periods of absence. This shows how a 'dual agenda' approach can work in practice and create a win-win situation both for employer and employees. Research also shows that the role of the trade unions is important as unionized workplaces are more likely to have policies and practices that support work–life balance (Dex and Smith, 2002). Further examples of integrating flexibility through a 'dual agenda' approach are outlined in Table 8.2.

We have discussed so far why work–life balance practices have become important for the workplace, what they involve, and how they can be developed through a 'dual agenda' approach. In the next section we consider whose role it is to develop work–life balance policies and practices.

Signpost to Chapter 11 Managing Age Diversity in the Workplace

The role of managers in developing and implementing work–life balance practices

The responsibility for initiating, supporting, and implementing work–life balance policies across an organization lies with different layers of management. Human resource managers, equality specialists, and trade union representatives are usually responsible for initiating the process of organizational change to embrace a work–life balance culture. This involves developing appropriate policies and practices and ensuring compliance with relevant legislation, as well as monitoring policy implementation and evaluating their impact. However, for such policies and practices to be effective, it is important that they are endorsed by senior management (Clake, 2005).

It is equally important that line managers 'buy in' to the work–life balance policies, to ensure that they are implemented and that they do not end up as 'empty shells' (Hoque and Noon, 2004). When it comes to policy implementation across an organization, line managers can hold the role of 'gate keepers'. As highlighted by several commentators, 'line managers have the power to either put real momentum behind the culture change or stop it dead' (Clutterbuck, 2003: 133) and the success of work–life balance initiatives largely depends on their attitudes, skills, and behaviour (Willmot, 2002).

However, to what extent are they equipped to manage flexible working and support a work–life balance culture? Research to explore the role of line managers in implementing

Table 8.2 Integrating company-oriented and employee-oriented flexibility

Company-oriented flexibility	Flexible working arrangements	Employees-oriented flexibility
Opportunity to extend daily working hours	Compressed hours	Opportunity to work a shorter week with no loss of income
Opportunity for temporary flexibility to deal with peaks and troughs	Annualized hours; term-time only work	Opportunity to have periods of time off work to coincide with school holidays or to have time off to pursue other interests
Full cover and continuity as a full-time job but with additional benefits: job-sharing employees can cover for each other during absence; the job can benefit from two sets of skills and expertise	Job-share	Opportunity to work part-time
Provide opportunities for job secondments to gain new skills or experience, while covering for an employee on leave	Maternity and parental leave, career breaks and sabbaticals	Take time off work for caring responsibilities or for other reasons
Reduction of costs for the running of offices	Homeworking	More control and autonomy over the working day; reduce need for commuting to and from work
Retain valuable skills and expertise create opportunities for retiring employees to pass on knowledge to successors	Flexible retirement	Reduce working hours as transition into retirement

work–life balance policies and flexible working shows that often line managers have limited knowledge and understanding of statutory company provisions for leave arrangements, have not received any training to implement flexible working, and have found themselves relying on their common sense to deal with staff's requests for flexible working (Bond and Wise, 2002; Lewis and Taylor, 1996; Yeandle et al., 2003). Their attitudes towards work–life balance and flexible working are likely to impact on the way employees experience work–life balance in their organization, as demonstrated by a survey investigating the experiences of work–life balance of about 500 employees in a UK university (Manfredi and Holliday, 2003: 47–48). This was part of an action research project to promote work–life balance. It highlighted that employees' experiences can vary significantly across the same organization, depending on line managers' attitudes, as evidenced by the following comments made by some of the respondents:

> 'I am lucky that my line manager strongly believes in work–life balance and encourages me to work flexible hours to suit my other commitments, and this helps to reduce stress and improve my performance at work.'

'I feel that Brookes is ideal for my particular circumstances, a lot of this is due to the flexibility of my line manager at departmental level.'

But the experiences of others can be very different ...

'There seems to be a mistrust of the idea of work–life balance with some level of manage-ment – almost a view that staff who are interested in it are somehow trying to take the university for a ride. This attitudes need to be dispelled if work–life balance initiatives are to be successful.'

'Some managers seem to look on people that do not put in excess hours as disloyal.'

The experiences of these employees clearly show that some managers view the idea of work–life balance with suspicion and scepticism, and that they are resistant to it. Some of the reasons for resistance might include concern about the cost implications of work-life balance practices, the lack of skills to manage flexible working patterns, and what might be perceived as loss of control over the staff they are supposed to manage. Line managers' compliance has also been identified as a type of barrier to organizational change that can be even more difficult to overcome than resistance. Clutterbuck (2003: 135) argues that 'compliance blocks discussion' as it generates the type of attitude that can be summed up as 'I'm doing what you want, so what's to talk about?' – and breeds a 'rule-book mentality', and this can be equally unhelpful. He also draws a distinction between 'reluctant compli-ance and exploratory compliance'. He defines reluctant compliance as a kind of resistance taken to a less overt level, as opposed to exploratory compliance, where managers take a neutral stance, and are prepared to experiment and assess how flexible arrangements can work in practice. This can lead to more positive outcomes as the involvement of line man-agers in the design and implementation of alternative working practices can help to over-come their initial resistance.

Demand for flexible working is likely to increase as the right to request to work flexibly is likely to extended because of demographic changes and the need for extending work-ing lives due to an ageing population. Therefore, it is important that organizations de-velop management capability to deal with the challenges posed by different working patterns. Research carried out by the Chartered Institute of Personal Development with several organizations in different employment sectors looked at a broader range of work–life balance practices, and found that most of these organizations did not believe that 'flexible working required an entirely new skillset – rather, that flexible working placed certain areas of management under the spotlight' (Clake, 2005: 29–30). Examples of management skills that are commonly identified as being essential in successfully managing flexible working are highlighted in Table 8.3 and are matched with mini case studies to help students understand their practical application.

It is also important to consider work–life balance issues for line managers. This group of staff is expected to implement flexible working and to promote a work–life balance culture, but their own work–life balance issues are often overlooked. Research shows that employees in managerial jobs are less likely to have requested to work flexibly, and that in some sectors, particularly in retail, full-time work is a condition for managerial and supervisory positions (Hegewisch, 2009: 24).

Table 8.3 Management skills required to manage flexible working

Communication. This is important for negotiating changes to working patterns and monitoring their effectiveness and impact on other members of the team. When staff work flexibly or remotely, two-way communication between managers and their staff is very important.	Sainsbury's, a major UK food retailer, needs to be able to respond quickly to changes in customer demand. Helen Webb, Retail HR Director, says 'Flexible working is paramount in retailing. We have to have conversations with people at least twice a year about moving their working hours to fit changing trading patterns. What's important in these conversations is being very clear about the "why" without dictating the "how".'
Fairness and consistency. These two elements are closely linked as consistency in the way requests for flexible working are dealt with by line managers is key to ensuring that employees feel that they are being treated fairly.	With government funding, Clock, a small, award-winning digital agency employing about 30 people, invested in advice to draw up policies on flexible working. 'One of the biggest challenges is the perception of fairness', says Nadim, the company's Chief Executive. 'If one person gets one thing, other people say "Why can't I have that?" Having policies makes it fair, workable, replicable and enforceable.'
Trust. Flexible working involves greater autonomy in the way employees perform their tasks and sometimes in the way responsibilities are delegated. This requires the existence of trust between employees and their line managers.	IBM has more than 115,000 mobile employees around the world. Alison Gregory is a Senior Managing Consultant in IBM's Human Capital Management Service in the UK. She has lots of experience managing people across different locations. She says it is important to give people responsibility. 'I have often said: "it is up to you when, where or how it is done – so long that it is on time, it is good and the client is happy.'
Planning and innovation. Managing a more flexible working environment means that line managers must be prepared to take a more creative approach to working patterns and plan their resources more carefully. A more team-based approach may be taken, involving employees in the design and implementation of flexible working arrangements.	When Sainsbury's in Camden, North London, had to change the working hours of staff in the bakery in order to respond to customer demand, the store manager, Ziggie Singh, sat down with the 15 bakers and explained what the business was trying to do. He asked them how they would achieve it if they were the management team. Bakery manager Lawrence Ijejh and his team of bakers went away and came up with a flexible system of 2–3 baking shifts a day to maintain a regular supply of fresh bread throughout the day.
Performance management. Setting clear expectations and objectives for individual staff is important in a flexible working environment so that performance can be managed by output. Line managers need to move away from the belief that it is important to see their staff in order to know how they are performing at work. It is also important that they avoid judging their staff on their reasons for working flexibly, provided that the job gets done.	In the case of IBM, where they have a large number of mobile employees (see above), Alison Gregory, Senior Managing Consultant explains that: 'Managing people who work flexibly or remotely ... means that you have to be more focused on outcomes, better at communication, more explicit about your expectations, more regular about checking that work is going the right way.'

Source: Adapted from Maitland (2009)

⮕ Student Activity 8.3

If you were the line manager, how would you deal with this situation?

Albert submits a request to you to work compressed hours (4 days a week) so that he can spend more time looking after his elderly parents. Susan also asks to work compressed hours (4 days each week) to do some voluntary work for a charitable organization. Due to operational reasons you can accommodate only one of these requests.

Identify what challenges this situation may pose for a manager and explain what response you would adopt and why. Here are some possible responses:

- You treat them equally and refuse both applications.
- You ask them to sort it out between themselves and with their colleagues and decide who should work compressed hours.
- You speak to both of them to explore whether a compromise can be reached, e.g. both of them work 4.5 days or they work compressed hours on alternate weeks.
- You ask them what they would do in your place.
- You agree to the request of the member of staff who you think needs the flexibility most.
- You agree to the request of the member of staff who you think ought to be rewarded most for his/her work.
- You consult with the rest of the team before making a decision.
- Or you can specify other options.

◉ End of Chapter Case Study Work–life balance policies at Oxford Brookes University

The Directorate of Human Resources at Oxford Brookes University in the UK carried out a project in partnership with the trade unions to develop work–life balance policies and practices. The university already offered some flexible working arrangements, enhanced maternity leave, and career breaks up to a period of three years. A bespoke project team was set up that included academics with expertise in the areas of human resource management and equality and diversity management, and human resource and equality practitioners, to draw on academic research to develop policies and practices. The team also included staff trade union representatives as well as representatives of staff who did not belong to the trade unions.

A university-wide survey was undertaken to gain an understanding of staff's experience of work–life balance, demand for flexible working, and to identify issues that needed to be addressed. The staff survey highlighted that respondents were overwhelmingly supportive of the idea of work–life balance and over 80 per cent of them believed that work–life balance enables people to work better. However, the survey results also showed that implementation of existing work–life balance practices was patchy across the university, and often staff were not aware of what was available. There was a demand for greater access to flexible working and, based on the findings from the staff survey, an action plan was drawn up with the following objectives:

- To extend the right to request flexible working to all employees
- To develop a package of work–life balance polices to include special leave arrangements and flexible working

- To ensure effective communication of work–life balance policies and practices to all employees across the university
- To design and deliver training for line managers to support work–life balance practices and implement flexible working
- To identify and share examples of work–life balance good practice across the university

A wide range of flexible working policies were introduced, including compressed hours, regular and occasional home-working, flexi-time, and part-year working to offer staff the opportunity to work a reduced number of weeks in a year. A university policy on career breaks was extended to all staff, not just those with childcare responsibilities, and enhanced study leave arrangements were introduced. All these policies were open all employees, subject to operational requirements and service delivery.

A key element of this project was to ensure effective communication to all staff of work–life balance policies and this was achieved by circulating a leaflet, attached to staff's pay slips, outlining all the work–life balance polices and practices offered by the university. A dedicated website was also set up, and a good practice guide was produce to highlight examples of good practice existing across the university.

Training and workshops for line managers and other key staff were organized to raise awareness about work–life balance issues, to update line managers on university policies and practice, and to develop their capability to manage flexible working.

The university has been monitoring the impact of this project on its workforce by using a staff satisfaction survey, which is regularly undertaken every two years. The latest staff survey shows that 76 per cent of respondents said that everyone is treated fairly with regard to helping them balance their work and personal commitments.

Further materials relating to this case study, such as the work–life balance policies and a guide to work–life balance good practice guide, are available on the online resources.

Case study questions

1. What kind of approach to do you think was adopted by this university to develop work–life balance policies and practices?

2. How important do you think it is for an organization to work in partnership with staff to develop work–life balance policies and practices?

3. Do you think that flexible working arrangements are equally accessible to all employees, or that it might be more difficult for some employees to access these arrangements compared to others, either because of the type of job they do or because of their position in the organization? Provide examples to justify your arguments.

4. Design a workshop to develop line managers' capabilities to manage flexible working. In the preparation of your work, address the following points:

   - The importance of work–life balance policies and practices in the workplace
   - Integrating company flexibility with employee flexibility
   - Communication
   - Fairness and consistency
   - Trust
   - Planning and innovation
   - Performance management

➕ Conclusion

Work-life balance issues have surfaced as a result of an increased participation of women in the labour market and other major changes, such as falling birth rates, an ageing population, and an increase in single-parent families. These issues have been placed on the public policy agenda of most industrialized countries, which have taken different approaches to promote work-life balance. In general terms, these have involved the adoption of different measures, including: the use of legislation to introduce leave arrangements and a right to flexible working for parents; a reliance on the social partners (employers and trade unions) to negotiate work-life balance arrangements in the workplace; and a reliance on the business case to encourage employers to adopt work-life voluntary initiatives.

We have seen through this chapter that the debate on work-life balance and academic research on this topic have developed, broadly speaking, along two main lines. On the one hand, there is the individual's perspective, which focuses on the gender dimension of work-life balance or on the more inclusive approach of work-life balance for all, which can be traced back to a diversity management ideology. On the other hand, there is the workplace perspective, which focuses on the challenge of integrating company-led flexibility, driven by the market and customer demands, with employee-led flexibility, driven by individuals' needs.

From an organizational perspective, particularly in the Anglo-Saxon countries, a lot of emphasis has been placed on the business case for work-life balance policies and practices, and the competitive advantages that these can offer in terms of staff recruitment and retention, and increased performance and productivity. However, research shows that there is no conclusive evidence to support these claims. Besides, economic pressure on companies to remain competitive, especially during a period of economic downturn, may lead to the marginalization of work-life issues. Furthermore, it is important to draw attention to the fact that from a global perspective, in the case of growing economies such as India, work-life balance is a western-imported concept, and a luxury that cannot be afforded. This demonstrates the need to move the debate on work-life balance beyond the logic of the business case and competitive advantage for companies, and to reframe it within the context of social justice, inclusive employment policies, and workplace practices that support people's participation in the labour market by helping them to combine paid employment with their personal lives.

Therefore, we think that the future of the work-life balance debate lies in a third line of argument, which has emerged in Europe, about socially sustainable work. As discussed in this chapter, this approach advocates the importance of considering the impact of the organization of paid work on individuals, local communities, and the wider society. Thus it can be concluded that work-life balance issues should be linked to the quality of life and human sustainability, but equally, as argued by Pitt-Catsouphes and Googins (2006), it should be acknowledged that they are of strategic importance to businesses and that they should be addressed at an organizational level through the principle of corporate social responsibility.

❓ Review and discussion questions

1. What are the main drivers that led to the development of the concept of work-life balance, and what types of approach have different countries taken to develop work-life balance policies and practices in the workplace?

2. Explain what is meant by 'experiences of work-life balance are gendered', and provide examples from academic literature and research to support your arguments.

3. Explain the concept of work-life balance from a diversity management perspective.

4. To what extent do you think that the expression work-life balance can capture the complexity of the relationship between paid work and other parts of people's lives?

5. Explain the border-crossing theory, and provide examples of how this can be applied in practice to the way in which people manage their work–life balance.

6. What does it mean to take 'a dual agenda' approach to develop work–life balance policies and practices in the workplace?

7. Discuss the role of line managers and what management capabilities are needed to successfully manage flexible working.

 For additional material on the content of this chapter please visit the supporting Online Resource Centre at **www.oxfordtextbooks.co.uk/orc/kumra_manfredi/**

Further reading

Gambles, R., Lewis, S., and Rapoport, R. (2006) *The Myth of Work–Life Balance.* Chichester: Wiley.

Kossek, E.E., Lewis, S., and Hammer, L.B. (2010) Work–life initiatives and organizational change: overcoming mixed messages to move from the margin to the mainstream. *Human Relations,* 63/1: 3–19.

Rapoport, R., Bailyn, L., Fletcher, J.K., and Pruitt, B.H. (2002) *Beyond Work–Family Balance.* San Francisco, CA: Jossey-Bass.

Sturges, J. (2008) All in a day's work? Career self-management and the management of the boundary between work and non-work. *Human Resource Management,* 18/2: 118–134.

References

Allard, K., Haas, L., and Hwang, P. (2007) Exploring the paradox: experiences of flexible working arrangements and work-family conflict among managerial fathers in Sweden. *Community, Work and Family,* 10/4: 475–493.

Beauregard, T.A. and Henry, L.C. (2009) Making the link between work-life balance practices and organizational performance, *Human Resource Management Review,* 19: 9–22.

Bond, S. and Wise, S. (2002) Family leave policies and devolution to the line. *Personnel Review,* 32/1: 58–72.

Bowen, G.L. (2000) Workplace programs and policies that address work-family and gender equity issues in the United States, in Haas, L., Hwang, P., and Russell, G. (eds), *Organizational Change and Gender Equity.* London: Sage, pp. 79–98.

Bunting, M. (2004) *Willing Slaves.* London: Harper Collins.

Clake, R. (2005) *Flexible Working: The Implementation Challenge.* London: CIPD.

Clark, S.C. (2000) Work/family border theory. *Human Relations,* 53/6: 747–770.

Clutterbuck, D. (2003) *Managing Work–Life Balance.* London: Chartered Institute of Personnel Development (CIPD).

Collinson, P. (2009) The benefits of a four-day week. *The Guardian,* Saturday 28 March.

Crosby, F.J. (1987) *Spouse, Parent, Worker: On Gender and Multiple Roles.* New Haven, CT: Yale University Press.

Department of Trade and Industry (2001) *The Business Case.* London: Department of Trade and Industry.

Dex, S. and Scheibl, F. (2002) *SMEs and Flexible Working Arrangements.* Bristol: The Policy Press/Joseph Rowntree Foundation.

Dex, S. and Smith, C. (2002) *The Nature and Patterns of Family-friendly Employment in Britain.* Bristol: The Policy Press/Joseph Rowntree Foundation.

Doherty, L. (2004) Work-life balance initiatives: implications for women. *Employee Relations,* 26/4: 433–452.

Doherty, L. and Manfredi, S. (2006) Action research to develop work-life balance in a UK university, *Women in Management,* 21/3: 241–259.

Equal Opportunities Commission (2007) *Working Outside the Box: Changing Work to Meet the Future*. Manchester: EOC.

Equality and Human Rights Commission (2009) Working better: fathers, family and work-contemporary perspectives. Research summary 41 available at http://equalityhumanrights.com/publications/a-z-of-publications/

European Foundation for the Improvement of Living and Working Conditions (2007) *Work–Life Balance: Solving the Dilemma*. Available online at http://www.eurofound.europa.eu/publications/htmlfiles/ef0789.htm.

Executive Office of the President, Council of Economic Advisers (2010) *Work–Life Balance and the Economics of Workplace Flexibility*. Available online at http://www.whitehouse.gov/files/documents/100331-cea-economics-workplace-flexibility.pdf.

Fleetwood, S. (2006) *Why Work–Life Balance Now?* Lancaster University Management School Working Paper. Lancaster: Lancaster University. Available at http://www.lums.lancs.ac.uk/publications/abstract/004344/ (retrieved 26/4/2011).

Gambles, R., Lewis, S., and Rapoport, R. (2006) *The Myth of Work–Life Balance*. Chichester: Wiley.

Gattrell, C. (2007) A fractional commitment? Part-time work and the maternal body. *International Journal of Human Resource Management*, 18/3: 462–475.

Gíslason, I.V. (2007) Parental leave in Iceland: bringing the fathers in. Developments in the wake of new legislation in 2000. Reykjavik: Ministry of Social Affairs and Centre for Gender Equality. Available online at www.jafnretti.is/D10/_Feles/parentalleave.pdf.

Haas, L., Allard, K., and Hwang, P. (2002) The impact of organizational culture on men's use of parental leave in Sweden. *Community, Work and Family*, 5/3: 319–342.

Haas, L. and Hwang, P. (2007) Gender and organizational culture. *Gender and Society*, 21: 52–79.

Hantrais, L. (2000) *Social Policy in the European Union*. London: Macmillan.

Hegewisch, A. (2009) *Flexible Working Policies: A Comparative Review*. Manchester: Institute for Women's Policy Research and the Equality and Human Rights Commission.

Hogarth, T., Purcell, K., and Simm, C. (1999) *Whose Flexibility? The Costs and Benefits of the Non-standard Working Arrangements and Contractual Relations*. York: Joseph Rowntree Foundation.

Hooker, H., Neathey, F., Casebourne, J., and Munro, M. (2007) *The Third Work–Life Balance Employee Survey*. Employment Relations Research Series No. 58. London: Department of Trade and Industry.

Hoque, K. and Noon, M. (2004) Equal opportunities policy and practice in Britain: evaluating the 'empty-shell' hypothesis. *Work, Employment and Society*, 18/3: 481–506.

Houston, D. (2002) *Work–Life Balance in the 21st Century*. Basingstoke: Palgrave Macmillan.

Hyman, J., Scholarios, D., and Baldry, C. (2005) Getting on or getting by? Employee flexibility and coping strategies for home and work. *Work, Employment and Society*, 19/4: 705–725.

International Labour Office (2009) *Eighth European Regional Meeting, Facts on Quality of Working Life*. Geneva: ILO. Available online at http://www.ilo.org/wcmsp5/groups/public/---dgreports/---dcomm/documents/publication/wcms_101648.pdf

Johnson, M. (2004) *The New Rules of Engagement: Life–Work Balance and Employee Commitment*. London: CIPD.

Jones, A. (2003) *About Time for Change*. Place: The Work Foundation in association with Employers for Work-Life Balance. Available online at http://www.theworkfoundation.com/assets/docs/publications/177_About%20time%20for%20change.pdf.

Kandola, R. and Fullerton, J. (1994a) *Managing the Mosaic*. London: Institute of Personnel Development.

Kandola, R. and Fullerton, J. (1994b) Diversity: more than just an empty slogan. *Personnel Management*, November: 46–49.

Levine, J. (1993) Men, childcare and the US workplace. Paper delivered at the 'Men as Carers' International Seminar, Ravenna, Italy, 21–22 May.

Lewis, S. (1999) How to voice the need to reconcile work and family, in Salmi, M. and Lammi-Tuskula, J. (eds), *European Diversities: Combining Work and Family Life*. Seminar Report. Helsinki: Stakes.

Lewis, S. (2006) *Gender, Parenthood and the Changing European Workplace. Final Report of the Fifth Framework Project*. Brussels: European Union.

Lewis, S. and Cooper, C.L. (1987) Stress in two earners couples and stage in the life cycle. *Journal of Occupational Psychology*, 60: 289–303.

Lewis, S., Gambles, R., and Rapoport, R. (2007) The constrains of a 'work–life balance' approach: an international perspective. *International Journal of Human Resource Management*, 18/3: 360–373.

Lewis, S. and Roper, I. (2008) Flexibility and work–life balance, in Muller-Camen, M. et al. (eds), *Human Resource Management*. London: CIPD.

Lewis, S. and Smithson, J. (2001) Sense of entitlement to support for reconciliation of employment and family life. *Human Relations*, 55/11: 455–481.

Lewis, S. and Taylor, K. (1996) Evaluation the impact of family-friendly employer policies: a case study, in Lewis, S. and Lewis, J. (eds), *The Work–Family Challenge: Rethinking Employment*. London: Sage.

Maitland, A. (2009) *Working Better: A Manager's Guide to Flexible Working*. Manchester: Equality and Human Rights Commission. Available online at http://www.equalityhumanrights.com/advice-and-guidance/here-for-everyone-here-for-business/working-better/working-better-a-managers-guide-to-flexible-working/.

Manfredi, S. and Holliday, M. (2003) *Work–Life Balance: An Audit of Staff Experience at Oxford Brookes University*. Oxford: Centre for Diversity Policy Research.

McRae, S. (1998) Part-time employment in a European perspective, in Drew, E., Emerek, R., and Mahon, E. (eds), *Women, Work and the Family in Europe*. London: Routledge.

Monks, J. (2001) *Changing Times*: A TVC guide to work–life balance. London: Trade Union Congress.

Moss, P. and O' Brien, M. (2006) *International Review of Leave Policies and Related Research*. Employment Relations Research Series. London: Department of Trade and Industry.

Natoli, G. (2005) *Teoria e prassi per la conciliazione lavoro e famiglia*. Roma: Ministero del Lavoro e delle Politiche Sociali.

Pillinger, J. (2002) The politics of time: can work–life balance really work? *Equal Opportunities Review*, 107: 18–21.

Pitt-Catsouphes, M. and Googins, B. (2006) Recasting the work–family agenda as Corporate Social Responsibility, in Kossek, E. and Lambert, S. (eds), *Work and Life Integration: Organisation, Cultural and Individual Perspectives*. Mahwah, NJ: Lawrence Erlbaum Associates.

Rapoport, R., Bailyn, L., Fletcher, J.K., and Pruitt, B.H. (2002) *Beyond Work–Family Balance*. San Francisco, CA: Jossey-Bass.

Storey, J. (1992) *Developments in the Management of Human Resources: An Analytical Review*. Oxford: Blackwell.

Webster, J. (2004) Working and living in the knowledge society: The policy implications of developments in working life and their effects on social relations. Report from the project 'Infowork', Department of Sociology, Trinity Colloge, Dublin.

Willmot, B. (2002) Line managers hold key to staff's flexible hours. *Personnel Today*, 4 September.

Wise, S. and Bond, S. (2003) Work–life policy: does it do exactly what it says on the tin? *Women in Management Review*, 18(/2): 20–31.

Yeandle, S., Phillips, J., Scheibl, F., Wigfield, A. and Wise, S. (2003) Line Managers and Family-friendly Employment: Roles and Perspectives. Bristol: The Policy Press/Joseph Rowntree Foundation.

9 Managing Sexual Orientation and Transgender in the Workplace

Learning objectives

- Appreciate the progress made in public and organizational life by those from lesbian, gay, bisexual, and trans communities
- Appreciate the approach to the issue taken by public and private sector organizations and identify similarities and differences between them
- Understand the concept of visible and invisible stigma and comment on its causes and consequences
- Understand the difference between the issues facing LGB people and those facing trans people
- Be aware of some of the key challenges that remain

Key terms

- **Bisexual:** a person who is sexually attracted to both sexes.
- **Gay:** a person whose sexual orientation is to persons of the same sex.
- **Lesbian:** a woman whose sexual orientation is to other women.
- **Pink pound:** refers to the amount of money that homosexual people have available to spend (Financial Times Lexicon, 2010).
- **Stigmatized groups:** members of stigmatized groups find themselves marginalized, the subject of negative social identities, and frequently the targets of discrimination. Examples of stigmatized groups are racial minorities and those with physical disabilities.
- **Trans:** the terms 'trans' people and 'transgender people' are often used as umbrella terms for people whose gender identity and/or gender expression differs from their birth sex, including transsexual people, transvestite/cross-dressing people, androgyne/polygender people and others who define as gender variant (Mitchell and Howarth, 2009: ii).
- **Transgender:** an umbrella term for people whose gender identity and/or gender expression differs from their birth sex. They may or may not seek to undergo gender reassignment hormonal treatment or surgery. The term is often used interchangeably with trans (Mitchell and Howarth, 2009: ii).
- **Transsexual:** a person who intends to undergo, is undergoing, or has undergone gender reassignment which may (or may not) involve hormone therapy or surgery (Mitchell and Howarth, 2009: ii).

Introduction

In this chapter we explore the issue of discrimination in respect of lesbian, gay, bisexual, and trans (LGBT) people. This is a research topic which many have observed requires further examination, as in comparison to other equality strands it remains a relatively new and under-researched topic. This is both in terms of academic study and organizational practice. LGBT is an umbrella term used to describe the group, but on examination we find that there are distinctions within each community and the needs and concerns differ by group. In this chapter we explore a number of these distinctions and seek to understand where progress has been made and how this has been achieved. We also focus on the areas where there is still work to be done. In terms of progress made, we look at the Stonewall (2010) *Top 100 Employers Index* and determine the steps that organizations have adopted to implement and progress the issues of their LGB employees. We also comment on progress made in respect of the mainstreaming of LGB people in both the private and public sectors. However, we continue to see a picture of LGBT people gaining access and entry to organizations, but once in them often being the targets of discrimination and harassment. We thus turn to explanations as to why this might be. We look at the work of Ragins et al. (2007) to understand the causes of discrimination through the concept of stigma, with a particular focus on the difference between visible and invisible stigmas and the conditions under which those with invisible stigmas, such as LGB people, are likely to remain silent and those where they are likely to disclose.

We also explore the experience of trans people. We see that a number of legislative regulations have come into force to protect trans people in the workplace, but that as a community they continue to face discrimination and harassment both in wider society, but also in the workplace. We conclude with a case study which provides an example of an organizational response to the issue, focusing on LGB people and the impact this has had on work practices at IBM.

Lesbian, gay and bisexual people's expectations of discrimination

Signpost to Chapter 2 An Outline of European and UK Equality Legislation

In 2008 Stonewall, an awareness-raising and lobbying group for the rights and equality of lesbian, gay and bisexual (LGB) people, commissioned a survey of 1,658 LGB people to explore their expectations and experiences of a number of key societal institutions. One of these was their treatment in the workplace. This was the first such study to be undertaken and revealed a number of issues. The study not only wanted to highlight how those from the LGB community experience society, but also the importance of expectations and how these frame and position our experience of treatment in society. The findings revealed that despite some years of legislation outlawing inequality in respect of LGB people, many continue to believe that if they are open about their sexual orientation it will hold them back in their interactions with a number of key societal institutions, such as the political system, the criminal justice system, in education and in the workplace (Stonewall, 2008).

The survey revealed that in the last five years, nearly one in five lesbian and gay people have experienced homophobic bullying in the workplace. One third of them think that lesbian and gay people who are open about their sexual orientation in the workplace are more productive, although coming out brings its own risks. It raises the possibility that the individual may become the subject of homophobic bullying and potentially less favourable treatment with respect to perks and promotion opportunities. The study reported that homophobic bullying occurs at all organizational levels. Line managers were responsible for bullying in 25 per cent of cases, fellow team members in 50 per cent of cases, and people in a more junior role in 30 per cent of cases (Stonewall, 2008).

Stonewall collected further data on the experience of LGB people in the workplace in 2010. As part of their *Workplace Equality Index*, employers wishing to be included in the index were required to seek feedback from their LGB staff. The sample consisted of 7,200 employees from 273 organizations. Results showed that 83 per cent of LGB employees were open about their sexual orientation to their colleagues and 65 per cent were 'out' to their manager. However, only 26 per cent were open with customers, service users, or clients. Of respondents, 38 per cent felt unable to be open about their sexual orientation with colleagues, their manager, or both, and 13 per cent have not disclosed their sexual orientation to anyone at work. Bisexual employees are eight times less likely than lesbians or gays to disclose their sexual orientation to anyone at work.

Seventy-five per cent of LGB staff agreed that their workplace has a culture which is inclusive of LGB people. The feeling is highest among those who are completely open about their sexual orientation at work (87 per cent) and among employees of those organizations in the top 25 companies in the Stonewall 2010 Index, where the figure is 82 per cent (see below). And 78 per cent of LGB staff said they would feel confident reporting anti-gay bullying behaviour at work. Once again, this feeling is highest among those who are fully open about their sexual orientation at work (89 per cent) and lowest among those who are not (56 per cent).

In terms of management, 64 per cent of LGB staff felt that their line manager supported them as an LGB employee, although this figure is lower among bisexual staff (34 per cent), and black and minority ethnic LGB staff (55 per cent). However, for staff who are not open about their sexual orientation in their workplace, only 9 per cent think they are supported by their line manager.

Senior management were felt to be supportive of LGB staff by 61 per cent of the sample. Here again, greatest support is felt by those who are fully 'out' in their workplaces (77 per cent) and those employed by organizations in the top 25 (71 per cent).

These figures show some room for optimism in respect of the workplace culture and support from managers and heterosexual colleagues for LGB employees, particularly those who are open with everyone in their workplace about their sexual orientation. However, the figures do need to be treated with some caution; they are taken from a self-selecting group – employers wishing to be included in the *Workplace Equality Index*. These employers are likely to be at the vanguard of policy, practice, and commitment to the issue. How representative these findings are of organizations at large remains debatable.

> ### Student Activity 9.1
>
> 1. In your view, what impact will these expectations have on those from the LGB community when they enter organizations?
> 2. What do you think their main fears will be?
> 3. Where do you think they are most likely to look for support?
> 4. What types of support do you think would be most effective and why?
> 5. What recommendations would you make to help overcome these expectations?

Understanding discrimination on the grounds of sexual orientation in the workplace through the concept of stigma

In order to understand how these expectations of discrimination are formed and why LGB employees may or may not disclose their sexual orientation, in this section we examine discrimination through the concept of 'stigma'. Along with religious belief, sexual orientation has been described as a peculiarly sensitive and to some extent a taboo topic (Colgan et al., 2007; Ward and Winstanley, 2003). This is because, unlike many other stigmatized groups (e.g. black and minority ethnic groups, or disabled and older workers), LGB stigmatization is generally one of the 'invisible' areas of diversity. It is a topic that has received much less research attention in the field of management than the visible forms of diversity, such as gender or race (Bowen and Blackmon, 2003).

According to Ragins et al. (2007), members of stigmatized groups find themselves marginalized, the subject of negative social identities, and frequently the targets of discrimination (Crocker et al., 1998; Goffman, 1974 [1963]). Some individuals and groups have readily discernible and visible stigmas, e.g. race or physical disability (Jones et al., 1984). Others, such as gay men, lesbians, and bisexuals, have invisible stigmas and face specific challenges (Clair et al., 2005; Pachankis, 2007; Quinn, 2006; Ragins, 2004).

A key challenge for those in organizations with invisible stigmas is whether to disclose their stigmatized identity to those in the organization (Ragins et al., 2007). This is an extremely stressful decision for an individual and it has been identified as one of the key career challenges facing LGB employees (e.g. Button, 2001, 2004; Chrobot-Mason et al., 2001; Griffith and Hebl, 2002; Ragins, 2004). This is because disclosure has been reported to result in verbal harassment, job termination, and, at the extreme end of the scale, physical assault (D'Augelli and Grossman, 2001; Friskopp and Silverstein, 1996). Thus the fear of disclosure may have a greater negative impact on employees than actually disclosing one's sexual orientation, which has been described by LGB employees as bringing a sense of relief (Griffin, 1992; Woods, 1994).

Studies examining the psychological and work outcomes of disclosing LGB identity at work have predicted generally positive outcomes. The rationale is that through disclosure the individual achieves congruence between their public and private identities (Ellis and Riggle, 1995) and is thus able to obtain psychological wholeness and well-being (Reynolds and Hanjorgiris, 2000). They will also be relieved of the strain of leading a double life (Fassinger, 1995; Griffin, 1992). While these assertions may seem intuitively reasonable, research evidence supports a more complex picture, with some findings indicating positive outcomes for the discloser and some negative (Ragins et al., 2007). Thus the decision to disclose is an ongoing process which is influenced by each social interaction. It requires judgement, weighing the psychological benefits of engaging in authentic relationships on the one hand, and the potential costs of social rejection on the other (Goffman, 1974 [1963]). Thus disclosure is not a binary choice, with disclosure or non-disclosure as the only options. Rather, it is a continuum which ranges from complete disclosure at one end to non-disclosure at the other (Ragins et al., 2007). The criteria by which those with invisible stigmas determine where they will position themselves along the continuum is examined through a number of conceptual models. Bowen and Blackmon (2003) used voice and silence to develop their model, explaining how fear and 'spirals of silence' impact the decision to disclose gay identity at work. Clair et al. (2005) use risk assessment and cost-benefit analyses to underpin their model, where the individual would assess the potential costs of disclosure against the perceived benefits.

Within an organizational setting, a number of factors have been found to support disclosure. These are as follows:

- **Presence of similar others:** the presence of similar others affects the perception of the stigma; it offers the possibility of group acceptance and support. Ragins (2008) noted that for those who have not disclosed their sexual identity at work, the presence of LGB colleagues or managers led to a social identity process (Tajfel and Turner, 1986) that would make disclosure more likely.

- **Support from dissimilar others:** interestingly, the decision to disclose is also positively influenced by the presence of individuals within the organization who do not personally share the stigma, but who are willing to publicly voice their support for those who do. Woods (1994) reported that a number of the gay men interviewed in his study gave the presence of gay co-workers and support from heterosexual peers and managers as key factors in their decision to disclose. There is evidence that this information has filtered through to organizations and is informing practice. For example, in the Stonewall 2010 *Top 100 Employers Index*, the Foreign and Commonwealth Office LGB Staff Network Group, (FLAGG) recently launched 'Friends of FLAGG'. This is a campaign which aims to gain support from Foreign Office colleagues who are not personally lesbian, gay, or bisexual, but who want to show their support for those in the organization who are, and who also support the work of the network (Stonewall, 2010).

The key factor that will hinder an individual's willingness to disclose will be if they have experienced discrimination due to disclosure in the past. For example, Woods (1994) reported that a number of those in his study commented that past discrimination in previous organizations had raised respondents' awareness, and in some cases their expectation, of discrimination in their current organization. Schneider (1987) found that in her sample of lesbians, those who reported losing their job due to disclosing their sexual orientation were understandably less likely to disclose in their present organization than those who had not had such an experience. Even less severe costs of disclosure, e.g. verbal comments and less preferential treatment than co-workers, were found to negatively influence individuals' decision to disclose in subsequent employment (Ragins et al., 2007). To reconcile this mixed picture, Ragins et al. (2007) undertook a study to take into account not just the individual drivers to disclose, but also the contextual situation within which the disclosure decision is made.

Drawing on social identity theory (Tajfel and Turner, 1986), Crocker et al., (1998: 505) defined stigmatized individuals as those who 'possess (or are believed to possess) some attribute or characteristic that conveys a social identity that is devalued in some particular context'. Thus, since stigma consists of perceived attributes viewed negatively within a particular social context, the environment is key in determining whether a particular characteristic is deemed a stigma (Ragins et al., 2007). Recent research drawing on 'stigma theory' has found that stigma shapes an individual's identity, behaviour and cognitions (Deaux and Ethier, 1998; Levin and van Laar, 2006; Miller and Major, 2000).

The findings of the study supported the expected relationships. Those who had not fully disclosed their sexual orientation in their workplaces because of fear of disclosure reported overwhelmingly negative consequences of their non-disclosure. These consequences were in relation to their careers, their workplace experiences, and their overall psychological well-being. Those reporting that they did not disclose their sexual orientation at work because of fear of social rejection had less positive job and career attitudes, received fewer promotions, and reported more stress-related symptoms than those who had fully disclosed (Ragins et al., 2007). We thus see that far from disclosure leading to uniformly positive outcomes for LGB employees, non-disclosure may be a necessary adaptive strategy that LGB employees adopt in unsupportive and potentially hostile work environments (Cain, 1991; Fassinger, 1995), emphasizing the importance of social context.

Co-worker support also emerged as a key finding of the study. Those in supportive work groups with supportive managers were far more likely to disclose their sexual orientation than those in either unsupportive or neutral work groups (Ragins et al., 2007). This indicates that supportive heterosexual colleagues enable LGB staff to bring their whole selves to work and work and perform in a coherent and consistent manner.

⊙ Student Activity 9.2

The following excerpts are adapted from two articles that covered a story which broke in May 2007 concerning Lord Browne, former Chief Executive Officer of BP, who was forced to resign after it became known that he had lied under oath about how he met his gay partner. He was attempting to obtain an injunction against a national newspaper which planned to print details of their four-year relationship. Read these excerpts and answer the questions that follow.

'For the last 41 years of my career at BP, I have kept my private life separate from my business life. I have always regarded my sexuality as a personal matter, to be kept private.' (Lord Browne's resignation speech, printed in *The Independent*, 2 May 2007, in an article by Robert Verkaik, Law Editor)

In an article in *The Times*, published on 2 May 2007, Matthew Parris discusses the issue. He speculates that Lord Browne may have felt the need to conceal his sexuality for business reasons, citing the attitudes of shareholders, employees, and business partners, particularly those in differing regions of the world. Matthew Parris also suggests that, although attitudes became more liberal over time, revealing Lord Browne's sexuality midway through his career could have caused significant attention.

1. What are the main factors which led Lord Browne to conceal his sexuality for so long?

2. Do you think his actions would have altered if the 2003 Regulations had been enacted earlier in his career?

Case study 9.1   Fair Treatment and Equal Employment Opportunities at BP

Consider the excerpt below from the BP *Code of Conduct*.

BP aspires to create a work environment of mutual trust and respect, in which diversity and inclusion are valued, and where everyone who works for BP:

- Knows what is expected of them in their job
- Has open, constructive performance conversations
- Is helped to develop their capabilities
- Is recognized and competitively rewarded for their performance based on merit
- Is listened to and is involved in improving team performance
- Is fairly treated, with respect and dignity and without discrimination
- Feels supported in the management of their personal priorities

Basic rules you must follow

In support of these aspirations, as a BP manager you must:

- Make sure your own decisions regarding recruitment, selection, development and advancement of employees are based on merit – qualifications, demonstrated skills and achievements. Do not allow factors such as race, colour, religion, gender, age, national origin, sexual orientation, gender identity, marital status or disability to influence your judgement
- Always seek to influence other parties with whom we work (contractors, agents, JVs) to do the same – particularly where we are the JV operator or hold a majority interest
- Follow all applicable labour and employment laws wherever we operate. In some areas where we operate, legal requirements are stringent. Familiarize yourself with any applicable additional local requirements with which you must comply.

Source: BP *Code of Conduct*, available at http://codeofconduct.bpweb.bp.com, p. 20 (accessed 5 October 2010)

Case study questions

1. Do Lord Browne's actions and resignation (as described in Activity 9.2 above) compromise BP's stated diversity policies and initiatives? Outline in what way(s) you think they do.

2. Provide your recommendations as to how BP can progress in overcoming these issues.

The organizational response for LGB equality in the public and private sectors

Having considered some of the concerns LGB employees may feel in respect of disclosing their sexual orientation in their workplace, we now turn our attention to the approach adopted to the issue within both public and private sector organizations.

Public sector organizations

The Employment Equality Directive (2000) signalled an important and ground-breaking advance in the protection of those from the LGB community from discrimination in employment based upon their sexual orientation. Enshrined in UK law in 2003 (in the Employment Equality (Sexual Orientation) Regulations), Colgan et al. (2009) [argue that the protection is long overdue. They cite evidence which indicates that LGB people experience discrimination and harassment at work (Colgan et al., 2008; Day and Schoenrade, 2000; Hunt, 1999). LGB people suffer costs to their health and quality of working life, and it has also been shown that those employers who do not seek to protect the rights of their LGB employees are likely to have to cope with the consequences of a demotivated and less productive LGB workforce (Day and Schoenrade, 2000).

Research evidence would indicate that it is the public services, and most particularly local authorities, which have led in respect of the inclusion and development of sexual orientation in parallel with other equality strands (Carabine and Monro, 2004; Colgan et al., 2007).

In their study, Colgan et al. (2009) argue that the impetus for the energy put into the equality and inclusion of LGB staff in the public services has been very much embedded within the overall 'modernization' agenda pervading public service provision. The modernization agenda within the public services encompasses a number of policy and practice initiatives, for example, the marketization of service provision and a range of managerialist interventions which focus on efficiency, effectiveness, and economy. These are underpinned by a variety of quantifiable outputs and performance targets to track progress, and the privatization or the adoption of private sector practices (McTavish and Miller, 2007; Newman and Clarke, 2009). The consumer has become central in service provision, and through the introduction of 'choice', consumer power is privileged as a means of securing equality and participation (Newman and Clarke, 2009). Colgan et al. (2009) thus argue that through the articulation of a business case embedded within the modernizing agenda, recognizing LGBT people as consumers and users of public services has supported and underpinned the policy and practice initiatives observed. This is clarified in guidance issued to local authorities in 2003 and revised in 2007 by the Improvement and Development Agency, which states that:

> Social inclusion and community engagement are at the heart of the modernizing agenda for local authorities. Recognizing lesbian, gay and bisexual people as equal citizens represents an exciting part of that agenda. (Creegan and Lee, 2007: 8)

To assess the relevance and impact of the approach adopted within the public services and its perceived effectiveness with a sample of LGB respondents, Colgan et al. (2009) reported on two studies. One was a pre-interview questionnaire issued to 154 LGB staff in 2006, and the other was interview-based data from the 154 respondents. The questionnaire revealed that respondents believed the public services were no longer at the forefront of promoting equality in relation to sexual orientation. Only 23.7 per cent of respondents 'strongly agreed' that they consider their employer to be LGB friendly in terms of organizational policy, compared to 46.2 per cent of private sector respondents and 33.3 per cent of voluntary sector respondents. Particular difficulties were reported in manual labour and male-dominated environments, where respondents feel it is particularly difficult to be open about their sexual orientation. Those working in schools, social services, and housing also experienced difficulties in respect of 'coming out' to clients, customers, and students (Colgan et al., 2006).

Of public service respondents, 23 per cent said they had experienced discrimination in respect of their sexual orientation, and 32.5 per cent reported experiencing harassment. Echoing the findings from the Stonewall (2008) study cited above, discrimination and harassment could come from line managers or colleagues, although Colgan et al. (2009) found students, clients, or the public were also potential sources of discriminatory or harassing behaviour.

In terms of public sector implementation of the 2003 Employment Equality (Sexual Orientation) Regulations, Colgan et al. (2009) found that LGB respondents felt that there had been minimal impact on organizational policy and practice. This was mainly because local authority employers were perceived to be 'ahead of the game', although organizations did report that they had audited their existing processes to ensure complete compliance with the regulations. However, LGB employees indicated that insufficient attention had been given to communicating and publicizing the regulations, in particular where policy changes had been made. This was felt to be particularly prevalent in respect of line managers, who were sometimes viewed as unable or unwilling to give the issue due attention in team meetings, where they were perceived to be uncomfortable in discussing the issue.

However, where the 2003 regulations are perceived to have had significant impact is in respect of an increased level of confidence felt by LGB workers. A gay male said that his decision to join the fire service in 2004 was influenced by the presence of the regulations. He commented: '... without that legal protection I wouldn't have gone into the Brigade ... even if I got in and had a bad time, I had the legal protection to pull me out of the situation' (Colgan et al., 2009: 289).

In respect of work to be done, two key areas emerged in the study. The first concerned the prioritization of the regulations alongside legislative requirements regarding other diversity strands, e.g. gender, race, disability, age, etc. It was recognized that resources for equality work within an already financially constrained public sector were limited. As an Equality Manager for a Local Authority commented: 'We have to prioritize meeting our statutory responsibilities. ... So if you were to ask me what proportion of our overall resources were devoted to LGB issues, it is actually, the honest answer, is less than on disability' (Colgan et al., 2009: 289).

The second issue concerns how realistic it is to impose performance standards against each of the equality strands on line managers who are already under substantial pressure to improve performance and efficiency across a number of their areas of operation. The modernizing agenda requires efficiencies and operational changes to be made through reorganization and the introduction of more flexible ways of working. To add to these highly complex organizational processes additional targets and measures linked to the achievement of the equality strands was perceived by equality managers as an additional burden on already stretched managers and resources. Interestingly, equality and diversity is enshrined in policy and thus should be mainstreamed through the performance management process (Colgan et al., 2009). One wonders why this issue is the one which is perceived as potentially 'expendable' where others clearly are not negotiable (e.g. reorganization and flexible working).

Private sector organizations

In the public sector, we thus see that the impetus for action in respect of equality for LGB employees has been a combination of compliance in meeting legislative requirements (particularly post 2003), but also the articulation of a business case emanating from the modernization agenda. Here the emphasis is on inclusion regarding service provision to individualized consumers who have choice for the first time in respect of their public services (Colgan et al., 2009). In the private sector, there has also undoubtedly been a great deal of attention paid to the issue. Here again, a key driver has been compliance with legislative requirements, but also evident is a clear business case. In the private sector, the business case has not been formed around service users and meeting their requirements. Instead it has been based upon the growing realization of a highly lucrative and relatively untapped market, that of LGB people who are less likely to have children and are thus likely to have higher disposable incomes than their heterosexual counterparts. Termed the 'pink pound', market researchers have put this market at approx £81 billion, and in times of economic downturn, many organizations are waking up to the fact that this is a market they ignore at their peril.

According to a recent spending and lifestyle study compiled by Gaydar.com (www.Gaydar. com), LGB consumers are staying afloat in the recession. They report high credit card usage among their sample and a high spend per month on cards – an average of £482 per person. Spending is largely on holidays (51.6 per cent), clothes (47.5 per cent) and internet shopping, excluding groceries (62.3 per cent). The respondents to the survey reported taking an average of 1.81 European short breaks, 1.46 European holidays, and one long-haul holiday in 2007. Figures like these have prompted holiday company Thomson to launch the first range of holidays aimed specifically at the gay, lesbian, and bisexual market.

◉ Case Study 9.2   Targeting the LGB market

Read the following excerpt and answer the questions below.

Thomson's Launch First Holiday Service Tailored for Gay Customers

Thomson Holidays have recently launched a new range of holidays tailored to the Gay market. The range, entitled the 'Freedom Collection', provides a distinctive offering in the marketplace. The collection is covered by the 'GayComfort' standard, which is an accreditation programme indicating that frontline hotel staff have been trained to meet the needs of gay travellers. The holidays are currently offered in seven locations, with some accommodation catering only to a gay clientele.

In launching the collection, Thomson's Innovation Manager, Phillippa Morgan, said: 'This is a hugely exciting launch for Thomson. There's definitely an appetite in the market for gay-friendly holidays that come with the security and peace of mind that only a big tour operator can offer. ... The reason we've taken this approach is because research has shown that three out of four gay or lesbian holidaymakers actively search out hotels they believe are genuinely welcoming. '

Source: Adapted from Sanders 2010.

Case study questions

1. What are the key drivers are behind Thomson's decision to launch their new range of holidays?

2. What are the advantages of such holidays for gay and lesbian travellers?

3. Do you think the values of diversity and inclusion underpinning the Sexual Orientation Regulations are advanced in the Thomson approach (i.e. identifying 'pink' destinations and offering gay exclusive hotels)?

4. Turner (2010) notes that the idea behind this range of holidays was originally mooted in 1991. Why do you think Thomson's have decided to go ahead with this range of holidays now? Would you recommend other organizations to follow Thomson's lead and launch products and services aimed only at a gay/lesbian market?

When reporting the findings from the 2008 Stonewall survey into LGB expectations of discrimination, a key finding was that LGB consumers would be more likely to buy from retailers showing LGB imagery in their advertising. There is some evidence that advertisers and marketers have realized this potential and are producing advertisements featuring lesbian and gay couples. For example, in the UK in 2008, Heinz produced an advertisement for its Deli Mayo product featuring a gay kiss. Lloyds TSB have produced a print advertisement in which a gay couple have been granted a mortgage from the organization and are buying a house together (Turner, 2010).

We thus see in the private sector that engagement with the LGB agenda is very much a business case and market-driven imperative. As traditional consumer market segments come under pressure and diminish, new market segments need to be identified. The pink pound shows clear evidence of holding steady even in recessionary times, and organizations are looking at ways to meet the needs of this group and develop their presence among a relatively poorly served and misunderstood demographic group.

Debate Box

Organize the class into two groups, one for the motion and one against.

The motion is:
Paying attention to LGB issues beyond what is required by law in private sector organizations should only be done if the activity can be justified and grounded in a sound, economically-determined business case.

Stages in the debate: (each stage is given with timings, the overall time for the activity is 55 minutes – allowing a few minutes for change over of presenters, etc.)

- Each group has 20 minutes to prepare their arguments either for or against the motion.
- Each group is given 5 minutes to present their opening statement (10 minutes in total).
- Groups reconvene for 10 minutes to prepare rebuttal arguments.
- Each group has 2 minutes to present rebuttal arguments.

A vote is taken and the winners of the debate announced; the casting vote goes to impartial observers: tutors, audience members not involved in the debate, or observers.

Benchmarking evidence: a mixed picture

To assess how well both sectors are performing in respect of their commitment to LGB staff and their organizational inclusion, benchmark evidence would support a mixed picture, showing strength for both sectors. Stonewall have for the last six years produced a *Workplace Equality Index*, which showcases Britain's top employers for LGB staff. The benchmark study not only requires employers to complete a highly detailed questionnaire covering nine key areas of organizational policy and practice in respect of protecting equality for LGB staff, but they are also required to demonstrate how their approach has a lasting impact on the workplace. Inclusion in the index is clearly recognized by employers as a desirable aim, as submissions for inclusion have more than doubled since 2006 (352 applications were made for inclusion in the 2010 index), and the score needed to gain entry to the index rose by 10 points in a year. In 2009, 56 points was sufficient to get into the top 100, by 2010 this had risen to 66.

Though the public services are well represented in the index, private sector professional service firms are the top-performing sector. Local authorities are the single biggest sector in the index and are doing particularly well in respect of police authorities. Central government is also among the top performers. The public sector accounted for the largest number of submissions, but the private sector made the most successful submissions: one-third of private sector submissions made the top 100 compared with a quarter of public sector submissions. The top three companies on the index for 2010 were Ernst and Young in third place, Hampshire Constabulary in second place, and IBM in first place. Accepting the award for IBM, Brendon Riley, CEO for UK and Ireland, said:

> IBM is extremely proud to accept this important accolade. ... Since last year's award, we have done much to re-evaluate and strengthen our LGB strategy as part of our overall commitment to diversity. We've looked more closely at the LGB network group – its value proposition and its life cycle – to ensure that it continues to deliver value both to the corporation and its members. We've also enhanced career monitoring for our LGB employees, to ensure that they are being treated equitably in career development and promotion opportunities, and to build a pipeline of future LGB executives.

> **Student Activity 9.3**
>
> 1. Why do you think employers want to be included in the Stonewall *Top 100 Employers Index*?
> 2. What benefits do you think they gain?
> 3. What value do you think these benchmarking exercises bring to organizations?
> 4. What value do you think benchmarking exercises contribute to the issue, in this case equality for LGB people in society?

Understanding the needs of 'trans' employees

A group who are also protected under legislation, but who have perhaps not received as much attention as LGB people, are those from the 'trans' community. The terms 'trans people' and 'transgender people' are both used for people who have a gender identity or wish to express their gender in a way which is contrary to their birth gender. This includes transsexual people (those who are intending to undergo, are undergoing or have undergone a gender reassignment process in order that they may live permanently in their acquired gender), transvestite or cross-dressing people (who wear clothes generally associated with the opposite gender either occasionally or permanently), androgyne or polygender people (those who do not conform to binary gender identities and do not see themselves as either male or female), and others defining themselves as gender variant (Mitchell and Howarth, 2009).

Signpost to Chapter 2 An Outline of European and UK Equality Legislation

At present there is not a clear official figure on the size of the trans population. No census in the UK asks if people identify as trans (Mitchell and Howarth, 2009). Estimates of the trans population range from 65,000 (Johnson, 2001) to 300,000 (GIRES, 2008). In the absence of an official estimate, it is impossible to determine levels of inequality, discrimination, or social exclusion experienced by trans people. However, there are indications that trans people experience and suffer due to transphobia. This takes a number of forms and can include: 'bullying, discriminatory treatment in schools, harassment and physical/sexual assault and rejection from families, work colleagues and friends; (Mitchell and Howarth, 2009: vi).

Public perception of the trans population evidences some negative attitudes. However, there is also room for some optimism. In 2006 The Scottish Social Attitudes Survey reported 50 per cent of respondents would be unhappy if a close relative were to enter into a long-term relationship with a transsexual person, and 30 per cent did not believe a transsexual person would be suitable as a primary school teacher (Bromley et al., 2007). In Wales, re-search found that 45 per cent of respondents would be unhappy if a close relative were to enter into a long-term relationship with a transsexual person, and 33 per cent did not believe a trans person would be suitable as a primary school teacher. However, 48 per cent did think that a trans person would be suitable as a primary school teacher (Equality and Human Rights Commission, 2008). Further research in the Northwest of England supports this more opti-mistic trend. Here 14 per cent of respondents felt negatively towards trans people, but 34 per cent felt positive. The majority (44 per cent) felt neutral (EHRC, 2008).

From an employment perspective, a number of legislative protections are available to this group. These are contained in the Sex Discrimination (Gender Reassignment) Regulations (SDA) 1999, the Gender Recognition Act (GRA) 2004, and the Equal Treatment Directive (2004/113/EC), which led to the Sex Discrimination (Amendment of Legislation) Regulations 2008. These regulations combine to require that employers ensure that in respect of gender reassignment those undergoing treatment, planning to have treatment, or those who have completed treatment receive due recognition of their acquired or chosen gender identity. It also protects them from discrimination in employment, and the 2008 regulations ensure pro-tection from discrimination in the provision of goods, facilities, and services (Mitchell and Howarth, 2009).

Despite legislative protection, research suggests that trans people are still experiencing dis-crimination and harassment at work. Only those undergoing, planning to undergo, or who have undergone gender reassignment are protected by employment law, but those who have yet to enter into the gender reassignment process are less protected. Whittle (2007) conducted a survey with trans people on their experiences of discrimination at work. He found that 29 per cent of respondents had experienced verbal harassment (derogatory comments) at work, and some had experienced verbal abuse (e.g. name calling). In their study, Keogh et al. (2006) found that problems at work were more likely to be experienced by trans people (33 per cent) than LGB people (13 per cent). In research by a:gender (2007), it was reported that over 50 per cent of trans people suffer discrimination and harassment at work. They also found that one in four find the treatment so severe that they leave the organization, and 42 per cent of those who have not yet entered the gender reassignment process but who wish to do so cite the likelihood of negative reaction in their workplace as the reason for not going ahead (Mitchell and Howarth, 2009). Research has also shown that trans people are more likely to be found working in the public sector, and this rose post-gender reassignment. A survey of 208 trans people conducted in 2000 found that, pre-transition, 28 per cent of respondents worked in the public sector. This rose to 42 per cent post-transition (Whittle, 2000). It also appears that trans people are more likely than the general population to be self-employed. Morton (2008) found that 19.7 per cent were self-employed. Though the study was unable to provide clear evidence as to why this was the case, it can be presumed that trans people may prefer a working environment over which they have more control and where they have more say on who they have day-to-day contact with (Mitchell and Howarth, 2009).

Within organizations, there has been some debate whether the issues affecting trans people should be considered alongside those affecting LGB employees. In research conducted by NatCen (2009), the view was taken that the issues should be separated. This was because each involves different issues. LGB people have issues concerning their sexual orientation, whereas trans people have issues in respect of their gender identity. Conflating such separate issues is to confuse matters and not fully address the needs of either group.

Debate Box

Organize the class into two groups, one for the motion and one against.

The motion is:

The needs of LGB and trans employees are sufficiently dissimilar to warrant their own strand in an organization's diversity policy.

Please follow stages in the debate as indicated above.

Implementing LGBT policy: organizational networks

One of the main ways in which organizations have sought to implement policy in respect of their LGBT employees is to establish networking groups for their LGBT employees. The purpose of these groups is to provide both individual benefits to the members themselves, but also organizational benefits in demonstrating clarity and focus for policy directions. The groups provide a forum for organizations to understand the issues of most concern to their LGBT employees, and through this to form an agenda for change.

Employees joining such groups may do so for a number of reasons. Some may decide to join to improve their self-esteem, and to enable them to be more honest and open about who they are in the work environment (Clair et al., 2005; Gedro et al., 2004). Professional reasons may also encourage some to join; here, the interest will be to build and enhance work relationships with colleagues (Clair et al., 2005; Humphrey, 1999). Another set of motivators may involve driving an agenda for social or political change (Colgan and Ledwith, 2000; Humphrey, 1999). A final reason for individuals deciding to join such groups is the possibility of influencing policy orientations and decision-makers (Githens and Aragon, 2009). The groups are useful, then, because they provide a forum in which the issues directly affecting LGBT employees can be aired and communicated through organizational channels to those who, first, need to be aware of the issue and, second, and perhaps more importantly, have the ability to take action to address the issue.

LGBT groups within organizations can take a number of forms. Githens and Aragon (2009) identify four main types (see Figure 9.1).

We thus see that there are a number of aims and objectives of LGBT groups. Some are seeking an activist agenda aimed at the overall betterment of society (Whittington, 2001). Others are looking to bring about organizational change at the more local level with the intention of improving organizational effectiveness. The groups will also vary in respect of whether they believe organizations tend towards order or chaos (Burrell and Morgan, 1979).

Emergent

Queer/radical approaches	Internally responsive informal approaches
For example, small groups bringing subversive change and informal labour groups.	*For example, informal networking groups and informal mentoring groups.*
Small, informal groups that work to bring change through overt or subtle, subversive action.They reject gay/straight binaries, work with broad coalitions, and integrate broader social issues into queer activism.	Unofficial groups for career development, social support among LGBT workers, and encouragement of diversity for competitive advantage.
Organized unofficial approaches	**Conventional approaches**
For example, LGBT union groups and LGBT law enforcement groups.	*For example, LGBT employee resource groups and diversity communities.*
Structured groups that are not sanctioned by the employing organization and that aim for social change in society and the organization.	Structured, formally sanctioned me groups that organize formal programmes and encourage discussion about diversity for the benefit of the organization.

Emphasize social change

Emphasize organizational effectiveness

Strive for order

(Githens and Aragon, 2009: 126)

Figure 9.1 Four types of LGBT network group within organizations (Githens and Aragon, 2009: 126)

If organizations tend towards order, the structure and composition of the group will tend to be orderly and tied in with overall organizational aims and objectives. If the organization is more free-flowing, the tendency will be to have a group formed around a set of relatively loose principles where key aims and priorities will emerge over time.

An organization which has greatly benefited from its LGBT group and other policy initiatives implemented to advance integration of LGBT employees is IBM. Their approach is detailed in our end of chapter case study.

 **End of Chapter Case Study** IBM's policy for LGBT employees

IBM is one of the world's oldest and most successful IT companies. Originally founded in the nineteenth century in New York, IBM is now involved in the invention, development, and manufacture of the industry's most advanced information technologies. Even before it was legally required to do so, the company had developed policies for LGBT staff that promoted equality and eliminated discrimination. Des Benton, IBM's UK Diversity and Inclusion Programme Manager, says that the company has a long history of equality, inclusion, and progressive action, both in the USA and the UK.

Without it being legally necessary, IBM had explicitly added sexual orientation to its non-discrimination policy. In 1991, it began to create networking groups for LGBT employees across Canada and the USA, and in 1998 it set up groups in the UK. Initially, the groups in the UK were established to help introduce changes to employee benefits for same-sex partners, ahead of the legislation which came into force in December 2003, although they have since focused more on social and business networking. While corporate social responsibility plays an important part in IBM's thinking, there was a clear business imperative behind its approach to LGBT equality too. Des explains:

As a large company, IBM feels a responsibility to 'give something back to the world', but that wasn't the only reason for this initiative, nor was the fact the law was changing. IBM, like many other employers, wants to have good diversity policies in order to attract the best people and to recruit from the widest possible pool of talent. We also believe that a workforce that looks like our customers helps us understand our customers better – and the government estimates that 6 per cent of the UK population is lesbian, gay, or bisexual.

In addition, several surveys have shown a powerful brand loyalty among gay and lesbian consumers. One survey showed that 87 per cent would remain loyal to companies who market directly to them, while 77 per cent would switch brands to companies with a positive stance to the LGBT constituency. So being known for our commitment to LGBT diversity would help us access this market, as well as being the right thing to do.

One change identified by the networking group was the need to introduce identical benefits for same-sex partners as those already received by partners and spouses of heterosexual staff. This was done across IBM's UK business in 2001, and included coverage by the company pension scheme and relocation expenses. In addition, a policy was drawn up outlining IBM's approach to diversity, and senior executives helped push initiatives forward. Communication with all employees about the value of the company's approach has also been important, so that IBM employees today see this approach as part of the norm.

IBM accepts that implementing the policy has not been cost-free. The company has spent money in supporting social activities for LGBT staff to network internally and externally. It has also sponsored and organized events to highlight what the company is doing – these range from internal events for IBM staff to two leadership conferences, exploring and building on the qualities of LGBT managers and future leaders. It has invested in specific advertising and sales efforts targeted at the LGBT community, including in 2001 setting up a full-time Sales and Talent team dedicated to the LGBT market. Perhaps most impressively, the company walked away from business where a client did not want LGBT employees working on the project, and it has also demoted managers who failed to follow policy or demonstrated poor behaviour relating to diversity issues.

However, Des is confident there is clear evidence of the success of the approach. IBM has been recognized as a leading employer for LGBT people, helping to attract and retain staff from LGBT backgrounds. In 2007 (and 2010), they topped the Stonewall *Workplace Equality Index*, which is the definitive national benchmarking exercise showcasing Britain's top employers for gay people.

> We're increasingly finding that diversity and inclusion policies are something other businesses look for when deciding whether to do business with IBM, and we've also been part of external activities such as Stonewall's Education for All campaign, aimed at tackling homophobic bullying in schools in the UK, which has prompted feedback from people outside the company. This all helps to promote us to LGBT customers, giving us the business advantage we're looking for.

Source: CBI, TUC, and EHRC (2008: 30–32),

Case study questions

1. Which of the four approaches to an LGBT employee network group identified by Githens and Aragon (2009) have IBM adopted? How do you know this?

2. What are the benefits of this approach for:

   a. members of the group?

   b. the organization?

   c. external stakeholders?

3. What are the components of IBM's 'business case' for LGBT equality and inclusion?

4. Do you think the organization is right to have an LGBT group? Are the needs of all these constituencies likely to be met equally?

✚ Conclusion

In this chapter, we have explored the issue of discrimination of the grounds of sexual orientation and transgender. We have seen that this is a topic in which research is very much at the early stages of developing a detailed understanding of the issues facing LGBT people and much remains to be done. We have examined views on the meaning and impact of appreciating and accepting those with alternative sexual orientations and diverse gender identities. We have explored the expectations of discrimination experienced by LGBT people in society as a whole, but specifically in the workplace. We have also sought to understand those areas in which progress has been made, and assessed where there is still work to be done.

In terms of progress made, evidence has been presented in respect of benchmarking data collected annually by Stonewall, which shows increasing numbers of organizations wishing to be included in their list of the Top 100 employers for LGB people. It raises the bar for those organizations seeking to make the list. Success has also been noted in light of a mainstreaming of the community through marketing initiatives from a diverse range of organizations which focus directly on the needs and requirements of LGB consumers. It may be argued that this comes from a business-based case perspective and that recessionary times have exacerbated energy in this area. Nevertheless, progress is evident.

However, we still see that individuals are put into a very difficult position within organizations and face decisions which will have repercussions whichever way they decide to act. For those who disclose their sexual orientation, there is the fear of discrimination, harassment, or worse. There is also the fear of marginalization and exclusion from key organizational work and social groups. For those who choose not to disclose, the constant fear of discovery is present, as is the everyday strain of maintaining a dual identity. For those from the transgender community, particularly those undergoing gender reassignment treatment, the option of whether to disclose or not is removed. The alterations to individuals are evident to see, and the stress of the process and the lack of sympathy received from work colleagues and organizations leads many people to leave their organizations and set up their own businesses so that they may work in a more supportive and accepting environment.

In the final section of the chapter we looked at one of the main approaches adopted by organizations to aid them in understanding and appreciating the needs and requirements of their LGBT employees. This is the formation of LGBT organizationally-based networks, which meet to plan action and determine priority issues for employees within the organization. The IBM case study illustrated the benefits of such groups, not only to their members, but also to the organization overall.

❓ Review and discussion questions

1. In your view, which sector is doing most to advance the agenda in respect of LGBT equality and inclusion – the public or private sector?

2. Is there any need for concern that private sector interest in LGBT diversity and inclusion is largely driven by a business case scenario and legislative compliance?

3. Is it right that LGBT employee groups are being relied upon by organizations to determine and advance the change agenda, and that there is no formal recognition of their contribution either in terms of monetary reward or organizational benefit, such as promotion?

4. Write a briefing document to your Diversity Director outlining the key issues facing trans people in the workplace. Include your recommendations of how the organization can best meet these challenges.

 For additional material on the content of this chapter please visit the supporting Online Resource Centre at **www.oxfordtextbooks.co.uk/orc/kumra_manfredi/**

Further reading

Bowen, F. and Blackmon, K. (2003) Spiral of silence: the dynamic effects of diversity on organizational voice. *Journal of Management Studies*, 40: 1393–1417.

Button, S. (2004) Identity management strategies used by gay and lesbian employees: a quantitative investigation. *Groups and Organization Management*, 29: 470–494.

Clair, J.A., Beatty, J.E., and MacLean, T.L. (2005) Out of sight but not out of mind: managing invisible social identities in the workplace. *Academy of Management Review*, 30/1: 78–95.

Colgan, F., Creegan, C., McKearney, A., and Wright, T. (2007) Equality and diversity policies and practices at work: lesbian, gay and bisexual workers. *Equal Opportunities International*, 26/6: 590–609.

Ragins, B.R. (2008) Disclosure disconnects: antecedents and consequences of disclosing invisible stigmas across life domains. *Academy of Management Review*, 33/1: 194–215.

Ward, J. and Winstanley, D. (2003) The absent presence: negative space within discourse and construction of minority sexual identity in the workplace. *Human Relations*, 56/10: 1255–1280.

 ## References

a:gender (2007) *Gender Identity and Employment Monitoring: Best Practice Recommendations*. London: a:gender.

Bowen, F. and Blackmon, K. (2003) Spiral of silence: the dynamic effects of diversity on organizational voice. *Journal of Management Studies*, 40: 1393–1417.

BP (2010) *Code of Conduct*. Available at http://codeofconduct.bpweb.bp.com (accessed 5 October 2010).

Bromley, C., Curtice, J., and Given, L. (2007) *Attitudes to Discrimination in Scotland: 2006 Scottish Social Attitudes Survey*. Edinburgh: Blackwell.

Burrell, G. and Morgan, G. (1979) *Sociological Paradigms and Organizational Analysis: Elements of the Sociology of Corporate Life*. London: Heinemann.

Button, S. (2001) Organizational efforts to affirm sexual diversity: a cross-level examination. *Journal of Applied Psychology*, 86: 17–28.

Button, S. (2004) Identity management strategies used by gay and lesbian employees: a quantitative investigation. *Groups and Organization Management*, 29: 470–494.

Cain, R. (1991) Stigma management and gay identity development. *Social Work*, 36: 67–73.

Carabine, J. and Monro, S. (2004) Lesbian and gay politics and participation in New Labour's Britain. *Social Politics*, 11/2: 137–156.

CBI, TUC, and EHRC (2008) Public recognition for diversity helps attract and keep customers: IBM case study, in *Talent Not Tokenism: The Business Benefits of Workforce Diversity*. London: Confederation of British Industry, Trades Union Congress and the European Human Rights Commission, pp. 30–32.

Chrobot-Mason, D., Button, S.B., and DiClementi, J.D. (2001) Sexual identity management strategies: an exploration of antecedents and consequences. *Sex Roles*, 45: 321–336.

Clair, J.A., Beatty, J.E., and MacLean, T.L. (2005) Out of sight but not out of mind: managing invisible social identities in the workplace. *Academy of Management Review*, 30/1: 78–95.

Colgan, F., Creegan, C., McKearney, A., and Wright, T. (2007) Equality and diversity policies and practices at work: lsbian, gay and bisexual workers. *Equal Opportunities International*, 26/6: 590–609.

Colgan, F., Creegan, C., McKearney, A., and Wright, T. (2008) Lesbian workers: personal strategies amid changing organizational response to 'sexual minorities' in UK workplaces. *Journal of Lesbian Studies*, 12/1: 31–46.

Colgan, F. and Ledwith, S. (2000) Diversity, identities and strategies of women trade union activists. *Gender, Work and Organization*, 7: 242–257.

Colgan, F., Wright, T., Creegan, C., and McKearney, A. (2009) Public service, equality and sexual orientation. *Human Resource Management Journal*, 19/3: 280–301.

Creegan, C. and Lee, S. (2007) *Sexuality: The New Agenda. A Guide for Local Authorities on Engaging with Lesbian, Gay and Bisexual Communities*. London: Improvement and Development Agency.

Crocker, J., Major, B., and Steele, C. (1998) Social stigma, in Gilbert, D., Fiske, S., and Lindzey, G. (eds), *The Handbook of Social Psychology* (4th edition). Boston, MA: McGraw-Hill, pp. 504–553.

D'Augelli, A.R. and Grossman, A.H. (2001) Disclosure of sexual orientation, victimization and mental health among lesbian, gay and bisexual older adults. *Journal of Interpersonal Violence*, 16: 1008–1027.

Day, N.E. and Schoenrade, P. (1997) Staying in the closet versus coming out: relationships between communication about sexual orientation and work attitudes. *Personnel Psychology*, 50: 147–163.

Deaux, K. and Ethier, K.A. (1998) Negotiating social identity, in Swim, J.K. and Stangor, C. (eds), *Prejudice: The Target's Perspective*. San Diego, CA: Academic Press, pp. 302–323.

Ellis, A.L. and Riggle, E.D. (1995) The relation of job satisfaction and degree of openness about one's sexual orientation for lesbians and gay men. *Journal of Homosexuality*, 30: 75–85.

Equality and Human Rights Commission (2008) North West Diversity Survey (unpublished data). Manchester: EOC.

Fassinger, R.E. (1995) From invisibility to integration: lesbian identity in the workplace. *Career Development Quarterly*, 44: 148–167.

Friskopp, A. and Silverstein, S. (1996) *Straight Jobs, Gay Lives: Gay and Lesbian Professionals. The Harvard Business School and the American Workplace*. New York: Touchstone/Simon & Schuster.

Gedro, J.A., Cervero, R., and Johnson-Bailey, J. (2004) How lesbians learn to negotiate the heterosexism of corporate America. *Human Resource Development International*, 7: 181–195.

GIRES (Gender Identity Research and Education Society) (2008) *Guidance for GPs, Other Clinicians and Health Professionals on the Care of Gender Variant People*. London: Department of Health.

Goffman, E. (1974 [1963]) *Stigma: Notes on the Management of Spoiled Identity*. New York: Simon & Schuster.

Griffin, P. (1992) From hiding out to coming out: empowering lesbian and gay educators, in Harbeck, K.M. (ed.), *Coming Out of the Classroom Closet: Gay and Lesbian Students, Teachers and Curricula*. Binghampton, NY: Haworth Press, pp. 167–196.

Griffith, K.H. and Hebl, M.R. (2002) The disclosure dilemma for gay men and lesbians: 'coming out' at work. *Journal of Applied Psychology*, 87: 1191–1199.

Githens, R.P. and Aragon, S.R. (2009) LGBT employee groups: goals and organizational structures. *Advances in Developing Human Resources*, 11/1: 121–134.

Humphrey, J.C. (1999) Organizing sexualities, organized inequalities: lesbians and gay men in public service occupations. *Gender, Work and Organizations*, 6: 134–151.

Hunt, G. (1999) *Laboring for Rights: Unions and Sexual Diversity across Nations*. Philadelphia, PA: Temple University Press.

Johnson, S. (2001) *Residential and Community Care of Transgendered People*. London: Beaumont Society.

Keogh, P., Reid, D., and Weatherburn, P. (2006) *Lambeth LGBT Matters: The Needs and Experiences of Lesbians, Gay Men, Bisexual and Trans Men and Women in Lambeth*. London: Sigma Research.

Levin, S. and van Laar, C. (eds) (2006) *Stigma and Group Inequality: Social Psychological Perspectives*. Mahwah, NJ: Lawrence Erlbaum Associates.

McTavish, D. and Miller, K. (2007) Public sector reform, modernization and gender: a case of further and higher education. Conference paper presented at Gender, Work and Organization, University of Keele, 27–29 June.

Miller, C.T. and Major, B. (2000) Coping with stigma and prejudice, in Heatherton, T.F., Kleck, R.E., Hebl, M.R., and Hull, J.G. (eds), *The Social Psychology of Stigma*. New York: Guilford Press, pp. 243–272.

Mitchell, M. and Howarth, C. (2009) *Trans Research Review*. Research Report 27. Place: Equality and Human Rights Commission.

Newman, J. and Clarke, J. (2009) *Publics, Politics and Power: Remaking the Public in Public Services*. London: Sage.

Pachankis, J.E. (2007) The social psychological implications of concealing a stigma: a cognitive-affective-behavioural model. *Psychological Bulletin*, 133: 328–345.

Quinn, D.M. (2006) Concealable versus conspicuous stigmatized identities, in Levin, S. and Van Laar, C. (eds), *Stigma and Group Inequality: Social Psychological Perspectives*. Mahwah, NJ: Lawrence Erlbaum Associates, pp. 83–103.

Ragins, B.R. (2008) Disclosure disconnects: antecedents and consequences of disclosing invisible stigmas across life domains. *Academy of Management Review*, 33/1: 194–215.

Ragins, B.R., Singh, R., and Cornwell, J. (2009) Making the invisible visible: fear and disclosure of sexual orientation at work. *Journal of Applied Psychology*, 92/4: 1103–1118.

Reynolds, A.L. and Hanjorgiris, W.F. (2000) Coming out: lesbian, gay and bisexual identity development, in Perez, R.M., DeBord, K.A., and Bieschke, K.J. (eds), *Handbook of Counseling and Psychotherapy with Lesbian, Gay and Bisexual Clients*. Washington, DC: American Psychological Association, pp. 35–55.

Sanders, J. (2010) Mainstream holiday company launch first gay-tailored service. *news.PinkPaper.com* (accessed 5 October 2010).

Schneider, B.E. (1987) Coming out at work: bridging the private/public gap. *Work and Occupations*, 13: 463–487.

Stonewall (2008) *Serves You Right: Lesbian and Gay People's Expectations of Discrimination*. London: Stonewall, UK.

Stonewall (2010) *Stonewall Top 100 Employers 2010: The Workplace Equality Index*. London: Stonewall, UK.

Tajfel, H. and Turner, J.C. (1986) The social identity theory of intergroup behaviour, in Worchel, S. and Austin, W.G. (eds), *Psychology of Intergroup Relations* (2nd edition). Chicago, IL: Nelson-Hall, pp. 7–24.

Turner, C. (2010) Why marketers should be tapping into the gay and lesbian pink pound. *UTalkMarketing.com* (accessed 5 October 2010).

Ward, J. and Winstanley, D. (2003) The absent presence: negative space within discourse and construction of minority sexual identity in the workplace. *Human Relations*, 56/10: 1255–1280.

Whittington, R. (2001) *What is Strategy – And Does It Matter?* (2nd edition). London: International Thomson.

Whittle, S. (2000) *Employment Discrimination and Transsexual People*. London: Gender Identity Research and Education Society.

Whittle, S. (2007) 'Sex changes'? Paradigm shifts in 'sex' and 'gender' following the Gender Recognition Act. *Sociological Research Online*, 12/1.

Woods, J.D. (1994) *The Corporate Closet: The Professional Lives of Gay Men in America*. New York: Free Press.

10 Managing Religion or Belief in the Workplace

Learning objectives

- Examine evidence of discrimination on the grounds of religious affiliation in the labour market
- Identify the main feature of the EU and UK legislation to protect religion or belief in the workplace
- Explain principled and pragmatic reasons that justify protection of religious freedom in the workplace
- Understand the interaction between religious freedom and other equality rights
- Define the different roles of public sector and private sector employers in relation to accommodating employees' religious practices
- Understand the implications for managing religious diversity in the workplace

Key terms

- **Dignity:** '[d]ignity is not a natural, empirical characteristic of human beings, but is a status conferred by humans upon themselves, to set them apart from other species' (Parekh, cited in Vickers, 2008b: 36–37). Consequently, this concept involves a moral judgement about the absolute intrinsic worth of human beings.

- **Discrimination on the grounds of religion or belief:** the terms 'religion' and 'belief' are defined as 'any religious belief or philosophical belief' and include a reference to a lack of religious belief. It is unlawful to discriminate on the grounds of religion or belief in relation to staff recruitment, employment, promotion opportunities, vocational training, and dismissal. Access to further and higher education is also covered by the legislation as part of the protection for vocational training.

- **Philosophical belief:** there is no clear definition under EU and UK law of what constitutes a 'philosophical belief'. The kinds of 'beliefs' likely to be protected by the law 'will need to have a certain level of cogency, seriousness, cohesion and importance' in accordance with the case law developed by the European Court of Human Rights (Vickers, 2006: 123).

- **Reasonable accommodation:** this involves accommodating employees' religious practices in the workplace, provided that it is reasonable and practicable to do so. Examples of reasonable accommodation could be allowing employees to adhere to a particular dress code (e.g. wearing a headscarf or a turban with a work uniform) or allowing some time off during the working day for prayers. Under EU and UK law there is no legal obligation for employers to accommodate employees' religious needs. However, failure to do so may result in indirect discrimination on the grounds of religion, which can be unlawful.

Introduction

In this chapter, we examine discrimination on the grounds of religion or belief and discuss the implications of protecting religion or belief in the workplace. The prohibition to discriminate on the grounds of religion in employment and occupation, except where religion is an inherent requirement of a particular occupation, was introduced in 1958 by the International Labour Organization Convention on Discrimination (Employment and Occupation). However, these provisions had a very limited effect until bespoke legislation was adopted by individual countries to this effect. In Europe, protection against discrimination on the grounds of religion or belief was introduced in 2000 by the Employment Equality Directive (2000/78/EC), which establishes a general framework for equal treatment in employment and occupation. This Directive plays a key role in the EU social policy agenda, addressing social and economic disadvantage which may be linked to prejudice and discrimination against certain groups. In the UK, the protection against discrimination on the grounds of religion or belief was incorporated into national legislation in 2003 and it has now become part of the 2010 Equality Act.

Issues around religion or belief in the workplace and the impact of the legislation do not appear to have been as well researched as some of the other equality strands discussed in this book. The boundaries between ethnicity and religion are not always clear and this makes it more difficult to explore to what extent discrimination may be linked to religious association. In this chapter, we examine some of the evidence that points to the existence of discrimination on the grounds of religion or belief in the labour market, particularly in relation to certain religious faiths. We then identify and discuss principled and pragmatic reasons, based on non-religious arguments, which justify the protection for religion or belief in the workplace. The multidimensional nature of religious discrimination is also explored as well as the potential for religious freedom to come into conflict with other equality rights, such as those of gender and sexual orientation. These conflicts can arise because of the way sexual orientation and the role of women in societies is viewed by some religious faiths. Conflict between rights can pose a complex dilemma and, as discussed in this chapter, the only way to address these issues is to find a balance between different equality interests.

In the final section of this chapter we consider the actual implications for managing religion or belief in the workplace and draw attention to the distinction between the role of public and private sector employers in their approaches to implement this equality strand.

Policy context: religious diversity and the labour market

Perceptions of discrimination on the grounds of religion or belief appear to be widespread in several European countries, as evidenced by the results of a survey carried out across all member states (European Commission, 2009: 17). In several countries, over half of the respondents believed that this type of discrimination is widespread, and these included the Netherlands (59 per cent), France (58 per cent), Denmark (55 per cent), Belgium (54 per cent), Sweden (53 pre cent), and Greece (51 per cent). However, only a small proportion of respondents thought that this type of discrimination is widespread in their country, including the Czechs and Slovakians (12 per cent), Latvians (13 per cent), and Lithuanians (14 per cent). Such marked differences about perceptions of discrimination on the grounds of religion or belief among European countries are likely to be explained by greater ethnic and religious diversity within the populations of some of these countries. This is partly due to their colonial past, for example in the case of France and the UK, and partly due to immigration patterns. In the UK, 45 per cent of respondents believed that discrimination on the grounds of religion or belief is widespread and, although this proportion is lower compared to some of the countries listed above, it is nonetheless higher than the EU average of 39 per cent.

Purdam et al. (2007: 148) highlights that 'the UK has one of the most religiously diverse populations in the European Union, both in terms of diversity within Christianity and different worlds religions' and that 'even minority religions have considerable diversity of traditions, cultures and languages'. Such religious diversity is also evidenced by the results of the 2007–2008 Citizenship Survey, which shows that 74 per cent of the population are Christian, 16 per cent declared themselves to have no religion, 4 per cent are Muslim, followed by Hindus and Sikhs, 1 per cent, Sikhs, 0.6 per cent, Buddhists, less than 0.5 per cent, and other religious groups such as Spiritualists, Pagans, Jain, Wicca, Rastafarian, Baha' i, and Zoroastrians where the percentages are very small.

It is not easy to examine how all these different religious or non-religious groups fare in the labour market since the boundaries between ethnicity and religion are not always clear. This may be partly explained by the fact that sometimes ethnicity is defined as including religious identity, and also that some religious groups are predominantly from one particular racial group (Vickers, 2006: 34). It follows that it can be problematic to establish to what extent discrimination based on people's religious association plays a part in the disadvantage that certain groups seem to experience in the labour market.

The availability of information from the 2001 UK Census has made it possible to explore the position of different religious groups as well as that of non-religious ones in the labour market. This has revealed that among men, Christians have the highest employment rate (77 per cent), followed by Jewish, Hindu, Sikh, and those with no religion (over 70 per cent), Buddhists (66 per cent), while Muslims have significantly lower rates of employment (56 per cent). This group also presents the highest rate of male economic inactivity (33 per cent) and unemployment (12 per cent), while men with no religion have the lowest rate of economic inactivity (17 per cent), and Jewish men have the lowest unemployment rates (4 per cent), followed by Christian and Hindu (5 per cent) (Bradford and Forsyth, 2006: 115).

Women's employment presents similar patterns with Christians having the highest rate of employment (69 per cent), followed by Jewish, Hindu, and Sikh (60 per cent or over), Buddhists (53 per cent), and Muslim with a significantly lower rate (27 per cent). Muslim women's rate of economic inactivity is also the highest (67 per cent) compared to lower rates in other groups (28 and 42 per cent respectively) (ibid.: 116).

Further analysis of these data by different ethnic groups with different religious affiliation shows a tendency for Muslims, across all ethnic groups, to have significantly lower rates of employment compared to those of other religions. For example, Black African Muslims of both sexes have the highest unemployment rates among all ethnic groups (28 per cent of men and 31 per cent of women); Indian Muslims have a lower unemployment rate (11 per cent of men and 12 per cent of women), which is, however, still significantly high compared to unemployment rates of other religious groups, as seen earlier (ibid.: 120). Bradford and Forsyth (2006: 121) compare employment rates among different religious groups belonging to the same ethnic group, namely Indians, and show that both Indian Muslim men and women have the lowest rates of employment compared to those belonging to other religions within the same group.

UK employment statistics (for 2004) also indicate the existence of horizontal and vertical occupational segregation within certain religious groups. For example, 37 per cent of Muslim men work in distribution and in the hotel and restaurant industry compared with 17 per cent of Christian men and no more than 27 per cent of men in any other group. Muslim and Sikh men are more likely to work in low-skilled jobs compared to Christian men. Also, Jews and Hindus are the most likely to work in managerial or professional occupations, about half in each group: Jewish men are more likely to work in the banking, finance, and insurance industry compared to any other religion, while Hindu men are more likely to be medical practitioners (one in 20) compared to Christian men (one in 200). With regard to women, between 16 and 20 per cent of Muslim, Hindu, and Sikh women are concentrated in sales and customer service jobs, compared to 12 per cent of Christians and of those with no religion. Sikh women are also most likely to work in low-skilled jobs, while Jewish and Buddhist women are the most likely to work in managerial and professional jobs. As a consequence of these employment patterns, Bond et al. (2009) highlighted the existence of pay gaps based on religion, including a negative pay gap for Muslims and a beneficial pay gap for Jews.

These employment trends seems to point to the fact that there are 'significant differences within ethnic groups, depending on religious association' and that Muslims seem to experience an 'unexplainable employment penalty relative to other non-white religions, over and above all other characteristics (including ethnic differences and language fluency)' (Lindley, 2002). This evidence suggests the existence of religious discrimination towards Muslims, although some of these differences may also be partly explained by other factors, such as attitudes towards work and motivation which may be difficult to measure (ibid.: 439). Sikhs too appear to have a disadvantaged position in the labour market, which may be partly due to religious discrimination.

Qualitative research commissioned by the UK government (Weller et al., 2001: 39) uncovered evidence of unfair treatment linked to religious affiliation. This study highlighted a number of areas where respondents reported having experienced unfair treatment, which included:

- dress restrictions (Muslims, Sikhs, inter-faith)
- working on religious days/holidays (Christians, Jains, Jews, New Religious Movement (NRM)s, Pagans)
- lack of respect and ignorance of religious customs (Hindus, Jews, Muslims, Zoroastrians)
- applications and recruitment practices (Christians, Muslims, NRMs, Sikhs, Zoroastrians, inter-faith)
- promotion prospects (Sikhs)

Moreover, research undertaken in the USA found that job applicants who wore Muslim religious identities were rated the least employable for high-status jobs, but most employable for low-status jobs (Ghumman and Jackson, 2009).

The evidence presented in this section suggests that there is a compelling case for the need to address discrimination on the grounds of religion or belief in the workplace, hence the introduction in the EU and other countries of legislation to protect workers against this type of discrimination.

A brief overview of the legislation

The EU Employment Equality Directive (2000/78/EC) establishes a general framework for equal treatment in employment and occupation which includes protection against discrimination on the grounds of religion or belief in employment, occupation, and vocational training. More specifically, this Directive protects against direct and indirect discrimination, harassment, and victimization on the grounds of religion or belief. There is no formal definition of religion or belief in this Directive. As noted by Vickers (2006: 4), on the one hand this is an advantage in that it provides a flexible concept that 'can adapt to reflect modern developments in our understanding of religion or belief'. On the other hand, the lack of formal definition of religion or belief can give rise to inconsistencies across member states about the way in which such concepts are defined. Vickers uses the example of Scientology, which is recognized in some member states but not in others. She also points out that the definition of what qualifies as 'belief' for the purpose of the protection afforded by this Directive is even more nebulous. As a guiding principle, she suggests that the kinds of 'beliefs' likely to be protected by the law 'will need to have a certain level of cogency, seriousness, cohesion and importance' in accordance with the case law developed by the European Court of Human Rights (Vickers, 2006: 123).

online
resource
centre

see online
resources for a
list of most
commonly
practiced
religions

The Directive was transposed into national legislation by the member states and regulations against discrimination on the grounds of religion or belief were introduced in the UK in 2003. These have now being included in the 2010 Equality Act. The terms 'religion' and 'belief' are defined as 'any religious belief or philosophical belief' and include a reference to a lack of religious belief. Under this legislation it is unlawful to discriminate on the grounds of religion or belief in relation to staff recruitment, employment, promotion opportunities, vocational training, and dismissal. The regulations also cover access to further and higher education as part of the protection for vocational training. Positive action, in the form of training to improve opportunities in the workplace for under-represented religious groups, is also permitted by the law (Vickers, 2008a).

Similar legislation was adopted in the USA much earlier compared to the EU, and anti-discrimination provisions are included in Title VII of the Civil Rights Act 1964. This makes it unlawful for employers to discriminate on religious grounds in relation to staff recruitment and termination of employment and, unlike the EU and the UK law, expressly requires employers to 'make a reasonable effort to accommodate employees' religious belief and practices unless such accommodation would impose an undue hardship on the employer' (Brown, 2010). We shall see later, that although a similar requirement is not included under EU and UK law, in practice failure to accommodate religious practices, when

Signpost to
Chapter 2 An
Outline of
European and
UK Equality
Legislation

it would be reasonable and practicable for an employer to do so, could amount to indirect discrimination.

In the following sections we discuss the main features of the legal protection against discrimination on the grounds of religion or belief, its theoretical underpinning, its relationship with other equality rights, and its practical implications for the workplace.

Debate Box

Belief in climate change

Tim Nicholson, an employee at Grainger PLC, Didcot, in the UK, was made redundant in 2008 from his job as head of sustainability. A judge ruled that he could claim unfair dismissal under the Employment Equality (Religion and Belief) Regulations 2003 (now part of the 2010 Equality Act) that covers 'any religion, religious belief or philosophical belief'. Mr Nicholson said that his belief in climate change had influenced his life to the extent that he no longer flies. He complained that his former employer did not take his concerns and belief about climate change seriously. His former employer has appealed against this decision as they argued that 'a belief about climate change and the environment... is not a religious or philosophical belief', and added that 'it is a political view about science and/or the world' (BBC, 2009).

Organize the class into two groups, one for the motion and one against it.

The motion is:
A belief in climate change is a political belief and not a philosophical one, and therefore it should not be protected by the law.

Stages in the debate: (each stage is given with timings, the overall time for the activity is 55 minutes – allowing a few minutes for change over of presenters, etc.)

- Each group has 20 minutes to prepare their arguments either for or against the motion.
- Each group is given 5 minutes to present their opening statement (10 minutes in total).
- Groups reconvene for 10 minutes to prepare rebuttal arguments.
- Each group has 2 minutes to present rebuttal arguments.

A vote is taken and the winners of the debate announced; the casting vote goes to impartial observers: tutors, audience members not involved in the debate, and observers.

Visit the Online Resource Centre for a link to the full article.

Why is religion or belief protected in the workplace?

Protection of religion or belief in the workplace is part of a wider debate that is taking place in many European countries where religious diversity is increasing as a result of immigration trends. The issue which is at the core of this debate is the extent to which different kinds of religious practices, for example the wearing of religious symbols or adherence to a particular dress code for religious observance, should be accommodated in western societies including in the workplace, given that by and large workplaces tend to be structured on a secular tradition.

There are robust arguments grounded in political liberal theory and in the human rights discourse that can justify the protection of religion or belief in the workplace without having to resort to religious arguments. Vickers (2008b) suggests that there are both principled and pragmatic reasons for protecting religion or belief in the workplace, and these are examined in the following sections.

Principled reasons: dignity, equality, and autonomy

Freedom of religion or belief is grounded in the concept of dignity, which involves a moral judgement about the absolute *intrinsic worth* of human beings. Therefore, by implication, all individuals deserve respect on the grounds of their innate humanity (Fredman, 2002). Hepple (2011: 15) argues that 'treating the individual with dignity also means respecting the differences between people that spring from their gender or sexuality or physical or mental abilities or cultural experiences, religion or belief', thus acknowledging that we all have multiple identities. Furthermore, it is suggested that the concept of dignity encompasses two other important principles: first, the principle of equality between humans, who although they 'may not be equal in their abilities and attributes', nonetheless 'they are equal in their humanity and human worth'; second, the principle of autonomy, according to which 'human beings should be able to develop their own ideas of good and exercise control over their life' (Vickers, 2008b: 37).

Thus dignity, equality, and autonomy form the basis for the protection of religious freedom or belief as a human right, which is enshrined in the European Convention of Human Rights (ECHR), and in many other fundamental charters. It follows that it is necessary to extend protection for religion or belief to the workplace in order to support an individual's dignity, equality, and autonomy, since participation in paid work is an important part of people's lives. Furthermore, participation in paid work is closely linked to the notion of citizenship, since it is viewed as a way of contributing to the economic welfare of society.

Although these arguments provide a robust theoretical basis to justify the protection of religion or belief in the workplace, some may view religion or belief as a matter of individual and personal 'choice'. Therefore, religion may not be seen on a parity with other equality rights which, unlike religion, are not chosen characteristics. This point was articulated in a recent decision of the UK Court of Appeal in the case of *Eweida v British Airways PLC*, where a female employee was not allowed to wear a small visible cross with her work uniform because it was against her employer's dress code, which prohibited jewelry to be visible over the work uniform. In this case, one of the judges stated that: 'one cannot help observing that all of these (protected characteristics) apart from religion or belief are objective characteristics of individuals; religion and belief alone are matter of choice' (Webster, 2010: 10). This argument, however, ignores the fact that some people do not view religion as a matter of 'choice', but rather as part of their self-identity. This idea is well exemplified by the words of Archbishop Dr John Sentamu, who wrote: 'asking someone to leave their belief in God at the door of their workplace is akin to asking them to remove their skin colour before coming into the office. Faith in God is not an add-on or optional extra' (cited in Webster, 2010: 10). Research findings based on an analysis of the Fourth National Survey of Ethnic Minorities in England and Wales appear to support this view as they shows that many South Asians identified their religion with their identity. Many Muslims, Hindus, and Sikhs also viewed their religion as a very important part of their lives, while less than half of white Anglicans felt that religion was important to the way they led their lives (Modood et al., 1997).

Thus, the reasons for protecting religion in the workplace are not based on a question of 'choice', but rather on the principles of autonomy, dignity, and equality, which include 'the view that individual autonomy requires that one remains free to live according to one's conscience' (Vickers, 2008b: 39). It is acknowledged that this argument can be used to justify protection for any belief that an individual may view as an important part of her identity. However, it is argued that only those practices and beliefs that help an individual to make sense of the world, and through which they develop a sense of good, should be legally protected on the grounds of dignity, autonomy, and equality (ibid.). Moreover, it ought to be pointed out that Article 9 of the European Commission of Human Rights establishes that protection of religious freedom is not an absolute right and that religious manifestation may be subject to restrictions in order to safeguard the rights of others. This means that respect for religion or belief is not intended to take priority over other characteristics which are also part of an individual's self-identity, such as gender, race, or sexual orientation, but that religion or belief should be protected along with these characteristics. This in some cases can be problematic because of competing claims which may occur between different equality rights, and we explore these below.

Pragmatic reasons: conflict resolution and social inclusion

There are also strong pragmatic reasons that justify the protection of religion or belief in the workplace. These are rooted in political and socio-economic arguments, such as conflict resolution and the need for promoting social inclusion and social cohesion.

To extend equal respect and legal protection to different religions is a key factor in maintaining peace and harmony in society. History is riddled with examples of wars being fought in the name of different religious faiths, and unfortunately modern societies are not yet rid of religious conflicts. Contemporary examples where a legal guarantee for religious equality has been part of conflict resolution are India, where this was included in the country's Constitution, and Northern Ireland. In the latter case, legislation for religious equality also includes provisions to promote equality of opportunities for both Catholics and Protestants to participate in paid employment.

Another important reason to justify legal protection for religion or belief in the workplace is the need to promote social inclusion. It is in the interest of society to prevent alienation and exclusion of minority groups because if they suffer discrimination and disadvantage this is likely to lead to conflict and undermine the fabric of society, thus jeopardizing social cohesion. For example, research suggests that some people may exclude themselves from job opportunities for fear of being discriminated against because of their religious affiliation (Weller et al., 2001). This demonstrates that it is in the interest of the state and society to encourage and support participation of all groups in the labour market by eradicating discrimination against religion or belief and by ensuring that people all have the same opportunities to access paid work and enjoy the benefits associated with it.

Having identified some of the main reasons, both principled and pragmatic, that justify protection on the grounds of religion or belief in the workplace, in the next section we examine the interaction between religion or belief, freedom of expression, and other equality strands.

The interaction between freedom of religion, other equality strands, and freedom of expression

The interaction between religion or belief, other equality strands, and freedom of expression can create complex dynamics which, in some cases, can lead to intersectional discrimination or to conflict between different equality rights. Intersectional discrimination can be broadly defined as a situation where 'the discrimination involves more than one protected characteristics and it is the unique combination of characteristics that results in discrimination, in such a way that they are completely inseparable' (Government Equalities Office, 2009: 10–11, see also Chapter 1). In this section we explore issues around intersectional discrimination with regard to gender, race, and freedom of expression, and examine how different equality rights can come into conflict.

Signpost to Chapter 1 Equality and Diversity Issues in the Labour Market

Religion and gender

The debate over the wearing of headscarves or the veil by Muslim women has been linked to gender equality. Banning the wearing of headscarves or veils in the workplace can indirectly discriminate not only on the grounds of religion, as it would not affect other religious faiths which do not require specific dress codes, but also on the grounds of gender, as it would affect Muslim women but not Muslim men. The latter shows how religion and gender can intersect and result in a 'unique combination' of discrimination that would affect only Muslim women and would likely hinder their participation in the labour market, thus frustrating the aim of achieving greater gender equality in the workplace. Furthermore, it can be argued that the wearing of a headscarf or veil can be seen as part of an individual's freedom of expression since it can be an important symbol carrying religious, but also, for some, political connotations. In this example, religion and gender intersect with the fundamental right of freedom of expression, thus resulting in a 'unique' combination of multiple jeopardy against the rights of Muslim women.

However, from a different perspective, some may argue that the wearing of headscarves or the veil can be seen by others as a symbol of women's subordination to men's power, stressing their inferiority compared to men, which is contrary to the right to gender equality. We can see here how freedom of religion can clash with gender equality.

This discussion shows the multifaceted nature of the ongoing debate that is taking place in several countries around the wearing of the headscarf or the veil. It highlights that this debate is far from being conclusive. Although the provisions of the European Employment Directive appear to suggest that a ban on wearing headscarves is potentially indirectly discriminatory, as it would disproportionately disadvantage Muslim women, who would find it more difficult to comply with the requirement of not wearing a headscarf compared to other groups, in practice this issues has been approached differently by different countries. For example, France has banned the wearing of the *burqa* in public places and headscarves in schools. However, in the UK, the wearing of headscarves is common in the workplace, but a teacher was banned from wearing the *jibab* when working at a school (for the details of this case, see Chapter 3). In Denmark, the decision of an employer to ban the wearing of headscarves with the workplace uniform was upheld by the Danish Supreme Court as it was accepted that the prescribed uniform was intended to convey the political and religious neutrality of the organization.

A similar conflict can emerge between gender equality and the beliefs of other religious faiths which do not view women as equal to men. For example, in some faiths only men are allowed to become religious ministers and, as outlined in Chapter 2, this is legally permitted as an exception to direct sex discrimination where employment is 'for the purpose of an organized religion'. However, some view these practices as an unjustifiable infringement of the right of women to gender equality.

Debate Box

Ordination of women in the Catholic Church is still forbidden

An announcement by the Vatican that the 'attempted ordination' of women is one of the gravest crimes in ecclesiastical law has caused anger and indignation among liberal Catholics and women's groups. Terry Sanderson, president of the National Secular Society, has been quoted as saying that this was 'one of the most insulting and misogynistic pronouncements that the Vatican has made for a long time. Why any self-respecting woman would want to remain part of an organization that regards their full and equal participation as a "grave sin" is a mystery to me.' (Guardian, 2010)

Organize the class into two groups, one for the motion and one against it.

The motion is:
In the twenty-first century the legal provisions that allow some religious faiths to ordain men only into the priesthood are no longer justifiable and they should be abolished.

Follow the stages for the debate as given above.

Religion and race or ethnicity

Race or ethnicity and religious affiliation can be closely linked as in several countries people with a particular religion tend to belong predominantly to a certain ethnic group. For example, in Cyprus, the division between Greek-Cypriot and Turkish-Cypriots can equally be drawn between Christian-Cypriots and Muslim-Cypriots. The implications of this link between religion and ethnicity would be that discrimination against Turkish-Cypriots would also amount to indirect discrimination on the grounds of religion. Furthermore, in some countries the definition of certain ethnic groups includes people who share the same religious identity. For example, Sikhs in the UK are defined as an ethic group, but they are also a religious group. The same can be said about Jews, who are defined as an ethnic and a religious group (Vickers, 2006: 34). In these instances, too, we can see the potential for religion and race or ethnicity to intersect and form a 'unique combination' of discrimination that can cause a double disadvantage for certain groups in the labour market.

Signpost to
Chapter 5
Managing
Ethnic
Diversity in the
Workplace

Sexual orientation

The relationship between religion and sexual orientation can be problematic, as a number of religious faiths consider homosexuality to be immoral, and this can lead to a conflict between two different equality rights. The difficulty here is that the legal protection for these two equality strands is informed by the same principles of dignity and autonomy, and therefore one equality ground cannot prevail over the other. An example of this type of conflict is well illustrated in the case of *Peterson v Hewlett-Packard* in the USA. In this case, Peterson, an employee at the Hewlett-Packard IT company, objected when the organization started a campaign in support of diversity that included hanging posters in the workplace which featured an HP employee identified as gay. Peterson's religious views included the belief that homosexual activities were against the commandments contained in the Bible, and he believed that he had a right to expose homosexuality as a sin. Consequently, he started to post Bible verses which explicitly condemned homosexuality in his cubicle at work. He was asked by the company to remove them as they infringed the company harassment policy and its commitment to support employee diversity, but he refused to so. He was dismissed and he lost his subsequent claim for wrongful dismissal against HP since the court upheld the employer's decision (Brown, 2010). We can see how in this case an employee's manifestation of his religious views infringed the dignity of other employees and their right for their sexual orientation to be respected.

We can conclude from this discussion that conflicts between freedom of religion and other equality rights can pose a difficult dilemma and there are no conclusive answers. In dealing with conflict between different rights, it is important to refer to the key principles examined earlier, of dignity, autonomy, and equality, and remember that freedom of religion is not an absolute right but one that is protected alongside other equality rights.

Signpost to Chapter 9 Managing Sexual Orientation and Transgender in the Workplace

Managing religion or belief in the workplace

It is clear from the issues explored so far that the protection of religious freedom presents a number of challenges for employers as accommodation of religious observance in the workplace needs to be balanced against freedom from religion and other equality interests of staff and service users (Figure 10.1). How these different interests should be weighted against one another partly depends on the nature of the employer and whether it operates in the public or in the private sector. This is an important distinction to draw (Vickers, 2008a, 2008b) because, to a certain extent, public sector employers represent the state and therefore need to take into account public policy. For example, as mentioned earlier, it is in the state's interest to combat social exclusion and promote greater participation of all different equality groups in the labour market. It follows that public sector employers ought to uphold social policy's objectives and reflect these in their policies and practices. This is reinforced by the 2010 Equality Act, which has placed a positive duty upon public sector employers to take action to advance equality in respect of the protected equality groups and eliminate discrimination (see Chapter 2). However, if public sector employers are expected to uphold social policy goals because they represent the state, for the same reason, they also need to retain a certain degree of religious neutrality to ensure that different faiths or beliefs, including non-religious belief, are equally respected. This means that there may be limitations, within public sector organizations, concerning the extent to which religious interests can be accommodated in order to maintain a degree of religious neutrality.

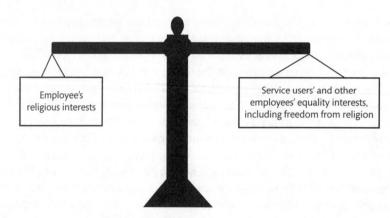

Figure 10.1 Balancing religious interests against other equality interests

Private sector employers, in contrast, are not expected to provide the same degree of support for the state's public policies, as also demonstrated by the fact that the positive duties to promote equality under the 2010 Equality Act do not extend to them. The implications of this are twofold: first, private sector employers may not provide the same level of protection for religious freedom as public sector organizations; second, they do not necessarily need to retain a certain degree of religious neutrality, and some may chose to adopt a specific religious ethos, for example a bookshop selling religious books.

In practice, the approach taken by private sector employers to balance religious interests against other equality interests will depend on the nature of the business, the size of their workforce, and of their customer base. For example, large utility companies, which provide essential services, such as the supply of water or gas, likely to employ a diverse workforce and to provide their services to the general public, may need to approach these issues in a similar way to large public sector employers.

There are three main aspects to the management of religion or belief in the workplace. The first is to ensure that employees and job applicants are not directly discriminated because of their religion or belief, save in those cases where it can be argued that there is an occupational requirement that objectively justifies it, and that this is proportionate to achieve a legitimate aim. The second is to avoid indirect discrimination on the grounds of religion or belief by accommodating employees' religious observance or belief in so far as it is reasonable and practicable. The third is about fostering harmonious and respectful working relations and providing a working environment where employees' religion, lack of religion, or belief is fully respected. Each of these aspects and their management implications are considered in turn in the following sections.

Direct discrimination and occupational requirement

Direct discrimination against an employee or a job applicant because of their religion or belief is unlawful, unless there is an occupational requirement that objectively justifies it. It is also important to stress that an occupational requirement is an exception to the general principle of non-discrimination and, as highlighted in Chapter 2, the requirement must be genuine and not a pretext to discriminate. It must be a defining aspect of the job and not just one aspect of it. Furthermore, the application of such a requirement must be proportionate to achieve a legitimate aim. In order to understand how this rule can apply in practice within the context of religion or belief, we examine a number of examples from across Europe.

The genuine occupational requirement exception appears to be most frequently used in cases involving religious employers, which, in order to preserve their religious ethos, may require their staff to adhere to the same religious faith or belief as that of the organization they work for. This has often been the case in education and, for example, in Greece, 'non-Orthodox teachers cannot be appointed to state kindergartens or primary schools unless there is more than one teaching post, so that another teacher shares the same religion as the majority of the children' (Vickers, 2006: 60).

In Spain, domestic legislation distinguishes between work that is defined as 'ideological' and work that is defined as 'neutral'. Employees in religious organizations are expected to adhere to the same religious faith as that of their employer, only in relation to those jobs that can be defined as 'ideological' and deemed to convey the religious ethos of that particular organization. Those employees who are instead expected to carry out 'neutral' jobs are not required to conform to the organization's religious ethos. Similar rules apply in Denmark where in the case of an employee who was dismissed from a cleaning job in a Christian humanitarian organization, it was decided that there was no genuine occupational requirement for cleaning work to be undertaken by people belonging to the same religious faith of the organization (ibid.).

These examples illustrate that a genuine occupational requirement must be a defining aspect of the job and cannot be used to justify direct discrimination on religious grounds in the case of work that does not involve transmission of religious values or of a particular belief, as in the Spanish and Danish examples above. It must also be proportionate to achieve a legitimate aim, as in the Greek example, where in kindergartens and primary schools, to preserve the ethos of the Orthodox faith (a legitimate aim), the requirement for teaching staff to adhere to that religious faith is applied in a proportionate way by reserving some of the teaching posts, but not all of them, for applicants who hold the same religious faith.

Indirect discrimination and reasonable accommodation

The EU Directive and the UK Equality Act 2010 do not impose a legal duty on employers to make 'reasonable accommodations' for religious practices in the workplace, as in the case of the US legislation which, as well as prohibiting discrimination on religious grounds in the workplace, also requires employers to 'make a reasonable effort to accommodate employees' religious belief and practices unless such accommodation would impose an undue hardship on the employer' (Brown, 2010). However, as highlighted by Vickers (2008a), since the European and UK legislation prohibits 'indirect discrimination', in practice, employers need to consider whether to make reasonable accommodations for the needs of religious employees, as failure to do so may result in indirect discrimination. Before we consider what 'reasonable accommodation' means in practice, it is important to understand the impact that lack of 'reasonable accommodation' could have on the experience of employees whose religious faith requires them to adhere to particular practices.

The relationship between an employer and an employee is based on a contract which is entered into voluntarily by both parties. Therefore, some may argue that if an employee finds that this relationship no longer suits her, because her employer is not prepared to accommodate her religious practice, she is free to resign and find alternative employment. In other words, people have a 'choice' as to whether or not to work for a particular employer. We can see that the argument around the notion of 'choice' is resurfacing here, although from a different angle compared to that discussed earlier. This argument ignores the fact, as pointed out by Marxists, that some people may be restricted in the kind of choices that they actually have due to their socio-economic circumstances. For example, we have already seen that many Muslim and Sikh workers tend to be concentrated in low-skilled jobs and their choices of employment may be very limited. Therefore, unless employers are prepared to accommodate religious needs, these workers may be faced with a choice between being able to work but not being able to comply in full with the requirements of their religious observance, or being free to follow their religious observance but not working at all. However, even when an individual may be in a position to have alternatives, Leader (2007) argues that people should not be confronted with such a dilemma, but they should be entitled to remain in their preferred organization. In support of his argument, Leader draws an interesting comparison with the situation working women used to find themselves in when they became pregnant, before equality legislation was introduced which made it illegal for employers to dismiss a pregnant employee. Prior to the prohibition to discriminate on the grounds of pregnancy, it was considered acceptable for employers to dismiss pregnant women since the common view was that they had a 'choice' between having children or keeping their job. What these situations all have in common is that individuals are faced with the dilemma of having to sacrifice one aspect of their life, such as religious freedom or motherhood, for another one, such as their professional aspirations, or vice versa. Thus, this potential conflict highlights the importance of helping individuals to balance different parts of their lives rather than having to keep them separate.

This discussion echoes some of the arguments outlined in Chapter 8 on work–life balance, and the importance for organizations to offer flexible working options to enable their employees to achieve a 'balance' between their personal and working lives. From this perspective, the notion of 'reasonable accommodation' can be compared to flexible working, which is provided to help people 'balance' important aspects of their personal life with paid work.

Some of the most common areas where the need for making 'reasonable accommodations' are likely to occur can include:

Signpost to
Chapter 8
Managing
Work–Life
Balance

- dress and grooming codes
- hours of work and time off for religious observance
- food and drinks

Dress and grooming codes

Several employers require their employees to wear a uniform, and although such requirement applies equally to all employees, it can indirectly discriminate against those whose religion observance require them to adhere to a particular dress or grooming code. For example, a Muslim woman may be indirectly discriminated against if she is not allowed to wear a headscarf at work. Similarly, a requirement for male employees to be clean shaven could indirectly discriminate against Sikh men, whose religion requires them to grow a beard. There are cases, however, where it may not be reasonable or practicable to accommodate an employee's religious need. For example, for health and safety reasons, men working as fire fighters need to be clean shaven in order to ensure that breathing equipment can be properly fitted to their face.

Hours of work and time off for religious observance

Flexible working arrangements may be used to accommodate an employee's request to change her hours of work in order to participate in religious observance, provided that it is reasonable and practicable to do so having had regard to the needs of the business. For example, some employees may need time off for prayers during their working day and flexi-time could be used to accommodate this request, thus enabling them to make up for the lost working time. Specific rules, which were introduced in the UK by the Employment Rights Act 1996 at the time when shop opening hours were extended to Sundays, apply to Sunday working. These regulations entitle employees working in the retail or betting trades to opt out from Sunday working by giving three months' notice to their employers. However, employees may be required to work on Sundays during the notice period. In addition, these regulations do not apply to job applicants, who could be disadvantage by a requirement to work on Sundays.

Food and drinks

For some people, it is contrary to their religion to eat certain types of food. For example, Hindus do not eat beef and Muslims do not eat pork. Similarly, alcoholic drinks are not permitted by some religious faiths. Therefore, where reasonable and practicable, organizations' catering services should provide a choice of food and make sure that soft drinks are available at work-related social functions.

➔ Student Activity 10.1

Reasonable accommodation for religious practices in the workplace

In groups, consider and discuss the following scenarios and answer the questions that follow:

A small finance company needs its staff to work late on a Friday afternoon to analyze stock prices in the American finance market. The figures arrive late on Friday because of the global time differences. During the winter months some staff would like to be released early on Friday afternoon in order to be home before nightfall – a requirement of their religion. They propose to make the time up during the rest of the week.

The company is not able to agree to this request because the American figures are necessary to the business; they need to be worked on immediately and the company is too small to have anybody else able to do the work. (Example adapted from ACAS (2009))

1. Do you think that the requirement of working on Friday afternoon in this company meets a legitimate business aim?

2. Do you agree with the company's decision or do you think that in this case, it would be reasonable and practicable for some employees to be absent from work on Friday afternoons? Provide reasons for your answer.

A Hindu employee working in a large public sector organization has lost a close relative and wants to take time off for bereavement. Hindu religion requires that following cremation, close relatives of the deceased will observe a 13-day mourning period, during which time they should remain at home. However, under the employer's policy, staff are allowed only two days off work for bereavement in the event of the death of a close relative. The employee asks his employer to take 13 days off work to observe his religious requirements and suggests that he takes the remaining 11 days from his annual leave entitlement.

This request is refused on the grounds that the organization's policy only allows for two days bereavement leave and the annual leave policy provides that this should be booked in advance and cannot be granted at short notice. This policy is to guarantee sufficient staff cover to ensure the efficient delivery of the service to the general public.

1   What are the issues in this case?

2.   What differences can you identify between this case and the previous one? How are they likely to impact on the employer and on the employee?

3.   Do you agree with the employer's decision, or do you think that in this case it would have been reasonable and practicable for the employer to accommodate the employee's religious need to observe a longer period of bereavement?

Fostering harmonious relations and respectful working relations: tackling harassment

Fostering harmonious and respectful relations in the workplace is fundamental to protect employees' dignity and autonomy and, by extension, that of service users. It is important to raise awareness among staff of issues relating to the protection of religion or belief in the workplace, and create an environment that supports religious freedom, but equally freedom from religion and other equality interests. Therefore, employers need to take reasonable steps to tackle any behaviour from either their employees or service users that can cause offence or humiliation to some staff because of their religious views or beliefs. This would involve the adoption of a harassment policy to protect employees against offensive behaviour. Such policies should cover the workplace as well as other work-related activities (e.g. a social gathering), and training sessions to raise awareness about these issues, particularly as sometimes unwelcome behaviour may be unintentional. In the specific context of religion or belief, such types of behaviour may include:

- unwanted comments or conduct aimed at an individual's religion or belief
- making offensive comments or jokes about religious groups
- making derogatory comments about religious clothing or other religious symbols worn by another employee
- teasing an employee for holding a particular belief
- physical assault on an individual because of their religious practices
- unwanted comments or conduct aimed at an individual's lack of religion or lifestyle
- persistent attempts to convert other employees
- criticizing, on religious grounds, the lifestyle or behaviour of other employees
- physical assault on an individual because of their lifestyle.

However, to identify in practice what might constitute offensive behaviour in relation to religion or belief can present some difficulties. This is because of a lack of shared or established understanding about the impact that certain behaviours can have on different religious groups or beliefs. In the case of other equality strands, such as race and gender, the case law has helped, over a period of time, to develop a common understanding about the types of conduct that are deemed to be offensive and degrading and likely to constitute harassment. However, in the case of religion or belief, given the wide range of religions or beliefs which can potentially be covered by the legislation, it is not always clear whether a set of views constitute a religion or a belief which is protected under the law. Consequently, it is not easy to establish what kind of conduct can cause offence (Vickers, 2008a).

A clear example of this is the case outlined in the first Debate box in this chapter, where an employment tribunal in the UK decided that a belief in climate change is a philosophical belief and therefore is protected by the law. Does this mean that, for example, the behaviour of a manager who strongly denies the existence of climate change and insists that employees travel either by plane or car, could create a hostile and intimidating working environment for those staff who believe in climate change, and therefore it could be perceived as a form of intimidation or harassment? The answer may be possibly yes, but one cannot be absolutely sure given that so far the question as to whether climate change is a 'philosophical belief' has only been examined in one case. This proposition would probably need further testing.

A second problem about defining what may constitute harassment in relation to religion or belief is the fact that someone's manifestation of religion, or lack of religion, may be another person's experience of harassment. For example, in a case in the USA, *Wilson v US West Communications*, a Catholic employee, motivated by her religious views about abortion, decided to wear a badge at work with the picture of an aborted foetus on it. Her colleagues found this behaviour offensive. She was dismissed by her employer and the US court held that the dismissal in this case was lawful (Vickers, 2008a: 36). Conversely, it can be argued that an overt display of lack of religion, through, for example, a culture of jokes about religion, can be offensive to some religious groups, and an employer would need to take action to protect religious employees from what could otherwise be perceived as a form of harassment.

A third problematic area is the relation between protection against harassment on the grounds of religion or belief and protection against harassment on the grounds of sexual orientation. As seen earlier in the case of Peterson, the manifestation of one person's religion can be another person's experience of harassment. In this kind of situation, protection of religion and freedom of religious expression can be restricted by parallel legal protection on the grounds of sexual orientation or other equality strands.

Investigating harassment claims, in relation to any equality strand, can be a complex task for employers, particularly as harassment can be unintentional. Where religion or belief are involved, harassment cases can present additional difficulties due to a lack of shared understanding of what might constitute harassment in these cases, as discussed earlier. So how should employers approach these issues, especially as organizations are responsible for the actions of their employees as well as being directly liable? The ACAS guide for employers and employees on religion or belief in the workplace stresses the importance of employers carefully considering all the circumstances of the case before reaching a conclusion, and particularly the views of the person making the claim since harassment is often subjective. Once all the evidence relating to the case in question has been collected, employers should ask themselves whether what has taken place can 'reasonably' be considered to have cause offence (ACAS, 2009: 7).

Workplace mediation, in some situations, may offer a way of resolving conflict between different equality rights, as for example, in the case of a clash between religious belief and sexual orientation. Mediation is a voluntary process where a trained mediator, who is a completely neutral third party to the case in question, helps the parties involved in the dispute to find a resolution. A mediator can be either an employee working for the same organization where the conflict is happening or an external mediator. In either of these examples, it is a key element of the mediation process that the mediator does not take sides or tell the parties involved in the dispute what they should be doing. The role of the mediator is to offer the opportunity to the parties to present their sides of the story, explain the impact that this conflict is having on them, and help them to discuss their issues and identify a way of resolving them. Mediation can be an effective tool to resolve harassment cases because often the offensive behaviour can be unintentional, the result of a misunderstanding, or of lack of awareness about other people's values (see the Further reading section at the end of the chapter for ACAS's Mediation: An Employer's Guide (ACAS and CIPD, 2009)).

In conclusion, in order to manage this equality strand effectively, employers need to take steps to create a working environment where all employees feel respected and able to express their religion or beliefs. This can be achieved by raising awareness through training and other initiatives about the importance of protecting religion or belief in the workplace, and by ensuring that organizational policies and practice promote equality and dignity for all.

⊙ Student Activity 10.2

An employees has added a personal email signature with religious connotations on to their work email – 'Helping hands are better than praying lips.'

1. What does this message suggest to you?

2. Do you think that employees should have the freedom to add this kind of messages to their work emails?

3. Do you think that this kind of message might create a problem in the workplace?

(To help you answer these questions see Email Signatures, Employers Forum on Belief, available at www.efbelief.org.uk/pages/email-signatures.html)

▣ End of Chapter Case Study Tower Hamlets Council: a London local authority

The London Borough of Tower Hamlets has the largest proportion of Muslim residents (36.4 per cent) of any local authority in the UK, almost as much as its Christian population (39 per cent), while the third largest group of residents are those with no religion (18 per cent). As a service provider as well as an employer, the Council needs to address issues of religion or belief to meet the expectations of its customers as well as managing what may be the conflicting demands of a diverse workforce. Thus the Council has produced a religion or belief equality scheme to identify issues, take steps to address them, and develop policies and practices to support freedom of religion or belief. We consider here briefly the main aspects of the process adopted by the Council to develop its religion or belief scheme and some of its outcomes.

Consultation with the stakeholders

In order to ensure that their scheme reflected the religious diversity of both its customers and its workforce, Tower Hamlets Council embarked on an extensive consultation process with all the major faith groups in the borough as well as with non-religious people. The following issues emerged:

- Some council officers expressed concern that unreasonable requirements were placed on faith-based organizations to adopt secular language to be allowed to tender for contracts to provide services on behalf of the Council.
- Others felt that the Council had too many ties with faith communities, which make it difficult for people with no religious belief or for those who wish to keep their belief private.
- Council employees believed that the workplace played an important role in bringing people of different backgrounds together to build positive relationships.
- Some employees identified factors that they felt had a detrimental effect on their ability to be open about their religion or belief such as world events, resulting in a negative portrayal of certain faith communities by the media.

Adoption of special provisions to accommodate religious needs

In order to accommodate different needs for religious observance, the Council has adopted a number of special provisions that include:

- Prayer room: although there is no legal requirement to provide a prayer room, the Council has two prayer rooms for its staff.
- Flexibility: this include a flexi-time system to enable employees to take time off for prayers during the working day and then make up the lost time; changing working hours to attend religious festivals or take longer holidays for religious trips; in recognition of the fact that not all its staff want to take leave at Christmas, the Council offers one day's concessionary holiday that can be taken some other times.
- Food and drink: vegetarian, halal, and kosher food as well as non-alcoholic drinks are made available at the Council canteen and social events.
- Dress code: guidelines are provided to ensure that decisions about dress code do not discriminate indirectly.
- Calendar of religious events: a calendar of major religious festivals and events is produced each year in conjunction with the local Inter-faith Forum. Various events are held to raise awareness about various religious issues, for example the Muslim Awareness week.
- Monitoring religion: data about employees' religious affiliation is collected and this has enabled the Council to identify pay differentials among staff with different religious affiliations. For example, while Christian staff are fairly consistent at all grades, Muslim staff are more likely to be concentrated in jobs that pay less than £20,000 a year.

However, the effort that Tower Hamlets Council took to support religion or belief received negative media coverage in a television programme which claimed that there was an entryist agenda by a Muslim organization with a base in the borough (*Dispatches*, 1 March 2010, Channel 4).

Source: Adapted from Godwin (2010)

online resource centre

An extract from
Tower Hamlets
Religion/
Belief Equality
Scheme
Objectives
can be viewed
on the Online
Resource
Centre.

Case study questions

1. Consider the issues that emerged from the consultation held by the Council with the stakeholders. In your view, do the actions taken by the Council to deal with religion or belief in the workplace suggest that those issues have been addressed effectively?

2. Based on the information provided, why do you think that the approach taken by this organization has attracted negative media coverage?

3. Draw an action plan for this organization to comply with its positive duty to eliminate discrimination on the grounds of religion or belief, to advance equality, and to foster good relations between people with different equality interests. When drawing your plan take the following into account:

   – Identify the organization's objectives by taking into consideration the nature of public sector employers and the issues raised by the consultation with the stakeholders.

   – Describe the type of action to be taken in order to achieve the set objectives.

 ## Conclusion

We have seen that perceptions of discrimination on the grounds of religion or belief are widespread in several European countries. This trend is probably linked to the ongoing debate about immigration in those countries and to an alarming increase of xenophobia and intolerance towards the religious faiths of some minority groups. These facts, compounded with evidence which points to the existence of discrimination in the labour market based on religious affiliation, and supported by the principles of dignity, autonomy, and equality, which are rooted in the human rights discourse, make a strong case for the need of legal protection against this type of discrimination.

However, the implementation of this equality right in the workplace can be problematic as it can potentially clash with other equality rights, such as sexual orientation and gender, because of the views held by some religious faiths on homosexuality and the role of women in society. There is no absolute right to religious freedom, as established by Article 9 of the ECHR, and therefore, in these situations, an employee's right to religious freedom will have to be balanced against other equality rights and the right to freedom from religion of other employees and service users. As highlighted by Vickers (2006: 5), where the balance lies may depend in part on the status of the employer, whether it has a religious ethos, or whether it is part of the public or private sector.

Another important feature of this equality strands is that it also covers 'philosophical belief', which appears to be an 'open-ended concept' since there is not yet a shared understanding of how this should be defined in practice. This is evidenced by the decision of the UK employment tribunal that a belief in climate change amounts to a philosophical belief and is therefore protected by the law. The uncertainty about how belief may be defined adds to the complexity for employers about managing this equality strand in the workplace. However, managing religious diversity in the workplace does not have to be onerous, and often requires some practical and inexpensive accommodations, for example allowing staff to wear a headscarf or providing for some flexibility during the working day. Thus, relatively small changes to daily working practices can play an important role in the development of a more inclusive work culture which can contribute towards social inclusion of minority groups and greater social cohesion.

Review and discussion questions

1. To what extent is there evidence of discrimination on the grounds of religion or belief in the labour market?

2. What are the main arguments that underpin protection of religion or belief in the workplace?

3. How can a 'philosophical belief' be defined?

4. Explain the reasons why this equality strand can potentially come into conflict with other equality rights and how such conflict may be approached.

5. What does 'reasonable accommodation' mean in the context of religion or belief? Are employers under a legal obligation to 'accommodate' an employee's needs for religious observance?

6. What kind of steps can be taken by employers to manage religious diversity in the workplace?

For additional material on the content of this chapter please visit the supporting Online Resource Centre at **www.oxfordtextbooks.co.uk/orc/kumra_manfredi/**

Further reading

Vickers, L. (2006) *Religion and Belief Discrimination in Employment – The EU Law*. Brussels: European Commission.

Vickers, L. (2008) *Religious Freedom, Religious Discrimination and the Workplace*. Oxford: Hart Publishing

Lindley, J. (2002), Race or religion? The impact of religion on the employment and earnings of Britain's ethnic communities. *Journal of Ethnic and Migrant Studies*, 28/3: 427–442.

ACAS and CIPD (2009) *Mediation: An Employer's Guide*. London: ACAS and the Chartered Institute of Personnel and Development. Available at http://www.acas.org.uk/index.aspx?articleid=1680.

References

ACAS (2009) *A Guide for Employers and Employees: Religion or Belief and the Workplace*. London: ACAS. Available at http://www.acas.org.uk.

ACAS and CIPD (2009) *Mediation: An Employer's Guide*. London: ACAS and the Chartered Institute of Personnel and Development. Available at http://www.acas.org.uk/index.aspx?articleid=1680.

BBC (2009) Appeal on climate change. *BBC News*, 7 October. Available online at http://news.bbc.co.uk/1/hi/england/oxfordshire/8294573.stm.

Bond, S., Hollywood, E., and Colgan.F. (2009) *Integration in the Workplace: Emerging Employment Practice on Age, Sexual Orientation and Religion or Belief*. Research Report No. 36. Manchester: Equality and Human Rights Commission.

Bradford, B. and Forsyth, F. (2006) Employment and Labour Market Participation. In Office for National Statistics *Focus on Ethnicity and Religion*. Basingstone: Palgrave Macmillan.

Brown, J. (2010) Peacemaking in the culture war between gay rights and religious liberty. *Iowa Law Review*, 95: 747–817.

Email Signatures, Employer Forum on Belief, available at www.efbelief.org.uk/pages/email-signatures.html

European Commission (2009) Discrimination in the EU in 2009. *Eurobarometer* (special issue) 317. Available at http://ec.europa.eu/public_opinion/archives/ebs/ebs_317_sum_en_pdf.

Eweida v British Airways plc [2010] EWCA Civ 80 CA.

Fredman, S. (2002) *Discrimination Law*. Oxford: Oxford University Press.

Ghumman, S. and Jackson, L. (2009) Between a cross and a hard place: religious identities and employability. *Workplace Rights*, 13/3: 259–279.

Godwin, K. (2010) Tower Hamlets Council: religion at work. *Equal Opportunities Review*, 199: 11–14.

Government Equalities Office (2009) *Explaining the Equality Bill: Dual Discrimination*. London: HMSO, pp. 10–11. Available at www.equalities.gov.uk.

Guardian (2010) Liberal Catholics share secular anger as church puts female ordination on par with sex abuse. *The Guardian*, 16 July.

Hepple, B. (2011) *Equality: The New Legal Framework*. Oxford: Hart Publishing.

Leader, S. (2007) Freedom and futures: Personal priorities, institutional demands and freedom of religion. *The Modern Law Review*, 70/5: 713–730.

Lindley, J. (2002), Race or religion? The impact of religion on the employment and earnings of Britain's ethnic communities. *Journal of Ethnic and Migrant Studies*, 28/3: 427–-442.

Modood, T., Berthoud, R., Lakey, J., Nazroo, J., Smith, P., Virdee, S., and Beishon, S. (1997) *Ethnic Minorities in Britain: Diversity and Disadvantage*. London: Policies Studies Institute.

No. 01-35795 *Peterson v Hewlett-Packard Co*, US, 9th Cir, Jan 6, 2004.

Purdam, K., Afkhami, R., Crockett, A., and Olsen, W. (2007) Religion in the UK: an overview of equality statistics and the evidence gap. *Journal of Contemporary Religion*, 22/2: 147–168.

Sheldon, L. (2007) Freedom and futures: personal priorities, institutional demands and freedom of religion. *The Modern Law Review*, 70/5: 713–730.

Vickers, L. (2006) *Religion and Belief Discrimination in Employment – The EU Law*. Brussels: European Commission.

Vickers, L. (2008a) *Religious Discrimination at Work*. Liverpool: The Institute of Employment Rights.

Vickers, L. (2008b) *Religious Freedom, Religious Discrimination and the Workplace*. Oxford: Hart Publishing.

Webster, S. (2010) Misconceptions about the nature of religious belief. *Equal Opportunities Review*, 119: 8–10.

Weller, P., Feldman, A., and Purdam, K. (2001) *Religious Discrimination in England and Wales*. London: Home Office Research Study 220. Available at http://rds.homeoffice.gov.uk/rds/pdfs/hors220.pdf.

No. 94-2752 *Wilson v US West Communications*, US, 8th Cir, July 10, 1995.

Managing Age Diversity in the Workplace

 Learning objectives

- Understand the demographic changes and ageing trends that have led to the introduction of legal protection against age discrimination and for the need to extend working lives

- Understand how equality is conceptualized in the context of age and employment, and to what extent the aims of the age equality agenda relate to organizational practice

- Define employees' perceptions and manifestations of age discrimination in the workplace

- Explain the concepts and strategic approaches to the management of age diversity in the workplace, and identify the benefits and issues that concern both different generations of workers and organizations

Key terms

- **Age discrimination:** treating a person or a group of people less favourably because of their age. For example, denying older workers access to training opportunities that are available to younger workers.

- **Flexible retirement:** this involves retiring on a part-time basis and starting to draw a pension while continuing to work for the rest of the time for the same employer. The feasibility of this arrangement depends on the rules of individual occupational pension schemes.

- **Work ability:** '[t]he development of human capital to meet the demands of the labour market' (Ministry of Social Affairs and Health (Finland), 2002: 24), which means that an individual's capabilities have to be matched with work demands. In order to maintain a balanced relationship between an individual's capabilities and work demands, these will need to be adjusted as a worker becomes older.

Introduction

In this chapter, we examine age discrimination and discuss the implications of managing age diversity in the workplace. Protection against age discrimination was introduced by the EU Equality Directive (2000/78). In the UK, the Age Regulations were adopted in 2006, and subsequently amended and incorporated in the 2010 Equality Act. We start by examining the policy context that led to the introduction of protection against age discrimination as part of a wider strategy to extend working lives. This has been the result of demographic changes and economic pressure placed on governments' social security systems and pension funds by an increasingly ageing population. We then explore the main theoretical perspectives that have been used to conceptualize age equality in the workplace. We also examine the likely impact of age discrimination on individuals' self-esteem, and how this can negatively affect their work motivation, by referring to a number of conceptual frameworks. The chapter concludes with an overview of management strategies to understand how organizations need to adjust their working practices in order to manage both age diversity and an older workforce effectively.

Policy context: demographic changes and ageing trends

The population in most industrialized countries is ageing at a fast pace as life expectancy has increased and fertility rates have dropped, resulting in a lower birth rate, as outlined by the projections shown in Table 11.1. However, although people are living longer, they tend to have shorter working lives, and many exit the labour market before reaching retirement age.

These demographic changes, combined with early retirement trends, have created what has been defined as 'the age/employment paradox' (Walker, 2001: 3). On the one hand, life expectancy has increased steadily since the 1950s; on the other hand, people's participation in the labour market has dropped significantly due to early retirement. These trends gradually became established between the 1970s and the 1990s as a result of economic recessions and the transformation from a manufacturing to a service economy. On a macro economic level, such trends were often encouraged by government policies and collective agreements with trade unions, in order to reduce unemployment. On a micro organizational level, they offered a convenient way to manage workplace restructuring and cost reduction through voluntary redundancies. As a consequence, governments are now presented with the imminent prospect of a population which consists of a proportionately higher percentage of retired people compared to the proportion of those who are in paid employment.

Table 11.1 Europe is ageing

Rate of the population of working age (aged 20–64) in 2050	52%
Rate of the population aged 15–24 in 2050	19%
Rate of the population aged 65 or over in 2050	29%
Dependency ratio in 2050 (this is the ratio of people aged 65 or over relative to the working age population of 15–64)	50%
Fertility rate in 2060 (below replacement threshold of 2.1)	1.68 children per woman
Life expectancy for women in 2060	89
Life expectancy for men in 2060	84.5

Source: European Commission (2008) EU27 The demographic future of Europe – from challenge to opportunity

A further cause for concern is the fact that many older people are at risk of suffering from poverty if they do not have sufficient pension income to support themselves. This can be particularly the case for women, whose life expectancy is comparatively longer than that of men, and whose economic contribution is more likely to have been, at least in part, through unpaid work, such as caring for children and adult dependants, and less through paid work. As a result, they are less likely to have built up a sufficient pension income. The International Labour Organization (2002: 8) has acknowledged that 'old age has a strong gender dimension', and that many women across the world could end up in poverty at the end of their lives.

These changes to the population profile will have an impact on the labour market, on governments' expenditure for social security and health care, and on the sustainability of pension funds. Therefore, it can be clearly understood how extending working lives and reversing trends of early retirement have become a priority within employment policies in the European Union, as well as in most industrialized countries. For example, in Japan, since 2006 it has become mandatory for employers to raise the retirement age to 65, and some companies have made plans to phase out the retirement age altogether (Japan Times, 2006). In the UK too mandatory retirement was recently abolished in October 2011. It is within this context that taking steps to prevent age discrimination in the workplace has been identified as a key element of employment policies aimed at extending working lives. This is equally relevant in policies which aim to support young people by helping them enter the labour market, and avoid the risk that they may 'embark on a life of permanent benefit dependency' (European Commission, 2009b: 8). These examples comprise aspects of the wider intention to promote equity across all ages.

➔ Student Activity 11.1

Compare and contrast the extent of demographic changes in two or more European countries by using Eurostat data, a link to which is available on the Online Resource Centre. Prepare a short presentation highlighting how these are likely to affect the labour market in these countries.

What is age equality in the context of employment?

This section provides a conceptual framework to understand equality in the context of age and employment. It draws from the work of Fredman (2003) to identify and explain some of the main concepts in support of age equality in the workplace as well as arguments put forward to justify limitations to the protection of age discrimination in employment.

There is a strong ethical case for age equality that is rooted in the general principle of equal treatment and human rights. Everybody has the right not to be treated less favourably because of their age, including older workers, just as other groups have the right not to be treated less favourably because of other characteristics, such as race, gender, disability, sexual orientation, religion, or belief. Fredman (2003) argues that age equality is underpinned by two substantive values: 'dignity' and 'participative democracy'. It is an affront to people's dignity to treat them less favourably because of their age, and this principle informs the EU Charter of Fundamental

Human Rights, which states in Article 25 that the elderly have a right 'to lead a life of dignity and independence' (ibid.: 45). On the basis of this principle, it can be argued that, within the context of employment, it is an affront to an individual's dignity to retire her once she has reached a particular age on the assumption that her capabilities have diminished because of her age. Negative stereotyping regarding older people's capabilities in relation to paid work is unwarranted. Gerontology, the science that studies the process of ageing and older people's health, demonstrates that 'individuals must be assessed as individuals and not assumed to possess the average properties of their age group' (Grimley Evans, 2003: 16). This assertion is further validated by commonplace examples of older people who occupy prominent positions in key aspects of public life, such as in politics, the judiciary, academia, and corporations. Furthermore, from a broader social perspective, age equality is also supported by the value of 'participative democracy', which aims to ensure full participation of all groups to 'all aspects of social life', thus combating social exclusion (Fredman, 2003: 46).

As seen in the previous section, both older workers and very young ones are more likely to be at risk of social exclusion, and age equality is key to ensuring their full participation in the labour market. However, it has been argued by some that age, which is a characteristic we all share, should be viewed differently from other protected characteristics which relate only to certain groups. This idea is based on the 'fair innings' argument, which draws on a distinction between equality at a given time and equality over a lifetime. The latter concept is based on the assumption that a particular life stage should not be considered in isolation as all of us will have the opportunity to experience some advantages and disadvantages at different stages of our lives, provided, of course, that we all live long enough. Consequently, it can be argued that older workers have already had a 'fair innings', as they have had the opportunity to benefit from paid employment and career progression, and therefore it is justifiable to retain a mandatory retirement age in order to ensure that younger people can enjoy these opportunities too. However, as highlighted by Fredman (2003), this argument is based on a number of flawed assumptions.

It is wrong to assume that everybody will have had the same opportunities to be in paid employment and to enjoy a series of benefits associated with this, including building up enough income for a retirement pension. A clear example of this can be seen in the work experiences of women, which are often patchy and interrupted by career breaks for child rearing, whereas men are more likely to have uninterrupted working lives. Furthermore, this argument also assumes that the number of jobs in the economy is limited, and, although it is acknowledged that this might be the case at the level of an individual organization, this is not the case for the whole of the economy. Fredman argues that this approach is 'known as the 'lump of labour' fallacy', as it 'ignores the fact that jobs can create further jobs, so that the size of the labour market is determined by the scale of demand for jobs, not the supply of jobs' (2003: 47). It can also be added that, on a macro economic level, there is no evidence which shows a link between people exiting the labour market and people entering it, 'as entry and exit flows in the labour market do not usually occur in the same sectors' (International Labour Organization, 2002: 7).

Different treatment on the grounds of age, especially in relation to older workers, is also explained from a neo-liberal perspective, as a result of market choices due to the higher costs of employing older workers compared to their younger counterparts (Urwin, 2006). Other neo-liberal viewpoints suggest that older workers themselves are to blame if they find it difficult to either remain in the labour market or access it because they do not keep their skills up to date and keep themselves competitive (Wood et al., 2008).

These arguments, however, can be contested as they do not take into account the value that older workers can bring to an organization in terms of knowledge and experience, which can compensate for the higher costs of employing them. Furthermore, it is not always the case that employing older workers is more expensive, as in many low-skilled and low-paid jobs it is unlikely that there is much difference in the costs of employing older workers compared to younger ones. Finally, there is an issue about access to training for older workers, as research discussed later in this chapter shows that older workers may not be given the same opportunities to train and to keep their skills up to date as their younger counterparts.

Can the business case deliver age equality?

The arguments presented above show that older workers may be discriminated against and that legal protection may not be sufficient to prevent this happening. Can the 'business case', as part of a diversity management approach, deliver age equality? We have seen that, from a macro economic perspective, a clear business case is pushing age boundaries in the workplace in favour of greater participation of older workers in the labour market. This is primarily to avoid shortages of labour, to reduce the government's expenditure on social security, and to sustain the viability of pension funds. From an organizational perspective, however, the business case can be used either way: in support of older workers, or against it. Depending on the business needs of a particular organization, it can be argued that, in order to retain valuable experience and expertise that older workers can offer, there should *not* be a fixed retirement age. Equally, it can be argued that there *should* be a fixed retirement age, for reasons of workforce planning or even to promote greater age diversity by employing younger workers. This not only demonstrates the contingent nature of the business case and the manner in which circumstances determine its usage, but also shows how the concept of diversity, when applied to age, can in practice, as argued by Sargeant (2005a: 634), legitimize 'continued age discrimination' by retaining a mandatory retirement age, thus undermining the 'human rights' argument, which advocates age equality for all.

From this discussion, one can see the complexity entailed in defining what equality means in relation to age in the context of employment, and the tensions between arguments rooted in the human rights discourse and those driven by more utilitarian and pragmatic reasons. Table 11.2 provides a summary of the conceptual frameworks and arguments discussed in this section.

⮊ Student Activity 11.2

Using the survey questions in Table 11.5 in the case study at the end of this chapter, undertake your own survey to examine the views of a sample of people as to whether a mandatory retirement age should be retained or not. You can work in teams and try to include in your survey people from different age groups (e.g. 25 and under, 26–35, 36–45, and so on). Each member of the team can take responsibility to survey between 10 and 20 people in a particular age group. Then compare the answers from the respondents in the different age groups to explore whether people of different ages may have different views about mandatory retirement.

Table 11.2 Conceptual frameworks for age equality

Concepts and values that support age equality in the workplace	Arguments to justify limitations to age equality in the workplace
Human rights argument based on the principle of equal treatment: no one should receive less favourable treatment on the grounds of their race, gender, disability, sexual orientation, religion or belief, and age. *Dignity:* it is an affront to an individual's dignity to treat her less favourably because of her age.	'Fair innings' argument distinguishes between equality at a given time and equality over a lifetime. We all experience advantages (e.g. opportunities to be in paid employment) and disadvantages over a lifetime (e.g. having to retire at certain age).
Participative democracy: all groups should be entitled to full participation in all aspects of social life, including participation in the labour market.	*Neo-liberal perspective:* age equality cannot be achieved because of the high costs for businesses of retaining older workers.
Business case: from a macro economic perspective, there is a need to extend working lives to address demographic changes. From an organizational perspective, older workers can offer valuable expertise and specialist skills.	*Business case:* there should be a fixed retirement age for workforce planning reasons, or even to promote age diversity by employing younger people.

Signpost to
Chapter 3
From Equal
Opportunities
to Managing
Diversity

The legal context

As mentioned at the beginning of this chapter the prohibition to discriminate on the grounds of age was introduce by the EU Directive (2000/78). However, unlike other discrimination grounds, the Directive contains an exception to the general prohibition of direct age discrimination, as stated by Article 6(1), in the following circumstances:

> Member states my provide that differences on the grounds of age shall not constitute discrimination, if, within the context of national law, they are objectively and reasonably justified by a legitimate aim, including legitimate employment policies, labour market and vocational training objectives, and if the means of achieving that aim are appropriate and necessary.

This article also lists a number of examples where such differences of treatment may be justifiable. Although this is not intended to be an exhaustive list, they include the fixing of a minimum age, professional experience, or seniority in service for access to employment, and the fixing of a maximum age for recruitment, which is based on the training requirement of a particular type of work.

The rationale for allowing the use of age-based criteria, provided that they can be objectively justifiable, reflects the fact that often age is used in the area of social policy and employment policy to serve some legitimate considerations. An example of this is the requirement of a minimum age to take up paid employment, which is intended to protect young people from exploitation and to uphold their right to receive an education. Another example could be a recruitment maximum age to train as a firefighter since this type of job requires a relatively long period of training. However, the most controversial aspect of this exception relates to the use of a mandatory retirement age and whether this can be objectively justified.

As discussed above, one of the main arguments in support of mandatory retirement is that of the 'fair innings'. However, some academics are very critical of this argument as it undermines the legal protection for older workers. It is useful at this stage to clarify that mandatory retirement refers to those clauses which can be contained either in a contract of employment or laid down by law and which provide that employees should be made to retire from their job once they have reached a specific age. Mandatory retirement should not be confused with pensionable age, which refers to the age when an employee would be entitled to start receiving a pension. Mandatory retirement is a form of direct discrimination and therefore potentially in breach of anti-discrimination law. However, many countries still use mandatory retirement and the question is to what extent this can be objectively justified.

Rules relating to mandatory retirement are being increasingly challenged, as evidenced by a growing number of cases that are been referred to the European Court of Justice (ECJ). For reasons of space we cannot engage here in an in-depth discussion of European case law that is developing in this area (see Manfredi, 2011), but we can provide a short overview of some of the main principles that have emerged from the ECJ decisions relating to retirement rules.

In a number of judgments the Court has ruled that a national retirement policy could potentially be objectively justified. For example, in the Spanish case of *Felix Palacios de la Villa* (2007), the Court found that a mandatory retirement age was objectively justified 'as part of a national policy seeking to promote better access to employment, by means of better distribution of work between the generations' (paragraph 53). Similar conclusions were reached in the German case of *Dr Domnica Petersen* (2010), which involved a challenge to a mandatory retirement age of 68 for dentists working in the public health sector. In this case, the Court accepted the argument presented by the German government that a mandatory retirement age was justified by the need to free up jobs and career opportunities for younger dentists. In the more recent judgment in the case of *Vasil Ivanov Georgiev* (2010), which involved a mandatory retirement age of 68 for academic staff working in Bulgarian universities, the Court accepted the argument presented by the Advocate General about the importance of universities maintaining 'a mix of different generations of teaching staff and researchers' (paragraph 46). The principle that can be extrapolated from these decisions is that the need to redistribute job opportunities among younger generations of employees can amount to a legitimate aim of employment policy that potentially could objectively justify the use of a mandatory retirement age, provided that this a proportionate way of achieving that aim.

In the UK case of Age Concern (2009), however, the Court ruled that a national law providing for a default retirement age of 65 was potentially objectively justifiable in order to assist employers with workforce planning. Nevertheless, the European Court referred the case back to the national court to decide whether the use of mandatory retirement was a proportionate mean of achieving such an aim. In the end the UK government decided in 2010 to phase out mandatory retirement and this was completely removed in October 2011. From that date, employers have either to manage their workforce without a fixed retirement age or, if they intend to continue to use a contractual mandatory age, this will have to be objectively justified. This means that not only do they have to demonstrate that it serves a legitimate aim, but also that it is a proportionate way of achieving that aim and that this cannot be achieved effectively in any other way.

This discussion shows that this is a complex area where there are 'diverging but legitimate interests', as highlighted by the ECJ in the German case of *Rosenbladt* (2010). These include the interest of older workers to continue to have an active working life, the interest of younger generations of workers to have access to jobs and careers opportunities, and the interest of employers to plan effectively for the management of their workforce 'against a complex background of employment relationships closely linked to political choices in the area of retirement and employment' (*Rosenbladt*, 2010: paragraph 68).

Debate Box

Still working at the age of 90

Professor Denny Mitchison, aged 90, was reported to be one of the oldest full-time professors in the UK. He is a pathologist and when asked whether he would ever retire, he commented 'Well I might if I get very ill. But how do you give up a major part of your life? I view it soberly, but it's a lot of achievement, and I continue to have what I think are really quite interesting and important ideas.' (Guardian, 2009)

Organize the class into two groups, one for the motion and one against.

The motion is:
When many young people face unemployment or struggle to find stable employment, it is fair to have a mandatory retirement age in the workplace.

Stages in the debate: (each stage is given with timings, the overall time for the activity is 55 minutes – allowing a few minutes for change over of presenters, etc.)

- Each group has 20 minutes to prepare their arguments either for or against the motion.
- Each group is given 5 minutes to present their opening statement (10 minutes in total).
- Groups reconvene for 10 minutes to prepare rebuttal arguments.
- Each group has 2 minutes to present rebuttal arguments.

A vote is taken and the winners of the debate announced; the casting vote goes to impartial observers: tutors, audience members not involved in the debate, and observers.

Age discrimination in the workplace

Ageism is a form of discrimination that, unlike other types of discrimination, is particularly insidious as it can potentially affect any person at any stage of her life cycle. Broadly speaking, it involves treating a person less favourably because of her age compared to someone else who is either younger or older, without an objective justification for such differential treatment. In this section we examine age discrimination within the context of the workplace, and in particular we explore how common age discrimination is, who is more likely to be affected by it, how it manifests itself, and how age discrimination is likely to impact on individuals.

How widespread is age discrimination and what categories of workers are more likely to be affected by it?

The existence of age discrimination is well documented by research (see Wood et al., 2008 for an extensive literature review on this subject), and statistical evidence suggests that it is likely to be more widespread compared to other types of discrimination. For example, a survey under-taken by the European Union shows the highest incidence of self-reported age discrimination (6 per cent) compared to other types of discrimination, for example gender and ethnic origin, which are both at 3 per cent (European Commission, 2009a). Research shows that workers who are more likely to report experience of age discrimination are the younger ones, under the age of 30, and older ones over the age of 50 (Duncan and Loretto, 2004; Snape and Redman, 2003).

A similar polarization of results was found by research undertaken in the Higher Education sector in the UK into employees' perceptions of age discrimination, across different occupa-tional groups employed in this sector, which include academics, professional and support staff, and manual staff (Manfredi, 2008). Although the evidence considered so far points to the fact that older workers, as well as younger ones, are more likely to experience age dis-crimination, the degree of negative stereotyping that can result in unfair discrimination may vary for different types of job and profession. Singer (2001: 629) conducted a study to inves-tigate job-related age stereotypes which indicated that views on older workers and their abilities vary according to different types of profession. For example, university academics and medical doctors were seen as 'significantly more similar to their younger counterparts' with regard to performance and interpersonal skills compared to other professions, such as accountants and computer scientists. This suggests that workers in certain jobs and profes-sions are more likely to be judged by their 'functional age' rather than their chronological age.

The concept of 'functional age' was introduced by an American scholar, Ross McFarland, who argued that age alone 'is a very uncertain indication of functional ability' (McFarland, 1955: 14). His assertion was based on research from experimental psychology which demon-strated that there are significant differences in the abilities and capacities of individuals of any given age. His research highlighted the importance of assessing functional age in relation to specific capabilities of an individual against the demands of specific jobs, rather than making assumptions based on chronological age. In addition, we suggest that there can also be envi-ronmental factors that contribute to influencing perceptions about who is considered an old worker. Environmental factors such as early retirement trends may contribute to create a tendency to consider workers 'old' at an earlier stage compared to other sectors where more people leave work when they reach the retirement age or even later.

How does age discrimination manifest itself in the workplace?

In the studies that investigated employees' perceptions of age discrimination in the work-place discussed earlier (Duncan and Loretto; 2004; Manfredi 2008; Snape and Redman 2003), recruitment and promotion were the types of employment practice most commonly cited by both younger and older employees where they believed that they had experienced age dis-crimination. These findings are hardly surprising since prior to the introduction of the age discrimination legislation, age-related criteria were commonly used by employers to make decisions about staff recruitment and promotion. A study undertaken for the UK Department for Work and Pensions (Metcalf and Meadows, 2006: 89–92) found that some employers had a maximum recruitment age in place below the age of 50, that years of previous work experi-ence were widely used as a selection criteria, and that some employers admitted that younger applicants under the age of 22, as well as older applicants aged 60 or over, were more likely to be disadvantaged in recruitment practices. Similarly, in-depth studies focusing on specific employment sectors have highlighted a number of practices potentially in breach of the age

Signpost to Chapter 2 An Outline of European and UK Equality Legislation

discrimination legislation (see Table 11.3). In addition, there is also evidence to suggest that younger employees may be treated less favourably with regard to pay, as those studies show that age may be used to fix starting salaries in several employment sectors (see Chapter 2 for a full discussion on the legal provisions about pay and benefits).

Access to training is also an area where older workers are likely to experience discrimination (see, for example, CIPD, 2003). Research found that with regard to access to training, many employers tend to favour younger workers, and that some believe that older workers are unwilling to train, although this claim does not seem to be supported by actual facts (McNair et al., 2007: 92). A common criterion which tends to act as a barrier to training opportunities for older workers is their proximity to retirement. Such an approach can be explained in the light of the theory on human capital, which suggests that employers are prepared to invest in their human resources as long as they can get a return on their investments. It has been argued, however, that the existence of a mandatory retirement age reinforces such discriminatory practices against older workers because the age of an individual is bound to impact on 'the viability of investment in human capital' as although 'previous commentators suggest that it is the time the individual has left at the firm that is important, not their age, mandatory retirement effectively makes the two indistinguishable' (Urwin, 2006: 93).

Age discrimination can also manifest itself in more subtle ways through stereotypical beliefs directed to either younger or older workers. For example, in the study undertaken in the Higher Education sector, experiences of ageist attitudes were reported by both younger and older employees, and these were categorized respectively as 'not being considered experienced enough', or 'being excluded from opportunities to take on new roles and responsibilities' (Manfredi, 2008: 26). Focus groups with 94 line managers, undertaken as part of the same research, validated these experiences as a number of them confirmed that they had to deal with complaints from younger colleagues who felt that they had not been taken seriously because of their age. Some of the managers themselves also had personal experience of age discrimination, and explained that they had encountered hostility from older staff who considered them to be too young to perform a management role. Ageist stereotypes against older workers also emerged from these discussions, as they were often

Table 11.3 Age-related discriminatory practices

Age-related discriminatory practices in the selection and recruitment of staff	Employment sector
Using length of experience as a selection criterion in recruitment for assessing competencies (this could disadvantage younger applicants)	Retailing, hospitality, construction, health and social care, other community sectors
Targeting particular age groups	Retailing
Providing age information of candidates when short-listing and interviewing staff	Retailing, hospitality, manufacturing, education
Using proximity to retirement and maximum recruitment ages to exclude job applicants	Transport and logistics

Source: McNair and Flynn (2006a, 2006b, 2006c, 2006d, 2006e, 2006f, 2006g, 2006h)

described as being resistant to change, less adaptable, and less productive compared to younger workers (Manfredi, 2008: 29). These kinds of negative, stereotypical beliefs against older workers are not uncommon, as is demonstrated by other studies on this subject, but they are often based on assumptions rather than facts (Taqi, 2002). For example, the most noticeable one is the presumed link between age and productivity and the belief that the latter declines with age. However, research findings on this subject are very mixed and so far no conclusive evidence has been produced to substantiate this claim (McEvoy and Cascio, 1989; Waldman and Aviolo, 1986). It can also be added that the concept of productivity, and how this should be measured, is very complex to define, not only because it depends on the type of job and work context, but equally because 'most jobs require the combination of various types of capabilities and the end result will not only depend on all these aspects, but also on the way these various capabilities are combined' (European Commission, 2006: 74).

Intersectional discrimination

A further dimension of age discrimination is represented by its possible intersection with other forms of discrimination, such as gender, race, and disability. Women are more likely to suffer a 'double jeopardy' because of their gender and because of their age. For example, their longer life expectancy, combined with a lower pension income, places them at a greater risk

---

⊙ Case study 11.1 Age is a core element of Centrica diversity strategy

Centrica, the international energy organization that includes British Gas and other businesses, has removed age as a factor from the selection process and has invested heavily in educating staff involved in recruitment in order to attract candidates with the right skills and attitudes from across the labour market. They commented that 'In our job descriptions we are not looking for years of experience. Rather we are looking for the skills attitudes and behaviours that we know are required in order to do a great job in our organization. Defining what and how we do things has been instrumental in removing the concept of age as a predictor of fit to a role.' They have also removed the upper age limits for the British Gas apprenticeship scheme, which 'has resulted in 30 per cent of our apprentice intake being over the age of 24', according to a spokesman.

Source: Anonymous (2009)

....

Case study questions

1. Do you think that there might be some jobs where it would be objectively justifiable to look for years of experience? Provide examples and explain how, in these cases, it would be objectively justifiable to measure experience by a certain number of years.

2. Why do you think British Gas had an upper age limit of 24 for their apprenticeship scheme in the past?

3. In addition to the 30 per cent increase in the apprentice intake of people over the age of 24, what other benefits do you think Centrica has derived from removing the upper age limit from their apprenticeship scheme?

of poverty in their old age. As highlighted earlier, old age presents a strong gender dimension, as women's participation in the labour market is more likely to have been limited due to their family responsibilities, and therefore they may not have had the opportunity to build up sufficient pension income. Socio-cultural factors also play a role in determining when women are considered to become an 'old' worker. Research reported by the International Labour Organization (2002: 8) suggests that 'women working in certain countries, such as those in the Baltic States and China, are especially vulnerable to age and sex discrimination'. However, women in western countries too are exposed to double disadvantage due to the interplay between age, physical appearance, and sexuality, either because of their perceived youth or because they tend to be considered older at an earlier age compared to their male colleagues (Duncan and Loretto, 2004; Granleese and Sayer, 2006; Itzin and Phillipson, 1995). Therefore, gender and age can be closely linked to one another and very difficult to disentangle.

Another form of discrimination that is closely associated with age is disability. The work of Sargeant (2004b: 24) shows that the prevalence of disability increases with age, as evidenced by significantly higher proportions of disabled people over the age of 50 in most European countries. For example, Germany and the UK have the highest proportion of disabled people aged between 50 and 54 (25.4 per cent and 24.9 per cent respectively) compared to an EU average of 21.1 per cent, while the UK, Germany, and France have the highest proportion of disabled people aged between 55 and 59 (35.7 per cent, 33.5 per cent, and 31.1 respectively) compared to an EU average of 28.9 per cent.

Impact of age discrimination

Age discrimination can have a negative impact both on individuals and organizations. From an individual's perspective, age discrimination can lead to material disadvantage, for example in terms of missed opportunities to gain promotion and higher earnings, or social exclusion if a person is denied access to employment because of her age. It can also have a negative impact on an individual's self-esteem, dignity, motivation, and in general on the relationship with her working environment. Desmett and Gaillard (2008) have used social identity theory to explore the impact of age discrimination on individuals. They start from the core premise of this theory, according to which individuals need to have a positive image of themselves, and explain that if the group individuals belongs to is devalued, for example because all people over the age of 60 are considered to be less productive at work, or all people under the age of 25 are considered to be inexperienced, they are likely to develop some cognitive and behavioural strategies to cope with this devaluation in their identity. They may choose to adopt a collective strategy to improve the image of the group they belong to, such as, for example, setting up an organization to campaign for the rights of older workers (e.g. the UK charity Age Concern), or they may react at an individual level. In the latter case, Desmett and Gaillard argue that an individual may develop a coping strategy by 'devaluing the domain where they are stigmatized', which, in our context, would be the workplace. This however, would lead to a loss of motivation and interest in their work, although they also point out that some individuals may react in the opposite way by increasing their commitment to their work 'to contradict the stereotype of age-related decline in motivation at work' (Desmett and Gaillard, 2008: 171).

Snape and Redman (2003: 80) found in their study about perceptions of age discrimination among employees in a UK local authority that there is 'a statistically significant association between an individual's perception of having suffered age discrimination and job attitudes' whatever the age of the individual. They refer to the social exchange theory, which suggests 'that affective commitment, defined as an individual's emotional attachment and identification with the organization (Meyer and Allen, 1997, cited in Snape and Redman, 2003) is related to the perception of a supportive and equitable exchange relationship (Shore and Wayne, 1993, cited in Snape and Redman, 2003), something that is likely to be violated by the experience of discrimination'.

We also argue that age discrimination, or any other type of unfair discrimination, can negatively affect the psychological contract between an employee and her employer, which can be broadly defined as a set of reciprocal obligations and entitlements that are perceived to exist between an employee and an employer. If it is perceived by an employee that this contract has been breached, for example as a result of age discrimination, this can lead to low morale and low motivation, and make an employee feel disengaged from her work. Therefore it is in the interest of organizations to eradicate age discrimination, to avoid the negative impact on their workforce's morale, motivation, and, ultimately, performance.

⊙ Student Activity 11.3

Conduct a focus group or short interviews with other students, friends, or colleagues to find out about their views and perceptions of age discrimination. Draw up a shortlist of questions to include the following:

1. At what age do you think a worker should be considered to be 'old'?

2. Does age matter for certain jobs? If you think that it does, can you give examples and explain why?

3. At what age do you think workers are more likely to be discriminated against because of their age (e.g. under 25 or over 50)?

4. Have you ever been discriminated against because of your age, or do you know someone who has?

5. If you have experienced age discrimination, how did it happen? How did it make you feel?

Discuss the results of your interviews with other students and consider whether any specific theme emerges from the answers (e.g. do most respondents seem to think that age discrimination affects mainly older workers?)

Managing age diversity in the workplace

Demographic changes are reshaping the composition of the workforce and this poses new management challenges for employers while at the same time presenting them with opportunities to introduce innovative approaches to their working practices and to the way they manage their human resources. The management of age diversity in the workplace is still developing, and employers have taken different approaches to it, as highlighted by a study carried out in a range of different employment sectors within 15 countries in the European Union (Taylor, 2007). This study shows that Nordic countries appear to have placed the emphasis on health and well-being as part of a more holistic general approach towards managing older workers; Belgium, France,

Italy, and Spain have instead focused on training, development, and flexible working, but placed little emphasis on workers' health: Austria, Germany, and the Netherlands have directed attention to training and development and less on flexible working; and the UK has adopted a more comprehensive approach. This research also highlighted that market forces appear to be the main driving factors for employers to engage with age management, to retain valuable expertise, to gain competitive advantage, and to tackle labour supply shortages, although public policy too plays an important role in encouraging employers to engage with age-related issues.

Health and well-being: the concept of work ability

The concept of work ability was developed in the late 1990s by the Finnish Institute of Occupational Health, and it can be broadly defined as 'the development of human capital to meet the demands from the labour market' (Ministry of Social Affairs and Health, 2002: 24). The Finnish government launched a national programme on ageing workers in 1997 in response to major demographic and structural changes which affected the country labour market, and it was within this context that the concept of work ability was researched, developed, and tested in a number of organizations.

Work ability is underpinned by the notion that an individual's capabilities have to be matched with work demands. It stresses the importance of maintaining a balanced relationship between these two factors as a key element to increase older workers' participation in the labour market. This echoes the work of McFarland (1955: 15), referred to earlier in this chapter, who highlighted the need for a continuous adjustment between the capacities of older workers and the requirements of their jobs, and also stressed that older people, when adequately motivated, can learn new activities and adjust to the changes caused by age. Medical evidence shows that while some physical functions decline with age, other cognitive functions can improve, such as 'control of use of language or the ability to process complex problems in insecure situations', which leads to the conclusion that as workers age, work should become less physically demanding and instead 'include more of the mental characteristics that improve during their career' (Ilmarinen, 2001: 548). The work ability concept has been illustrated using the metaphor of a house (see Figure 11.1).

The external environment that surrounds the house is occupied by society, family, and friends, which can influence what happens in the house. The latter is built on four floors: the first floor includes health and functional capacities; the second floor competencies, including knowledge and skills; the third floor values, attitude, and motivation to work; and the fourth floor relates to the work environment. What happens on this floor is determined by employers and how they organize the workplace, and in order to maintain work ability, a harmonious relationship must be maintained between this floor and the other floors in the house. This balance is no longer achieved only by adapting the workers (e.g. through training), but also by adjusting the work because, as highlighted by Ilmarinen, 'we have been blaming the wrong source – the human beings – saying "you are poor" – although really it's the job that is poor' (BBC, 2004).

Various interventions have been identified to maintain work ability and prevent early retirement through ill health. These include:

- The use of a work ability index based on a self-assessment questionnaire
- The development, through training, of management capability to deal with work ability

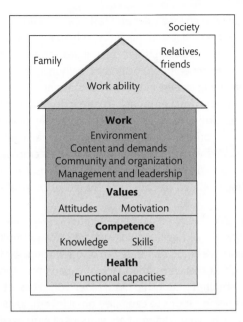

Figure 11.1 The concept of work ability (Ilmarinen, 2006)

- Workplace programmes to promote exercise and physical well-being
- Improvement of the workplace environment
- Training programmes for older workers to ensure that they keep up to date, particularly with new technology.

The use of the house metaphor conveys very clearly the importance of placing work ability at the core of any strategy to manage an older workforce, because if the foundations of the house are weakened by poor work ability, any other intervention is likely to be ineffective.

A holistic approach to age management

A holistic approach to managing age diversity should look at different aspects of human resource management and how these are likely to impact on age, but equally it should take a life-cycle perspective. This means that age management issues should be considered in relation to the life cycle from the perspective of an employee and of the employment relation, rather than from a set of specific circumstances relating to a particular age group, such as, for example, training for younger workers, career progression for middle managers, or retraining for older workers (European Commission, 2006). Such an approach should include a number of practices, ranging from monitoring the age profile of the workforce to promoting internal mobility and intergenerational activities.

Internal mobility can be achieved by employing different practices that partly depend on the size of an organization. These might include task rotation, the use of secondments to take up new roles, and assignments to specific projects. The development of internal mobility presents a number of advantages from an employer's and employee's perspective. Offering employees the opportunity to change roles and tasks can sustain older workers' motivation and performance, but it is also suggested that it can help to retain younger employees by offering them the opportunity to build up their capabilities and develop their careers. In fact, internal mobility can help to generate opportunities for 'horizontal' career moves, which are particularly useful in managing careers in those organizations where 'vertical' career opportunities may be limited. A 'horizontal' approach to career development can avoid fuelling the 'fair innings' argument, according to which, as discussed earlier, older employees should retire to make space for their younger colleagues. Moreover, it can contribute towards the development of a multi-skilled workforce, thus responding to employers' needs for greater flexibility in the way they provide services and products, and ensuring that 'future generations of workers will be better prepared to cope with the need for greater mobility' (European Commission, 2006: 138).

Research by Henkens (2003) shows that intergenerational teams are important in eradicating the negative stereotypes held against older workers, for example, about their level of productivity. By extension, we argue that they can also reduce negative stereotypes against younger employees, such as their presumed lack of experience. Another way to promote good intergenerational working relationships is for older workers to act as mentors to younger colleagues. This enables organizations to capitalize on older employees' expertise and facilitate the flow of knowledge between different generations of employees.

Flexible working

Flexible working and flexible retirement are considered to be key elements in increasing the rate of participation of older workers in the labour market, and to help with the transition from full-time employment to retirement. Moreover, flexible working involving a reduction in working hours can contribute to maintaining good work ability. A good work–life balance

---

◉ Case study 11.2 Generation Y

'I want it all and I want it now!'

This sentiment typifies the challenging new attitude that Generation Y (those born in the 1980s and 1990s) are bringing to the workplace. Research undertaken by the Employers' Forum on Age (EFA) found that this generation represents 22 per cent of the workforce, yet nearly half of all graduates leave jobs within two years, with the resulting recruitment, retention, and management implications. This group wants a career lattice rather than a career ladder. Young people do not have the same linear career expectations as their predecessors. They do not see life in straight lines. This does not mean they aren't ambitious. According to the EFA research, employers will need learning and development opportunities to be dynamic and flexible and they will need to allow this age group to seek out their own creative challenges too. Ultimately, they equate success not with status but with autonomy and flexibility. The EFA suggests that this is a group of people, to whom portfolio careers, switching industries, taking career breaks, travelling, working with different kinds of people, and flexible working will become the norm. They know that there is no job for life. This is a generation of multi-taskers, and they can juggle email on their Blackberrys while talking on mobile phones while trawling online.

Source: Employers' Forum on Age (2008)

Case study questions

1. Do you agree with this assessment of the so-called Y generation?

2. What aspects of a holistic approach to managing age diversity could be useful to manage this generation of workers?

3. To what extent do you think that the needs of this generation of workers and those of older workers can be met by similar working practices?

Table 11.4 Types of flexible working

Life stage	Type of flexible working
Family building, childcare responsibilities	• Maternity/paternity leave • Career break • Part-time work, job-sharing • Compressed hours (working a shorter week by compressing the weekly working hours into longer days) • Work in term-time only (working only during school terms and be off work during school holidays) • Working from home • Flexi-time (to chose, within limits, the time when to start and finish work)
Approaching retirement, eldercare (i.e. looking after elderly relatives)	• Career break, unpaid leave • Part-time work, job-sharing • Compressed hours • Annualized hours (the period of work is defined over the whole year) • Working from home • Flexi-time • Bridge jobs (change of role and responsibilities, often including a reduction in working hours)
Flexible retirement	• Retire part-time and start drawing a pension while continuing to work for the rest of the time for the same employer. The feasibility of this option depends on individual occupational pension schemes regulations • Seasonal employment (working only during busy periods of the year, such as at Christmas and in the summer)

is important at every stage of people's lives and careers, and Table 11.4 outlines how different types of flexible working and leave arrangements can support employees' work–life balance at different stages of their life.

Flexible working when approaching retirement and flexible retirement are popular options, as highlighted by the 2001 Eurobarometer survey (European Commission,), which indicated that nearly three out of four people in the European Union are in favour of the idea of gradual retirement from paid work (Kohl, 2002, cited in Platman, 2004). Research commissioned by the UK Department for Work and Pensions (Hedges et al., 2009) found that, although the idea of gradual withdrawal from the labour market through flexible work-ing was generally popular with people, many did not think that it would be a realistic pros-pect for them as opportunities may be limited in practice. In fact, flexible working is not always commonly available, and employers in the private sector are less likely to offer flex-ible working compared to those in the public sector. Furthermore, Platman (2004: 187) has highlighted that some forms of flexible working involve low levels of employment protec-tion and present the risk, for some older workers, of ending up in insecure forms of employ-ment and being marginalized in the same way as other vulnerable groups. Besides, workers on low pay may not be able to afford flexible working if this involves a reduction in their pay.

In conclusion, if flexible working is going to play a more prominent role in the transition between full-time work and retirement, there is a need to ensure that people are better in-formed about their pension entitlements, and the financial implications of deferring their pension. Equally, flexible working needs to become more widespread and issues around managing an increased level of flexibility must be addressed at organizational level. Finally, it is important for flexible working to be protected by employment rights if it is to meet the public policy aims of extending working lives.

Signpost to
Chapter 8
Managing
Work–life
Balance

▶ Student Activity 11.4

Examine Figures 11.2 and 11.3 below, which show the age profile of the workforce in the retail sector and in the health and social care sector, respectively. Working in teams, compare and contrast the age profile in these two sectors and identify possible challenges in terms of their workforce age. Imagine that you have been asked by employers in one of these two sectors to develop a strategy to manage age diversity. Prepare a PowerPoint presentation to outline your proposal. This should include the following points:

- the importance of monitoring the workforce age profile
- areas where age discrimination may occur and examples of how to avoid it
- depending which sector you have chosen, suggestions on how to attract and retain either younger or older workers
- suggestions for a holistic approach to managing age diversity, including examples of how this can be achieved and its benefit for an organization.

Prior to the preparation of your PowerPoint presentation, you may wish to find out more about general working patterns in these sectors, e.g. shift work, 24/7 service delivery, and whether there are any existing examples of good practice that can help you to devise a diversity management strategy.

The end of retirement?

As seen earlier in this chapter, the UK is probably one of the few countries within the European Union that has decided to abolish mandatory retirement. Many employers, however, have voluntarily removed mandatory retirement, thus offering the opportunity to their employees of prolonging their working lives. In most cases these decisions have been driven by business needs, such as labour shortages and the need to retain particular expertise. It has been reported that those employers who have removed mandatory retirement have experienced a number of benefits, including improved customer relations.

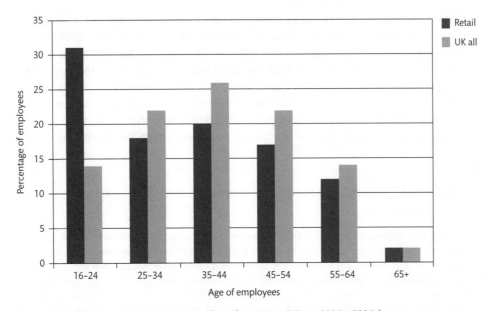

Figure 11.2 The age profile of the retail workforce (McNair and Flynn, 2006a, 2006e)

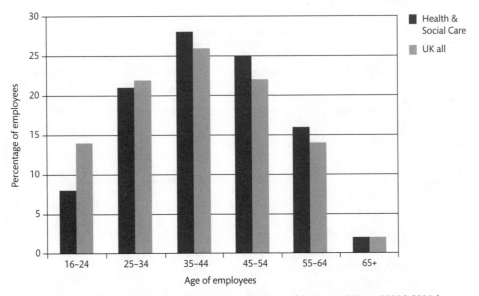

Figure 11.3 The age profile of the health and social are workforce (McNair and Flynn, 2006d, 2006e)

An example of this is the case of JD Wetherspoon in the UK, which has benefited greatly from boosting the proportion of older workers on its staff. They found that they have been able to cover some key shifts that are not so attractive to younger workers, such as busy weekday lunchtimes. They have re-educated their managers to be more flexible in their hiring and that has helped their staff retention. They also found that older workers are a hit when it comes to customer service. One of their managers commented, 'Older people are good at doing that they like talking to people and are willing to spend that bit more time making sure customers are having a good experience.'

JD Wetherspoon has attracted older staff by running a publicity campaign to make it clear that there are no barriers to them getting on in the company (Institute of Directors and the Department for Work and Pension, 2009: 25). The UK-based retailer Marks and Spencer (M&S) removed its retirement age in 2002. This move was driven by the need to retain highly effective customer sales advisers. At the same time, more employees were expressing the wish to continue to work past retirement age. The key benefits experienced by the company, since they removed the retirement age, have been improved flexibility offered to both the business and employees, and the increased loyalty of employees who valued the choice (Line, 2007).

End of Chapter Case Study Retirement policies in the Higher Education sector

The Higher Education Funding Council for England funded a project in 2007–2008 which aimed to support Higher Education institutions to develop good practice in managing age diversity in employment. This involved an investigation of age-related issues in the sector via an Age Staff Survey to capture employees' attitudes towards retirement and perceptions of age discrimination. A series of focus groups were also conducted with line managers to explore their views about retirement and other age-related matters. Twelve Higher Education institutions took part in this research, and over 7,000 employees responded to the Age Staff Survey. Table 11.5 shows the distribution of employees' opinions regarding a fixed retirement age.

Table 11.5 Age Staff Survey administered in Higher Education institutions

	Strongly agree	Agree	Neither agree nor disagree	Disagree	Strongly disagree
It is important to have a fixed retirement age in order to enable younger employees to progress their career ('Fair innings' argument)	4.2%	15.5%	33.9%	**36.2%**	10.2%
A fixed retirement age unfairly discriminates against older employees (Age equality argument)	13.6%	**45%**	26.4%	13.4%	1.6%
It is important to have a fixed retirement age in order to enable under-represented groups, such as ethnic minorities and women, to progress their careers (Competing claims with other equality strands argument, e.g. race and gender)	1.2%	5.2%	32.8%	**43.4%**	17.4%
It is important not to have a fixed retirement age in order to enable HEIs to retain valuable expertise and specialist skills ('Business case' argument in support of no mandatory retirement age to tap into the resource of older workers)	15.5%	**46.1%**	26.3%	10.5%	1.5%

Table 11.5 (*continued*)

	Strongly agree	Agree	Neither agree nor disagree	Disagree	Strongly disagree
It is important to have a fixed retirement age in order to enable HEIs to manage their workforce effectively ('Business case' argument in support of a fixed retirement age for workforce planning)	1.7%	13.4%	**37.9%**	37%	9.9%

These results indicate that well over half of the respondents supported the age equality argument, and just over 60 per cent supported the 'business case' in favour of no mandatory retirement age. Conversely, there was very little support for the 'fair innings' argument, or for the other arguments in favour of mandatory retirement age. Furthermore, a significant proportion of respondents – 34.8 per cent of men and 24.6 per cent of women – indicated that they expected to retire after the age of 65.

The findings from the focus groups with line managers provided a mixed picture of the impact of retirement policies. Several line managers, particularly among academics, expressed concern at the prospect that some of their colleagues wished to continue to work beyond the age of 65. They believed that if academics did not retire, there would be a stagnation of the internal labour market that would reduce opportunities for younger staff to progress their career or enter academia. High salary costs of older staff were also cited as a problem for retaining them.

Line managers of professional and support staff were concerned with the fact that many of their staff (from the 'baby boom generation') were approaching retirement and the effect that mass retirees could have on the level of staff in their departments. Their experience was that staff in this cohort wanted to leave even before they reached the retirement age, and this raised issues about succession planning, or rather, the lack of it. It also emerged from the discussion with this group of managers that their institutions had contributed to raise such expectations, as, in the past, they had often made use of early retirement packages to restructure departments.

Line managers of manual staff were more sympathetic towards some of their staff's intentions to work beyond the age of 65, and several of them already managed staff over that age. The costs of retaining older staff were not an issue for these managers as manual staff tend to be on low pay. Health and safety were cited as possible issues, as some manual jobs can be physically demanding, but it was noted that these difficulties could be overcome by making adjustments to roles and responsibilities. Overall it was reported that it has been common practice for several manual staff to continue to work past retirement age, either for financial reasons or because work provides them with social interaction, or both.

Source: Manfredi and Vickers (2009)

Case study questions

1. What are the main issues in this case?

2. Which theoretical frameworks relating to age equality are reflected by the concerns of line managers if staff do not retire at a fixed age?

3. In the light of the findings presented in this case study, consider whether it would be objectively justifiable for universities to continue to have a fixed retirement age, particularly in relation to academic staff. (Refer to the concepts of legitimate aim and proportionality discussed earlier in this chapter.)

4. To what extent does this case study reflects some of the issues discussed in the section about the policy context?

Conclusion

The introduction of legal protection against age discrimination and measures designed to extend working lives appear to have been driven primarily by market forces and economic pressure on governments' social security systems and pension funds, caused by an ageing population and low birth rates. Other types of discrimination, such as gender and race discrimination, have gained prominence as a result of people's liberation movements and are well grounded in the human rights discourse, while age discrimination seems to have been prompted by economic pressure. This will have significant implications for employment policies and will impact on the workplace. Furthermore, as people's awareness of age discrimination increases, ageist employment practices will become more open to challenges, thus raising the profile of age equality in the workplace. Age policies in the workplace are still an evolving area and there is a need for organizations to develop strategies to manage age diversity effectively, as this has implications for several aspects of human resource management, as considered in this chapter.

It is important to note that managing age diversity is not a new concept, since an organization's workforce is always likely to be made up of workers of different ages. However, the introduction of legal protection against age discrimination and policies aimed at extending working lives has brought into focus the need for developing a strategic approach to the management of age diversity. This should take a holistic approach, as discussed in this chapter, over the career of a worker and of the employment relationship in order to create positive synergies between different generations of workers and harness the skills and the talents of all ages.

To conclude, we argue that the introduction of this equality strand with its management implications challenges the linear progression from education to work and retirement, and opens up spaces to reformulate employment practices and the way in which people participate in paid work. This may become increasingly more interspersed with periods of time to care, to study, or to undertake voluntary activities or leisure breaks during the course of an individual's life, thus creating a new workplace context where chronological age becomes irrelevant, and the focus is placed entirely on people's competencies and abilities.

 ## Review and discussion questions

1. Explain what the 'age/employment paradox' means and how this can be linked to the introduction of legal protection against age discrimination.

2. Discuss the ethical and pragmatic reasons that support the case for age equality in the workplace.

3. Critically review the 'fair innings' arguments and its implications for age equality in the workplace.

4. How is age discrimination likely to manifest itself in the workplace and who is more likely to be affected by it? Provide examples to support your arguments.

5. Explain what the concept of work ability means and discuss its practical application at an organizational level.

6. Discuss what management approaches may be taken to manage effectively an age diverse workforce.

For additional material on the content of this chapter please visit the supporting Online Resource Centre at **www.oxfordtextbooks.co.uk/orc/kumra_manfredi/**

 ## Further reading

CIPD (Chartered Institute of Personnel and Development) (2001) *Age Discrimination at Work.* London: CIPD.

Sargeant, M. (2007) *Age Discrimination in Employment.* Aldershot: Gower.

Sargeant, M. (2010) The default retirement age: legitimate aims and disproportionate means. *Industrial Law Journal*, 39/3: 244–263.

Taylor, P. (2008) *Ageing Labour Forces: Promises and Prospects*. London: Edward Elgar

References

Anonymous (2008) *The Demographic Future of Europe: From Challenge to Opportunity*. European Commission. Available online at http://europa.eu/legislation_summaries/employment_and_social_policy/disability_and_old_age/c10160_en.htm.

Anonymous (2009) Diversity policies fuel business success at Centrica: company wins award for anti-ageism initiatives. *Human Resource Management International Digest*, 17/2: 21–24.

BBC (2004) Moving the Finnish line at work. *BBC News*, 8 December. Available online at http://newsvote.bbc.co.uk/mpapps/pagetools/print/news.bbc.co.uk/1/hi/world/europe

CIPD (Chartered Institute of Personnel and Development) (2003) *Who Trains at Work?* London: CIPD.

Desmette, D. and Gaillard, M. (2008) When a 'worker' becomes and 'older worker': the effects of age-related social identity on attitudes towards retirement and work. *Career Development International*, 13/2: 168–185.

Duncan, C. and Loretto, W. (2004) Never the right age? Gender and age-based discrimination in employment. *Gender, Work and Organisation*, 11/1: 95–115.

Employers' Forum on Age (2008) *The Gap in the Workplace: Generation Y*. London: The Employers' Forum on Age.

European Commission (2001) Social Exclusion and Modernisation of Pension Systems, *Eurobarometer*, 4671. Brussels. Available online at http://www.esds.ac.uk/findingData/snDescription.asp?sn=4761&print=1.

European Commission (2006) *Ageing and Employment: Identification of Good Practice to Increase Job Opportunities and Maintain Older Workers in Employment. Final Report.* Brussels: Directorate-General for Employment, Social Affairs and Equal Opportunities. Available online at http://ec.europa.eu/employment_social/emplweb/news/index_en.

European Commission (2008) *Demography Report 2008: Meeting Social Needs in an Ageing Society*. Brussels: European Commission.

European Commission (2009a) Discrimination in the EU in 2009. *Eurobarometer* (special issue) 317/Wave 71.2 – TNS Opinion & Social. Available at http://ec.europa.eu/public_opinion/archives/ebs/ebs_317_sum_en_pdf.

European Commission (2009b) *Communication from the Commission to the European Parliament, the Council, the European Economic and Social Committee and the Committee of the Regions. Dealing with the Impact of an Ageing Population in the EU*. Brussels: European Commission. Available online at http://ec.europa.eu /publications/publication14996_en.htm.

Fredman, S. (2003) The age of equality, in Fredman, S. and Spencer, S., *Age as an Equality Issue: Legal and Policy Perspectives*. Oxford: Hart Publishing.

Granleese, J. and Sayer, G. (2006) Gender ageism and 'lookism': a triple jeopardy for female academics. *Women in Management Review*, 21/6: 500–517.

Grimley Evans, J. (2003) Age discrimination: implications of the ageing process, in Fredman, S. and Spencer, S. (eds), Age as an Equality Issue: Legal and Policy Perspective. Oxford: Hart Publishing, pp. 11–20.

Hedges, A., Sykes, W., and Groon, C. (2009) *Extending Working Life: Changing the Culture. Qualitative Research into Effective Messages*. Research Report No. 557. London: Department for Work and Pension.

Henkens, K. (2003) *Stereotyping Older Workers and Retirement: The Managers' Point of View*. WANE Working Paper 5, Workforce Ageing in the New Economy. The Hague: Netherlands Interdisciplinary Demographic Institute, pp. 1–20.

Ilmarinen, J.E. (2001) Ageing workers. *Occupational and Environmental Medicine*, 58: 546–552.

Ilmarinen, J. (2006) Promotion of work ability and employment of ageing workers in Finland. Paper presented at the seminar: Finland–a country that cares about its Human Potential. Institute of Public Affairs, Bratislavia, Slovakia, 15 November.

Institute of Directors and the Department for Work and Pensions (2009) *Extending Working Lives: A*

Director's Guide. London: Institute of Directors and the Department for Work and Pension.

International Labour Organization (2002) *An Inclusive Society for an Ageing Population: The Employment and Social Protection Challenge*. Second World Assembly on Ageing, Madrid.

Itzin, C. and Phillipson, C. (1995) Gendered ageism: a double jeopardy for women in organizations, in Itzin, C. and Phillipson, C. (eds), *Gender, Culture and Organisational Change: Putting Theory into Practice*. London: Routledge, pp. 81–90.

Japan Times (2006) Workforce gears up to take in growing number of seniors. *The Japan Times*, 2 August. Available online at http://search.japantimes.co.jp/cgi-bin/nn20060802f2.html

Line, F. (2007) *The End of the Line for Retirement Ages: The Business Case for Managing without a Retirement Age*. London: The Employers' Forum on Age.

Manfredi, S. (2008) *Developing Good Practice in Managing Age Diversity in the Higher Education Sector: An Evidence-based Approach*. Oxford: Centre for Diversity Policy Research and Practice, Oxford Brookes University. Available online at www.brookes.ac.uk/services/hr/cdprp/age.

Manfredi, S. (2011) Retirement, collective agreement and age discrimination: implications for the Higher Education sector in the UK. *International Journal of Discrimination and the Law*, 11(1/2): 65–80.

Manfredi, S. and Vickers, L. (2009) Retirement and age discrimination: managing retirement in Higher Education. *Industrial Law Journal*, 38/3: 343–364.

McEvoy, G.M. and Cascio, W.F. (1989) Cumulative evidence of the relationship between employee age and job performance. *Journal of Applied Psychology*, 74/1: 11–17.

McFarland, R. (1955) The psychological aspects of ageing. Paper presented at the 28th Graduate Fortnight on Problems of Ageing of the New York Academy of Medicine, New York. Available online at www.ncbi.nlm.nih.gov/pmc/articles/PMC1805831.

McNair, S. and Flynn, M. (2006a) *Managing an Ageing Workforce in Retail: A Report for Employers*. London: Department for Work and Pensions.

McNair, S. and Flynn, M. (2006b) *Managing an Ageing Workforce in Hospitality: A Report for Employers*. London: Department for Work and Pensions.

McNair, S. and Flynn, M. (2006c) *Managing an Ageing Workforce in Construction: A Report for Employers*. London: Department for Work and Pensions.

McNair, S. and Flynn, M. (2006d) *Managing an Ageing Workforce in Health and Social Care: A Report for Employers*. London: Department for Work and Pensions.

McNair, S. and Flynn, M. (2006e) *Managing an Ageing Workforce in 'Other Community' Sectors: A Report for Employers*. London: Department for Work and Pensions.

McNair, S. and Flynn, M. (2006f) *Managing an Ageing Workforce in Education: A Report for Employers*. London: Department for Work and Pensions.

McNair, S. and Flynn, M. (2006g) *Managing an Ageing Workforce in Manufacturing: A Report for Employers*. London: Department for Work and Pensions.

McNair, S. and Flynn, M. (2006h) *Managing an Ageing Workforce in Transport and Logistics: A Report for Employers*. London: Department for Work and Pensions.

McNair, S., Flynn, M., and Dutton, N. (2007) *Employers Responses to an Ageing Workforce: A Qualitative Study*. Research Report No. 455. London: Department of Work and Pensions.

Metcalfe, H. and Meadows, P. (2006) *Survey of Employers' Policies, Practices and Preferences Relating to Age*. London: Department of Work and Pensions.

Ministry of Social Affairs and Health (2002) *The Many Faces of the National Programme on Ageing Workers*. Helsinki: Ministry of Social Affairs and Health.

Platman, K. (2004) Flexible employment in later life: public policy panacea in search for mechanisms to extend working lives. *Social Policy and Society*, 3/2: 181–188.

Sargeant, M. (2005a) For diversity against discrimination: the contradictory approach to age discrimination in employment. *The International Journal of Comparative Labour Law and Industrial Relations*, 21/4: 629–644.

Sargeant, M. (2005b) Disability and age-multiple potential for discrimination. *International Journal of the Sociology of Law*, 33: 17–33.

Singer, M.S. (2001) Age stereotypes as a function of profession. *The Journal of Social Pshychology*, 126/5: 691–692.

Snape, E. and Redman, T. (2003) Too old or too young? The impact of perceived age discrimination. *Human Resource Management Journal*, 13/1: 78–89.

Taqi, A. (2002) Older people, work and equal opportunity. *International Social Security Review*, 55/1: 107–120.

Taylor, P. (2007) *Employment Initiatives for an Ageing Workforce in the EU 15*. Dublin: European Foundation for the Improvement of Working Lives. Available online at www.eurofound.europa.eu/publications/htmfiles/ef0639.htm.

Urwin, P. (2006) Age discrimination: legislation and human capital accumulation. *Employee Relations*, 28/1: 87–97.

Waldman, D.A. and Aviolo, B.J. (1986) A meta-analysis of age differences in job performance. *Journal of Applied Psychology*, 71: 33–38.

Walker, A. (2001) *Towards active ageing in the European Union*. Paper prepared for the Millennium Project Workshop–Towards Active Ageing in the 21st century. Tokyo: The Japan Institute of Labour, 29–30 November.

Wood, G., Wilkinson, A., and Harcourt, M. (2008) Age discrimination and working life: perspectives and contestations – a review of the contemporary literature. *International Journal of Management Reviews*, 10/4: 425–442.

Judgments of the European Court of Justice

Judgment of the ECJ of 16 October 2007, Case C-411/05 of *Felix Palacios de la Villa v Cortefiel Servicios SA*

Judgment of the ECJ of 5 March 2009, Case C-388/07 of *The Incorporated Trustees of the National Council for Ageing (Age Concern England) v Secretary of State for Business Enterprise and Regulatory Reform*

Judgment of the ECJ of 12 January 2010, Case C-341/08 of *Dr Domnica Petersen v Berufungsausschuss fur Zahn fur den Bezirk Westfalen-Lippe*

Judgement of the ECJ 12 October 2010, Case C-45/09 of *Rosenbladt v Oellerking Gebaudereinigungsges.mbH*

Judgment of the ECJ of 18 November 2010, Joined cases C-250/09 and C-268/09 *Vasil Ivanov Georgiev v Technicheski universitet*

# 12

Conclusion and Emerging Themes

The purpose of this short concluding chapter is to offer some final thoughts about issues and themes which have emerged from this book and that are likely to shape the equality and diversity agenda in the future, both within the context of the wider labour market and of the workplace. In particular, we focus on: the challenges for policy makers arising from changing patterns of disadvantage and discrimination; aspects of recent equality legislation that could have a significant impact on the advancement of equality in the next decades; the concept of corporate social responsibility as a possible future drive for promoting equality and diversity initiatives within organizations; future directions in the conceptualization of diversity through an analysis of 'inclusion'; and the challenges and opportunities posed by global diversity management.

Patterns of inequalities and challenges for policy makers

Overall, the content of this book shows a mixed picture in relation to the advancement of equality in the labour market and in the workplace. On the one hand, it points to the fact that significant progress has been made, as demonstrated by several examples discussed in this book. These include greater participation of different social groups in the labour market, the extension of equality legislation to protect a wider range of individual characteristics, and changes to working practices to accommodate and value workforce diversity.

However, it also shows that patterns of inequalities still persist across different social groups. For example, as discussed in Chapter 1, there are still significant differences within the European Union between the rates of employment of men and women. Female rates of employment continue to be significantly lower, at 59 per cent, compared to those of men, at 73 per cent. Equally, as seen in Chapter 6, a significant gender pay gap still persists in almost every country, although with some degree of difference between countries. Furthermore, for certain groups, inequalities can be aggravated by the economic downturn. This appears to be particularly the case for younger people aged 15–24 who are neither in education nor in employment or training (NEETs) (The Social Situation in Europe, 2009). In some countries, for example the UK, young people defined as NEET seems to be disproportionately represented among some ethnic groups with a particular religious affiliation. In the UK, as seen in Chapter 1, 42 per cent of young Muslim people are classified as NEET (Equality and Human Rights Commission, 2010). This suggests that the combination of certain characteristics, namely age, ethnicity, and religious affiliation, can lead to a greater risk of social exclusion, disadvantage, and discrimination.

Younger people are also more likely to be found in the category of the so-called 'working poor', particularly in Northern European countries (see Chapter 1). These are people who are in paid work, but who have an income which is below 60 per cent of the national median. In the UK, the working poor are disproportionately represented among Bangladeshi households since one in three of them have an income below 60 per cent of the national median (Equality and Human Rights Commission, 2010).

Strong patterns of disadvantage and discrimination have also emerged in relation to migrant workers. Cross-national studies about the working conditions of migrants within the European Union show that this group, particularly from a non-western background and from countries which are outside the EU, are more likely to suffer disadvantage and discrimination (see Chapter 1). Legal protection for migrant workers who come from countries outside the European Union, referred to as *third country nationals*, is limited both under EU law and under the UK Equality Act 2010. The implications of this are that they constitute 'ill-defined' groups such as 'immigrants', 'asylum seekers', or 'foreigners', who, although admitted into the EU, nonetheless are treated as 'an underclass of sub-citizens' (Hepple, 2011: 39–40). The European Commission has been working to develop a framework policy to facilitate the integration of this group within their host countries (European Commission, 2007). However, the emergence in several European countries of extreme nationalist movements, coupled with the current economic downturn, is making the position of migrant workers even more vulnerable. Racist and xenophobic attitudes have also been fuelled by a public debate that portrays immigrants as a drain on national resources, taking jobs away from country nationals, and disrupting local communities. There is a serious risk that these kinds of attitudes can contribute to the spreading of racism and intolerant views to national ethnic minority groups too. Perceptions of discrimination on the grounds of ethnic origin are already very common across Europe, as evidenced by an EU survey which shows that 61 per cent of respondents believed discrimination on the grounds of ethnic origin is widespread (European Commission, 2009).

These are all very challenging issues that policy makers are facing and, unless they are tackled in the next few years, they stand to pose a serious risk to social cohesion.

A new generation of equality legislation

There have been significant developments in equality legislation both at the level of the European Union and at a national level over a number of decades. In the UK, equality legislation has evolved since the creation in the 1970s of the individual right not to be discriminated against on the grounds of race and gender, with the addition of disability in 1995. The past decade has seen the introduction of the public sector duties from 2001 onwards, and in 2010 the introduction of the Equality Act. One of the distinctive features of this Act is that it brings together all the different protected characteristics and it takes a much more integrated approach to equality (see Chapter 2).

It has also been suggested that the Equality Act represents a 'new generation of legislation' which takes a transformative approach to equality (Hepple, 2011). Some of its new measures include provisions to take more proactive positive action and the public sector equality duty. The latter introduces a single equality duty to cover all the protected characteristics. One of its key objectives is to 'advance' rather than 'promote' equality, as stated under the previous legislation. As highlighted by Hepple (2011: 134), this 'change of wording to "advancing" is significant' since it signals an approach which is intended to be more focused on outcomes and real progress. This change of emphasis also addresses criticism that was levelled at the operation of the previous generation of equality duties. Under the former legislation these were seen as placing too much emphasis on processes to the point of risking becoming a 'tick box' exercise rather than helping to achieve real progress.

However, the most 'transformative' provisions included in the original draft of the Equality Act have not been enacted by the current UK Coalition government. Nevertheless, it is still worth mentioning them briefly. These included provisions to tackle intersectional discrimination and a legal duty which would have required public bodies, such as local authorities, to have due regard to ways of reducing inequalities resulting from socio-economic disadvantage. The latter would have been achieved by the application of this duty to the decision-making processes exercised by public bodies in relation to policies and allocation of resources. The significance of this duty is that it represented an attempt to reduce inequality by tackling socio-economic disadvantage which, as seen above, represents a serious challenge for policy makers. Although deep-seated socio-economic disadvantage cannot be resolved by legislation alone, the socio-economic public duty could have played a significant role in tackling these issues. By requiring policy makers at a local level to assess the impact of their decisions on the most disadvantaged groups, it could have contributed to breaking the 'vicious circle' of disadvantage and discrimination (see Chapter 1; Makkonen, 2002).

The drafted provisions to tackle intersectional discrimination were limited to the combination of only two protected characteristics, such as age and gender. In reality, however, intersectional discrimination may not be limited to two characteristics but it may involve a number of them. For example, we have seen in the section above that young Muslim men are more likely to be represented in the category of those who are neither in education nor in employment or training (NEET). This suggests the possibility that young Muslim men are discriminated against in staff recruitment practices by employers because of their age, their religious affiliation, and their gender. These three characteristics combined together can act in way which is inextricably linked and creates a unique form of discrimination unlikely to be experienced by other groups, for example young white Christian men. This is just an example of the possible dynamics that can lead to intersectional discrimination and it shows that in reality this phenomenon is frequently not simply confined to just two protected characteristics (see Chapters 10 and 11 for other examples). The choice to limit the provisions in the Equality Act to only two protected characteristics was motivated by a political decision in the face of opposition from the business lobby. However, in spite of these limitations, as suggested by Hepple (2010: 62), 'the Equality Act represents the beginning of legal protection for intersectional discrimination'. Thus, even if the Act did not go far enough, its provisions could have helped to raise awareness about intersectional discrimination among policy makers and within organizations.

The Act also provides for more proactive positive action. Employers will be able to take measures to overcome disadvantage or take steps to increase participation of under-represented groups in the workplace (see Chapter 2). In particular, within recruitment processes this meas-ure will allow employers in a tie-break situation to appoint the candidate from an under-repre-sented group. Potentially this type of measure, which has been permitted under EU law for quite some time (see Chapter 2), could help employers, if they decide to use it, to tackle discrimina-tory attitudes and unconscious bias which can influence decisions about staff recruitment and promotion. It could potentially contribute towards tackling 'horizontal' occupational segrega-tion (e.g. appointing more male teachers in primary schools where they are under-represented) as well as 'vertical' occupational segregation (e.g. appointing more women in senior roles within an organization). In particular, it will be interesting to see whether, following the Davies (2011) report, commissioned by the UK government to assess the causes of women's under-represen-tation on listed company's boards, this type of positive action will be used to achieve the recom-mended increase to 25 per cent of women on company boards by 2015.

It is also worth noting that the issue of women's under-representation on the boards of private listed companies has prompted a debate across Europe about the use of quotas to address what in most countries is still a significant gender imbalance. The European Commis-sion is debating whether to introduce legislation to impose quotas if not enough progress is made in this area (Davies, 2011). A growing number of European countries are resorting to the use of quotas following the example set by Norway which in 2006 introduced legislation requiring private listed companies to raise their proportion of women at board level to 40 per cent, and this was successfully achieved in 2010 (Storvick and Teigen, 2010).

In conclusion, the distinctive characteristic of this new generation of equality legislation seem to be a greater focus on equality of outcomes for different social groups. Furthermore, we are also witnessing a growing trend across Europe towards a more radical use of legislation to impose quotas to close the gender gap in decision-making roles. It will be interesting to see how, in the next decade, this new generation of equality legislation will be implemented in practice and how the quota debate will evolve.

Reframing the equality and diversity agenda as part of corporate social responsibility?

The single equality duty applies to public sector employers and educational establishments. It does not apply to private sector organizations. This is a significant limitation because the public sector is shrinking as a growing number of services are being contracted out to the private sector. This means that the ability of the public sector to influence the equality and diversity agenda in the private sector, through procurement laws, is going to be significantly restricted. The future of the equality and diversity agenda in the private sector will continue to rely primarily on employers' voluntary initiatives, which are often driven by a business case approach. However, as discussed in Chapter 3, significant criticism has been levelled at the use of the business case to advance equality. It has been argued that the business case is selec-tive, partial, and contingent (Dickens, 1999), and it can only justify limited action on equality (Kirton and Greene, 2010). Thus many academics and commentators are calling for the need to move beyond the business case. However, the question is what can encourage business organizations to advance this agenda, particularly at a time when many businesses will be concerned about the implications of the economic downturn?

Some academics and commentators have started to link equality and diversity issues to the corporate social responsibility (CSR) agenda, as reported in some of the chapters in the second part of this book. For example, in Chapter 8 on work–life balance, Pitt-Catsouphes and Googins (2006) suggest that work–life balance issues, which are linked to the quality of life, are of strategic importance to organizations and they should be seen as part of their CSR agenda. In Chapter 7 on disability, research by Dibben et al. (2002) points to a possible link between disability practices in organizations and an expressed commitment to CSR. Also in the context of age equality, Line (2007) argues that supporting older workers and helping them to continue to stay in paid work should be seen as part of an employer's CSR.

The concept of CSR presents an internal dimension that includes responsibility towards employees (European Commission 2001; see also Parkinson, 1995, for a comprehensive literature review on CSR) but also an external dimension which has been defined as *social activism* (Parkinson, 1995). The latter refers to organizations' initiatives to pursue philanthropic purposes or to address social issues. Moreover, CSR can also be analyzed from the perspective of stakeholder theory (see, for example, Freeman, 1984, 1994), according to which organizations can affect through their practices the life and interests of a wide range of people including their employees. These traits of CSR offer scope for a progressive interpretation of this concept, which can lend support to the argument that organizations have a role and a responsibility to promote social justice both as part of their internal employment practices, but equally as part of their external relations. A good example of how the equality and diversity agenda can be linked to CSR can be seen in the case study of EnterpriseMouchel at the end of Chapter 1. This company received the Excellence Award 2010 for their approach to CSR. As that case shows, the company achieved the award by adopting a number of initiatives to promote equality and diversity which ranged from a review of their internal practices (the internal dimension of CSR) to initiatives relating to their external relations with sub-contractors (the external dimension of CSR) and to the wider community in which they operate (social activism).

There is, however, another interpretation of CSR which proposes that organizations should only engage in CSR activities to the extent that they support profit maximization, as it is in this way that business organizations contribute to the welfare of society (Friedman, 1970). From this perspective, equality and diversity initiatives may be part of CSR but only in so far as they contribute to maximizing profit. It follows that the link between the equality and diversity agenda and CSR would be just another version of the business case.

Whether CSR can drive the equality and diversity agenda in the private sector and take it beyond the business case depends on how this concept is interpreted. The European Union is trying to promote a progressive concept of CSR and 'encourage businesses to adopt good practices in the social field on a voluntary basis' and 'to invest in human capital' (http://europa.eu/legislation_summaries/employment_and_social_policy/employment_rights_and_work_organisation/n26039_en.htm). From this perspective, equality and diversity practices should be placed at the core of CSR. Furthermore, in a global economy CSR can become a powerful vehicle to extend equality standards and uphold human rights, particularly in developing economies. However, what in practice CSR means to organizations remain to be seen. Whether CSR can provide a new framework for the development of the equality and diversity agenda will depend on extent to which organizations are willing to acknowledge their role in the promotion of social justice, or whether they see CSR just as another marketing tool in order to gain a competitive edge.

Building on diversity: the concept of inclusion

As the diversity field has evolved, researchers have been seeking to determine the processes and practices through which diversity can be leveraged to achieve greater organizational benefit (Gonzalez and De Nisi, 2009). In Chapter 3, we discussed the development of the concept of diversity management and some of the key theoretical frameworks which have been advanced to understand it. Through this discussion it becomes apparent that a theme they all have in common is an intention to identify and explain the advantages accruing to organizations by broadening the range of identity groups they have within them. However, more recently, commentators have observed that theories of diversity have assumed that simply broadening the range of identity groups will automatically mean individuals from across those identity groups will feel equally 'included' (Roberson, 2006). To explore this notion of 'inclusion' further, a research stream has developed to determine the factors required to build work environments in which individuals from diverse backgrounds, experiences, and segments of the community can feel included and equally valued (Bilimoria et al., 2008; Roberson, 2006).

Interestingly, though the concept of inclusion is receiving increased attention, it is still relatively new and we are some way to reaching a consensus on the nature of the construct and its theoretical underpinning (Shore et al., 2010). This can be seen in the variety of definitions available. For Pelled et al. (1999: 1014), inclusion is defined as 'the degree to which an employee is accepted and treated as an insider by others in a work system'. For Roberson (2006: 217), inclusion refers to 'the removal of obstacles to the full participation and contribution of employees in organizations', while Lirio et al. (2008: 443) view inclusion as 'when individuals feel a sense of belonging and inclusive behaviours such as eliciting and valuing contributions from all employees are part of the daily life in the organization'. Avery et al. (2008: 6) follow in similar vein as their definition states that inclusion is 'the extent to which employees believe their organizations engage in efforts to involve all employees in the mission and operation of the organization with respect to their individual talents'. For Shore et al. (2010), there are two common themes evident in the above definitions. The first alludes to a sense of 'belongingness', as indicated by words such as 'belonging', 'accepted', and 'insider'. The second refers to the ability of members of diverse identity groups to feel they are valued as unique individuals and not just representatives of their groups. This theme is indicated by phrases such as 'valuing contributions from all employees' and 'individual talents'.

Moving beyond definitions of inclusion to the organizational processes and practices which evidence its presence, the most common to be identified are those articulated in Pelled et al. (1999). In their study they looked at the relationship between demographic heterogeneity (e.g. gender, race, tenure, education) and three indicators of inclusion. These were the degree of influence that employees have over decisions affecting them at work, the degree to which employees feel they are kept well informed about the company's business strategy and goals, and the likelihood employees will keep their jobs. The findings showed that all three factors are indicators of organizational inclusion, but there is a difference in the extent to which those from the various identity groups feel they have access to each of the factors. It is thus evident from this study that even where diversity in terms of heterogeneity of identity groups within the organization has been achieved, it does not automatically follow that inclusion has occurred and obstacles to the full participation and contribution of employees have been removed (Roberson, 2006).

Shore et al. (2010) base their conceptualization of inclusion on the combined constructs of 'belongingness' and 'uniqueness'. They argue that much of the diversity literature has focused on group-based diversity and the organizational benefits to be gained by broadening the range and scope of identity groups. However, the focus on group-based diversity has meant that each individual's need to be recognized and accepted for the unique talents they bring tends to be overlooked and may lead to individuals being viewed as 'representatives' of a particular identity group rather than individuals with multiple social identities and a unique blend of experiences, abilities, skills, and talents. It is important to recognize the complexity of the individual, who can simultaneously create uniqueness and similarity with identity group members (Shore et al., 2010). So, for example, the same person can be unique in terms of their gender (e.g. a woman in an all-male team), while at the same time gaining 'insider' status through their race (e.g. Caucasian) (Roccas and Brewer, 2002). To focus only on one of the constructs, either 'belongingness' or 'uniqueness', has inherent dangers as it means that individuals are discouraged from expressing and sharing their unique and personal characteristics, such as their background, education, and experiences, which make them who they are (Hewlin, 2009). Shore et al. (2010) thus encourage a combining of the two constructs as through this will come a better understanding of the concept of inclusion and advances in the research and practice of diversity management can be made.

In terms of the impact on organizational practice, broadening the lens from a single focus on diversity to a view encompassing the concept of 'inclusion' may be instructive in understanding why it is, despite over 40 years of legislation in respect of ensuring equality of opportunity in the workplace and 20 years of diversity management research and organizational effort, there is still some way to go to achieve true equality in the workplace.

For example, in a recent study by Kumra (2010), consultants in an international management consulting firm were interviewed to elicit their views in respect of how merit is socially constructed within the firm. The findings showed that both male and female consultants agreed that there exists within the firm a very clear articulation of the meritocratic, who are perceived as those who are able to commit completely to the firm and work long hours. The following quotes illustrate this issue:

> We do expect a huge amount of our consultants. We pay them to work 35 hours per week but nobody does, because that is our culture, I suppose, and it is not uncommon to walk around this building at 8 o'clock in the evening and you will find huge numbers of people still working. It is a drawback if you do not like doing that. It is a bit hard on people and particularly people who have family commitments or other commitments. (Male Director)

> [Question: What would be the consequences to someone if they weren't prepared to do that and thought as far as I'm concerned, I'm prepared to give the business 10 hours a day, but that really is enough and then I want to go home and have a life?] I think in general terms that would be supported, but when you're really up against it and you're all trying to make something happen, you understand it when someone's got an appointment or something, but I don't think you could be in this job if you wanted to work like that. (Female Principal Consultant)

However, for those unable to conform to this mode of working, there are clearly consequences. One such group identified in the study is that opting for the firm's highly publicized work–life balance policy by working a reduced-hours week. This is one of the key pillars of the firm's diversity policy. It is viewed as a key mechanism in the recruitment and retention of (most usually) talented women. The experience of women working in this way does not live up to the espoused organizational rhetoric. The following quotes articulate these women's views:

> I'm a bit disappointed that they don't quite live up to the flexible image that they like to portray. We talk here about being your employer of choice, this wonderful phrase to throw about and they are your employer of choice because if you ask for something they will do their utmost to give it to you ... but it would tend to be internal work and people would not see that as being as important as the client facing work. Therefore you don't get promoted on it. (Female Consultant 3)

> ... it's interesting that it doesn't appear to feed to my generation [early 30s]. It's interesting that the number of men who are still under the same delusions, so it's not feeding down particularly quickly, even those we were talking about earlier. Their wives are affected by these choices and yet they walk into work and although you might be the most caring, loving attentive father and concerned about their wives' careers, they won't have a look at the women they're working with. Why should she get this, why should she get that. If she can't hack it the way that I have, then she shouldn't be here. (Female Principal Consultant)

> Again, I don't have any evidence of this, but the perception is that part-time is looked on as if you're checking out of the system a bit, so I think I may have a bit of work to do on that one, enabling people to make choices about working part-time without trashing their careers. (Female Director)

From these quotes it is evident that women working part-time perceive their decision to do so, although formally sanctioned by the firm, gives a signal to key decision-makers that they are not totally committed to the firm and this has implications for their career development and advancement. They are often removed from client-facing work and put on internal projects, which are unlikely to lead to promotion. They feel resentment from their colleagues, who perceive they are not doing their fair share and so should not reap the same rewards as others. They also feel let down by the organization which honours the letter of the policy (i.e. providing flexible working opportunities to those who ask for it), but not the spirit of it, in that their career opportunities are reduced and they are excluded from core activities and removed from key networks. We thus see from the study that moves to enhance diversity may indeed do so. The firm in question can rightly say that they have made efforts to increase the diversity of their workforce and have made some progress towards achieving this. However, when we look at the outcome of these policies, it is clear that they do not achieve 'inclusion'. Those opting to work in non-standard ways do not feel included and valued for their contributions; rather, they are marginalized and made to feel that they do not contribute as they should and their choice to work flexibly is having negative impact on both the firm and their colleagues.

Global diversity management

Another emerging issue is that of global diversity management. Opportunity Now (2010) have recognized the lack of development in the field and indicated that although they see this as a key issue, they are at a very early stage in developing their understanding and approach to the topic. To progress the issue, they have established a Business in the Community workplace roundtable discussion forum on Global Diversity to assist them in determining the nature of the issue, plan priorities and key stages, and disseminate the findings to interested parties.

Evidence of the importance of the issue is also available from the USA, where a survey of Fortune 500 companies was conducted and all of the companies perceived global diversity management to be an important or very important issue (Dunavant and Heiss, 2005). Interestingly, though, only 50 per cent of the organizations surveyed consulted their global stakeholders when determining their diversity strategy, just 39 per cent provide extensive multicultural training for all employees, and only 27 per cent regularly evaluate progress in respect of the achievement of diversity goals. A further, and perhaps the most concerning finding of all, is that it is not uncommon within these organizations for their diversity programmes to be based on the assumption that domestically developed targets and objectives can be automatically transferred internationally across all operations.

In assessing the main objectives of global diversity management, Nishii and Ozbilgin (2007) identify two key issues. The first concerns the management of diversity across countries, with the aim of determining how each country may differ, and define and conceptualize diversity given their individual social, political, and legal perspective. Through such an analysis it is possible to see the extent to which western/US-based approaches to diversity management are appropriate. The second concerns the management of cultural diversity in respect of employees and countries. Critical here are issues such as how can multicultural teams be managed to ensure that they meet their aims and objectives, how do we ensure effective and fruitful interactions among global employees and business units, and how do we develop global and cultural competence across the organization.

Organizations will undoubtedly need to develop policy for each key area of the business, dependent on local conditions. So, for example, it may be wholly inappropriate to set ethnic diversity targets in an environment where the population is rather homogeneous (e.g. Japan). It may also be of limited value to impose performance management techniques based on individual reward and recognition in cultures which value collective-based effort and reward. An example of this came in a study by Kumra (2008), where interviews were conducted with a number of organizations with international operations to understand their experiences. A key learning point for an international bank emerged when they exported their UK-developed, individually-based performance-related pay system to their Singapore operation. The first difficulty involved actually trying to persuade employees to talk about their individual achievements. Singapore is a collectivist culture, and as such, employees prefer to work in groups and teams. Unlike in the UK (which is an individualistic culture), they do not seek to stand apart from the group. The bank persisted and managed to gain some measure of individual performance and allocated individual bonuses accordingly. It then came to the attention of HR managers that informally members of teams were taking their individual bonuses, pooling them, and allocating them equally among team members. Through this experience, the bank realized the need to localize practice to better reflect prevailing cultural norms and work values.

However, Nishii and Ozbilgin (2007) caution that a process of localization cannot be allowed to develop in an unfettered and *ad hoc* manner. It will need to be embedded within an overarching policy framework which balances local needs with the achievement of globally developed values and objectives. They argue that it is important that the organization has in place definitions of global diversity which take into account the socio-historical power discrepancies within each cultural setting (Cavanaugh, 1997) and do not assume that a definition derived in one context will automatically be applicable and acceptable in others. They further recommend that as local diversity policy initiatives develop, they should be vetted to ensure they meet with the overall goals and objectives of the organization's global diversity initiative, and that they are consistent across global units. This will ensure that the organization's overall objective of fostering and maintaining diversity is capable of achievement and does not become fragmented.

For additional material on the content of this chapter please visit the supporting Online Resource Centre at **www.oxfordtextbooks.co.uk/orc/kumra_manfredi/**

References

Avery, D., McKay, P., Wilson, D., and Tonidandel, S. (2008) Unequal attendance: the relationships between race, organizational diversity cues and absenteeism. *Personnel Psychology*, 60: 875–902.

Bilimoria, D., Joy, S., and Liang, X. (2008) Breaking barriers and creating inclusiveness: lessons of organizational transformation to advance women faculty in academic science and engineering. *Human Resource Management*, 47: 423–441.

Cavanaugh, J. (1997) (In)corporating the other? Managing the politics of workplace difference, in Prasad, P., Mills, A., Elmes, M., and Prasad, A. (eds), *Managing the Organizational Melting Pot: Dilemmas of Workforce Diversity*. Thousand Oaks, CA: Sage.

Commission of the European Communities (2001) *Promoting a European Framework for Corporate Social Responsibility*. Brussels: Commission of European Communities. Available online at http://europa.eu.int/eur-lex/en/comgpr/2001/com2001_0366n01.pdf.

Commission of the European Communities (2007) *Communication from the Commission to the Council, the European Parliament, the European Economic and Social Committee and the Committee of the Regions*. Third Annual Report on Migration and Integration. Brussels: Commission of European Communities.

Davies, M. (2011) *Women on Boards*. Department of Business, Innovation and Skills. Available online at http://www.bis.gov.uk/assets/biscore/business-law/docs/w/11-745-women-on-boards.pdf.

Dibben, P., James, P., Cunningham, I., and Smythe, D. (2002) Employers and employees with disabilities in the UK: an economically beneficial relationship? *International Journal of Social Economics*, 29/6: 453–467.

Dickens, L. (1999) Beyond the business case: a three-pronged approach to equality action. *Human Resource Management Journal*, 9/1: 9–19.

Duvanant, B. and Heiss, B. (2005) *Global Diversity 2005*. Washington, DC: Diversity Best Practices.

Equality and Human Rights Commission (2010) *How Fair is Britain?* Manchester: EHRC. Available at http://www.equalityhumanrights.com/key-projects/triennial-review/.

European Commission (2009) Discrimination in the EU in 2009. *Eurobarometer* (special issue) 317/Wave 71.2 – TNS Opinion & Social. Available at http://ec.europa.eu/public_opinion/archives/ebs/ebs_317_sum_en_pdf.

European Commission (2010) The Social Situation in the European Union. Directorate-General for Employment, Social Affairs and Equal Opportuinities. Brussels: European Community.

Freeman, R.E. (1984) *Strategic Management: A Stakeholder Approach*. Boston, MA: Pitman.

Freeman, R.E. (1994) The politics of stakeholder theory: some future directions. Business Ethics Quarterly, 4: 409–421.

Friedman, M. (1970) The social responsibility of business is to increase its profits. *The New York Times Magazine*, 13 September. Available at http://www.colorado.edu/studentgroups/libertarians/issues/friedman-soc-resp-business.html.

Gonzalez, J. and De Nisi, A. (2009) Cross-level effects of demography and diversity climate on organizational attachment and firm effectiveness. *Journal of Organizational Behavior*, 30: 21–40.

Hepple, B. (2010) The new single Equality Act in Britain. *The Equal Rights Review*, 5: 11–24.

Hepple, B. (2011) *Equality: The New Legal Framework*. Oxford: Hart Publishing.

Hewlin, P. (2009) Wearing the cloak: antecedents and consequences of creating facades of conformity. *Journal of Applied Psychology*, 94: 727–741.

Kirton, G. and Greene, A.M. (2010) What does diversity management mean for the Gender Equality Project in the United Kingdom? Views and experiences of organizational actors. *Canadian Journal of Administrative Sciences*, 27/3: 249–262.

Kumra, S. (2008) *Lessons from the East*. Working Paper No. 22. Oxford: Oxford Brookes University.

Kumra, S. (2010) Social construction of merit in a professional services firm: guardian of equality of veil for inequity? Paper presented at the Gender in Management Track at the British Academy of Management Conference, Sheffield.

Line, F. (2007) *The End of the Line for Retirement Ages: The Business Case for Managing without a Retirement Age*. London: The Employers' Forum on Age.

Lirio, P., Lee, M., Williams, M., Haugen, L., and Kossek, E. (2008) The inclusion challenge with reduced-load professionals: the role of the manager. *Human Resource Management*, 47: 443–461.

Makkonen, T. (2002) *Multiple, Compound and Intersectional Discrimination: Bringing the Experience of the Most Marginalized to the Fore*. Abo, Finland: Institute of Human Rights.

Opportunity Now (2010) *Global Diversity Management: Agenda for Action*. London: Opportunity Now.

Parkinson, J.E. (1995) *Corporate Power and Responsibility: Issues in the Theory of Company Law*. Oxford: Oxford University Press.

Pelled, L., Ledford, G., and Mohrman, S. (1999) Demographic dissimilarity and workplace inclusion. *Journal of Management Studies*, 36: 1013–1031.

Pitt-Catsouphes, M. and Googins, B. (2006) Recasting the work–family agenda as corporate social responsibility, in Kossek, E. and Lambert, S. (eds), *Work and Life Integration: Organisation, Cultural and Individual Perspectives*. Mahwah, NJ: Lawrence Erlbaum Associates.

Roberson, Q. (2006) Disentangling the meanings of diversity and inclusion in organizations. *Group & Organization Management*, 31/2: 212–236.

Roccas, S. and Brewer, M. (2002) Social identity complexity. *Personality and Social Psychology Review*, 6: 88–106.

Shore, L., Randel, A., Chung, B., Dean, M., Ehrhart, K., and Singh, G. (2010) Inclusion and diversity in work groups: a review and model for future research. *Journal of Management*, 32/1: 1–28.

Storvick, A. and Teigen, M. (2010) *Women on Board: The Norwegian Experience*. Oslo: Institute for Social Research: Friedrich, Ebert, Stiftung. Available online at http://www.socialresearch.no/Publications/Other-reports/2010/2010-004.

Glossary

Affirmative model of disability: this model seeks to promote a positive discourse on disability by moving away from the notion that disability is a 'personal tragedy' (Swain and French, 2005). It also suggests that an impairment should be viewed as an 'ordinary characteristic' of human experience rather than as an 'extraordinary characteristic' (Cameron, 2008).

Age discrimination: treating a person or a group of people less favourably because of their age. For example, denying older workers access to training opportunities that are available to younger workers.

Bisexual: a person who is sexually attracted to both sexes.

BME: stands for black and minority ethnic, a term coined to encompass a number of minority groups within society.

Business case: a set of arguments which for the first time promoted the diversity evident within organizations in respect of the demographic make-up of employees as a positive asset to business; something which, if managed and leveraged effectively, could provide organizations with much needed competitive advantage.

Change management: a process through which organizations adapt to and meet the demands presented by increasingly turbulent and volatile markets.

Dignity: '[d]ignity is not a natural, empirical characteristic of human beings, but is a status conferred by humans upon themselves, to set them apart from other species' (Parekh, cited in Vickers, 2008b: 36–37). Consequently, this concept involves a moral judgement about the absolute intrinsic worth of human beings.

Direct discrimination: less favourable treatment of a person because of a protected characteristic. Direct discrimination cannot be justified, except in the case of age and disability. Discrimination based on a stereotypical assumption made by the employer will be direct discrimination.

Disability: this can be defined as 'a consequence of processes that exclude people from society' (Howard, 2003: 4).

Disadvantage: with regard to employment, disadvantage encompasses a situation where an individual, because of her personal characteristics, is not able to participate in paid work in the same way as others. An example of this is a person with a disability who may not be able to work unless some adjustments are made to the working environment.

Discrimination: amounts to unfavourable treatment which cannot be objectively justified.

Discrimination on the grounds of religion or belief: the terms 'religion' and 'belief' are defined as 'any religious belief or philosophical belief' and include a reference to a lack of religious belief. It is unlawful to discriminate on the grounds of religion or belief in relation to staff recruitment, employment, promotion opportunities, vocational training, and dismissal. Access to further and higher education is also covered by the legislation as part of the protection for vocational training.

Diversity: being different or varied.

Diversity champion: an individual, usually senior within the organization, who is given the role of communicating the key aims, objectives, and policy initiatives in respect of diversity management both inside and outside the organization.

Diversity Council: body charged with developing and then implementing the local response to strategic objectives in respect of diversity management emanating from the Global Diversity Forum.

Employee networks: groups formed, usually by employees themselves, at which issues of common interest to members of the group can be debated, discussed, and explored.

Equal pay: the principle that men and women are entitled to equal pay for equal work. This includes doing the same or similar work or work of equal value. Pay includes basic wages and salary as well as other contractual benefits such as company cars, annual leave, and pension contributions.

Equality: the Universal Declaration of Human Rights states that: 'All human beings are born free and equal in dignity and rights', which means that they are all equal in their humanity and moral worth and they all share an essential dignity as human beings.

Ethnicity paradigm: within the ethnicity paradigm key areas of study are immigration and the social patterns and experiences of usually European immigrants (Omi and Winant, 1986). The debate within the paradigm has focused on two opposing themes: assimilation versus cultural pluralism, namely incorporation or separation of ethnic groups.

'Everyday' racism: this is defined as 'those subtle and pervasive manifestations of racism faced by Blacks on a daily basis in the workplace' (Essed, 1991, in Deitch et al., 2003: 1300).

Family-friendly employment: refers to a mix of flexible working patterns and leave arrangements, such as maternity, paternity, and parental leave, that can be made available to working parents in the workplace.

Flexible retirement: this involves retiring on a part-time basis and starting to draw a pension while continuing to work for the rest of the time for the same employer. The feasibility of this arrangement depends on the rules of individual occupational pension schemes.

Gay: a person whose sexual orientation is to persons of the same sex.

Glass ceiling: one of the most dominant metaphors used to explain women's absence in senior organiza-tional positions. The glass ceiling has been defined as 'a barrier so subtle that it is transparent, yet so strong that it prevents women and minorities from moving up in the management hierarchy' (Morrison and von Glinow, 1990: 200).

Glass cliff: a term coined by Ryan and Haslam (2007) to explain the higher than average number of women being appointed to the boards of organizations experiencing under-performance and financial difficulty. The 'glass cliff' is a term used to denote the precarious nature of the positions and the gendered processes embedded within their allocation to women.

Global Diversity Forum: a decision and policy-making body that works through key actors within the organization's diversity structure to provide information from both outside and inside the organization on which decisions in respect of future directions for diversity strategy can be based.

Harassment: unwanted conduct which has the purpose or effect of creating an intimidating, hostile, degrading, humiliating or offensive environment, or of violating dignity. Harassment can occur on the basis of any of the protected characteristics.

Impairment: this can be defined 'as problems with the function or structure of the body' (Howard, 2003: 4).

Indirect discrimination: the application of a provision, criterion or practice to all staff equally, but which puts groups with a protected characteristic at a disadvantage compared with others. For example, a requirement may be imposed on both men and women but it may put women at a disadvantage compared with men.

Institutional racism: defined in the Macpherson report as: 'The collective failure of an organization to provide an appropriate and professional service to people because of their colour, culture, or ethnic origin. It can be seen or detected in processes, attitudes and behaviour which amount to discrimination through unwitting prejudice, ignorance, thoughtlessness and racist stereotyping which disadvantage minority ethnic people' (Macpherson, 1999: para. 6.34).

Labyrinth model of women's leadership: the labyrinth symbolizes a complex journey towards a goal of value to the individual. To negotiate a labyrinth is not a simple or direct endeavour. It requires persistence, an understanding of progress, and careful analysis of the challenges that lie ahead. It is this message they seek to give to women as they aspire to leadership positions. There are routes to the top, but there are many twists and turns that have to be negotiated along the way – both expected and unexpected – but because all labyrinths have a route through them, the ultimate goal is attainable.

Lesbian: a woman whose sexual orientation is to other women.

Medical model of disability: a model that locates the issue of disability with an individual.

Occupational requirement: where it is crucial to a particular job that a person be of a particular sex, race, disability, religion or belief, sexual orientation, or age, etc., then there is an occupational requirement for the job. This provides an exception to the general non-discrimination rule and allows an employer to impose a requirement that the holder of the job must have the particular characteristic. For example, for reasons of privacy it may be that a public changing room attendant should be of the same sex as those using the changing room.

Occupational segregation: this relates to a situation where people from a particular social group are concentrated in certain occupations or in certain employment sectors. Occupational segregation can be horizontal (e.g. women predominantly working in administrative and clerical jobs across different sectors of employment) or vertical (e.g. women segregated in lower-status jobs and under-represented in senior jobs).

Philosophical belief: there is no clear definition under EU and UK law of what constitutes a 'philosophi-cal belief'. The kinds of 'beliefs' likely to be protected by the law 'will need to have a certain level of cogency, seriousness, cohesion and importance' in accordance with the case law developed by the European Court of Human Rights (Vickers, 2006).

Pink pound: refers to the amount of money that homosexual people have available to spend (Financial Times Lexicon, 2010).

Positive action: measures to promote equality based on a recognition that for some disadvantaged groups there may be a need to 'catch up', in terms of their access to skills development and education. Within Codes of Practice issued by the Equal Opportunities Commission and Race Relations Board (now both merged into the Equality and Human Rights Commission), recommendations are made in respect of policy initiatives which enable this to be done, for example, implementing management development programmes targeted only at members of ethnic minorities, to increase the number of ethnic minority managers.

Preference theory: emanating from longitudinal research conducted in the USA and Europe which charts lifestyle preferences and values as key determinants of the employment decisions men and women make, the assertion of preference theory is that it advances a new explanation for labour market participation and employment outcomes, particularly for women.

Protected characteristic: these are the characteristics which are protected by UK discrimination law. They are: age, disability, gender reassignment, marriage and civil partnership, pregnancy and maternity, race, religion or belief, sex, and sexual orientation.

Race relations cycle: developed by Park (1939/1950), the 'race relations cycle' has four key stages: contact, competition, accommodation, and eventual assimilation. For Park, the cycle is progressive and irreversible, though he does acknowledge that any particular stage may be prolonged. At the heart of Park's work is the view that assimilation is the logical and natural antidote to racism and ethnocentrism.

Reasonable accommodation: this involves accommodating employees' religious practices in the workplace, provided that it is reasonable and practicable to do so. Examples of reasonable accommodation could be allowing employees to adhere to a particular dress code (e.g. wearing a headscarf or a turban with a work uniform) or allowing some time off during the working day for prayers. Under EU and UK law there is no legal obligation for employers to accommodate employees' religious needs. However, failure to do so may result in indirect discrimination on the grounds of religion, which can be unlawful. For example, the requirement not to wear a headscarf with a work uniform could disadvantage Muslim women as they would find it more difficult to comply with this requirement compared to other religious or non-religious groups. This will be unlawful unless it can be objectively justified.

Reasonable adjustment: (applies to disability discrimination only) the legal duty to make reasonable adjustments to try to remove disadvantages faced by disabled workers. Examples include changing the physical environment to enable access to a building, providing specialist equipment to help disabled workers, or changing working hours to make work possible for a disabled worker.

Sex-role stereotyping: research evidence that supports the contention that there are distinct characteristics, attitudes, and temperaments that can be attributed to men and others which can be attributed to women.

Social dialogue: social dialogue is defined by the European Trade Union Confederation as 'the process of negotiation by which different actors in society (or "social partners") reach agreement to work together on policies and activities'. The social dialogue can bring together representatives of employers and employees but it can also involve government or European Union representatives.

Social model of disability: this model distinguishes between the notion of impairment and disability and, unlike the medical model, it locates the issue of disability with society. It is based on the idea that 'it is not individual limitations, of whatever kind, which are the cause of the problem, but society's failure to provide appropriate services and adequately ensure that the needs of the disabled people are fully taken into account in its social organization' (Oliver, 1996: 32).

Socially sustainable work: relates to the importance of considering the impact of the organization of paid work on the wider society.

Stakeholder: an individual or representative of a group of individuals with an interest in the processes, practices, and outcomes of the organization. Stakeholders can be both inside (e.g. employees, managers, etc.) and outside (e.g. shareholders, consumers, customers) the organization.

Stigmatized groups: members of stigmatized groups find themselves marginalized, the subject of negative social identities, and frequently the targets of discrimination. Examples of stigmatized groups are racial minorities and those with physical disabilities.

Trans: the terms 'trans' people and 'transgender people' are often used as umbrella terms for people whose gender identity and/or gender expression differs from their birth sex, including transsexual people, transvestite/cross-dressing people, androgyne/polygender people and others who define as gender variant (Mitchell and Howarth, 2009: ii).

Transgender: an umbrella term for people whose gender identity and/or gender expression differs from their birth sex. They may or may not seek to undergo gender reassignment hormonal treatment or surgery. The term is often used interchangeably with trans (Mitchell and Howarth, 2009: ii).

Transsexual: a person who intends to undergo, is undergoing, or has undergone gender reassignment which may (or may not) involve hormone therapy or surgery (Mitchell and Howarth, 2009: ii).

Victimization: this occurs where a person is treated badly because he or she has, in good faith, taken action or supported someone else's actions relating to an equality claim, for example, being treated badly for bringing a discrimination claim or for agreeing to give evidence in the hearing of a discrimination case.

Work ability: '[t]he development of human capital to meet the demands of the labour market' (Ministry of Social Affairs and Health (Finland), 2002: 24), which means that an individual's capabilities have to be matched with work demands. In order to maintain a balanced relationship between an individual's

capabilities and work demands, these will need to be adjusted as a worker becomes older.

Work–life balance: broadly defined as a set of policies and practices to help individuals to achieve a balance between the demands arising from paid work and their personal lives.

Work–life harmonization: this concept has been proposed as an alternative to that of work–life balance, which implies a separation between the domain of paid work and that of personal life. It has been suggested that work–life harmonization can better capture the multiple challenges faced by individuals at different stages of their life cycle, to combine paid work with other parts of their life (Gambles et al., 2006).

Index